MEDIEVAL FRENCH TEXTUAL STUDIES
In Memory of
T.B.W. Reid

ANGLO-NORMAN TEXT SOCIETY

OCCASIONAL PUBLICATIONS SERIES

NO. 1

MEDIEVAL FRENCH

TEXTUAL STUDIES

IN MEMORY OF

T. B. W. REID

EDITED BY

IAN SHORT

LONDON
published by the
ANGLO-NORMAN TEXT SOCIETY
from Birkbeck College, London WC1E 7HX
1984

© *Anglo-Norman Text Society 1984*
ISBN 0 905474 10 4

Set in IBM Baskerville
and printed in Great Britain by
Express Litho Service (Oxford)
and bound by
The Green Street Bindery Limited

ACKNOWLEDGEMENTS

It is particularly appropriate that the Anglo-Norman Text Society should choose to inaugurate its Occasional Publications Series by honouring the memory of its late President with a volume of essays contributed by friends and colleagues from Britain and abroad. More than any other single factor, it was Tim Reid's long and energetic service to ANTS, especially after 1963, that ensured that the Society continues to command a high international reputation, and is now in a position to expand its publishing activities. This token of our appreciation of him as a scholarly editor, both modern and medieval, serves as a collective expression of thanks from the whole of the ANTS membership.

Since this book was first projected, Mrs Joyce Reid has taken an active interest, and indeed played an important part, in its preparation, and it is a pleasure to place on record here the Society's gratitude to her. Our thanks are due also to the volume's contributors and subscribers, as well as to the Curators of the Taylor Institution, Oxford, who made a grant from the Gerrans Fund, the President and Fellows of Trinity College, Oxford, and the Modern Humanities Research Association for generous subventions in aid of publication.

CONTENTS

PREFACE

T.B.W. Reid 6.iii.1901—30.viii.1981

In honouring the memory of Tim Reid, we pay tribute to one of the most learned Romance philologists of his time, to a man who inspired colleagues and pupils alike by his example of meticulous scholarship and selfless commitment. This volume, the second collection of essays to be dedicated to him, is intended to reflect in particular Reid's activities as a textual critic and as President of the Anglo-Norman Text Society from 1963. Following his retirement from the Oxford Chair in 1968 (he had been elected Professor of the Romance Languages there in 1958 after thirteen years in the Chair of Romance Philology at Manchester), Reid was presented with a volume in his honour entitled *The History and Structure of French*. Those unfamiliar with the details of his biography will find, in D. M. Stewart's prefatory essay to this 'Festschrift', a full account of his academic career spanning the years 1929 to 1971, together with a list of his publications.

Retirement in no way diminished Reid's scholarly activity; on the contrary, the period between 1968 and 1981, much more an Indian summer than an autumn, saw him flourish despite the increasing burden of indifferent health which he had long since contrived to ignore. His productivity is to be measured not so much in terms of publications under his own name (though his *The 'Tristran' of Beroul: a Textual Commentary* appeared in 1972, and an important article on textual criticism in *Medium Aevum* in 1976) as in unremitting work behind the scenes on the annual volumes of the Anglo-Norman Text Society and, more importantly, on its joint publication with the Modern Humanities Research Association, the *Anglo-Norman Dictionary*.

The full extent of Reid's contribution to the success of the *AND* is known only to those most closely involved with the final drafting and preparation for the press of the first two, and most of the third, fascicles. It was he who, from 1976, assumed

xi

overall responsibility for ensuring that this long-standing project finally became a reality. Far from merely supervising the enterprise, however, Reid, with characteristic commitment, undertook a full-scale revision of a large number of the Dictionary entries, to the extent that it soon became his full-time occupation. On the day of his death, he spent many hours hard at work revising the last letter of the third fascicle. This was his first venture into lexicography proper, and he brought to it, in addition to his linguistic expertise, two essential qualifications: he was painstaking and exceptionally well-informed. The skill and thoroughness with which he accomplished this enormous task can be gauged not only from the printed results, but also from the scores of long, minutely-detailed letters which he exchanged with his collaborators at every stage up to the final page-proofs — and often beyond.

The Times obituarist described Reid very aptly as a "man of wide culture and broad sympathies, sociable, blessed with a sense of humour, and, by the same token, tolerant and devoid of pedantry". Others have written of his "remarkable modesty" and "genuine indifference to adequate recognition". (Indeed, it was with great difficulty that he was persuaded to allow his name to figure on the title-page of the *Anglo-Norman Dictionary* as an editor.) But these qualities do not explain his willingness to devote the last years of his life to so much onerous, and often tedious, editorial work. This dedication was directly attributable to the main driving-force of his character: a passionate (one might almost say uncontrollable) commitment to the truth, and hence to strict accuracy and clarity in scholarship — or, to put it less pompously, as he himself would certainly have done, an urge to get things right. He would pursue problems tenaciously, and not rest until he had solved them to his entire satisfaction. Increasingly throughout his career, this commitment led him away from his own work as colleagues, editors of learned journals, and publishers came to appreciate his learning and editorial acumen and to turn to him for advice and guidance in a wide variety of fields. It was a distraction which he welcomed as a challenge, to which he responded generously. On these occasions, he would express himself with characteristic trenchancy; it was not in his nature to prevaricate when his opinion was sought. His criticism was all-embracing and merciless, but offered with a goodwill that quickly extinguished resentment. Mistrustful of enthusiasm and exaggeration, he rarely lavished praise, but was scrupulous in his judgement of others and their achievements.

Nor did he exempt himself from criticism. A past master of understatement, he described himself, in a short speech of thanks·which he gave on the occasion of the presentation of his 'Festschrift', as "a non-teacher, a rotten linguist, and a scholar of limited scope". He doubted whether he had actually taught anyone anything at the post-graduate level; at most he had let them get on with what they wanted to do and tried to keep them out of error by applying certain simple principles of analysis, rationality and scepticism. He claimed to have no ear for speech-sounds, no gift for mimicry, no spontaneous command of any language, even English. Much of what he had published, he said, consisted of flotsam from the wreck of larger, perhaps over-ambitious, projects. Among these he singled out a history of the expression of negation in French; the material which he had assembled for this study was, to judge from his surviving papers, enough to fill two large volumes at least, and it is a real cause for regret that what would certainly have been a major contribution to this aspect of French syntax never saw the light of day.

As for the course which his research had taken, Reid explained that over the years he had grown more and more preoccupied by. the simple desire to understand some of the things that individual human beings had said and written, to find out, as exactly as possible, what a particular word or form or construction, and especially an idiom or proverbial expression, was intended to, and actually did, convey. He suggested that any success that he had had in this endeavour was perhaps due to his shortcomings as a linguist, for when, by dint of much toil and trouble, conscious analysis and comparison, he worked himself into the comprehension of a word or expression, he possibly came to understand it rather better than those whose perception was more immediate and direct. This applied particularly, in his view, to a dead language like Medieval French, and particularly also to the situation where the original utterance was accessible only through the intermission of a perhaps erroneous scribal copy.

It was indeed in the allied arts of textual exegesis and editing that Reid's scholarship showed to its best advantage, and in this area that he excelled. The hallmark of his research was meticulousness, a habit of a lifetime that he may well have acquired while reading for his degree in law at Trinity College, Dublin. His methodology was analytical, rationalistic, and founded on uncompromisingly philological principles: he had little patience with the sort of critic who lays claim to superior insight into an author's psyche but does not understand his syntax, who expatiates on the beauties of a poet's verse but does not understand his metre. To problems of textual criticism he brought a seemingly instinctive feeling for what was linguistically possible and what was likely to be the result of scribal interference or corruption. In fact, however, intuition played no part whatever in his ability to recognise deviations from authentic Medieval French; a profound knowledge of its grammar, derived from the close reading of a wide range of texts over many years, underpinned his detection of scribal error, and was the foundation on which, by interventionist emendation exploiting all available evidence, both external and internal, he set about reconstructing the original reading.

Reid made no secret of his hostility to the editorial school which, in the name of textual conservatism, reduces the role of the scholarly editor to that of a timid transcriber of isolated manuscripts. While fully recognising the dangers inherent in the wholesale rewriting and reconstruction of medieval texts, he found himself much more in sympathy with the editorial tradition exemplified by Wendelin Foerster, whose textual criticism, particularly on Chrétien de Troyes, he had come to appreciate through his work on *Yvain*. Far from nostalgically advocating a return to the past, however, Reid was looking to the future in the full conviction that the way ahead lay in the direction of empiricism rather than positivism; and to this extent he was a scholar with a mission — to rally the textual critics and editors of his day to the cause of what he saw as 'true philology'. Time will tell whether they are confident enough to respond to the call.

It was entirely in character for Tim Reid, when summing up his own achievements at the end of his university career, to have attributed what success he had had to a combination of "good luck, good friends, and, above all, a good wife". What is needed to complete this picture is, of course, the fact that he was an exceptionally good scholar. His lightly-worn, self-effacing erudition will long be remembered by those who had the privilege of working with him and learning from him. We commemorate the scholar and the man with admiration, affection and gratitude.

THE RIGHT TO EMEND

T. B. W. REID_____

[The lecture on which this article is based was originally delivered at a
meeting of the Society for the Study of Mediaeval Languages and Literature at Merton College, Oxford, in March 1974. Thereafter it was twice
revised, and read, in October of the same year, at the 100th meeting of
the University of Manchester Medieval Society, and subsequently, in March
1976, at the Seminar on Editing and Textual Studies at King's College,
London. It is not clear whether Professor Reid intended eventually to
publish this lecture in article form. Had he done so, however, it is certain,
given his working habits and the uncompromisingly high standards which
he set himself, that he would not have allowed it to appear in print without subjecting it to yet further revisions and improvements. Whatever alterations of substance he might have made, he would undoubtedly have adapted
his presentation to satisfy the more formal requirements of the traditional
scholarly article. It is in order to go some way to meeting this need in
particular that, in publishing this paper posthumously, it has been thought
permissible to introduce certain minor changes in wording here and there,
and to supply a full range of footnote references. In all other respects,
however, the text faithfully reproduces the tone and content of the lecture
in its final revision.]

The 'right' in question in this paper is that of the editor of an
Old French text to emend some of the readings of his sole or
base manuscript. It may be that, in the case of happier languages,
the editor's right to emend his medieval Spanish, English or
German text has never been questioned. But this right certainly
has been questioned — indeed, almost abolished — as regards the
texts in my own field. I am thinking mainly of some of those
texts which are preserved in a single manuscript, such as the
Tristran of Beroul and, in a sense, the Oxford *Chanson de Roland.*
I shall also be referring to a few texts of which there are several
or many manuscripts, such as the romances of Chrétien de Troyes,
on the assumption that they are now normally edited by select-
ing a single manuscript as base.

Of all the extant manuscripts of Old French texts, there is
not one that anybody would maintain to be a completely faithful copy of the original. Every scribe made some mistakes (even

1

if he was the author copying his own work[1]); some scribes made many, and in the process of transmission the mistakes inevitably multiplied. When these Old French texts came to be taken seriously as works of linguistic, literary or historical importance, medievalists of great learning and perspicacity published editions of them in which, after careful analysis and comparison, they did their best to correct the errors of the manuscript copies and to restore what they believed to be the original form of the works. The scholars in question included, for example, Gaston Paris and Paul Meyer in France, Hermann Suchier and Eduard Koschwitz in Germany; the many editions included those of the *Roland* by Theodor Müller and others, of most of the romances of Chrétien de Troyes by Wendelin Foerster, of Beroul by Ernest Muret. These editions provided the student of Old French literature with texts of very high quality: practically every line was comprehensible, plausible in its context, and consistent with all that was known about the linguistic and literary usage of writers of the relevant period and region of origin. No doubt they were occasionally open to the suspicion of owing just a little too much to the editor, who might sometimes be thought to have indulged in what Vinaver has called "disguised

---

[1] Cf. the case of Frère Angier, on whose holograph (MS Paris BN fr. 24766, dated Oxford 1213) see Paul Meyer in *Romania*, XII (1883), 145–208, M. K. Pope, *Etude sur la langue de Frère Angier* (Paris, 1903), and M. D. Legge in *Romania*, LXXIX (1958), 512–14. Matthew Paris's *Vie de seint Auban* also survives in an autograph copy (MS Dublin Trinity College 177 [*olim* E.1.40] of *c.* 1230–57); see A. R. Harden's ed., ANTS XIX (Oxford, 1968), p. xiii, and F. McCulloch in *Speculum*, LVI (1981), 761–85. Textual corruption through scribal unreliability has, of course, been recognised since Antiquity. Martial articulated the problem with characteristic pungency when he wrote:

Si qua videbuntur chartis tibi, lector, in istis
sive obscura nimis sive Latina parum,
non meus est error: nocuit librarius illis
dum properat versus adnumerare tibi.
Quod si non illum sed me peccasse putabis,
tunc ego te credam cordis habere nihil. . . .   (*Epigr.* II, 8)

['If any passage in these sheets seems to you, reader, either too obscure or composed in questionable Latin, the fault is not mine: it was the copyist who spoiled them in his haste to complete for you his stint of verses. But if you should think that I am the guilty one, not he, then I will believe that you are quite devoid of intelligence. . .'].

collaboration with the author"[2] — but it was widely felt that this was not really a very high price to pay for the labours of a good editor.

This happy state of affairs was brought to an end almost entirely by the influence of a single distinguished scholar, Joseph Bédier. Although Bédier had expressed objections to the traditional type of critical edition in his editions of the *Lai de l'Ombre* (the first as far back as 1890 and the second, with more explicit criticisms, in 1913), it was really the publication of his edition of the *Chanson de Roland* in 1921, followed by his commentaries in 1927,[3] that inaugurated the revolution in editorial methods which some have called 'Copernican'. Bédier showed, not only to his own satisfaction but also to that of many other critics, that the text of the *Roland* poem contained in the Oxford manuscript Digby 23 represents one family, and all other versions a single second family, and therefore that the Oxford text has as much authority as any of the others, or all the others together. This had already been maintained by Theodor Müller, but Bédier went on to argue very persuasively that, where there is disagreement between the two families, the Oxford text is nearly always much the better, and in his view the more likely to have preserved the original reading. He therefore edits the *Chanson de Roland* almost exactly as if Digby 23 were the only extant manuscript; his rare corrections owe practically nothing to the other versions of the poem. In the case of the *Lai de l'Ombre*, where there are seven manuscripts of roughly equal merit, which do not lend themselves to the construction of a stemma, Bédier's method was to choose the one which showed the fewest individual variants and treat that in the same way as he was later to treat the Oxford version of the *Roland*.

[2] In his article 'Principles of Textual Emendation' in *Studies . . . presented to Professor Mildred K. Pope* (Manchester, 1939), pp. 351–69, here 368 [repr. in C. Kleinhenz (ed.), *Medieval Manuscripts and Textual Criticism* (Chapel Hill, 1976), pp. 139–59].

[3] J. Bédier, *Le Lai de l'Ombre . . .* (Fribourg, 1890), SATF (Paris, 1913) (cf. also Bédier in *Romania*, LIV, 1928, 161–96, 321–56); *La Chanson de Roland* (Paris, 1921; 6th definitve ed. 1937), *La Chanson de Roland commentée* (Paris, [1927]) (cf. also Bédier in *Romania*, LXIII, 1937, 433–69, LXIV, 1938, 145–244, 489–521).

Now, Bédier was undoubtedly a great medievalist; and though his actual editions of texts make up only a small part of his published work, his prestige was such that his editorial principles have dominated the attitudes of editors of Old French texts for the past half-century, at any rate in France and in England. Because of Bédier, anyone editing a text of which there are several manuscripts has felt obliged to choose one of them as his base and to edit it as if it were the only one extant. Any attempt to correct the base manuscript with the help of others (whether based on a stemma or not) is considered to produce a 'composite' text — and 'composite' has become a dirty word. Whether the edition is based on one manuscript chosen from among several, or on the sole extant manuscript, the gospel according to Bédier requires the readings of that manuscript to be "reproduced as faithfully as possible", or "modified as little as possible".[4] As is well known, Bédier summed up the spirit of his principles in a dictum which he attributed to the "archéologue Didron": "Il faut conserver le plus possible, réparer le moins possible, ne restaurer à aucun prix".[5] The implication of Bédier's reference to Didron was, I suppose, that anyone who tried to restore a text was comparable to Didron's better-known contemporary Viollet-le-Duc, whose heavy-handed rebuilding of medieval cathedrals and castles (and especially, perhaps, of the Cité de Carcassonne) was and remains a grisly warning to restorers. But Bédier himself must surely have realised, not only that the line between repairing and restoring is a very difficult one to draw, but also that the whole analogy between the editor of a medieval text and the archaeologist or architectural expert dealing with a medieval building is really rather misleading. The medieval church or castle that survived to undergo the ministrations of Didron or Viollet-le-Duc was not a copy of one that had disappeared, whereas Bédier's editorial principle actually depends on the fact that the original of our extant copy has indeed disappeared without trace: "la leçon primitive, celle du manuscrit archétype, à jamais perdu, demeure hors de nos prises".[6]

---

[4] John Orr in his ed. of the *Lai de l'Ombre* (Edinburgh, 1948), p. xx.
[5] *Ed. cit.*, pp. ix—x.
[6] *Ibid.*, p. vii.

This observation that the original text is irrecoverably lost, with its counterpart that in a case like the *Chanson de Roland* "la copie d'Oxford est unique, elle est notre seul bien tangible, réel",[7] leads Bédier to what seems to me a counsel of despair. The copyist of the Oxford *Roland*, as Bédier himself says, has transposed a Continental French original of probably somewhere about the year 1100 into the forms of Anglo-Norman usage of about 1170; he has obviously made a great many careless mistakes, and has left us at least fifty lines which are incomprehensible as they stand. But Bédier argues that we do not know enough about the linguistic, narrative or metrical usage of the author to justify us in making any substantial change in the scribal text, even where a much more plausible reading is offered by one or more of the collateral versions. His corrections of the Oxford manuscript are usually confined to what he calls "des fautes serviles, fausses lectures ou erreurs de la plume".[8] But he never tells us just how these trivial errors are to be distinguished from other errors (or indeed how errors of any kind are to be recognised as being errors). I have examined the corrections which he makes in the first 250 lines of the poem. In each of seven words, he supplies missing letters, from one to three in number; in each of three other words, he changes one letter; in one line he inserts the missing verb *ad* 'has'. But his only emendations of any substance, in these 250 lines, are those in the following three passages:[9]

1) 116—18   La siet li reis ki dulce France tient.
            Blanche ad la barbe e tut flurit le chef,
            Gent ad le cors e la cuntenance fier [*corr. to*
                                 e le cuntenant fier]

2) 144—47   'Li reis Marsilie est mult mis enemis:
            De cez paroles que vos avez ci dit,
            En quel mesure en purrai estre fiz?'
            'Voet par hostages,' ço dist le Sarrazins [*corr. to*
                                 Vos par hostages]

---

[7] *Ibid.*, pp. viii—ix.
[8] *Ibid.*, p. ix.
[9] Except where indicated, examples here and below are given with the original wording of the base MS, but with the transliteration and punctuation of the editors.

3) 202   De ses paienveiat quinze [*corr. to* paiens
                                        enveiat]

In particular, Bédier makes no emendations for grammatical or metrical reasons alone. The manuscript text of these 250 lines shows nearly thirty abnormalities of declension and some dozen irregularities of syllable-count, but all these are left in the edited text as they stand in the manuscript. So in example 3 above, although the line is emended to make sense, it remains two syllables short.

This is a brief illustration of Bédier's practice as an editor. It would not be a serious exaggeration to say that every editor of an Old French text in France or in England, from the early twenties to the present day, has come under the influence of his ideas, whether directly or indirectly. One of the most influential exponents of the Bédierist, or non-interventionist, doctrine was Mario Roques, director of the *Classiques français du moyen âge* from the foundation of the series in 1910 until his death in 1961. Notable examples of his editorial methods are the editions in that series (usually under Roques's name, though he cannot have done all the work himself) of successive branches of the *Roman de Renart* (from 1948 on), based on the single manuscript BN fr. 371, and of the romances of Chrétien de Troyes (from 1952 on), based on the single manuscript BN fr. 794 (the one copied by the scribe Guiot). Disciples of Bédier in England have included, for example, John Orr, Alfred Ewert, and Eugène Vinaver, and through them their pupils, such as Frederick Whitehead. They all repeat, with very slight variations, the formula that the editor has modified the text of his manuscript "as little as possible". But 'as little as possible' is a highly subjective concept, and in practice it proves to be a very elastic quantity. For one thing, two editors of equally strong Bédierist views can take opposite decisions about the 'possibility' of a given manuscript reading. It is interesting to compare in this respect the *Roland* editions of Bédier himself and of Whitehead.[10] Consider, for instance, line 147 in example 2 above. Here Whitehead retains the manuscript reading (only modifying *Voet* to *Voelt* because this appears to be what the scribe first

---

[10] *La Chanson de Roland* (Oxford, 1942; 2nd ed. 1946).

wrote), making the comment: "*Voelt par hostages* ('he will do it by giving hostages' or 'he wishes it to be done by an exchange of hostages') involves a violent ellipsis, but it is far from an impossible reading".[11] Bédier, however, considers that it is indeed an impossible reading and emends to *Vos par hostages*, with a use of the subject-pronoun in a verbless reply formula that is well attested in Old French.[12] There is a similar disagreement over line 325:

4) Li duze per, por qu'il l'aiment tant [*Bédier corr. to*
por ço qu'il]

Again Whitehead keeps the manuscript text, with an extremely rare use of *por que* in the sense of 'because' which leaves the second hemistich one syllable short; but Bédier silently emends to *por ço qu'il*, which is both grammatically and metrically normal. On the other hand, in lines 601–2, it is now Bédier who retains the manuscript text:

5) Quan l'ot Marsilie, si l'ad baisét el col,
Puis si cumencet a venir ses tresors [*Whitehead corr. to*
a uvrir ses]

Bédier apparently interprets 602 as 'Then his treasure (nom. sing.) begins to arrive' (he omits the line in his translation, but in his commentary[13] he cites two passages from the much later romance of *Guillaume de Dole* in which *venir* is used of jewels and relics being produced). Whitehead here follows the other editors in assuming that the subject of *cumencet* is *Marsilie*, and that *ses tresors* is not nominative singular but accusative plural; he therefore corrects *venir* to *uvrir*, which is the verb that appears in several of the other versions.

Not only do Bédierists sometimes disagree among themselves; individual Bédierists sometimes change their minds about what is and what is not 'possible'. Thus the *Roland* manuscript, at lines 451–52, has the following reading:

---

[11] *Ibid.*, p. 119.
[12] See A. Tobler, *Vermischte Beiträge zur französischen Grammatik*, I, 3rd ed. (Leipzig, 1921), 4ff.
[13] *Op. cit.*, p. 147.

6) Tuit li preierent li meillor Sarrazin
    Qu'el faldestoed s'est Marsilies asis [*Bédier corr. to*
                                            Tant li preierent]

Bédier in his commentary[14] declares that there is no need to
emend *Tuit* ('all', masculine nominative plural) to *Tant* ('so
much, so long'), with some of the other versions and most of
the editors, because *que* alone, without correlative, can have the
sense of 'so that'; this is, of course, true in principle, though not
very plausible in this context. But in Bédier's definitive edition
it is *Tant* that appears both in the text and in the translation
('Tant l'ont prié les meilleurs Sarrasins que sur son trône Marsile
s'est rassis').[15] This is a common construction in the poem, and
occurs in exactly the same two-line form, with *Tant* beginning
the first line and *Que* the second, in at least two passages
(402–3, 405–6). A similar hesitation is shown by Whitehead in
lines 1421–22:

7) Ne reverrunt lor peres ne lor parenz
    Ne Carlemagne ki as porz les atent [*corr. to* per(e)s; *but
        cf.* Ne reverrunt lor meres ne lor femmes 1402]

In his edition Whitehead followed some previous editors in
emending *peres* to *pers*, understood as 'peers', which gives a
metrically correct hemistich; but in his last article[16] he argued
that the parallelism with 1402 required the retention of *peres*
in spite of the metrical irregularity.

Somewhat similar discrepancies between two Bédierist editors
are to be found in the treatment of the text of the *Tristran* of
Beroul in, respectively, Ewert's edition of 1939 and the revised
fourth edition of Muret published in 1947 under the name of
"L. M. Defourques", that is Mario Roques and Lucien Foulet.
As I have said, Ewert is a thoroughgoing Bédierist, and he rejects
the majority of Muret's original emendations in order to return
to the readings of the manuscript wherever he can possibly
attach a meaning to them. 'Defourques', in spite of his Roques

---

[14] *Ibid.*, p. 145.
[15] *Ed. cit.*, p. 41.
[16] 'Comment on Three Passages from the Text of the Oxford *Roland*' in *History
and Structure of French: Essays in Honour of Professor T. B. W. Reid* (Oxford, 1972),
pp. 257–62.

component, retains more of Muret's corrections, no doubt because his edition is, after all, presented not as a new work but as a revision of Muret's. In the first 1,000 lines of the poem, I have counted some fifteen cases where Ewert reverts to the manuscript reading while 'Defourques' keeps Muret's emendation; but there is also one case where Ewert emends though 'Defourques' does not, and there are five passages where both editors find it necessary to reject the manuscript text but adopt different corrections. Like Bédier and Whitehead in their treatment of the *Roland*, Ewert also sometimes changed his mind about what was 'possible' in Beroul; in his commentary of 1970, he occasionally accepts a new emendation or at least mentions it with guarded approval, but almost as often he suggests abandoning one of his own few emendations in favour of a return to the manuscript.

Bédier and his disciples do not, then, always agree (even with their own previous opinions) about what constitutes a 'possible' reading of the manuscript, which must be retained, and what constitutes an 'impossible' reading, which may be emended. In a well-known article of 1939, 'Principles of Textual Emendation',[17] Vinaver attempted to provide the objective criteria of 'impossibility' that had hitherto been lacking. In doing so, he seems to me to out-Bédier Bédier, for he transforms the not very systematic approach of his master into a matter of stern logical principle. He examines the successive movements of the scribe's eye in the actual process of copying, as he looks from his model to his copy and back again to his model; and he analyses and contrasts the various scribal errors that may arise from the intrinsic nature of that process — errors such as misreading (mistaking one letter or abbreviation for another), or homoeoteleuton, or dittography, and so on. Vinaver's analysis and classification is clearly accurate and acute; but the claims which he makes for its utility in deciding whether a reading can be emended are much exaggerated. His basic theory is summed up in the following dictum: " 'Impossible' readings are those which can be shown to result from scribal errors; such readings it is our duty to correct. 'Improbable' readings may or may not

---

[17] *Art. cit.* above note 2.

be due to the author, and those we have obviously no right to alter"[18] Now, everybody would no doubt agree that it is our duty to correct, if we can, all readings that "can be shown to result from scribal errors". But what Vinaver here seems to overlook is the fundamental point that a reading does not automatically reveal itself as faulty at the scribal level. Before any reading can be "shown to result from a scribal error", it must be identified, on grounds quite unconnected with the mechanics of copying, as being a faulty, or at the very least an unsatisfactory, reading. One of Vinaver's examples is a passage from the Oxford *Folie Tristan*, lines 99—101:

> 8) Tiltagel esteit un chastel
>   Ki mout par ert e fort e bel,
>   Ne cremout asalt ne engin ki vaille.

Line 101 in the manuscript means literally 'it did not fear any assault or siege-engine that avails'. Here both the editors who had published the text, Bédier and Hoepffner,[19] had assumed that there was a lacuna of a line and a half, and had printed the passage in such a way as to suggest that the word *engin* had occurred twice in the model and that the scribe had leapt from the first to the second instance by homoeoteleuton. Vinaver proposes a simpler, or at least briefer, correction, depending on a slightly different type of scribal error.[20] His hypothesis is that in the model the second word in line 101 was *cremt* (present indicative, 'fears'), but that the scribe, after writing the *m*, looked back at the model where his eye caught the *m* of *mout* in the previous line, with the result that he completed the word as *cremout* (a form of the imperfect indicative, unusual — but possible — in the scribe's Anglo-Norman); he then looked back at the model and carried on from the *t* of *cremt* with *asalt*, etc. Now, it is possible that this is what actually happened in the scriptorium (though Vinaver's explanation requires us to assume that in the model the adverb *mout* was written in full, whereas in fact it was usually abbreviated to *mlt*). But even if

---

[18] *Ibid.*, p. 368.
[19] J. Bédier, *Les deux Poèmes de la Folie Tristan*, SATF (Paris, 1907); E. Hoepffner, *La Folie Tristan . . .* (Paris, 1934).
[20] *Art. cit.*, pp. 358—60.

this is how the scribe came to write *cremout*, it does not justify
the claim that Vinaver proceeds to make. He declares that "we
have in this instance corrected a corrupt line in the *Folie
Tristan* by a mere reproduction of the mechanism of copying,
without the aids of versification and grammar, but that our
emendation has produced a reading which is both linguistically
and metrically sound". Now, it is simply not true that Vinaver's
correction has been carried out "without the aids of versification and grammar". For why did Bédier, and Hoepffner, and
Vinaver, all want to emend the manuscript reading in the first
place? Why did Bédier and Hoepffner suggest that there was a
lacuna, and Vinaver produce his elaborate account of the scribe's
eye-movements? Precisely because the manuscript text of line
101 is metrically unacceptable: even assuming elision in *n'engin*,
it has nine counted syllables instead of eight. It is this metrical
irregularity that first impels an editor to question the authenticity
of the line as written by the scribe. He then begins to consider
where the excessive syllable might be located. If at this stage he
picks on the word *cremout*, that is because it is grammatically
abnormal (though not impossible): it is an Anglo-Norman
hybrid form of imperfect indicative (for Continental Old French
cremeit, later *cremoit*), and the imperfect indicative, furthermore, would not normally be followed in the subordinate
clause by the present subjunctive *vaille*. It is only at this late
stage in his examination that the editor may look round to see
what kind of copying error might have led the scribe to write
cremout, instead of the present indicative form that would
have justified *vaille* in the subordinate. The normal present
indicative form is *crient*, but in an Anglo-Norman copy this
might be written *cremt*. Having made this observation, the
editor may reflect that the presence of the word *mout* in the
previous line explains how a copyist might have erroneously
written *cremout* instead of *cremt*. But this does not mean that
the presence, in the neighbourhood, of the very common adverb
mout contributes anything whatever to the detection of the
error, which is an indispensable preliminary to its correction.
And the position is very similar with many of the other passages
where Bédier, or Vinaver, is prepared to emend the manuscript
reading on the ground that it is due to a purely scribal error.

What enables the editor to detect the existence of an error is something that has in itself nothing to do with the activity of the scribe in the process of copying: it is the observation, which must be made by the Bédierist editor in exactly the same way as it would have been made by any old-fashioned editor before the 'Copernican' revolution, that the versification, or the grammar, or the sense, of the passage as it appears in the manuscript is not such as can be reasonably attributed to the author. Any editor, when he makes any emendation, considers himself to be intervening on behalf of the author against the scribe; and in some cases, like those cited by Vinaver, he may be able, at the second stage of the editorial process, to identify the particular copying error made by the scribe. But if there is nothing in the grammar or versification or sense of the passage to arouse suspicion, there is no possible ground for making accusations against the scribe: one cannot go through the whole manuscript text suspecting that every time the same letter sequence (such as *mout*) occurs twice within a short space there must have been a scribal contamination. Still less can one go through it suspecting that every time a word (such as *engin*) is not repeated within a short space, a passage ending with another instance of that word must have been omitted as a result of homoeoteleuton.

The analysis of the scribal process, then, does nothing to help an editor to detect scribal errors in a manuscript. If he is to make any corrections, he must be prepared, like a Gaston Paris or a Hermann Suchier, to set himself up as a more reliable authority on the language, versification, and meaning of the original work than the scribe. And this is not so presumptuous as it may at first appear. It must be remembered that the scribe was usually copying for a living and therefore working at speed, that he was sometimes imperfectly experienced in writing the vernacular, ignorant of dialects other than his own, and uncertain about literary forms, and for all these reasons liable to serious lapses of attention. The editor, on the other hand, is working at his leisure, has ample comparative data at his disposal, has had some professional training and has usually developed a genuine interest in what he is doing, so that his full attention is brought to bear on his task. If such an editor is prepared to edit, he is

certain to detect a number of unsatisfactory readings; but only
a small proportion of them are likely to be of the types that the
Bédierist recognises as depending on the intrinsic nature of the
scribal process, and therefore emendable. Most of them, though
equally unsatisfactory as segments of the work which is the
editor's concern, are doomed by a non-interventionist such as
Vinaver to remain for ever uncorrected, simply because Vinaver
can see no reason why the scribe, as a scribe, should have made
this particular error. If the error does not come within the scope
of Vinaver's rules, then the scribe, he seems to imply, cannot
have made it. For example, in an article of 1973,[21] discussing a
highly controversial passage in Beroul, the account of Tristran's
leap from the clifftop chapel, he maintains that the poet cannot
have meant to say that Tristran *chiet en la glise* 'falls in the
mud', because the manuscript has not *chiet* but *sont*, and
"there is no reason why a scribe should write *sont* for *chiet*" —
not "I can see no reason why", or even "the principles that I
have laid down do not explain why", but flatly "il n'y a aucune
raison pour que . . .".

Now, as far as these commoner errors are concerned, the ones
that cannot be accounted for by a specific scribal process such
as homoeoteleuton or dittography, most editors of the last
generation or so, even if they do not express themselves as
uncompromisingly as Vinaver, refuse to assume the responsibility
of knowing better than the scribe, and insist on leaving things as
they stand in the manuscript. I would not wish to deny them
the right to remain thus passive if they so desire; but I do resent
the 'holier-than-thou' attitude that they adopt towards anyone
who ventures to be more active in the matter of emendation.
That is why I feel it necessary to point out that in reality these
conservative editors are not nearly as conservative as they pro-
claim themselves to be: quite often they quietly abandon their
declared principles. This appears only occasionally in the actual
emendations that they make. Consider, however, my first
example (*Roland* 118): both Bédier and Whitehead regard *e la
cuntenance fier* as an 'impossible' reading, yet as far as I can see,

---

[21] 'Remarques sur quelques vers de Béroul' in *Studies . . . in memory of Frederick
Whitehead* (Manchester, 1973), pp. 341–52, here 344.

the writing of *la cuntenance* instead of *le cuntenant* does not come under any of the types of purely scribal error recognised by these editors or by Vinaver. It would surely be far-fetched to suggest that the scribe wrote *la* because there is *la barbe* in 117, and *-ance* because there is *France* in 116. We cannot bring the case under Vinaver's Error 1, "Misunderstanding of the original",[22] because — apart from the fact that the scribe has not misunderstood the original — this is defined as mistaking one letter or abbreviation for another, and if we extended that to cover mistaking *le cuntenant* for *la cuntenance* it would cover almost any putative error, and would therefore destroy Vinaver's whole argument. Since there is little doubt that the two words are synonyms, the reading *la cuntenance* cannot be criticised on grounds of sense; the only justification for the correction is, in fact, grammatical and metrical: *cuntenance* is feminine, but *fier*, which assonates correctly with *tient*, *chef*, etc., is masculine. *Cuntenance* also makes the hemistich a syllable too long. For myself, I should of course have no hesitation in making the emendation; but I should have expected both Bédier and Whitehead to reject it as arbitrary and illegitimate, since they refuse to correct so many other lines which are equally irregular grammatically or metrically; and Vinaver would no doubt say that there is "no reason" why a scribe should miscopy *le cuntenant* as *la cuntenance*.

Doubtful emendations like this are, as I have said, comparatively rare. Much more important are the unavowed changes which these editors make in defiance of their own stated principle of "reproducing the readings of the manuscript" or "allowing the extant texts to speak for themselves".[23] By the very fact of printing the text in accordance with modern conventions of alphabet and diacritics, resolution of abbreviations, capitalisation and punctuation, they are imposing on it interpretations which are simply not expressed in the manuscript, and which may be quite different from what the author intended. Like editors of all schools, they distinguish between *i* and *j*,

---

[22] *Art. cit.*, p. 361; cf. also p. 354: "Errors arising from movement *a*", 1.
[23] A. Ewert, 'On the Text of Beroul's *Tristran*' in *Studies . . . Pope, op. cit.*, pp. 89—98, here 89.

between *u* and *v*, between *c* and *ç* (before back vowels), between
e and *é*, and also between comma, semi-colon, colon, and full
stop, and between the presence and the absence of question-
marks, quotation-marks, and so on. In all these respects (which
can affect phonology, morphology, syntax, and vocabulary),
even the most conservative editor, whether he realises it or not,
is constantly changing the manuscript text and forcing his own
view of its meaning on the reader, to the exclusion of other
possible meanings. Professor Rothwell, in his article in the
Whitehead volume,[24] has given many examples of clearly
erroneous choices made by editors of Anglo-Norman texts; but
the same thing can happen in perfectly respectable Continental
texts. Thus Ewert, in an edition which professes to give us an
"unvarnished" Beroul,[25] follows Muret in printing lines 1991—92
as:

> 9) Li reis en haut le cop leva,
>   Iré le fait, si se tresva.

He thus takes the first word of 1992 as the past participle *iré*
'angered', although elsewhere in the text this participle appears
with a diphthong as *irié* and would here be expected to take the
nominative singular form *iriez*. He also transcribes the last word
of the line as *tresva*, present indicative of *tresaler* (which means
either 'go beyond, pass on' or 'swoon, faint'), although elsewhere in the text the 3rd singular present indicative of the verb
aler is always *vet*, not *va*. But in fact, the first word may well
be the noun *ire* 'anger', and the last word may well have been
in the original *tresüa*, 3rd singular preterite of *tressüer* 'sweat',
which occurs in a similar context in 4431. The editors, by their
spellings, have imposed on the line the interpretation 'Angrily
he does it, and swoons away/passes on' (though there is nothing
in the context to suggest that he does either). It is at least

---

[24] 'Appearance and Reality in Anglo-Norman' in *op. cit.* above note 21, pp.
239—56.
[25] A. Ewert, *The Romance of Tristran by Beroul . . .*, I, *Intro., Text, Glossary*
(Oxford, 1939), II, *Intro., Commentary* (Oxford, 1970). The quotation is taken
from II, 43. E. Muret, *Béroul, Le Roman de Tristan . . .*, CFMA, 3rd ed. (Paris,
1928), 4th ed. rev. by 'L. M. Defourques' (Paris, 1947). Emendations discussed in
examples 9 to 14 are taken up in Reid's *The 'Tristran' of Beroul: a Textual Commentary* (Oxford, 1972), respectively pp. 73—74, 136, 44—45, 109, 112—13, 62.

equally likely that it meant in the original 'Anger caused him to do it, and he broke out into a sweat' (so Albert Henry[26] for the first half and Brian Blakey[27] for the second; Vinaver also now tells us that he proposed *tresüa* to Miss Pope as long ago as 1921[28]). The situation is somewhat similar in line 4180:

10) C'a esté fait, c'est sor mon pois

Although both Ewert and 'Defourques' mention the possibility that the initial letter was intended as a soft *c*, equivalent in the scribe's pronunciation to *s*, all editors print *c* without cedilla. This means that they take it as representing the conjunction *que*; but *que* is not used in this construction elsewhere in the text (nor, I believe, in Old French generally). The *C'* here is undoubtedly intended as a spelling for the conjunction *se* 'if' ('If it has been done, it is against my will' — a construction used several times in the text), and should be printed with a cedilla.

The same sort of pre-emptive strike by the editor (it might almost be called a confidence trick) may also result from his punctuation of the manuscript text. The editors of Beroul print lines 1105–8 (part of the appeal of Tristran's friend Dinas to Mark) as:

11) A vos ne mesferoit il mie.
  Mais vos barons, en sa [*MS* vos] ballie
  S'il les trovout, nes vilonast,
  Encor en ert ta terre en gast.

Ewert translates 1106–8 as 'But if he got your barons in his power or assaulted them, your land will yet be laid waste in consequence'.[29] This forces the sense of *trovout* (it means 'found', not 'got'); it takes *nes* as an otherwise completely unattested combined form of the conjunction *ne* 'or' plus *les* 'them'; and it assumes an asymmetrical disjunction of *trovout*, imperfect indicative, and *vilonast*, imperfect subjunctive, which is also illogical ('found them' or 'assaulted them'), and an abnormal hypothetical sentence construction

---

[26] *Etudes de syntaxe expressive* (Paris, 1960), p. 64, note 2.
[27] 'On the text of Beroul's *Tristan*' in *French Studies*, XXI (1967), 99–103, here 100ff.
[28] *Art. cit.* in the Whitehead volume, p. 351.
[29] *Op. cit.*, II, 147.

with these two past tenses in the protasis and the future *ert*
in the apodosis. I have very little doubt that the punctuation to be inserted at the end of 1107 should be a question-
mark, not a comma, and that 1106—8 were intended by the
author, and also by the scribe, to be a rhetorical question, of
a type common in the poem: the passage means 'To you he
would do no harm; but your barons, if he found them in his
power, would he not ill-treat them? Your land will yet be ravaged
as a result'.

These examples are enough to show, I think, that there is
really no such thing as a genuinely non-interventionist treatment of a medieval work, short of printing a purely diplomatic
text. Yet the professedly non-interventionist editors, who in
matters of spelling, accentuation and punctuation, are constantly
intervening between the reader and the manuscript text, will
often refuse to make the most obvious corrections to the wording on the ground that, however improbable the manuscript
reading may seem to the well-informed editor, it must be preserved "as long as it is possible that it comes from the original".[30]
Well, I suppose there are comparatively few sequences of words
in any language that can be said to be absolutely impossible; but
such extraordinary ingenuity is shown by some Bédierist editors
in attaching a sense, of sorts, to certain scribal readings that one
is bound to suspect that the ingenuity is perversely misapplied
and that the readings are in fact 'impossible'. This seems to me
to be true in some cases even of Ewert; I choose two examples
which can be fairly briefly discussed. The first is lines 3150—52,
describing Mark's return, alone, to his palace after an ominous
confrontation with three disaffected barons:

12)   A Tintajol, devant sa tor,
      Est decendu, dedenz s'en entre:
      Nus ne set ne ne voit son estre.

Here Ewert and 'Defourques' both keep the manuscript text;
Ewert's only comment on the passage[31] is to list the rhyme
entre:estre as one of the "imperfect" rhymes which he attributes to the author. But even apart from the rhyme (which is,

[30] Vinaver, *art. cit.* in the Pope volume, p. 368.
[31] *Op. cit.*, II, 31.

indeed, very imperfect), the implied meaning of 3152, 'no one knows nor sees his mind/condition', can hardly be said to make sense, for Mark is immediately greeted by Iseut. There is no doubt, I think, that *son estre* is, as Gaston Paris saw,[32] a pure scribal error for the adverb *soventre* 'behind', and that the scribe has also, as in other cases, dropped the preconsonantal *l* of *nel* and the *u* of *seut*, and probably also the titulus of *n'en*; the line meant for the author 'no one follows him or goes along behind him' (it has just been mentioned that he had returned alone). The locution *en vet soventre* occurs in the text, again rhyming with the verb *entre*, in 1988, though here with *en vet* miswritten as *entre*. My second, and similar, example is lines 3313—14, in the passage where the squire Perinis assures Iseut that he will give Tristran her secret message (that he is to appear, disguised as a leper, at the scene of the òath):

13) Dist Perinis: 'Dame, par soi,
     Bien li dirai si le secroi.'

Ewert attempts to justify the manuscript reading *par soi* by interpreting it as meaning "'by himself', i.e. in confidence".[33] But though *par lui* could in Old French mean 'by himself' in the sense of 'alone', it did not mean 'in confidence'. Though *soi* was sometimes used in Old French where Modern French would have *lui*, it could not be so used in a clause with a subject in the first person; moreover, neither *par lui* nor *par soi* would be separated from the verb by an adverb like *bien* here. On the other hand, the scribe has often mistaken initial *f* for *s*, and there are in the text two other cases (1318 and 1326) where he has written *soi* for *foi*, in one of which (1318) Ewert himself makes the correction. He should certainly have followed Muret and 'Defourques' in correcting also in 3313 and 1326, where the manuscript again has *par soi* for the common locution *par foi* 'in faith'.

There is at least one passage in Beroul where Ewert and Vinaver agree in rejecting an emendation which I had proposed,

---

[32] Cf. ed. Muret, CFMA, p. vi: "Les corrections proposées par Gaston Paris en marge des épreuves de l'édition de 1903 . . . ont été largement mises à profit", though this particular emendation had been dropped by the 4th ed.

[33] *Op. cit.*, II, 229 (cf. also 45).

but Vinaver also rejects Ewert's interpretation of the manuscript text, and I believe Vinaver's own interpretation to be quite unfounded. The lines in question (1648—50) occur in the account of the flight of Tristran and Iseut through the forest of Morrois (Vinaver describes it as one of the finest passages in the poem,[34] which it might well be if we knew exactly what it meant):

14) Longuement par Morrois fuïrent.
    Chascun d'eus soffre paine elgal,
    Qar l'un por l'autre ne sent mal.

Ewert's paraphrase of 1649—50 was: 'The sufferings of the lovers are shared equally: for neither of them feels their pangs because of the other'.[35] Vinaver objects to this because he believes that *soffre paine* refers to the fact of undergoing physical hardships, whereas *ne sent mal* expresses the lovers' spiritual unconsciousness of these miseries. He therefore cannot accept the interpretation of *Qar* 1650 as 'for', and in an article of 1961[36] he proposed to understand it as either 'and so' or 'with the result that, so that'; in support of these alternative translations he cited a note that I had put together for him.[37] My findings, however, were that the very few Old French instances of a co-ordinating *quar* meaning something like 'then' or 'consequently' are confined to the *Saint Alexis* and the *Mystère d'Adam* (here in a different syntactical context), while the use of a subordinating *quar* 'so that' is late (13th century) and predominantly North-Eastern; nothing at all like either of these uses has been adduced from any of the numerous literary texts of the second half of the 12th century whose language is similar to that of Beroul. I therefore suggested[38] that the *Qar* of Beroul 1650 might be a

[34] *Art. cit.* in the Whitehead volume, pp. 346ff.

[35] *Op. cit.*, II, 173.

[36] 'Pour le commentaire du vers 1650 du *Tristan* de Béroul' in *Studies in Medieval French presented to Alfred Ewert* (Oxford, 1961), pp. 90—95.

[37] The surviving correspondence between Reid and Vinaver contains long and detailed exchanges on this particularly contested interpretation. It has been necessary to exclude such passages from the edited extracts from the letters in the Appendix below.

[38] 'On the Text of the *Tristran* of Beroul' in *Medieval Miscellany presented to Eugène Vinaver* (Manchester, 1965), pp. 263—88, here 281 [repr. in *Medieval Manuscripts and Textual Criticism, op. cit.* above note 2, pp. 245—71].

scribal error, and I compared 1784—85 where two very similar lines are connected by the conjunction *mais*:

> Fu ainz mais gent tant eüst paine?
> Mais l'un por l'autre ne s'e[n] sent.

Vinaver replied,[39] maintaining his interpretation. He declares that *quar* in the sense of 'so that' ('de sorte de que') is so common in Old French that there is no need to look for examples from the period and region of Beroul, but does cite one from Beroul himself:

> D'Iseut grant joie demenoient,
> De lui servir molt se penoient;
> Quar, ce saciez, ainz n'i ot rue
> Ne fust de paile portendue (2965—68).

All I can say is that, in my opinion, the only sense conveyed to any unprejudiced reader by this *Quar* in 2967 would be its normal sense as a causal conjunction 'for'. Here, as quite frequently, what it introduces is not the external cause of the state of affairs indicated in the previous sentence, but the speaker's evidence or justification for the statement he has just made: 'They were rejoicing over Iseut and taking great pains to show her honour; for there was not a street, I assure you, that was not hung with silk'. Even if there were any other evidence that for Beroul *quar* could mean 'so that' (which there is not), the imperfect tenses *demenoient* and *penoient*, and the apostrophe *ce saciez*, would make that interpretation very unlikely here. Returning to my example 14 then, Vinaver's interpretation of the manuscript text involves the arbitrary imposition of a sense of *quar* which is the opposite of its only attested sense in Beroul and his contemporaries. My suggested emendation (about which I was very tentative) merely assumes that the scribe carelessly wrote the wrong conjunction here, as all editors of Beroul agree that he did in half a dozen other cases.

I find what seem to me even more grotesque examples of fidelity to the manuscript at all costs in the *Classiques français du moyen âge* editions of the romances of Chrétien de Troyes, especially the *Erec* (1952) edited by Roques himself and the

---

[39] *Art. cit.* in the Whitehead volume, pp. 348ff.

Cligés (1957) edited by Alexandre Micha. I take two examples from *Erec*[40], the first being lines 495—97:

15) L'eve lor done an deus bacins;
    Tables, et napes, et bacins,
    Fu tost aparellié et mis. [*ed. Foerster* napes, pains et vins]

This is one of some dozen passages in the text where the scribe Guiot's copy shows an 'identical rhyme' or *rime du même au même*, that is, the same word appears at the end of both lines of a couplet, and in the same grammatical function. Now, the general concensus of the manuscripts of Chrétien's poems shows that he did not use rhymes of this kind; the same word does occasionally appear at the end of both lines of a couplet, but always in different grammatical functions (for example, *pas* noun 'step' and *pas* complement of negation). Roques, however, argues[41] that the repetition of *bacins* here might be justified by the slightly different senses which he says are required: basins for washing the hands in 495 and bowls for serving food (a most unusual sense, incidentally) in 496. But he does not seem to believe this himself; for he goes on to say that if the second *bacins* was introduced by the scribe Guiot, this may have been because the reading of his model (which Roques now tacitly assumes to have been that of all the other manuscripts, printed by Foerster), with its reference to 'wines' in the plural, seemed to him inappropriate for the household of a poor vavassour. But this will not do either; for though *tables* and *napes* are plural forms (feminine nominative plural), the *pains* and *vins* of the other manuscripts are not plurals but

---

[40] The editions referred to are: M. Roques, *Les Romans de Chrétien de Troyes*, I, *Erec et Enide*, CFMA (Paris, 1952); W. Foerster, *Christian von Troyes sämtliche Werke . . .*, III, *Erec und Enide* (Halle, 1890). One of Reid's last articles is devoted entirely to Roques's edition of *Erec*, on which he brings to bear the full critical weight of his long experience as a textual scholar; see 'Chrétien de Troyes and the Scribe Guiot' in *Medium Aevum*, XLV (1976), 1—19. This article, together with that in the Vinaver volume (see note 38 above), represent Reid's most cogent expressions of his editorial convictions. On textual criticism with reference to Chrétien, see Tony Hunt, 'Chrétien de Troyes: the Textual Problem' in *French Studies*, XXXIII (1979), 257—71, and Ph. Ménard's article on F. Lecoy's ed. of *Le Conte du Graal*, cited in note 52 below.

[41] *Ed. cit.*, p. 215.

masculine nominative singulars — as Guiot would certainly have recognised, even if Roques did not. The lines mean, in the version of all the other manuscripts and of Foerster's edition, 'tables and cloths, bread and wine, was quickly prepared', the verb *fu* being singular to agree with the nearest of a group of co-ordinated subjects, as commonly in Old French. So Roques admits by implication that the archetype of all our manuscripts had *pains et vins*, and he says nothing to suggest that this was not also Chrétien's original version (which it undoubtedly was). When Guiot changed it to *et bacins*, repeating the last word of the previous line, he was committing a scribal error of a very common type; but instead of recognising the negligence and correcting it, Roques prefers to concoct a fanciful and invalid explanation on the hypothesis that Guiot was consciously trying to improve on his model.

My second example, lines 2084–87, comes from the description of the preparations for a tournament:

16)   La ot tante vermoille ansaigne,
       Et tante guinple et tante manche,
       Et tante bloe, et tante blanche,
       Qui par amors furent donees.

This is one of some fifteen cases where Guiot presents the lines of a couplet in reverse order from that in all the other manuscripts. Roques admits that the order with *Et tante bloe, et tante blanche* following on and referring to *ansaigne* 'pennon', and *Et tante guinple et tante manche* immediately followed by the clause about the wimples and sleeves being bestowed as love-tokens, "seems more natural"; but he then proceeds to argue that "*bloe* et *blanche* peuvent se rapporter à *guimple* ou à *manche*, et le désordre apparent et piquant qui en résulte a pu séduire un rédacteur".[42] Well, I think the only person to whom the logically and linguistically abnormal sequence in Guiot's text has ever appealed is Roques himself, and I feel sure that Guiot, if he had noticed what he had written, would immediately have corrected it.

These are only two examples out of some thirty where

---

[42] *Ibid.*, p. 221.

Roques in his critical notes to *Erec* seems to me to defend a
quite indefensible reading in Guiot's version; and there are
probably at least as many more where he simply prints Guiot's
very inferior reading without comment. What he sees as inten-
tional subtleties of style I believe to be in most cases straight-
forward scribal blunders. His procedure therefore seems to me
to constitute a *reductio ad absurdum* of the whole Bédierist
approach. I suppose that he began with the genuine intention
of producing an edition of the romances of Chrétien, and chose
the Guiot copy as his base because it is on the whole the best
manuscript that we have. But when it came to actually editing
the texts, he simply abdicated; falling a victim to the insidious
dogma of non-intervention, he forgot Chrétien de Troyes and
gave us Guiot with all his faults. And yet this edition of Chrétien
was enthusiastically received. In reviewing the first volume, an
eminent scholar remarked that it "gives us at last a genuine
medieval copy of *Erec*" (which would have been truer if Roques
had provided a *diplomatic* reprint); others went much farther,
hailing this as the modern edition to replace the "outmoded"
edition of Foerster. And it is, in fact, being more and more
frequently cited as the standard edition; for example, in the
Whitehead volume of 1973, all five of the contributors whose
articles deal with Chrétien normally cite him in the *Classiques
français du moyen âge* edition. This is very unfortunate for
Chrétien, for I have no doubt that one gets much closer to
what he actually wrote in the 'composite' and 'outmoded' editions of Foerster than in those of Roques and Micha.

It will no doubt have become evident before now that in all
the passages which I have cited I am on the side of the editor
who is prepared, where necessary, to emend. More generally, I
think editors of Old French texts should do much more emending than is at present usual. This applies particularly to the
editor like Roques who out of several manuscripts has selected
one to serve as his base: where this base is clearly faulty, the
necessary emendation can very often be provided, or suggested,
by the readings of other copies. I think that it applies also,
however — though perhaps more venturesomely —, to the
editors of single-manuscript texts like the *Jeu de saint Nicolas*
or the *Tristran* of Beroul, on which I happen to have worked

myself and to both of which I have proposed emendations.[43]
And even where there are two or more manuscripts, I feel sure
that it will sometimes be not merely permissible, but necessary,
to emend against the agreement of all the manuscripts. I give one
example of such a case, from one of the innumerable Old
French saints' lives, the Anglo-Norman *Vie de saint Laurent*,[44]
lines 174—79. The pagan emperor Decius is threatening Pope
Sixtus (II):

17) (*A*) Decius dit: 'O nos dunc vien,

Sacrefise a deu feras	fras *B*
Ou ce non, ici morras.'	U si ço nun *B*
Syxtus respunt: 'Lui sacrefis?	Lur s. *B*
Deu sacrefierai toz dis;	
A vos deus ne ferai sacrefice. . .'	frai *B*

Here it is obvious that, even though *A* is the base manuscript,
it must be emended in 176 to *B*'s reading *si ço nun* 'if not,
otherwise'. But it seems to me equally necessary to correct
175, against the agreement of both manuscripts, to *Sacrefise
a nos deus feras* 'you will sacrifice to our gods'; the pagan gods
are referred to below in 179, as contrasted with the Christian
God in line 178, and the plural required in 175 is correctly
taken up by the *lur* of *B* in 177, which again must be substi-
tuted for the *lui* of *A*. The correction of 175 against both manuscripts is confirmed by the metre (though in this text, as preserved, metre is not a very safe guide), but I can see no reason
arising from the process of copying why the common ancestor
of *A* and *B* should have written *a deu* for *a nos deus* (except in
so far as any copyist is capable from time to time of completely
misunderstanding his model). In a case like this, we simply have
to accept the fact that we know better than any of the scribes
concerned.

How far, you may ask, do I really feel these emendations to
be justified? Well, there are two distinct questions here. In all
the cases which I have discussed, and in scores of others, I am

---

[43] 'On the text of the *Jeu de saint Nicolas*' in *Studies . . . Ewert, op. cit.*, pp.
96—120, and, of course, his textual commentary on Beroul, *op. cit.* above in note 25.

[44] Subsequently edited by D. W. Russell, ANTS XXXIV (London, 1976). The
emendations suggested by Reid here were in fact adopted by Russell in his edition.

100% certain that the reading which I am rejecting is not what
the author wrote or intended to write. In such cases, the very
least an editor should do, in my opinion, is to leave a blank
in his edited text. As for the emended readings which I propose, I
believe the probability that they represent what the author wrote
is somewhere within the range of, say, 80 to 100%. I am bound
to admit, however, that this view is not universally adopted.
Most of my emendations to the text of the *Jeu de saint Nicolas*
have been accepted by Professor Albert Henry, but in the case
of Beroul, Ewert accepted very few of those which I had published before he completed the second volume of his edition.
Others he has rejected as "unnecessary" or "uncalled-for", or
"gratuitous", or in one case "bold". My Beroul *Commentary*
was described by one reviewer as continuing with my "pragmatic
approach to textual criticism".[45] Vinaver found the same
approach "bureaucratic", which is not far from the opposite: I
should have thought that 'bureaucratic' was a term less applicable
to my methods than to those advocated in his own 'Principles
of Textual Emendation'. His comment was made in the course
of a discussion which we have long been conducting by correspondence[46] (and occasionally in print). It arose in connection
with Ewert's rather surprising claim (in his Pope volume article,
published at the same time as the first volume of his edition)
that a good Bédierist, by correcting identifiable scribal errors in
a text such as that of Beroul, could arrive at "a substantially
faithful reproduction of the original".[47] Vinaver and I of course
agreed that all we can do by correcting these errors is to get a
little closer to the original. Where I completely parted company
with him was when he added: "A partial reconstruction is all we
can and should aim at".[48] It may well be that in many cases a
partial reconstruction is all that we can achieve, but I fail to see
why we should adopt the defeatist attitude that it is all we are
ever entitled to aim at. Once we are satisfied that a manuscript
reading is faulty, we should bring to bear all available evidence

[45] R. A. Lodge in *The Year's Work in Modern Language Studies*, XXXIV (1972),
50.
[46] See Appendix below.
[47] *Art. cit.* in the Pope volume, p. 98.
[48] See Appendix below.

of every kind, with the aim of establishing the original reading.[49] Often, of course, we shall fail, but sometimes we shall be able to say, with a high degree of probability, that this emended reading is what must have stood in the original — and probability is all that we can ever attain in human sciences like history, and literature, and even linguistics.

The doctrine of non-intervention in the editing of Medieval French texts has no doubt served its purpose in helping to curb certain exaggerations, but, at least in its more extreme forms, I hope and believe that it has now had its day. Certain aspects of its history were very well summed up by Whitehead in his article in the Ewert volume on 'The Textual Criticism of the *Chanson de Roland*'. He shows that Bédier really started it all more or less by accident: he was "at heart an empiricist"[50] (as is indeed shown by the emendations to the text of the *fabliaux* proposed in the appendix to the first edition of his thesis), and it was only because he happened to edit the *Roland*, where there is a probably unique relation between the Digby manuscript and the rest, that he set up the principle of defending the manuscript reading "wherever possible". This doctrine, when systematised by a Roques or a Vinaver, makes the editor the advocate of the scribe. Whitehead himself wants to see the editor resuming his original role of an impartial judge between scribe and author.[51] As I have already indicated, I would go further: since the scribe's case is there for all to see, I feel that the only hope of justice lies in the editor's intervention on behalf of the author. And I think this 'interventionist' approach may now be coming into fashion again after its long eclipse. I note that in dealing with the text of the *Chanson de Guillaume* Mme Wathelet-Willem has adopted a much less conservative attitude than that of McMillan in his edition for the Société des Anciens

---

[49] On the prime importance of establishing textual parallels, see Reid's commentary on Beroul, *op. cit.*, p. 4, and Appendix below.

[50] *Art. cit.* in the Ewert volume, pp. 76–89, here 85. Cf. Whitehead's later article, written in collaboration with C. E. Pickford, 'The Introduction to the *Lai de l'Ombre*: Sixty Years Later' in *Romania*, XCIV (1973), 145–56 [repr. in *Medieval Manuscripts and Textual Criticism, op. cit.*, pp. 103–15].

[51] *Art. cit.*, p. 84.

Textes Français.[52] The *Chanson de Guillaume* has a particular significance for me: it was the first complete Old French text that I ever studied as an undergraduate. We read it, of course, in the edition of Elizabeth Stearns Tyler, which is one that encourages emendation. The urge to emend (or intervene, or interfere) has never since left me. I am glad to see that it appears to be at last becoming respectable again.

---

[52] A useful historical perspective on changing editorial attitudes in Medieval French textual scholarship (and a good bibliography) is provided by A. Foulet & M. B. Speer, *On Editing Old French Texts* (Lawrence, Kansas, 1979), esp. pp. 1–39. In 1965, in his Vinaver volume article (p. 288), Reid had concluded that "the only really satisfactory form of edition is therefore one that gives [a plain transcription and an edited text] side by side in parallel columns or on facing pages. Thus presented, the editor's reconstruction of the original can be seen in its proper perspective, as the fruit, not of a presumptuous disguised collaboration with the author, but of a tentative and undisguised collaboration with the scribe". In this context it is interesting to note that the printing of synoptic editions, generally on non-interventionist lines, seems to be becoming an increasingly favoured solution to the problems posed by texts preserved in several MSS; for example, C. Régnier's *Prise d'Orange* (Paris, 1966), Jean Rychner's *Lanval* (Genève, 1958), *Fabliaux* (Neuchâtel, 1960), *Du Boucher d'Abevile* (Genève, 1975), Y. Lepage's *Couronnement de Louis* (Genève, 1978). C. Segre's important edition of the *Chanson de Roland* (Milano, 1971), though sharing *grosso modo* the stemmatic convictions that Bédier adopted, makes fuller use of collateral readings and does not hesitate to correct scribal error. Other modern editors of the Oxford *Roland*, however, are still carrying Bédier's textual conservatism to zealous extremes, notably G. Moignet (Paris, 1969; 3rd ed. 1972), and, *a fortiori*, G. Brault (Pennsylvania State Univ. Press, 1978) (for a review of the latter's editorial excesses, see *Romance Philology*, XXXIV (1981), *46–*63). Though a non-interventionist editor himself, A. J. Holden has been moved to take exception to the methodological conservatism of S. Sandqvist, who seems to assume that doubtful MS readings, if found paralleled elsewhere, in some way cease to pose editorial problems; see Holden's 'Nouvelles remarques sur le *Roman de Rou*' in *Revue de Linguistique romane*, XLV (1981), 118–27, and Sandqvist's earlier articles in *Romania*, XCIX (1978), 433–83 (on the *Roland*), and *Revue de Linguistique romane*, XLIII (1979), 287–309 (on the *Rou*). On the Continent, Ph. Ménard is one of the rare scholars to express reservations about the continuing vitality of the Bédier-Roques tradition; see his 'Note sur le texte du *Conte du Graal*' in *Mélanges . . . Pierre Jonin* (Aix-en-Provence, 1979), pp. 449–57 (written in much the same spirit as Reid's *Medium Aevum* art. of 1976), and pp. 165–66 of his contribution to the present volume. J. Wathelet-Willem's bold reconstructionalist approach in her ed. of the *Chanson de Guillaume*, 2 vols. (Paris, 1975), which provides a plain transcription opposite a critical text, remains more or less isolated, though L. Formisano's ed. of the *Destruction de Rome* (Firenze, 1981), for example, is interventionist on a wide scale.

APPENDIX

Set out below, in an edited form, are relevant extracts from the correspondence referred to in the course of the article. These letters are of particular interest in that they provide explicit statements from three distinguished textual scholars on the editorial procedures of which they were advocates and exponents.

A. Ewert to Reid (commenting on an early draft of an article
 which ultimately appeared in the Vinaver volume; [1964?]):
If, as your formulations suggest, your object is that the 'better' readings which you indicate should be incorporated in the text of an edition, then I am bound to say that I would have to dissent nearly all along the line. To begin with, it is not clear what exactly the edition which you envisage seeks to achieve: recover the original text of the author? or reconstruct the archetype? or produce a readable and coherent text? I have long been convinced that, in a case like Beroul, one ought to reproduce the MS with the absolute minimum of change, eliminating only what are indisputably scribal blunders, and 'correcting' the text only when it does not make sense, or if metrical criteria reveal a corruption — although even in respect of this criterion one must allow not only for the licences commonly tolerated (e.g. certain optional elisions), but also for the possibility that not merely the scribe but the author too allowed slightly imperfect lines or rhymes to stand (a possibility which is too often not even envisaged by editors).

. . . A scribe may be content to transcribe without serious regard to meaning, or he may be concerned that what he writes shall at least make sense (as he sees it), or he may introduce clarifications, or he may produce what is in effect a revised edition of the work that he is reproducing — and he may do some or all of these things in turn in the course of transcribing a single work. In these circumstances, how are we to know that a particular scribe has less literary taste and is less meticulous than the author whose work he is transcribing (at first or second hand)? I am therefore bound to question what I take to be some of your criteria:

1. I cannot agree that, if an editor has to choose between two readings, he is entitled to regard as alone genuine (and to prefer) the one which makes the better sense (or which he regards

as 'better' for other reasons), and to introduce this into the text
at the expense of the authentic MS reading.

2. I cannot agree that mere linguistic abnormality (in syntactic or other usage) should serve to invalidate a MS reading. I
feel that much of what has been said about 12th-century French
in the past 100 years is based upon doctored evidence. How can
it be otherwise if abnormalities are carefully combed out and
relegated to a set of variants which, more often than not, are
ignored completely? One all too easily gets a rule by just eliminating abnormalities.

3. I do not attach much weight to the fact that a particular
expression or construction runs counter to what appears to be
the poet's practice in other parts of the same work.

. . . To sum up my own view on this whole matter: I think
that while we can never have too much elucidation and textual
criticism, it is generally speaking wrong (at any rate in a case
like that of Beroul) to incorporate all the results of such criticism
and re-creation in a 20th-century edition, however convincing
the suggested emendations may be in themselves and taken
individually or seriatim. The prime consideration is that such an
edition should present a text which is as near as may be *authentic*, concessions to the modern reader — or critic — being largely
confined to the notes, except of course the harmless moderniza-
tion of the use of capitals and the like . . .

E. Vinaver to Reid (acknowledging receipt of The 'Tristran' of
   Beroul: a Textual Commentary; *3.xi.1972):*
In following your dialogue with Ewert, I feel on the whole
closer to his point of view than to yours, even though there are
many things in his commentary and glossary with which I do
not agree at all. I honestly do not think, however, that you have
made out a case for the somewhat bureaucratic approach to
criticism that you advance in your introduction. Where, after
all, do you find your "parallels"? In critical editions in which
readings "not paralleled elsewhere" have been excluded from
the text and from the glossaries? In dictionaries based on such
editions? And are you not forgetting that, even if the entire
manuscript tradition of medieval vernacular writings were made

available to us, it would represent only about a quarter of what was actually produced in France between 1100 and 1500?

I also disagree, as you know, with your theory of emendation, and particularly with the way in which you apply it to Beroul in this book. Here, of course, Ewert is an easy prey because of the way in which he put his 'non-interventionist' case. He should not have said, as he does, that his method would leave us with a text "which can fairly be considered a substantially faithful reproduction of the original". Nobody can say that once we have corrected the identifiable scribal errors in the MS we shall get a faithful reproduction of Beroul's poem; but what we can say is that we shall then get a little closer to that poem, and as close as we can in the present state of our knowledge of the manuscript tradition and of scribal technique. A *partial* reconstruction is all we can and should aim at. But if we simply put in what we think Beroul should or might have said, we run the risk of getting further away from him . . .

Reid to Vinaver (7.xii.1972):
I feel quite unable to accept the views about editorial procedures in your letter: the 'agreement to disagree' must, I fear, subsist. In insisting on the importance of finding 'parallels', I am not forgetting that the MSS now available to us represent only a small fraction of what was written down in French between 1100 and 1500 (and an infinitesimal proportion of what was spoken — much of which would be equally significant for our editorial purposes if we had access to it). But the situation of the medievalist is not in this respect essentially different from that of the reader or critic of contemporary literature. He too can understand a given text only by virtue of his acquaintance with 'parallels', though those that he knows can constitute only an infinitesimal proportion of the written and spoken material that might, if it were accessible, be relevant to the interpretation of that text — parallels, too, which like those of the medievalist are sometimes distorted by the accidents of transmission (mispronunciations, mis-spellings and misprints; mishearings and misreadings of various origins; faults of memory, failures to consider the physical or social context, and so on). As compared

with the modernist, the medievalist is more dependent on his dictionaries and glossaries, but this is largely because he has no speakers of the language to act as informants. If he is a scholar, however, he should use both the dictionaries and the critical editions primarily as indexes or concordances enabling him to find the most useful parallels as they actually stand in the MSS. The whole institution of language, after all, whether considered in relation to speaker or hearer, writer or reader, rests on the comparison of parallels as its basis.

I have never, I hope, denied that if we did no more than correct the identifiable scribal errors in the Beroul MS we should get a little closer to the poem of Beroul than if we merely printed a diplomatic text. I cannot, however, agree that this is "as close as we can get to it in the present state of our knowledge. . .". When I read the *Guardian*, I often have to treat its printed text as I would treat the diplomatic text of Beroul, for there are many passages that do not make sense (as judged by all the Modern English parallels that I have in my memory). Some of these can be corrected by assuming that a writer or a compositor has made what corresponds to a purely scribal error (e.g. a haplography). But that is not the nearest the ordinary newspaper reader can get to what the journalist intended to convey; many non-scribal errors can be quite confidently corrected by comparison with other passages in the same article, or with the help of information from independent sources. You say that "a *partial* reconstruction is all we can and should aim at": both in the case of Beroul and in that of the newspaper, a partial reconstruction may sometimes be all that we can achieve, but I do not think that we should adopt the defeatist attitude that it is therefore all we are ever entitled to aim at . . .

Vinaver to Reid (14.xii.1972 & 5.i.1973):
I think that it is a pity that the fortieth year of our friendship should find us so sharply divided over fundamental issues in a field which, in different ways, you and I have made our own. But here is a brief *mise au point* for what it is worth. Perhaps some good may come of it . . .

I find the parallel between your 'editing' of the *Guardian* articles and your efforts to emend Beroul particularly misleading. You are equating quantitatively data which belong qualitatively to different orders of things, and so producing an equation which is plausible in appearance but false in substance. You have, of course, heard and read only a fraction of what has been said and written in English in the last hundred years, and the fraction may well be smaller than that which expresses the proportion of extant Old French material to the total output of spoken and written Old French. But you know English in a totally different way, and you can therefore correct faulty English without any conscious reference to what you have heard and read. Neither you nor anybody else in this century can claim to know Old French like that. Only a living language can be mastered in a manner comparable to the acquisition of the mother tongue . . .

NIHIL IN TEXTU NISI QUOQUE IN INTELLECTU: THAT $\bar{n}$ *lostanit* PASSAGE IN THE STRASBOURG OATHS

F. J. BARNETT_____

There will always be a tension — a salutary tension — in textual criticism between those who believe in the dictum, quoted by Postgate,[1] that it is better to leave in the text "what if not the original reading is at least the remains of it", and those who hold that it is better "to present to the reader something which the author *might* have written than something he could not". As far as the criterion of intelligibility is concerned, the opposition could be expressed as between, on the one hand, those who believe in the "forcible extraction from the text of a meaning which is not in the words, and which would be admitted not to be in them, were it not seen to be required by the context" (Postgate again); and, on the other hand, those who believe that, where a reading defies understanding, it is legitimate, indeed necessary, to try to emend it — with, of course, prudence and in accordance with established palaeographical principles. This latter, as we know, is the kind of approach Tim Reid favoured. It is the one that I have adopted in this article.

The celebrated $\bar{n}$ *lostanit* crux[2] has come in for renewed

---

[1] J. P. Postgate in his article *Textual Criticism* in the *Encyclopaedia Britannica* (11th edition), from which the quotation later in this sentence is also taken. The quotation in the following sentence is from Postgate's contribution on the same subject in *A Companion to Latin Studies* ed. J. E. Sandys (Cambridge, 1910), p. 804.

[2] For ease of reference, I reproduce here the second oath in its French and Germanic versions, following the text as printed in Albert Henry's *Chrestomathie de la littérature en ancien français*, 3rd revd. ed. (Bern, 1965), p. 2, which capitalizes the names, divides the words and punctuates in accordance with modern practice; the *locus* itself, however, I present (in italics) as it appears in the MS:

Sacramentum autem, quod utrorumque populus, quique propria lingua, testatus est, romana lingua sic se habet:

Si Lodhuuigs sagrament que son fradre Karlo iurat conseruat, et Karlus, meos

discussion in recent decades,[3] mainly as a result of the attention which scholars have given the *Oaths* in line with current interest in the emergence of written Romance vernaculars. In the debate, the two critical approaches mentioned have again been in evidence, new and very determined efforts being made

---

sendra, *desuo partᾱ lostanit*, si io returnar non l'int pois, ne io ne neuls cui eo returnar int pois, in nulla aiudha contra Lodhuuig nun li iu er.

Teudisca autem lingua:

Oba Karl then eid, then er sinemo bruodher Ludhuuuige gesuor, geleistit, indi Ludhuuuig min herro then er imo gesuor forbrihchit, ob ih inan es iruuenden ne mag: noh ih noh thero nohhein, then ih es iruuenden mag, uuidhar Karle imo ce follusti ne uuirdhit.

[3] A lengthy separate article would scarcely suffice to discuss at all adequately the numerous attempts that have been made to explain or emend this *locus*. Some of them are worthy of serious consideration, and I should certainly have discussed at least these here had space permitted. On the other hand, this article would obviously not have been written if I had not considered them less persuasive than my own proposed solution. Here I shall merely recall that the interpretations (much canvassed at one time) which see in *tanit* some form of the verb *tenir* have met with serious objections on phonological, morphological or syntactic grounds (sometimes on all three), and remark that the *s* of *stanit* can in any case hardly be the reflexive pronoun, the nuance of intimate involvement which its use conveys being out of place in a legal document. The basic weakness of other suggestions is that: either they propose emendations whose corruption to the MS reading is not credibly explicable, especially as concerns the embarrassing presence of an unaccountable negative particle; or they postulate the presence of words, or meanings, or both, that are not otherwise attested in French and whose idiosyncratic character is foreign to the general ordinariness (allowance made for the legal content) and immediate intelligibility of the language of the *Oaths*.

Again for reasons of economy, I shall not attempt to give more than broad, but I hope sufficient, bibliographical indications. A full bibliography of *Oaths* studies down to the time of writing was appended by A. Ewert to his article in the *Transactions of the Philological Society* of 1935. Another especially useful older source is Foerster and Koschwitz's *Altfranzösisches Übungsbuch* (and its *Nachträge*), 7th ed. (Leipzig, 1932). Since the War, particularly in the 1960s and 1970s, a considerable number of further contributions on general *Oaths* topics have been published by distinguished scholars, including A. Castellani, A. B. Chernyak, Robert J. Hall, Roy Harris, H. Lüdtke, and P. Wunderli. Those relating more particularly to our *locus* have appeared mainly in the journals *Vox Romanica* (*VRo*) and the *Zeitschrift für romanische Philologie* (*ZrPh*), and in the series *Travaux de linguistique et de littérature publiés par le Centre de philologie et de littératures romanes de l'Université de Strasbourg* (*Tra Li Li*). They include: in *VRo*, articles by H. L. W. Nelson (1966), G. Hilty (1966, 1973, 1978) and S. Becker (1978); in *ZrPh*, by H.-E. Keller (1969) and S. Becker (1978); in *Tra Li Li*, by G. Hilty (*Mélanges Imbs*; 1973), and A. Castellani (*Mélanges Rychner*; 1978). See also A. B. Chernyak in *Lingvisticheskie Issledovaniya* (Moscow, 1973); V. Drašković in *Linguistika*, XV (1975) (Ljubljana); S. Becker, *Untersuchungen zur Redaktion der Strassburger Eide*, 1972 (reviewed by A. B. Chernyak in *Fololjogicheskie Nauki*, Moscow, 1975); and W. Kesselring, *Die französische Sprache im Mittelalter* (Tübingen, 1973).

particularly on the side of extracting a meaning from the text as it stands. I think that it is a fair comment that — for all the learning and ingenuity deployed — these various attempts at elucidation have failed to win general acceptance. The scholars concerned have at any rate failed in the main to convince one another. Perhaps the reason is that, whether defending the MS reading or emending it, they have concentrated primarily upon the obscure sequence of letters $\bar{n}$ *lostanit*, either regarding the other anomalous features of the *locus* as of secondary importance or neglecting them entirely. These features are: the illogical *lo* in the $\bar{n}$ *lostanit* phrase, which, as a succession of commentators have noted, seems to refer to the oath sworn by Louis, and not, as the situation demands, to the one sworn by Charles; the masculine form *suo*[4] accompanying the feminine noun *part*; and, for those who see in *stanit* some verb meaning 'breaks' or 'is false to', the presence of $\bar{n}$, which, interpreted as a contraction of the negative particle, would give a meaning contrary to that required by the context. The solution which I propose here not only takes account of all those anomalous features, but seeks to use them as positive clues in reconstructing the original reading, my contention being that their presence is only explicable if they are vestiges of a wording different from that contained in our manuscript.

My point of departure, then, is acceptance of the fact that, in view of the several indications of corruption in this *locus*, emendation is unavoidable. This conclusion is reinforced by the lack of success, referred to above, which scholars determined to

---

[4] *Suo* cannot plausibly be regarded as a feminine form in this text. Here we find the retained (and off-glide) atonic final vowels represented by a variety of graphies: etymological *o* in *poblo, nostro, Karlo* (two occurrences), etc., etymological *u* in *Karlus*, etymological *e* in *fradre* (three occurrences), etymological *a* in *cosa, aiudha*, etc., non-etymological *a* in *fradra* (one occurrence) and in *sendra* (off-glide), and non-etymological *e* in *Karle* (one occurrence). But it will be seen that, while *e* and *a* are used both etymologically and non-etymologically, *u* and *o* are used only etymologically (for masculines). This is in line with later French scribal practice, whereby final neutral *e* is represented by the letter *e* (and for a time, particularly in some areas and some texts, by *a*), whereas final *u* and *o* appear only in diphthongs (or triphthongs) or monosyllables, and only in masculines. There is, as far as I know, no instance in the Early Old French texts — and none, of course, in later French texts — of the use of *-o* corresponding to a Latin *-a*, a fact that has led some editors of the *Oaths* to correct *suo* to *sua* or *sue* in our passage.

avoid emendation have had in their attempts to extract from the text as it stands a meaning that is both philologically credible and appropriate in the context.

Now, about the general sense to be conveyed there can, fortunately, be no doubt — which gives us a solid basis to build on. The French and Germanic oaths embody undertakings by Charles's army and Louis's, respectively, that they will not support their leader against his brother if the brother concerned is true to his oath and their leader false to his. It is at this basic sense that all attempts to deal with this crux, whether by elucidation of the MS reading or by emendation of it, must arrive, and it is noteworthy that this sense is expressed clearly and straightforwardly in the Germanic oath. That is why — together with the close correspondence of the French and Germanic texts throughout the greater part of the two sets of oaths — many scholars have looked to the wording of the Germanic oath for guidance in reconstructing the original reading of the French text at the point under discussion. So to proceed does not involve the assumption that the French version was translated from the Germanic — although some studies of the *Oaths* suggest that this may have been the case — or that there must necessarily be a very close verbal correspondence at this point; it is merely to take into account a likelihood, namely that the two texts were couched in similar terms here as at most other points. Now, the Germanic text, literally translated, runs: 'If K. carries out the oath which he swore to his brother L., and L., my lord, breaks (*forbrihchit*) that which he swore to him . . .'. It was this fact, as well as the general force of the context, that led Suchier as long ago as 1874, followed by Meyer, Bartsch, Constans and others (possibly, indeed, the majority of those who have studied the text), to see in *stanit* some form of the verb *fraindre* 'to break', whether *franit* or *fraint*, both of which are palaeographically plausible.[5]

---

[5] The positive expression 'breaks, violates' is, in any case, much more natural in this context than a negative 'does not keep, stand by, uphold' (the meanings which some scholars seek to extract from n̄ *tanit, stannit* or *stanit*). It does not involve the pointless switching of synonyms: 'if Louis *observes* . . . and Charles . . . does not *keep* (stand by, uphold)'; and it fits in harmoniously with what follows: 'if I cannot deter him therefrom (i.e. from breaking (violating) his oath)'; whereas a negatived

This conjecture, based as it is upon the recognition of the presence in this passage of a familiar verb (as opposed to a postulated hapax), used in a familiar meaning, entirely appropriate in the legal context, and being the precise semantic equivalent of the corresponding verb in the Germanic oath, would very probably have gained universal acceptance if it had not been for the troublesome presence of the apparent negative contraction n̄. I propose to take it as the basis of my own suggested solution.

This is that, instead of *de suo part n̄ lostanit*, we should read *de sua part lo suon infraint* (or *infranit*).[6] This reading has two obvious advantages, apart, of course, from providing an entirely

---

verb would clash badly with what follows: 'deter him . . . (from *not* keeping (etc.) his oath)'. Is it really likely that the official responsible for drafting this legal text would have chosen such a contorted way of phrasing it when an entirely unexceptionable alternative, such as is found in the Germanic oath, lay so obviously to hand? The reading *franit* supposes only a miscopy of *st-* for *fr-*, graphies of similar shape in Caroline minuscule; *fraint* would suppose a further mistake, -*in*- miscopied as -*ni*-, a familiar confusion. In *franit*, the -*ni*- would presumably represent a palatalized nasal (< **frangit**), the otherwise unattested stage preceding the familiar *fraint*, in which yod has been disengaged.

[6] The phrase *sacramentum infringere* is attested in the near-contemporary oath sworn by Louis and Charles in 854: ". . . si Hludowicus frater noster illud sacramentum, quod contra nos iuratum habet, infregerit vel infringit . . ." (*Monumenta Germaniae Historica, Legum Sectio II*, p. 78). The syntax of this Latin oath is interesting, being decidedly popular in character: note the 'article' *illud*, while the *Strasbourg Oaths*, although vernacular, have no article in "si Lodhuuigs sagrament que son fradre Karlo iurat conseruat", and the popular perfect *iuratum habet* contrasting with the conservative past definite *iurat* of the *Oaths*. The Latin oath is in these respects more popular than the vernacular *Oaths*! The *infregerit vel infringit* shows both Latin and Romance syntax, represented as alternative constructions. French *enfreindre* (older form *enfraindre*) derives not from *infringere* but the recomposed form *infrangere*. This latter is entered in the index to *MGH Leg. Sect. II*, but does not, as far as I can see, appear in any of the passages to which the index refers. It is found in the glosses (Goetz, II 308, 49). See also the *infringo* entry in the *Thesaurus Linguae Latinae*. *Enfreindre* has, of course, remained a legal term down to the present day. Here I print the words separated by spaces, whereas below I print *suoninfraint* run together. It is probably otiose to recall that such runnings together of words, written or printed separately in modern practice, are frequently found in medieval manuscripts. Several examples occur in the *Oaths* MS, including in the *locus*, which is written *desuo partn̄ lostanit*. There are also examples in the *Oaths* MS of the separation of parts of a single word, also a common scribal practice, e.g. *cad huna* for *cadhuna*. Scribe A may even have found *lo suonin fraint* in his model, and he may have written *suo nin* in his interlinear correction. Such groupings would have facilitated the process of corruption which I postulate; they are not essential to it.

acceptable meaning, dependent in no way on otherwise unattested senses or otherwise unattested words: firstly, *lo suon*
(originally suggested by Gaston Paris in 1886) removes the
ambiguity of reference of *lo* standing alone, since it is now
clearly indicated that the oath that Charles might break is his
own, not Louis's; secondly, it replaces masculine *suo* with an
appropriate feminine form *sua* (more likely than *sue* in view of
the *-a* in the other feminines in this text). But, attractive as this
reading is, that fact alone would not, of course, entitle it to
acceptance as the probable original wording. For it is a well-
known and well-founded principle of textual criticism that a
link must be established between a conjectured reading and the
one that it replaces, i.e. it must be shown that a conjectured
original could by credible errors on the part of a copyist or
copyists have produced the reading judged corrupt.[7] It is only
because I believe that my proposed emendation fully meets
this reasonable requirement that I am putting it forward here.

In order to explain the corruption, we need suppose only two
copyists: scribe A copying *de sua part lo suoninfraint* jumps
from *de sua part lo* to *fraint*, omitting *suonin* by the fault of
haplography (or homoiographon) familiar to all palaeographers
and proof-readers, the similarity of *suo(nin)* to *sua(part)* giving
him the impression that the former had already been copied.
The slip would have been facilitated in this case by the fact that
de sua part lo fraint makes a kind of sense, provided that you
are not attending closely. But when his copy is read over, either
he or a reviser notices the omission and writes in the missing
sequence of letters between the lines (just as scribe B was to
add the omitted *d* in *aiuha* in the second oath), their position
possibly being determined by the fact that the tall letters *l* and
f did not leave room to write *suonin* directly over *lofraint*, thus:

suonin

de suapart lofraint

---

[7] Cf. Postgate in the *Encyclopaedia Britannica* article referred to in n. 1 above:
"No alteration of a text . . . is entitled to approval unless, in addition to providing the
sense and diction required, it also presents a reading which the evidence furnished by
the tradition shows might not improbably have been corrupted to what stands in the
text".

This, or something like it, was, I conjecture, the state of the passage as B, the scribe of our manuscript, found it. Being a conscientious man, as the various corrections which we find in his own manuscript show, he no doubt made every effort to produce a true and faithful copy; but, faced with a text composed some century and a half earlier — the interval between 842 and the date assigned to the *Oaths* manuscript by the palaeographers —, he was ill equipped to deal with any problem that called for more than the mechanical reproduction of the text as it stood in his model. For there had, of course, been considerable changes in the French language over that period; and the graphies of the *Oaths* are, in any case, archaic even for the ninth century, as a comparison with the *Eulalie* manuscript, which dates from only 40 years later (*c.* 880), shows. He must have found the language of the *Oaths* outlandish and remote, and he was certainly in no position to judge what would have been admissible or not admissible in the original text. Accordingly, interpreting the superscript letters as a correction instead of an insertion, he dutifully replaced the *sua* of *de sua part* with *suo*; and he readily contracted *nin* to *n̄*, equating it with the negative particle *nen* of his own time in virtue of what must have seemed to him an obvious correspondence of *i* in the *Oaths* in such words as *in, ist, cist* and *int* to the *e* of his contemporary French (*en, est, cest, ent*), just as he slipped into writing *en* for *in* in the first oath before noticing his mistake and correcting it with an expunctuation line. He can have seen no deterrent in the other forms of the negative particle found in the oath — *non* and *nun* (each occurring once) — precisely because they would suggest that it was variable in form.

Although, as we have seen, there are strong reasons for supposing that the MS *stanit* (or *ftanit*, as some palaeographers have deciphered the reading) must represent a *franit* (or *fraint*) of the original, there are no such strong pointers to the stage at which the corruption occurred or to the mechanism involved. In Caroline minuscule, the similar shape of the letters makes it easy to confuse the *st* and *fr* combinations. So did scribe A inadvertently write *stanit* (*ftanit*) as well as (at first) omitting *suonin*? In which case scribe B will merely have copied what he had before him. Or did *franit* (or *fraint*) still stand in the text B was copying? In which case he must: either have simply misread it as *stanit* (*ftanit*) and written down unreflectingly what he thought that he had before him; or have decided that, in view of the presence of the presumed negative particle, *franit* (*fraint*) 'breaks' could not be right and that some verb unknown to him (presumed obsolete?) must have been intended, whereupon he plumped for *stanit* (or *ftanit*) *en désespoir de cause* as the nearest graphical alternative. In any event, if we accept, as surely we must now do, that *stanit/ftanit* yields no credible meaning, we are obliged to assume that at some stage a copyist, unwittingly or witlessly, wrote down the sequence of letters that we find in our MS.

What I would claim for this conjecture is: that it restores a reading which is intelligible, unambiguous, appropriate in the context (compare the corresponding Germanic wording), and phraseologically appropriate (compare the wording of corresponding Latin legal texts); that it postulates no lexical or semantic hapax; that it remedies all defects of the MS reading (illogical *lo*, inadmissible masculine *suo*, unintelligible *stanit*, inappropriate 'negative'); and that it is readily and credibly 'corruptible' to the MS reading. I do not, of course, claim certainty for it; it is the essence of emendation based on conjecture to deal in probabilities not certainties.

THE LIFE OF SAINT MELOR[1]

A. H. DIVERRES

National Library of Wales Bettisfield MS 19 is a roll composed of three strips of vellum of varying length.[2] The first piece is badly mutilated at the top and was originally longer than it is now. An examination of the Latin Lives suggests that some fifteen lines of the beginning of the text may have been lost.[3] The poem is written in a single column, and 337 lines have been preserved in part or *in toto*, 213 on the front of the roll and 124 on the back, out of a probable total of around 370. While the front is very legible, the back has suffered badly from wear and has also been stained with gall, so that sections are only partly decipherable. There appear to have been at least three scribes, and their hands are typical of the middle or second half of the fourteenth century, a date which is confirmed by the orthography and by the metrical irregularities of the Anglo-Norman alexandrine rhyming couplets in which the poem is written.

Saint Melor, a young Breton prince whose ancestors were linked with the British emigrations to Armorica, was widely venerated in Brittany up to modern times. His cult had a certain vogue in Cornwall in the Middle Ages, but, from the eleventh century to the Reformation, its main centre in Britain was at the abbey church of Amesbury, which claimed to house his

[1] I wish to thank Drs A. Lodge, Ceridwen Lloyd-Morgan and Ian Short, who have checked parts of my transcript of the manuscript, and Professor W. Rothwell for providing me with information on some lexical forms.
[2] They are 197, 525 and 433 mm. long. For a fuller description, see my article entitled 'An Anglo-Norman Life of Saint Melor' in *The National Library of Wales Journal*, XV (1967), 167–178.
[3] Four medieval Latin Lives of Melor are extant. The earliest is preserved in MS Paris BN lat. 13789, and was edited by Dom Plaine in *Analecta Bollandiana*, V (1886), 165–176. For details of the others, see my article mentioned in n. 2 above.

body.[4] The earliest surviving *Vita* situates the story unequivocally in Brittany, but by the end of the thirteenth or the beginning of the fourteenth century, versions set in an insular context appear. The Anglo-Norman Life is one of these, and in it Armorican Cornubia and Dumnonia have become Cornwall and Devonshire.

The Bettisfield 19 account of Melor's life is generally more diffuse than the *Vitae*, and so it is impossible to reconstruct the undeciphered sections with certainty; hence the *lacunae* in the last third of the text. But since a comparison with the *Vita* in B.N. lat. 13789 allows their content to be described with reasonable accuracy, summaries have been included in the Notes to the Text.

The transcription conforms to the modern treatment of Anglo-Norman texts, and the convention of distinguishing between *i* and *j*, *u* and *v*, *c* and *ç* has been followed. The acute accent has been added to tonic *e* to avoid confusion with atonic forms, but no use has been made of the diaeresis to indicate vowels in hiatus. The abbreviations, which are orthodox, have been expanded in accordance with the orthographical practices of the scribes. Superscript *9* has been transcribed as *us*, and superscript *r* as *ur*, for *u* is the normal symbol for [u]. Only the relative pronouns have posed a problem. Since, in the case of *qui*, the full form is either *qui* or *ki*, *q* with superscript *i* has been transcribed *qui*. On the other hand, the full forms of *que* are usually *ke* or *qe*, rarely *que*, and so *q̄* has been transcribed *qe*. Every emendation not enclosed in square brackets is accompanied by the original MS reading at the foot of the page.

....................esu............... *f. 1r*
...............noun Danyel............

[4] The standard studies of his cult are: G.H. Doble, *Saint Melor* (Cornish Saints Series, n° 13, 1927); D.B. Grémont, 'Recherches sur saint Melar, Melor ou Meloir' in *Bulletin de la Société Archéologique du Finistère*, CI (1973), 285–361. See also J. Chandler, 'Three Amesbury Legends' in *Hatcher Review*, VI (1978), 12–23; A.H. Diverres, 'St. Melor, what is the truth behind the legend?' in *The Amesbury Millennium Lectures*, ed. J. Chandler (Amesbury, 1979), pp. 9–19.

. . . . [d'e] speye e d'armes cra[venté] .

4 . . . . [B] udich out noun

. . . . [p] ere Meliaus qe fu encheson

. . . . [sey] nt Melor par dreite reyson.

Cestuy Me[lia] us lors estoyt duk de Cornwaylle.

8 Prist dunkes a feme une noble dame to Bretayne:

De Deveneshyre ele fu nee, e nomee Auraylle;

Fille de un noble counte nomé Judec esteyt,

Atray de cele gent qe ly Engleys d'Yrlaunde ameneyt.

12 Luy avaunt dit Budich deus fiz avoit:

Meliaus fu ly premers, qui puys pere estoit

Seynt Melor ly martirs. Pur luy Dieu fesoit

Miracles plusurs, qe utre tuz lowé soyt.

16 Ly autre Ryvaud fu apelé, le frere Meliau,

Qui uncle f[u] verreyment a seynt Melor le bon.

Le premer an qe Meliaus la duchee ust de Cornwaylle

Naquit Melor de l'avaundite dame Auraylle.

20 E aprés tint ly duk Meliaus set aunz la terre saunz faylle:

Avint qe en le[s] set aunz ne plovoit jour ne nuyt,

Ne glace en la terre ne gelee aparust;

E nepurquant la terre ne lessa pas son bon fruyt,

24 Einz fu abundaunte en tuz byens qu Meliau ust.

E par ceo ben aparust qe Dieu de luy apaé fust.

Ly enemys, qe a tut dis ageyté cum lere,

D'envie enflauma le quer Ryvaud, le puysné frere,

28 De occire le dux Melyau, qui prince fu de la terre

De Cornwaylle; ceo sachez, mut yert de bone afere.

Puys avynt qe luy ducs Meliaus, qe pensa de byen fere,

Un parlement fist crier pur graunt prou de la terre.

32 A quel parlement vint Ryvaud, armé cum a guere,

Sy occist Meliaus, e pur luy regna a veyre

Tost aprés qe par douns ke sovent enchacent dreiture *f. 2r*

E violent les jugementz par une fause p[ar] lure;

36 De çoe les juges verreyment trop en prenent cure.

La terre de Cornwalle out Reyvaud a cele dreiture,

Lors estoit Melor heir ly ducs Meliaus;

E cely gayta Rayvaud l'enfaunt de set auns,

36 parvent cure

40   Par tote la terre ly espya com il luy put occire.
Taunt fu ly desleaus Reyvaud feru de graunt yre,
Kar il se dota se il y certeynement quidoit
Qu'il la terre chalengereyt si atint de pleyne age sereit.

44   Mes li avynt decevablement qe a dereynt luy prist
E luy amena en un leu qe lors oust noun Cobloyd
En Cornwaylle, e la ensemblout ly desleaus un parlement
De prelaz de la terre e des barons ensement.

48   En cest parlement voleyt luy tyraunt occire
Ly juvene enfaunt, seint Melor, si cum Meliau le pere.
Mes ly graunz seignurs de la terre, qe lors i furent,
Qe il ne occirent l'enfaunt ententivement prierent.

52   Taunt requisterent qe il graunta qe yl ne occyreit mye,
Mes un autre torment ly purvea: taunt vesquit en envie
Que il ly copereyt saunz pité plenement la meyn destre
E ly privereyt ensement del pié senestre.

56   Tost aprés fesoit ly glorious Rey saunz nule obstacle
Pur l'enfaunt, ly duz Melor, un mut bel miracle,
Kar il ly rendi apertement pur la mein trenchee
Une meyn d'argent bele e byen ordinee,

60   Dreyt de la fourme de l'autre meyn clere e lusaunte,
E ben joygna a braaz, e asseiz fust pliaunte.
Auxi un pié de arein ly rendi Jhesu Crist,
Pliaunt e movaunt cum nerf e char i fust.

64   Cest myracle ne fu veu unke mes ne oy
De homme que nus sachoum, qe Dieu feseyt pur ly.
E par ceo aparust ben qe Dieu ly ama cher,
Que vers tuz autres ly voleit issi honurer.

68   Ly seint enfes crust adés e s'amendoit:
De jour en jour cleregie aprist, si cum Dieu voloit,
E il fu norry en Cornwaylle en une abbaye
De cortesie ben, en doctrine e auxi de cleregie.

72   Taunt passa le tens qe ly glorious enfaunt
Seint Melor fu tut dreit de quatorze aunz.
En cel tens ly duz Melor a mervaylle beaus devint,
Bons e ben endoctriné e sagement se tint;

76   E tut adés ly enfes a bones ovres fructifiout,
Celeement e devotement sovent Dieu priout.
A graunt plenté de lermes yl ne vout qe l'en veit

Ke aparsoust de nule part la penaunce qe il fesoit.
80 E requist Dieu qe il meist en son comencement
Bone fin, sur tote rein mut plorout tendrement,
E ostat de son quer le amur de cet mund
E ly meist la soue amur en sun quer parfund;
84 Kar tut dys ly fust avis qe il deveit suffreer
La mort, si cum sun pere Meliaus, qe mut fust noble ber,
Qui li tiraund aveit occis par mut graunt utrage:
Feroit a ly cum un enemy a mut graunt damage.
88 Ly Creatur, qe de duçur est large e debonere
A tuz iceus qe sunt laus e de bone afere,
Qui de quer fin sunt enclin en sun servise,
E beneient e concreent la fey de seinte eglise,
92 Ad oy, pur veir vus dy, Melor sun jovene seint.
Pur ly norer e aforcer, myracle fesoit sovent,
E qe il dust saver qe tut cler sa priere fust oye
E ové amur tendre, loaunges rendre a Jhesu le fiz Marie.
96 Le seint ceo vi a entendi e amerousement
Ly merciout, si cum il sout, mut ententivement.
Ky lors veit e oyst sa grant beneyçun,
E sa parole duce e mole e de parfunde resun,
100 E les diz, ke pleyn de lyz ben ja fleirent,
Furent hauz e celestiaus ke del seint oyrent.
S'en vayst e sovent dist ke il saveyt ben taunt
Ke nostre Syre Deu elu icel jovene enfaunt
104 De aver honur a tuzjours e corone saunz flestre.
Pur ceo l'onurs nus utrer touz Jhesu le verrey prestre.
Sa voiz fuit jour e nuit sy plene de melodie,
Mut plesaunte, e tut dis louauté le Rei glorie
108 Si pleisaunte del jovene enfaunt fu la parole.
De li escoter lay e escoler e mestre de l'escole
A ly corust jour e nuyt, ne se poust nul sauler,
S'en merveylerent qe ly abunderent les reysouns si cler.
112   Si avint en un jour de aust qe alerent a boys
Entre ly e ses compaynouns pur quiller noiz;
Ly firent present de lur noiz cum a lur seygnur.
Volentirs les resçuit, e ové mut graunt amur,

91 ceo creent   98 Ly; denceyun   99 parolo

116　E les munda ové sa meyn qe d'argent fu mut cler;
　　　Les deis esteient longes e sotyls e delycius a veer.
　　　Fyre mervaylle estoit de ceo regarder,
　　　E de cele mayn ben clore, overer e plier.
120　Ly seint devaunt ses compaygnuns, suffrez qe jeo vous die,
　　　Se i va ové ses noiz dunt acuyn aveit envie.
　　　E les autres qe i furent mut mercierent Dieu
　　　Du miracle qe il fesoit pur seint Melor sun dreu.
124　Unkes ne tocha le quer de luy orgoil saunz faille,
　　　De taunt qe il vit en luy qe Dieu fesoit mervaille,
　　　Mes plus estoit humble, e quant hom en parlout,
　　　'Cest miracle ne vint ja de manience,' se disout.
128　　　Un jour avint qe des compaygnuns se estoit emblé
　　　E longement solun sa coustume aveit prié.
　　　Sy revieint a ses compaygnuns e se feist semblaunt
　　　De joye e de feste grant e tut ala juaunt,
132　Ke il ne dusent aparceire qe il venyst de plorer.
　　　Lors prist sa perre plate, dunt yl soleit juer
　　　O les autres, la getout tut haut en le eir.　　　　　　　　*f. 3r*
　　　E ele vola largement une demye lywe,
136　E afichout au descendre sur une perre nuwe.
　　　E pus Melor la prist suis, e meintenaunt saillout
　　　A graunt frois de caillo, sy cum Dieu voloit,
　　　Une fontayne vive de ewe duce e clere
140　Ke dure jekes au jour de huy; grant ben fet a la terre.
　　　Cest miracle glorius ly desleaus Ryvaud oist,
　　　Ke taunt fust desparpilé, tut jour grant duel fist,
　　　E s'en doloit nuyt e jour, e ceo utre mesure,
144　Ke il n'out Melor occis quaunt il le pout occire,
　　　Mes il le lessa aschaper par la ententive requeste
　　　De grauntz seyngnurs, qe prierent qe il ne copast la teste.
　　　Il se doloit durement, kar sa fausine fesoit,
148　E quida que ly enfes sun heritage receveroit
　　　Ke il tint mavesement e de luy chalengeroit.
　　　　　Lors apela a sei Ryvaud le mestre l'enfaunt,
　　　Ky out nun Cerialt, e luy diseit taunt:
152　'Si tu veus ly juvene Melor, tun desciple, occire,

134 E les

Jeo te durra grant guerdun e te fray riche sire,
Les teres a les purpris qe tu verras entur
E la montayne u tu es hore, ové tute la honur.'
156 Cerialt ly respondi qe il se conseilereit
E le matin ly dirreit respouns coment la chose irreit.
Cerialt a sa femme vint, la purmesse luy demoustra
Si il occist sun deciple, en conseyl luy demaunda
160 Que ly fust a fere de ceo e qe ele loua.
Ele otria [l] a richesce, e le guerdun voleit ben,
Ke il hastat a Ryvaud e ceo affermast sur tot ren
Le covenaunt purparlé qe fust mut profitable:
164 Tut issi trahi covetise le un e l'autre saunz fable.
Lors s'en vint Cerialt al maners duk Ryvaud,
Une symayne ové luy demora, lur covenaunt affermount.
La norice de seint, qe out ceste novele oye
168 De tele treson purparle[e], ové l'enfaunt s'en fuye
De Cornwaylle en un pays pres u l'aunte l'enfaunt
Demorast, en Deveneschire, qe il ama taunt;
Kar la norice quida tut issi sa mort desturber
172 E de la desleauté purparlee de le tut eschaper.
Quaunt Melor estoit venuz, sa aunte e sun barun,
Ke estoit konte noble e mut de graunt renoum,
De la venue le duz Melor grant joye avoient
176 E de la presence de luy ben reconfortez estoient.
'Melor, beau, tres duz,' dist ly quens, 'je te durra cest chastel
E te fray ducement norer et ben servyr e bel
Jekes tu seies de age, e te serra abaunduné
180 E quaunt qe jeo ay en cest mund te serra doné.'
Seint Melor luy mercia de ceo mut durement
E de cele corteisie gré luy rendi ducement.
Ly dux Ryvaud, ceo oy dire, durement se coressout
184 Ke Melor en Deveneschire a sa aunte fuy estoit;
Venir a sey Cerialt hastivement fesoist.
'Fuy s'en est Melor a s'aunte,' ly disoist.
'Jeo tey [di] pur que tu luy occies, ja ne targes mye,
188 Kar ne puis jeo joye aver, que qe l'en die.
Me semble qe jeo n'ay ren taunt cum il est en vie.

161 querdun 184 Cornwaylle

Le occiez, e mettras mun quer en graunt leesce;
Jeo tun guerdun dublerei pur veir, e ma premesse.'
192 Le covenaunt entre eus estoit lors renovelé:
Ky, quaunt Cerialt la teste Melor a luy ust presenté,
Le jour meimes, avaunt le solayl reconsaunt,
Avereit sun guerdun doblé qe luy fu promys avaunt.
196   Lors s'en parti del dux le desleaus breban;
Prist ové luy un sun fiz qe out noun Juxtan,
Ke fust grant bachelers, et vindrent a chastel
U Melor demorast. Mut furent de quer cruel!
200 Melor esteit prest cum aignel a sacrifise;
Corust a sun mestre, qe fu enemy de seinte eglise,
E luy tote la joye qe il sout fesoit,
E sun fiz Juxtan acoloit e beisout.
204 La aunte seint Melor, qe de tresoun ren ne sout,
Lur fesout feste e joye taunt cum ele sout.
Au seir voleit Melor en lyt sun mestre dormer,
Pres de luy e sun fiz Juxtan cele nuyt cocher.
208 Sa norice, qe de treson se douta tut dys,
Luy retint maugré le seon tut les dues nuys.
La terce nuyt issi fut qe le hure apruchoit
Que de ceste vie le seint parter devoit.
212 A grant lermes sa norice, qe congé luy donast
Pres de sun mestre e Juxtan cele nuyt grauntast
. . . .   *f. 1v*
. . . . dire . . . .
216 . . . . meres metre . . . .
. . . . esperit ceo . . . .
. . . . ava[n] t[uré]
. . . . de seint esperit partut est enturé
220 . . . . out
. . . . asprement disout
. . . . la espeye . . . .
. . . . Melor d'un cop d'es[peye] . . .
224 . . . . ly angles ne descenderent
. . . . oy . . . .
. . . . du martir oir mut grant honur

194 recorisaunt

Q . . . . de saint vost grant amur
228   . . . . de corone mut bele
      . . . . freche e novele
      . . . . fuy ke . . . . . . e
      . . . . ceste valee nus cui ennemie
232   . . . . ces tenebres aver cele grace
      . . . . clerement veoms ta [fac] e.
      Tost aprés Cerialt e Juxstan le cruel,
      Il pristrent la teste e amblerent du chastel.
236   En avalant du muer a une perre cesti,
      Juxstan le fiz Cerialt de la roche chay,
      Brisa soun coel en dous e morust sodeinement,
      E retint pur sa desfaute sun lower daugnement.
240   Cerialt, ke oust sun fiz tut issi perdu,
      Esteit dolent, mes, pur ce ke il ne fu aperceu,
      Hastout sey de aler ové la teste du martirs,
      Ke il porta en sun pan; mut fu fier e chers.
244   Cerialt vint hors du chastel e ala, tote la nuyt,
      De fere en haste sun present a Ryvaud le duks,
      De furneir li servise dont graunde covetise
      Destragna forment le poour de seint eglise.
248   Au matin vint la norice del glorius martyr
      E vit le corps senglaunt saunz chef gisir.
      Ele se plourout e criout cum forcenee:
      'Hore est la flur de cest mund de la teste privee.'   *f. 2v*
252   Mes ly martirs sa dolour doresnavant abregga,
      Kar les seinz aungles vit a l'oil, ki demorent la,
      E tuz le corps, ke luisa celestial lumere.
      Ceste vewe bien asuaja sa dolour ciere
256   . . . . d'avauntage e bien le savoit
      . . . . nubles e cher estoit.
      Cerialt . . . . il ala desiraunt son louer,
      Kar . . . . de seofh que il quida morer.
260   Cerialt . . . ., fesaunt pleinte grieve,
      . . . . al . . rez plus que nule vive
      . . . . mur fu perdu
      . . . . aschaper e qe unques [J] heisu
264   S . . . . la seinte teste dist
      . . . . apertement vist,

Par le . . . . la bouche oen ouvri,
Ki parlout de parole fine e dist tut issi:
268   'Cerialt, en la terre tost tun bastun fichez,
Te saudra la fontayne, dunt tu seras ben rasasez,
E aschaper peril de mort par soeif, çoe sachez.'
Qant Cerialt . . . . , il trambla cum a la mort,
272   Mes . . . . la soef li . . . . . e ly . . . . . si fort,
Se voleit asaier, si . . . . toz arieire.
Prist sun bastun e le fichout parfund en la terre.
. . . . qe se espaundoient
276   . . . . sur le bastun braunches . . . noient
. . . . bastun . . . . ent
Les fruits e le . . . . . . plusor . . . . costoient.
Or de la racine une fontayne . . . . sallout
280   . . . . sa . . . . e voissaus plus fesoit
. . . . ben e cler aprés graunt profit.
Cel miracle fesoit Deus la pur Melor sun eslit.
Cerialt sutivement a graunt plenté bevout,
284   Force e vigur a tut sun corps a mervaille dunout.
Puis prist il la teste qe il alout presenter;
Ja unques pur cest miracle ne voloyt repenter
Taunt ly destregnout l'ardur de covetise
288   E de tute la graunt richesce ki ly fu promise.
Il presenta la teste a Ryvaud . . . . ly requist,
Ke il ly tenist avenaunt e sa purmesse rendist.
     'Cerialts, tu as ben fet e mon quer mis en joye.
292   Hore je ay ta purmesse, tu averas la moye.
Tost munte ceste muntaigne, tost saunz delay;
Tere a vile qe tu verras a touzjours te doneray.'
Cerialt, qe estoit de si graunt chose joyus,
296   Le sommet de cele munta, mult leger fu e pruz.
Ses [iouz], cum il turna, cheirent a ses piez,
. . . . . . cum cere a . . . . ens les eouz
. . . . mere perdre o mult graunt tristesce
300   Ly . . . . tre sa veue . . . . la purmesse.
La nurice . . . . eust,
Kar chey sur la . . . . . . e devaunt le duc just.
La char du seint corps tuz destrete emana en la voie
304   . . . . . . dire defit . . . . chey . . . . . .

Ceste mort fu nunciee a l'aunte du martyr;
Car comme sun barrun ke l'ameit mult cher,
Il vindrent au corps du martir e le aparillerent.
308 En la meison u il esteit descolé a graunt honur le sevelerent.
Mes au matin tut de suys truverent le corps
Pres de fosse le seint martir gisaunt tut dehors.
Mes il porté fut la pres a une esglise,
312 E le sevelerent dignement ou sollempnus servise.
Le secund jour le martirs tut issi cum avaunt
Troverent dehors la tumbe tut autrefoyz gisaunt.
La terce foyz en un autre lieu fu il enterré,
316 A l'endemeyn ensiwaunt dehors la tumbe trové.
De sufrir mervailles trestuz s'en baiss[er]ent;
Pus qe il ne savoient u l'enterrer, ensemblement leverent
E mistrent par commun asent en un char le corps
320 Jeskes la u le char resteroit, e trere de .ii. tors.
Li tors trairent le char u le corps estoit;
Cil . . . . esturent pur veer ke avendroit.
Quaunt le char vient bien loinz, lors se resturent,
324 Ne voleient avaunt aler; duncks firent la endroit
Une riche sepulture e ensevelerent o graunt honur
Le glorious martirs, ly duc seint Melor.
E la fesoit Deus par ly sovent graunt deinté,
328 A la louange de son seint miracles a graunt plenté.
En le pays u la teste seint Melor demorout
Mult merveillouses vengaunces sovent Dieu fesoit,
Kar qui ke uncks parjure o deit nul faus serment,
332 Use de sa . . . . de reverense, çoe sachez verreyment,
Cil aragast hastivement e moreist sodeynement.
  Hom porta la teste, a devant Ryvaud la mist;
E quaunt il la visout, une deverie le si prist,
336 E le tiers jour aprés, savrez, occi . . . leis e le . . . morust,
Ki [trist]ur e dolours pur sa tresun resçust.

306 ameient   308 la sevelerent

Notes to the Text

1—5. The presence of the names of Melor's grandfather and great-grand-
father (or great-great-grandfather), Budic and Daniel, indicates that the

text opened with the saint's genealogy. For a reconstructed version of this, see the beginning of Dom Plaine's edition of the text of BN lat. 13789 (p. 166). According to the legend, Budic had two sons, Meliavus and Rivodius. Meliavus inherited the Armorican Dukedom of Cornubia and married Aurilla, the daughter of Judocus, the Count of Armorican Dumnonia. **11.** *Yrlaunde.* This is the only version of the legend to state that Melor's mother was of Irish extraction. Since she is described as "de genere Britannorum" in the Breton versions (see Dom Plaine's ed., p. 166), the detail is an adaptation to indicate to an English public that her ancestors came from overseas. The *Vitae* which situate the legend in an insular context omit the detail. **26.** *ageyté* i.e. *aguaiter* 'to lie in wait for'; cf. *Anglo-Norman Dictionary*, 17. **44.** *il* i.e. Melor. **45.** *Cobloyd.* Since the missing beginning of the *Vita* edited by Dom Plaine stretches beyond the first hundred lines of this text, we do not know whether it contained the name of the place at which Rivodius held his council. None of the other surviving medieval *Vitae* gives it. However, a version published in a breviary printed at St. Malo in 1537 and which also situates the story in a continental setting, names it *Gobroidus*, clearly the same. The place has not been positively identified. Dr Donatien Laurent of the Department of Celtic at the Université de Bretagne Occidentale at Brest had the following comment to make in a letter to me: "Je me demande s'il ne pouvait y avoir une graphie fautive pour *Colroyd* ou *Colloyd*. On a en effet dans trois chartes datées 857 (n° 80), 863 (n° 61) et 865 (n° 208) dans le *Cartulaire de Redon* le nom de lieu, *Aula Colroit* ou *Lis Colroit*, qui devient plus tard, *Les Colroet* (de *Coliretum* pour *Coriletum* =. la Couldraie). C'était à cette époque la cour du roi Salomon de Bretagne." Dr Laurent adds that the source of this information is his colleague B. Tanguy, a specialist in Breton place-names. **98.** Change of scribe. It must be admitted that the 16 lines in the hand of this copyist give few grounds for thinking that he was a careful transcriber. **105.** *L'onurs* appears to have been copied in error from the previous line; emend to *vout? Utrer* = OF *oltrer.* **114.** Change of scribe. **116.** *munda* 'cleaned'. **117.** *manience* 'manual skill'. **136.** *nuwe*, fem. of *nu*. **136—37.** It is possible that there is a *lacuna* of two lines here. Dom Plaine's text reads: "Postea vero, fixis in oratione genibus diu longeque perorans, cum praesentaneam adesse sibi divinam sensisset clementiam, accepta puerilitatis framea, quae vulgo vocatur petraria, avolare eam fecit quasi stadio dimidio aut eo amplius, infixitque eam supra petram durissimam, quasi super ceram mollissimam" (p. 168, lines 25—30). **137.** *la prist suis*, i.e. *la prist sus* 'picked it up'. **154.** *purpris* 'closed fields'. **155.** *honur* 'feudal right'. **171.** *desturber* 'hinder'; cf. *AND*, 181. **175.** *duz* here, and earlier at 74, could be either the Anglo-Norman spelling for *doux* (cf. 177) or *duc* (cf. 326). **187.** Change of scribe, possibly back to the first one. **193.** *Ky* i.e. Ryvaud. **194.** *reconsaunt* 'setting'. **196.** *breban* is from the Medieval Latin *brabanus* 'Brabanter'; see *Dictionary of Medieval Latin from British Sources* (O.U.P., 1975), pp. 211—12. The men of Brabant often found employment as mercenaries, and so their name became synonymous with 'plunderer' or 'thug'. **209.** *maugré le seon* 'against his will'. The *Vita* edited by Dom Plaine reads: "Sed nutrix ejus, eorum perversitatem metuens, ex multis indiciis quae ventura erant conjiciens, eum prima et secunda nocte, vellet nollet, secum retinuit ac ei ne cum ipsis quiesceret omnino interdicit" (p. 170, lines 14—17). **214ff.** The whole of the text on the back may have been copied by the second scribe. A certain number of lines, approximately fifteen, appear to be missing, followed by twenty which are largely illegible because of wear and staining with gall. Only the very bottom of the letters in 214 has survived, and so they are totally illegible. To make matters worse, there are a number of small holes, some of which seem to have existed before copying, though others, such as the one at the end of 233, which obliterates the last word, are more recent. The passage describes Melor's decapitation, but it is a far fuller account than the one in Dom Plaine's text (p. 170). **239.** *daugnement* is not listed in the *AND*. It would appear to be derived from the same root as *daunerie, dauneure*, both glossed as 'effrontery, immodesty'; cf. *AND*, 140. **247.** *destragna* 'harassed'. **256—82.** Several lines are only partially legible. After Juxtan had broken his neck, Cerialt fled with Melor's head. He was overcome by so great a thirst that he felt death close at hand. Melor's head then spoke, instructing Cerialt to thrust his staff into the ground. As soon as Cerialt had obeyed, the staff changed into a beautiful tree with fruit-bearing branches. A spring gushed forth from its foot; see *Vita*, ed. Dom Plaine, p. 171. **259.** *seofh* 'thirst'. **297—305.** The illegible beginning of 297 must contain forms of *ses yeux*. The passage describes how Cerialt lost his two eyes and died. Both the Dom Plaine and the Capgrave versions state that his flesh melted like wax in fire. The passage continues with the discovery by the governess of the saint's body surrounded by celestial light. **301—2.** A large hole between these two lines existed when the text was copied, as the interspace has been increased. The scribe also avoided it in copying 85 on the first side by writing to the left and right of it. **302.** *duc* i.e. Melor, not Ryvaud. **331.** *deit* 'says'.

TRADUCTION EN OIL DU TROISIEME SERMON SUR LE *CANTIQUE DES CANTIQUES*

ALBERT HENRY

Ce troisième sermon fait partie d'une traduction en oïl des 44 premiers sermons de saint Bernard sur le *Cantique des cantiques*, traduction conservée dans le manuscrit V du Musée Dobrée à Nantes. Elle a été faite dans une abbaye cistercienne du nord-est de la Galloromania, Orval, me semble-t-il, et, très probablement, au cours du dernier quart du XIIe siècle.[1]

Dans son premier sermon, saint Bernard soulignait le caractère particulier du *Cantique des cantiques*; il expliquait le titre du poème et abordait l'étrange début du livre: *par lo baisuel de sa boiche moi baist.* Il consacrait ensuite tout le deuxième sermon à l'élucidation des divers sens de cette formule.

Dans ce troisième sermon, il va établir la hiérarchie des trois baisers au Seigneur:

(i) le baiser des pieds, le seul auquel les pénitents sincères peuvent prétendre;

(ii) le baiser des mains, qui, pour les âmes plus avancées sur le chemin de la vertu, mais ayant honte encore de leur état et se souciant des oeuvres de piété, sera une transition salutaire vers

(iii) le baiser de la bouche, union de l'âme parfaite avec le Christ, union à laquelle nous devons aspirer de toutes nos forces.

En ce qui concerne la langue du traducteur,[2] quelques faits intéressants sont à souligner dans ce troisième sermon:

---

[1] Pour plus de détails concernant cette traduction, sa date et sa localisation, cf. *Bibl. 19* [= no. 19 de la Bibliographie ci-dessous en appendice].

[2] Premier essai de synthèse sur la langue, cf. *Bibl. 19*, 101—6. Pour la commodité de la lecture, j'attire simplement l'attention sur les faits suivants: *ei* pour *e < -á-* en graphie centrale: *leveir, seveir, queil, volenteit* — *ei* pour *i: peihs, peiz, leisons* — *ie* pour *i: paisieble, plaisieble, saintieblement* — *o ~ oi: boiche, atoichier, aproichemenz*

des calques lexicaux: *confuse* au sens de 'éblouïe' (2.2 *confuse des lumieres del ciel = confusa in luminaribus coeli*); le substantif *dignation* [1. *dignatio*] 'bonté' en 5.1, le traducteur lui substituant, en 5.9, une formation d'oïl, *dengement* (voir la note au texte); *exquist* [1. *exquisivit*] 6.1 'chercha';

le composé *avant alement* (6.3; voir la note);

à côté des indéfinis déjà connus (*queiz ke il soit unkes*, traduisant *quodcumque est*, en 5.5; *qui ki unkes es*, traduisant *quaecumque es*, en 2.3; cf. *Bibl. 19*, p. 105, *Poème Moral, Dial. Greg.* et *Job*), il faut relever l'adjectif indéfini *quel que plaist*; l'expression figurant plusieurs fois dans notre traduction, on peut parler de métasématisation: *a queil ke plaist home* 1.4 [1. *cuiusvis hominum*]; ailleurs dans le ms., *queiz ke plaist felonie* en 30c, S. 11 [1. *quaevis*], *les princeries et kez que plaist dignitez* en 59d, S. 19 [1. *quaslibet*], *kel que plaist abit* [1. *qualemcumque habitum*]; à ma connaissance, cet indéfini n'a pas été signalé jusqu'ici;

des mots régionaux (voir les notes au texte).

Nous reproduisons, dans le texte que nous éditons ci-dessous, les divisions en parties et paragraphes (nos chiffres romains et chiffres arabes entre crochets droits) telles qu'on les trouve dans l'édition 'romaine' du latin original (voir *Bibl. 3*); pour permettre de situer les notes sans trop de difficulté, nous ajoutons des chiffres qui numérotent les phrases à l'intérieur des paragraphes. Nous imprimons en caractères distinctifs, comme dans l'édition citée, les citations des textes sacrés faites par saint Bernard: on en trouvera les références précises dans la même édition.

Les graphies *del, al, dele* de l'article contracté sont gardées telles quelles dans tous les cas. Les abréviations ont été résolues selon les formes majoritaires (mais il faudrait étudier la graphie de la traduction entière).

— *ui* ~ *oi*: *puisons* — **paucu** > *pau* — -*eal* < -**ell**-, -**ill**-: *eas, peal, ceaz, bealtez* — *promier* < **primariu**; cf. *FEW*, IX, 376b — *un*(*m*) ~ *on*(*m*): *unkes, solunc, cum, repunse, hunte* — *lh* = *l* mouillé (?): *failhe, filhes, tailhanz* — *ng* = *n* mouillé: *devenges, avenget, ensenge moi, dengement* — -*t* final maintenu dans divers cas: *relievet, enforcet, serat, pardoneit, nunciet, vertut, pieteit* — *z* ~ *c*: *rezieut, graze* — réduction de *iee* à *ie*: *chargie* — pas de *e* prosthétique, parfois, devant *s* impure: *sperance, splendor* — absence de -*d*- intercalaire: *penre, penras* (pendre) — article déf. m. sg. rég. et pronom pers. m. sg. rég. *lo* — article déf. f. sg. souvent identique au masc., *li/le* — *lei* < **allaei**, et, par analogie, *celei* dém. f. rég. — pour certaines formes verbales, voir les notes au texte — forme tonique du pronom personnel devant le verbe.

[I. 1.] **1** Nos leisons hui el livre d'esprovance. **2** Repairiez
a vos mimes, et si esgard chascuns sa conscience sor cez
choses qui a dire sunt. **3** Ge vulh encerchier se unkes a alcun
de vos fut otroiet que il pouist ensi ke il lo sentist dire: *Del
baisuel de sa boiche moi baist.* **4** Car n'atient mie a queil ke
plaist home ce dire de volenteit; mais se alcuns at une foiz
rezieut de la boiche de Crist lo spirituel baisuel, senz
failhe sa propre esprovance lo resomunt, et il lo requiert
volentiers. **5** Ge aesme nului pooir savoir / ce que soit, se
celui nun ki lo prent. **6** Car ce est la manne repunse, et cil
soulement ki la manjout arat encor fain. **7** Ce est la fontaine
saelee a cui estranges n'at communion, et cil solement ki
en boit arat encor soif. **8** Oiez celui ki l'avoit essaïe coment
il la redemandoit: *Rend a moi*, fait il, *la leece de ton salut.*
9 Ce ne prendet mie a soi li anrme chargie de pechiez,
semblanz a la moie, qui encor est sozmise az passions de la
char, ki ancor ne sent mie la suaviteit del espir, ki ne seit et
ki n'at esproveit les deventrienes joies.

[2.] **1** Nekedent a celei ki teile est mosterrai je lieu
covenable a soi el salut. **2** Ne soi elliet mie folement a la
boiche del tres pieu espous, mais tres paürouse gecet avoec
moi az piez del tres. seveir sanior, et tremblant avoec lo
publican esgard la terre, non lo ciel, ke la face ki aconstumee
est es tenebres ne soit confuse des lumieres del ciel et
apressee de glorie, et ke ele ne soit renvolepee lo parés el
avoglement de plus espesse obscurteit, cant ele serat
re / batue par les nient aconstumees splendors dele majesteit.
3 Ne toi semblet mie, anrme qui ki unkes es teile, ne toi
semblet vilz et despitables cilz lieus u la sainte pecheresse
mist jus ses pechiez et vestit la sainteeit. **4** La muat li
Ethiopisse la peal et ele, restablie en novele blancor,
respondoit ja dunkes segurement et vraiement a ceaz qui
li reprovevent la parole: *Ge sui noire, mais bele, filhes de
Jerusalem.* **5** As tu mervelhe par kel art ele ce pooit faire u
par queilz merites ele l'out? **6** A pau de parole l'entent. **7**
Ele plorat amerement, et cant ele trahoit de ses profundes
entrailhes les lonz sospirs et soglotoit saintieblement
dedenz lei mimes, si vongeat ele fors les humors del fiel.
8 Li celestes mides li socorut tres hinelement, car *isnele-*

f. 8c

f. 8

f. 8

ment cuert sa parole. **9** N'est dunkes puisons la parole
Deu? **10** Oïl, vraiement fors et trenchanz et encerchanz les
cuers et les rains. **11** A la parfin *est la parole Deu vive et
faisanz et plus tresperzanz ke nule espee a dous tailhanz,
et atoichanz deci ke al departement del anrme / et del espir,*   *f. 8d*
et des jointures et des meoles, et deviseresse des penses. **12**
Giers solunc l'exemple de ceste bieneürouse repentant,
abaisse toi, chaitive, ke tu laisses a estre chaitive: abaisse
toi en terre, enbrace les piez, apaisente les de baisuez, leive
les de larmes, et nequedent nes laveras mie, mais toi, si ke
tu devenges une dele herde des tondues qui montent fors
dele lavendiere, si ke tu lo viaire covert de honte et de
larmes n'oses mie anzois leveir dont se *toi serunt pardoneit
tei pechiet,* ke tu oies: *Lieve toi, lieve toi, chaitive filhe
Syon; lieve toi, escou toi fors dele purriere.*

[II. 3.] **1** Giers, cant tu aras pris lo promier baisuel az
piez, ne toi oseras mie manés ellever al baisuel de la boche;
anz feras ta voie a un moien baisuel, cui tu penras el secund
lieu a la main: et de celui apren teil raison. **2** Se Jesuchrist
moi dist: *Toi pechiet toi sunt pardoneit,* ke moi valt ce, se
je ne laisse a pechier? **3** Ge ai devestie ma cote: se je la
revest, cumbien ai je esploitiet? **4** Lo parés, se je mes piez
cui je / avoi lavez remboe, valdrat moi dunkes riens ce que   *f. 9a*
je les avoi lavez? **5** Ge sordeilhouse de totes manieres de
visces, ai longement gieut en palud de lies: mais se je i
rechai, peihs moi serat ke cant ju i gisoi. **6** A la fin, moi
ramembret ke cil qui moi fist salf moi dist: *Elevos tu es
sanez, va t'en et si ne peche desormais, ke alcune peiors
chose ne toi avenget.* **7** Et cil ki donat la volenteit de
repentir, mestiers est ke il doinst la vertut de contenir, si ke
je ne face chose ki a repentir soit et ensi soient mes dairienes
choses peiores des promieres. **8** Car guai a moi repentant,
se manés sortrait sa main cil senz cui je ne puis riens faire;
nient vraiement, car ne repentir ne contenir. **9** Dentaprés
ge oi ce ke li Sages conseilhet: *Ne dobler mie,* fait il, *ta
parole en l'orison.* **10** Ge ai paür de ce ke li jugieres manacet
al arbre ki ne fait fruit. **11** Par tant, bien lo gehis, ne moi
vraiement est mie assez la promiere graze par cui je sui ja
repentanz des malz, se je l'altre ne / pren, ke je face fruiz   *f. 9b*

dignes de penance et desorenavant ne repaire mie a ce ke
je avoi vongiet.

[4.] 1 Giers ce moi covient promiers et proier et penre
ke je ose plus haltes et plus saintes choses atoichier. 2 Ne
vulh mie sodainement halz devenir: petit et petit vulh
esploitier. 3 Tant cum li ultrages del pecheor desplaist a
Deu, tant li plaist li huntes del repentant. 4 Tu l'apaisentes
tost, se tu gardes ta mesure et se tu ne quiers mie plus haltes
choses de toi. 5 Lonz et halz est li salz des piez a la boiche,
mais neaz covenables aproichemenz n'est ce. 6 Et quoi
altre chose? 7 Atoicheras les sainz viaires, tu ki ancor es
arrosez de novele purriere? 8 Seras tu hui presentez al
viaire de glorie, ki hier fus trahiz fors del palut? 9 Parmi
la main est tes trespassemenz: cele toi terdet promiers,
cele toi elliet.·10 Coment elliet? 11 Donant ce dont tu
soies taissie. 12 Que est ce? 13 La bealtez de continence et
li fruiz dignes de penance: ce sunt oevres de pieteit. 14
Cez choses toi elleveront / fors des fins en la sperance de
oser meilhors choses. 15 Et cant tu rezois lo don, si baise la
main, ce est: nient a toi, mais a son non done glore. 16
Done li une foiz et done li l'altre, or par les pardonez
pechiez, or par les otroïes vertuz. 17 U certes voies dont tu
armeras ton front encontre cez colz ke li Apostles dist:
*Que as tu, hom, ke tu n'as pris? Et se tu l'as pris, por coi
en as tu glore alsi cum tu nel aies mie pris?*

[III. 5.] 1 Ja a la parfin, cant tu es dous baisuez as la
doble esprovance de la divine dignation, puescelestre
n'aras mie honte d'entaissier plus saintes choses. 2 Car tant
cum tu creis en graze, tant t'enlarges tu en fiance. 3 De ce
avient ke tu aimes plus ardanment et huches plus fiement
por ce ke tu sens qui toi falt. 4 Mais *a celui ki huchet serat
aovert.* 5 Ge cui ke cil soverains baisuez, queilz ke il soit
unkes, de la sovraine dignation et de mervilhouse suaviteit,
ne serat mie denoiez a celui qui telz serat. 6 Ceste est la
voie, ciz est li ordenes. 7 Promiers nos / culchons az piez,
si plorons, davant lo Sanior ki nos fist, ce ke nos avons fait.
8 Aprés si querons la main de celui ki relievet et ki enforcet
les floibes genoilhes. 9 Aprés cant nos avons ce conseüt par
pluisors larmes et proieres, a la fin, puescelestre, si osons

f. 9

f. 9

ellever lo chief al viaire de glorie, poürous et tremblanz lo di, nient solement por esgarder mais por baisier: car *Christ li sires est espirs davant nostre face*, a cui se nos fumes conjoint el saint baisuel, devenons uns espirs par son dengement.

[6.] 1 A toi, sire Jehsu, a toi dist a droit mes cuers: *Toi exquist ma face; ta face, sire, requerrai je.* 2 Car tu moi fesis main oïr ta mercit, cum tu a moi promiers gisanz en pulriere et baisant tes honorables piez pardonas ce que je avoi malement vesquit. 3 Aprés, el avant alement del jor fesis tu l'anrme lie de ton serf, cant tu el baisuel de la main moi otroias la graze de bien vivre. 4 Et ce ke i at plus, beaz sire, se ce nun ke tu moi rezoives el ardor del espir, en la planteit de lumiere el baisuel mimes de / la boiche, si moi aemplisses de leece avoec ton viaire? 5 Ensenge moi, tres sueiz et tres pieus, *ensenge moi u tu geices, u tu paisses en meidi.* 6 Sanior frere, bon nos est ci estre, mais elevos li malisces del jor nos enrehuchet. 7 Cil hoste de cui nunciet nos est ke il nos sunt sorvenut, nos destrendent rumpre, miez ke finer, lo paisieble sermon. 8 Nos eisterons fors az hostes, ke alcune chose ne defailhet az offices dele cariteit de cui nos parlons, ke par aventure n'avenget ke hom de nos oiet dire: *Il dient et si ne font mie.* 9 Vos, orez endementręs, ke Deus facet bien plaisanz les volentries paroles de ma boche a nostre edifiement et a la loenge et a la glore de son non.

f.10a

Notes au Texte

1.3. *vulh*: cf. *vuilh* dans *Job*. **1.5.** *pooir*: dans le ms., chacun des deux *o* porte un accent; le copiste a-t-il voulu marquer les deux syllabes? — *Ge aesme [. . .] pooir [. . .]*: proposition infinitive calquée sur l'original latin. **1.6.** *manjout*: forme analogique, sans *e* désinentiel (cf. Fouché, *Verbe*, p. 137). **1.9.** *prendet*: sur cette forme du subj., cf. Fouché, *Verbe*, pp. 106−7. ⊥ *anrme* < **anima** est la graphie courante dans le ms. des *Sermons*. — *deventrienes joies* [1. *internorum penitus gaudiorum*]: *deventrien* 'du dedans, intérieur' figure aussi dans le sermon 26 et ailleurs; T.-L. cite uniquement *Dial. Greg.* et *Job*; cf. *FEW*, XXIV, 33a et b: "(wallon. lothr. 12−13 jh.)". **2.2.** *lo parés* traduit ici et en 2.3 et 3.4 *rursus*, 'de nouveau' ou 'de même'; l'expression est fréquente dans nos sermons; elle est surtout "wallon." et "lothr." selon *FEW*, VII, 648b. — *nient aconstumees*: les composés négatifs avec *nient-* ou *non-* sont fréquents dans Dobrée V; cf. *Bibl.20*. **2.3.** *pechiez*: le ms. porte, par erreur, *piez*. **2.4.** *ja dunkes*: on pourrait songer à corriger en *adunkes*, comme je l'ai fait en *Bibl.4*, mais il semble que le traducteur ait voulu rendre le *jam tunc* de l'original. — *segurement*: pour la forme, cf. *Bibl.19*, p. 102. — *reprovevent*: sur cet imparf. de la première conjugaison en Wallonie et en Lorraine, cf. *Bibl.19*, p. 103. **2.6.** *l'entent*: *l* a été ajouté, par la même main, dans l'interligne supérieur. **2.7.** **trahoit** (de *traire*!): le *h* marque l'hiatus et souligne les deux syllabes; cf. *trahiz*, en 4.8. **2.8.** *mides* 'médecin'; on trouve dans les *Sermons* les formes *meide, mide* et *mie*, toutes caractéristiques de la région wallonne; cf. *FEW*, VI, 604a et *Bibl.19*, p. 106. **2.12.** *giers* 'donc' traduit *igitur* (ici), ou *itaque* (3.1), ou *ergo* (4.1); il apparaît fréquemment dans Dobrée V; son usage n'a pas dû dépasser de beaucoup la fin du XIIe siècle: cf. les ex. de God. et de T.-L., et *FEW*, III, 27b. — *apaisenter* traduit, ici et en 4.4, *placare*; en *Bibl.6*, 43, *pacificare*; les exemples relevés par T.-L. proviennent de *Dial. Greg., Ezechiel, SSBern*, Jean de Condé; le *FEW*, VII, 459a considère que **pacentare* est surtout représenté dans le nord et l'est du domaine d'oïl. — *lavendiere* [1. *lavacrum*] : ce sens de 'lavoir' n'est, à ma connaissance, pas attesté ailleurs. — A la fin de la phrase, le texte latin est: *ita sane ut suffusum pudore ac maerore vultum sustollere non ante audeas quam audias et ipsa: Dimittitur tibi peccata tua, quam audias: Consurge [. . .]*; le traducteur semble avoir sauté après *levier dont* les mots *ke tu oies*, corrélatifs de *ainzois*. **3.1** *anz feras ta*: le ms. porte *ferat*. **3.2.** *toi pechiet*: sans doute erreur pour *tei*, forme courante. **3.3** *cumbien ai je esploitiet* traduit *quantum profeci*. **3.5.** *sordeilhouse* [1. *sordens*] ; dans le sermon 26, le subst. *sordelhes* traduit *sordes* 'saletés'; l'adjectif n'est connu, jusqu'ici, que par notre traducteur (cf. *FEW*, XII, 108a). — *rechai*: cf. wallon mod. *rtšé*. **3.7.** *dairienes* (graphie *deriene* en *Bibl. 5*, 74, à côté de *derraine, ibid.*, 80) cf. T.-L. s.v. *daërrain*. **3.9.** *dentaprés* 'd'où, aussi' traduit *proinde*; chez notre traducteur, on trouve: *dent* 'd'où'; *dentapres* a) 'ensuite', b) 'd'où, aussi, donc'; *dentenaprés* idem; *dentenavant* 'désormais'; *dent* est, si je ne m'abuse, le **deinde** latin; cf. *Bibl.17*. — *Ne dobler mie* traduit *Ne iteres* de *l'Ecclésiaste* VII, 15; la citation veut dire qu'il ne faut pas demander deux fois la même grâce. **4.1.** *ke* 'avant que': dans le texte latin, *prius* et *quam* sont séparés, et le traducteur semble avoir considéré *prius* comme un adverbe indépendant (comparer la phrase 9 ci-dessous); peut-être son *ke* signifiait-il alors pour lui 'afin que'. **4.5.** *neaz*, qui traduit *nec*, corespond au *neïs, nes* courant en ancien français; cette forme *neaz* ne figure, ni dans God., ni dans le *FEW*, VII, 72b, et T.-L. ne l'a relevée que dans *Job*; cf. *Bibl.14*, p. 169 et *Bibl.19*, p. 105. **4.6.** *Et quoi altre chose?* Le traducteur a considéré que le *Quid enim* de l'original était une véritable question, alors qu'il correspond à notre *Comment donc* affectif. **4.7.** *les sainz viaires: ora sacra* serait plutôt, ici, le saint viaire. **4.8.** *trahiz*: participe passé faible de nature analogique, dont je ne peux rapprocher que *traeit*, chez Frère Angier et dans *Dial. Greg.* (cf.

Fouché, *Verbe*, p. 368); pour le *h* et sa valeur, cf. *trahoit*, ci-dessus, 2.6.
4.11. *soies taissie* traduit *praesumas* 'viser haut' (en te donnant ce grâce
à quoi tu viserais haut). Pour *taissier*, a) 'donner l'audace de faire', b)
'faire fond sur', et *entaissier* en 5.1, a) 's'approprier', b) 'oser entreprendre',
c) 'présumer', d) 'oser', inconnus des dictionnaires, et abondamment attestés
dans notre traduction, avec, en outre, les substantifs *taisiere* et *taisserie*, cf.
Bibl.15. **4.14.** *fins* 'fumier'. T.-L. n'enregistre pas cette forme, à côté du
courant *fiens; fins* se trouve dans la langue d'oïl écrite en Wallonie et
subsiste dans certains dialectes de la Belgique romane: cf. *Bibl.14*, p. 168,
et *ALCB*, III, carte 883, point 12, ce point étant Muno, en Belgique romane.
4.16. On pourrait croire que le copiste s'est trompé d'abréviation (et c'est
probablement ce qui s'est passé ici): il a écrit l'abréviation de *par* au lieu de
celle de *por* (l'original latin a *pro*); mais la confusion *par/por* est fréquente,
entre autres, dans la scripta de Wallonie (cf. *Poème Moral*, p. xciii, et
Bibl.21, p. 244). **5.2.** *creis* [1. *crescis*]: cf. wallon mod. *cré*. – *toi*
enlarges [1. *dilataris*]; les dérivés verbaux en *en-* sont nombreux dans notre
traduction: ici même, *entaissier, enforcier, enrehuchier* (?); ailleurs, *en-*
covrir, enfaire, enhoster, enmovoir, enoïr, enconforter, encacier, ensongier
[= *ensoingnier*], *enconoistre*, etc.; cf. *Bibl.5*, p. 355. **5.5.** *qui telz serat*
traduit un peu vaguement *sic affecto*. **5.8.** *floibe*: cf. *floibe, floive,*
floibeteit en *Bibl.5*, p. 355, et *Bibl.6*, p. 107; *floibes genoilhes* traduit
genua dissoluta; floibe est "awall." et "apik." selon le *FEW*, III, 615b;
T.-L. ne relève la forme *genoilhes* que dans *Dial. Greg.* et *Ezéchiel*. **5.9.**
dengement [= *degnement*], qui traduit aussi *dignatio* (comme *dignation* en
5.1), paraît inconnu des dictionnaires. **6.1** *exquist*, calque de *exquisivit*
'a cherché'; comp. *exquisiteur* et *exquisition* dans God. **6.2.** *cum*
'lorsque': le traducteur reprend le *cum* latin; mais cf. graphies *un/on,*
um/om dans notre traduction. – le ms. porte *pardonanz*, inadvertance
pour *pardonas* [1. *remisisti*]; – *avoi vesqui* [1. *vixeram*]: sur le type
vesquir (notamment en Wallonie), voir *FEW*, XIV, 579b. **6.3.** *avant*
alement [1. *progressus*]: composé d'un 'modèle sémantique' inhabituel
en français moderne (sauf erreur, je ne trouve pas son correspondant
parmi les types dégagés pour le français contemporain par P. Wunderli
dans *Festschrift Kurt Baldinger*, Tübingen, 1979, 330–60), et même,
sous certains aspects, en ancien français; que *avant* ait ici son sens spatial
est en accord avec l'histoire de *avant* et de *devant*; mais on ne pourrait
pas, si je reprends la façon d'analyser de P.W., paraphraser *avant alement*
en "→ *X* est avant l'*alement*", ni "→ l'*alement* est avant *X*"; en somme,
il ne s'agit pas ici d'une référence extérieure, mais d'un vecteur interne:
alement dans la direction *en avant* (voir, mais avec un verbe, les expressions
aler avant, traire avant, etc.); il faut se tourner, pour la comparaison, vers
le latin et les langues germaniques; même en ancien français, *avant coure-*
ment, qui est la formation la plus proche que je connaisse de la nôtre,
signifie 'action de devancer' (résultant, certes, du fait de courir en avant,
mais c'est la référence relative qui s'impose); en *Bibl.6*, 56, *devant coriers*
[1. *praecursor*] peut s'analyser "→ le *corier* est avant *X*" (cf. P.W., *loc.*
cit., type 2), comp. afr. *avant marchant*. **6.6.** *li malisces*: masc., comme

souvent dans les textes du nord d'oïl; cf. *Berte as grans piés*, éd. A. Henry, v. 287. — *enrehuchet* (plutôt que *en* [= *de ci*] *rehuchet*); le traducteur a dû ne pas comprendre exactement le verbe latin *avocat* ('la malice du jour nous en écarte'); il a vu dans ce verbe simplement *vox*, d'où *huchier*; sur les verbes en *en-*, cf. 5.2.   6.7. *destrendent* [1. *cogunt*]; noter la désinence et cf. *prendet* ci-dessus. — *paisieble* [1. *gratum*], aussi en *Bibl.7*, 70 [1. *pacificus*]; je ne retrouve cette graphie que dans *Dial. Greg.*; cf. *plaisieble* [1. *gratiosus*], *Bibl.6*, 18 et note, et *Bibl.19*, p. 105.   6.8. *parlons*: avec *l* ajouté par la même main dans l'interligne supérieur.   6.9. *volentries* [1. *voluntarias*]; *volentri* est donné comme hapax par le *FEW*, XIV, 613a (sans doute d'après God., *Livre de Job*). — Le texte de Rome porte *ad vestram ipsorum aedificationem; nostre*, avec un *n* très net dans le ms., est-il une inadvertance du copiste?

INDEX LEXICOLOGIQUE[3]

apaisenter 2.12*, 4.4 — **atient** 1.4 [1. *est* + génitif] 'il appartient' — **atoichanz** 2.11 [1. *pertingens*] — **avant alement** 6.3* — **ce ke** 6.4 [1. *quid*, interrogatif] — **celei** 2.1, cf. Intro. note 2 — **creis** 5.2* [1. *crescis*] — **cum** 6.2* — **cumbien** 3.3* — **dairienes** 3.7* — **dengement** 5.9* — **dentaprés** 3.9* — **destrendent** 6.7* — **deventrienes** 1.9* — **deviseresse** 2.11 [1. *discretor*] — **dignation** 5.1. [1. *dignatio*], cf. Intro. — **dobler** (ne ~ mie) 3.9* — **dunkes** 2.4* [1. *tunc*] — **eisterons** (nos ~) 6.8 [1. *ego exibo*] — **elliet** 2.2, 3.1, 4.9, subj. pr. de *ellever* [1. *assurgat* ou *erigat*] — **encerchanz** 2.10 [1. *scrutans*] 'fouillant'; **encerchier** 1.3 [1. *explorare*] 's'enquérir' — **enforcet** 5.5 [1. *roborat*] — **enlarges** 5.2* — **enrehuchet** 6.6* — **entaissier** 5.1, voir *taissie* — **escou toi** 2.12 [1. *excutere*] 'secoue-toi' — **esprovance** 1.1 [1. *experientia*] 'expérience' — **exquist** 6.1* — **faisanz** 2.11 [1. *efficax*] — **fins** 4.14* [1. *stercus*] — **floibe** 5.8* — **fiement** 5.2 [1. *fidenter*], cf. God., s.v. — **gecet** 2.2, **geices** 6.5 [1. *iaceat* et *cubes*], cf. *Bibl.19*, p. 103 — **genoilhes** 5.8* — **giers** 2.12*, 3.1, 4.1 — **ke** 'pour que, afin que' 2.2 (peut-être, ici, 'de peur que'), 2.12, 3.6, 3.11, 6.9 et 10; 'avant que' 4.1* — **laissier a** 2.12 [1. *desinere*] — **lavendiere** 2.12* — **malisces** 6.6* — **manjout** 1.6* — **mides** 2.8* — **neaz** 4.5* — **nient aconstumees** 2.2* — **paisieble** 6.7* — **parés** (lo ~) 2.2*, 2.3, 3.4 — **petit et petit** 4.2 [1. *paulatim*] — **prendet a soi** 1.9 [1. *sibi arroget*] — **proier** 4.1 [1. *petere*] — **puisons** 2.9 [1. *potio*] — **queil que plaist** 1.4, **queilz que** [. . .] **unkes** 5.5, cf. Intro. — **qui ki unkes** 2.3, cf. Intro. — **quoi** 4.6* — **rebatue** 2.2 [1. *reverberata*] — **rechai** 3.5* — **renvolepee** 2.2. [*soit r.*, 1. *obvolvatur*] — **reprovevent** 2.4* — **repunse** 1.1, de *repon(d)re* 'cacher' [1. *absconditum*] — **saintieblement** 2.6 'd'une manière sanctifiante, salutairement' [1. *salutaribus singultibus*] — **salf** 3.6 [1. *sanum*] — **segurement** 2.4* — **sordeilhouse** 3.5* — **taissie**

[3] L'astérisque renvoie à une note.

4.11* — terdet 4.9, subj. pr. de *terdre* [l. *tergat*] — toi pour *tei* (?) 3.2* — trahiz 4.8, trahoit 2.7* — vesqui 6.2* — volentries 6.9* — vongeat 2.7, vongiet 3.11, de *vongier* (< vomicare), cf. *Bibl.4*, p. 183, n. 12 — vulh 1.3*, 4.2.

BIBLIOGRAPHIE

Contributions à l'étude du ms. Dobrée V
et de sa traduction des *Sermones super Cantica canticorum*

1. Léopold Delisle, 'Un troisième manuscrit de sermons de saint Bernard en français' dans *Journal des Savants*, 1900, 148–64 [Voir G. Durville, *Catalogue de la bibliothèque du Musée Thomas Dobrée*, I, *Manuscrits* (Nantes, 1904), 223–61].

2. Michel Zink, *La prédication romane avant 1300* (Paris, 1976), pp. 30, 65, 338.

3. *Sancti Bernardi opera*, I: *Sermones super Cantica Canticorum 1–35*, ad fidem codicum recensuerunt J. Leclercq, C. H. Talbot, H. M. Rochais (Rome, 1957); sur les rapports entre notre traduction et les diverses recensions des *Sermones*, cf. *Bibl.5*, 353–54.

4. Extrait de ce troisième sermon dans Albert Henry, *Chrestomathie de la littérature en ancien français* 1e éd. (Berne, 1953), 6e éd. (1978), I, 199–200, et II, 60–61.

5. Albert Henry, 'Traduction en oïl de la déploration de saint Bernard sur la mort de son frère, extrait du sermon 26' dans *Mélanges de langue et de littérature médiévales offerts à Pierre Le Gentil* (Paris, 1973), pp. 353–65 [repris dans A. Henry, *Automne, Etudes de philologie, de linguistique et de stylistique, rassemblées et publiées par des collègues, des élèves et des amis de l'auteur* (Gembloux-Paris, 1977), pp. 77–94].

6. 'Traduction en oïl du deuxième sermon sur le *Cantique des cantiques*' dans *Miscellanea codicologica F. Masai dicata* (Gand, 1979), pp. 273–78.

7. 'Traduction en oïl du premier sermon sur le *Cantique des cantiques*' dans *Etudes de philologie romane et d'histoire littéraire offertes à Jules Horrent* (Liège, 1980), pp. 175–82.

8. 'Notes lexicologiques d'ancien français' dans *Etudes de langue et de littérature du Moyen Age offertes à Félix Lecoy* (Paris, 1973), pp. 197–211.

9. 'Ancien français "meis(s)ir"' dans *Medioevo Romanzo*, I (1974), 111–14.

10. 'Ancien français "raiz" (*Jeu d'Adam*, v. 860)' dans *Romania*, XCII (1971), 388–91 [repris dans *Automne, op. cit.*, 59–62].

11. 'Encore "raiz" (*Jeu d'Adam*, v. 489)', *ibid.*, XCVI (1975), 561–65.

12. 'Ancien français "ciemes, cinme"' dans *The Canadian Journal of Romance Linguistics La Revue Canadienne de Linguistique Romane*, I (1973), 24–25.

13. "Ruteler", du wallon au franco-provençal' dans *Revue de linguistique romane*, XXXVIII (1974), 276—83 [repris dans *Automne, op. cit.*, 67—75].

14. 'Notes lexicologiques d'ancien français (II)' dans *Études de langue et de littérature françaises offertes à André Lanly* (Nancy, 1980), pp. 121—25.

15. 'Ancien oïl "taissier, entaissier" ' dans *Romania*, C (1979), 121—25.

16. ' "Burir" et sa famille en ancien français' dans *Festschrift Kurt Baldinger zum 60. Geburtstag* (Tübingen, 1979), pp. 511—22.

17. 'La descendance du latin "deinde" en ancien français' dans *Mélanges Jacques Pohl* (Bruxelles, 1980), pp. 109—14.

18. 'Une recette de "claré" en pays wallon vers 1200' dans *Mélanges offerts à M. Arnould et P. Ruelle* (Bruxelles, 1981), pp. 287—92.

19. 'Saint Bernard traduit vers 1200 en pays wallon' dans *Mélanges de philologie wallonne* (= *Les Dialectes de Wallonie*, VIII—IX), 1981, pp. 96—111.

20. Christine Platz, 'Edition d'un sermon anonyme de la Magdeleine' dans *Bulletin des jeunes romanistes*, XIII (1966), 14—18, et 'Sermon de la Magdeleine, Etude de la langue et index des mots', *ibid.*, XV (1968), 16—35.

21. Robert Taylor, 'Sermon anonyme sur sainte Agnès, texte du XIIIe siècle' dans *Travaux de linguistique et de littérature* [Strasbourg], VII 1 (1969), 241—53 (M. R. Taylor prépare une édition des 44 sermons sur le *Cantique des cantiques*).

22. Robert Taylor, 'Les préfixes de négation *non-* et *nient-* en ancien français' dans *Actes du XIIIe Congrès international de linguistique et · philologie romanes* (Québec, 1976), I, 647—58.

Abréviations utilisées:
God. (= Godefroy), T.-L., *FEW*;
Dial. Greg. = Li Dialoge Gregoire lo Pape, éd. W. Foerster (Halle, 1876);
Job = Moralium in Job fragmenta, en annexe à l'édition précédente;
Sprache Greg.-Job = Leo Wiese, *Die Sprache der Dialoge des Papstes Gregor, mit einem Anhang, Sermo de Sapientia und Moralium in Job fragmenta* (Halle, 1900);
Poème Moral = Le Poème Moral, Traité de vie chrétienne écrit dans la région wallonne vers 1200, édition complète par Alphonse Bayot (Bruxelles, 1929);
Fouché, *Verbe* = Pierre Fouché, *Le Verbe français, Etude morphologique* (Paris, 1931);
ALCB = Atlas linguistique de la Champagne et de la Brie.

UNE PETITE SUME DE LES SET PECHEZ MORTEUS (MS LONDON BL HARLEY 4657)

TONY HUNT

MS British Library Harley 4657 measures 231 mm. x 155 mm., and dates from the first quarter of the fourteenth century. It is a collection of religious and didactic treatises, and from a note on f. 1r (*Sir Thomas Tempest Baronet*) it is apparent that it was owned in the seventeenth century by the Sir Thomas Tempest who was 4th Baronet of Stella in County Durham.[1] The northern origins of the MS may be confirmed by a list of donations (*Ista sunt dona mihi data*) written in a fifteenth-century hand on f. 104r and which includes the names of *Mascam* (Masham), *Gisbourn* (Gisburn), *Poklyngton* (Pocklington) and *Hesaw* (Hessay), all in Yorkshire.[2] The contents of the MS are as follows:

1. ff. 1va – 4va: *Apocalypsis Goliae*[3] Inc. *A tauro torrida lampade scincii*; explic. *Mentis vestigia fecissent lubrica*. The text is written 34

---

[1] See C. E. Wright, *Fontes Harleiani* (London, 1972), p. 325, and *Complete Baronetage* ed. G[eorge] E[dward] C[okayne], I, 1611–25 (Exeter, 1900; repr. Gloucester: Alan Sutton, 1982), p. 217. The Durham books in the Harley collection which were once owned by Sir Thomas Tempest are all collections of religious texts, only two containing vernacular works. A copy of the *Manuel des Péchés* of William of Waddington is found in MS Harley 3860 and in MS Oxford Bodleian Library Rawlinson Poetry 241, both at one time in the possession of Tempest.

[2] Further names point to County Durham, e.g. Graystayns, Wessyngton (Washington) and Morden. It is possible that Bursea (E. Yorks) is intended by *de bursare*. Masham, Gisburn, Graystayns and Pocklington are all associated with 14th-century owners of Durham books; see A. B. Emden, *A Biographical Register of the University of Oxford to A.D. 1500*, II (Oxford, 1958), 1240, 844, 814, 1489 respectively, and N. R. Ker, *Medieval Libraries of Great Britain* 2nd edn. (London, 1964), pp. 255, 257.

[3] The MS was known to the poem's first editor, Thomas Wright, *The Latin Poems commonly attributed to Walter Mapes*, Camden Society, 16 (London, 1841), pp. 1–20 (two English translations from the 16th and 17th centuries are included on pp. 271–92). A more recent edition is that by Karl Strecker, *Die Apokalypse des Golias* (Rom/Leipzig, 1928).

lines to a column, the stanzas are marked by red paragraph signs, and there are red initials. Lines 201–4 of Wright's edition are omitted. The text is accompanied by marginal signs in red marking the seven chapters of the Book of the Seven Seals as follows: [f. 2rb] 1. 125 capitulum 1; [f. 2va] 1. 153 capitulum 2; [f. 2vb] 1. 185 capitulum 3; [f. 3ra] 1. 221 capitulum 4; [f. 3rb] 1. 252 [= Wright 256] capitulum 5; [f. 3va] 1. 288 [= Wright 292] capitulum 6; [f. 3vb] 1. 336 [= Wright 340] capitulum 7.

2. f. 4va: miscellaneous didactic verses.
Ad mensam residens noli nimium fore ridens,
pauca loqui studeas, cum quibus es videas.[4]
Nec nimium taceas nec verba superflua dicas.[5]
Et cadat in placitum quicquid erit positum.
Tu debes memori mente tenere mori.[6]
f. 4vb
Rufum ne foveas, quem namque fovebit egenum,
pro granis paleas reddet, pro melle venenum.[7]

3. f. 4vb: a macaronic poem to the Virgin,[8] written out as prose with red paragraph marks to indicate the stanzas.
En mai ki fet flurir les prez,
et pululare gramina,
e cist oysels chauntent assez,
iocunda modulamina,
li amaunt ki aiment vanitez
querent sibi solamina,
je met ver vus mes pensers,
O gloriosa domina!

En vus espair solaz truver,
propinatrix solaminum,
ki sovent soliez alegger
gravatos mole criminum.
Surement poet il esperer
medicinam peccaminum,
ki ducement voet reclamer
te lucis ante terminum.

---

[4] Cf. H. Walther, *Proverbia sententiaeque* ... 20861.
[5] Walther 16229.
[6] Walther 31632 (this MS only).
[7] Walther 26963 (this MS only).
[8] Printed by T. Wright and J. O. Halliwell, *Reliquae antiquae. Scraps from Ancient Manuscripts illustrating chiefly Early English Literature and the English Language*, I (London, 1841), 200–2 (ed. Wright). The poem is briefly discussed by Carol J. Harvey, 'Macaronic Techniques in Anglo-Norman Verse' in *L'Esprit Créateur*, XVIII (1978), 70–81, esp. 74.

Duce rose, sul saunz per,
virgo decora facie,
en ki se pount amirer
cives celestis patrie,
en vus voet Deus esprover
vires sue potencie,
quant se força de vus furmer,
splendor paterne glorie.

Taunt de bunté en vus assist,
et tanta speciositas,
ke a pain mendif remist,
neque prodigalitas;
mes quant si grant enprés pris[t]
illius liberalitas,
de vus, çoe crai, le cunsail prist,
O lux beata trinitas!

Dame, sur tutes le pris avez,
et gaudes privilegio,
de honur, valu e buntez,
et hoc requirit ratio,
quant cil ki pur nus arusé
cruore fuit proprio,
de vus nasqui, li desiré,
Jhesu nostra redempcio.

Mere, pur la duzur Jhesu,
[vostri] dilecti filii,
qui nasqui, quit, par vertu
ab omni labe vicii,
defens nus seez e escu
contra fulmen iudicii,
par vus nus mist en salu
summi largitor premii.

4. more didactic verses.

Simia, ninfa, canes, lira, nummus avesque rapaces
sunt ludi laicis, sunt idola religiosis.[9]
Fortiter expende, dum sit tibi copia rende!
Nummis si queris parcere, pauper eris.[10]

5. ff. 5ra — 85ra: a complete text of the *Manuel des Péchés*.[11] Inc. *Ici comence le manuel de peché*; explic. *Icy finist la soume del manuel*

---

[9] Walther 29636.
[10] Walther 9830.
[11] See E. J. Arnould, *Le 'Manuel des Péchés'. Etude de littérature religieuse anglo-normande (XIIIe siècle)* (Paris, 1940). The MSS are described on pp. 359—98.

de peché. Written 33—34 lines to a column, the text is written in a new, large hand in black ink. There are regular rubrics in red, red and blue paragraph marks and initials, and numerous corrections and insertions. At the top of f. 61vb there is written in red *Del jugement* referring to the section lower down the column beginning "Ore escotez del jugement/Coe ert al jur de juise". Dry-point rubrics are found on ff. 8v, 9r, 14r, 24v, 26r, 71r. Rubrics in ink occur on ff. 31r, 32r, 33v, 37v, 43v, 46r, 52r, 55r, 56r, 60v, 66r, 68v, 69v, 70r, 70v.

6. ff. 85ra — 86rb/86va—b: two insertions, each in a different and later hand, relating to the *Manuel des Péchés.* The first, with *renvoi* to f. 77vb, comprises 11. 11465—688 (Bk 8); the second, written out a couplet to a line, has a *renvoi* to f. 78ra and is made up of 11. 11706—806.

7. f. 86v: a later hand has copied out the runic alphabet at the bottom of the page, below the Abc.

8. ff. 87ra—97rb: an anonymous Anglo-Norman translation of the *Disticha Catonis* in 1076 lines; the four main books are rendered in 152 stanzas.[12] The text is written in double columns, 34 lines to a column, with the Latin provided throughout (each line having a red initial). Red paragraph marks accompany each vernacular stanza, which is composed of six six-syllable lines rhyming aabccb. With the exception of f. 88v and the last stanza on f. 97rb, where the third and sixth lines are written out beside the couplets, the text is written out in metrical lines. There is no formal division of the four books. A fifteenth-century hand has made some corrections to the Latin text. After the *Epistula* and *Breves Sententie* there is a red rubric *Incipit hic Cato dans castigamina nato (f.* 88va). After the last line on f. 97rb the following has been added in the hand of the text at the bottom of the page: *Hic finit Cato dans castigamina nato,/ostendens quare mundum non debet amare./Ici finist le liver de Catun/ki aprent sun fiz sen et resun.*

9. ff. 97va—98rb: a prayer to the Virgin.[13] Inc. *Preciuse dame, sainte Marie,/Mere Deu, espuse e amie;* explic. *E de tuz mauz nus deliverez. Amen.* Written in the same hand as the preceding item, 34 lines to the column.

[12] Edited by Stengel in *Maître Elies Überarbeitung der ältesten französischen Übertragung von Ovids Ars Amatoria* herausgegeben von H. Kühne und E. Stengel nebst Elies de Wincestre, eines Anonymus und Everarts Ubertragungen der Disticha Catonis herausgegeben von E. Stengel, Ausgaben und Abhandlungen aus dem Gebiete der romanischen Philologie 47 (Marburg, 1886), pp. 106—58. I am preparing a new edition from the unique copy.

[13] See J. Sonet, *Répertoire d'incipit de prières en ancien français* (Genève, 1956), 1700, and K. V. Sinclair, *Prières en ancien français* (Hamden, Connecticut, 1978), p. 123 (1700). Neither volume records that in the present MS the text ceases at 1. 140 of the edition published from MS Trinity College Dublin 312 (C.4.2) by M. Esposito in *Modern Language Review*, XIII (1918), 312—18.

10. ff. 98va–99ra: another prayer.[14] Inc. *Duz sire Jhesu Crist ke par vostre saint pleisir/De femme deignastes nester e hom devenir*; explic. *E venir a la joie ke saunz fin dait durer. Amen.* Same scribe as above, 34 lines to the column.

11. f. 99rb: *Ici cumencent les .xxxvi. mestres folies e ki ben les entent/ .36. sens aprent.* One of seven known pieces on a variable number of 'folies'.[15] There are 36 lines which, with the exception of lines 13 and 16, rhyme in pairs. At the foot of f. 99ra–rb there is added a coda of 10, mostly much shorter, lines. The whole piece is written in a slightly later hand, and in slightly darker ink, than the preceding item.

12. ff. 99va–103vb (incomplete): a treatise in octosyllabic couplets on the Seven Deadly Sins which begins with a red rubric *Ci comence une petite sume de les set pechez morteus.* The text, reproduced below, is written 44 lines to the column. It has been corrected in the ink of the text by what appears to be the same hand (except f. 102va where *suffretur* seems to be in a different hand).[16] The initial letter of the first line is in red, and there is a red splash over the paragraph mark and initial letter at 1. 81. There are frequently accents over vowels in hiatus (see below).

On the final leaf (f. 104r) a fourteenth-century hand has written

Crapula premeditacio langor et humor habundans
in sompnis maculant extrema duo sine culpa.

Treatises on the Seven Deadly Sins take their place, of course, in the penitential movement which led to the production of countless manuals of instruction for confessors.[17] Paul Anciaux provided a detailed account of the achievements

---

[14] See Sonet, *supra* 541, and Sinclair, *supra* p. 61 (541).

[15] The MSS are: Cambridge Gonville and Caius Coll. 408, p. 323 (30 *Folies*); Oxford Bodleian Library Selden supra 74, f. 59vb (30 *Folies*); Cambridge U.L. Gg.I.1, f. 629ra (32 *Folies*); London BL Harley 957, f. 27v (33 *Folies*); Florence Bibl. Laurenz. Plut. XVIII. dextr. 7, f. 270va (35 *Folies*); London BL Harley 4657, f. 99rb (36 *Folies*); London BL Arundel 507, ff. 99va–100ra (60 *Folies*). The first, second and fourth of these versions remain unpublished. The Harley 4657 text was inaccurately published by Achille Jubinal, *Nouveau Recueil de contes, dits, fabliaux et autres pièces inédites des XIIIe, XIVe, et XVe siècles* . . ., II (Paris, 1842), 372–4 (falsely attributed to Harley 4677). Only the Florence version is mentioned in *GRLMA* VI/2 (Heidelberg, 1970), p. 296, no. 7248. The Cambridge U.L., Florence and Harley 4657 versions form a closely related group. A version was used in Robert de Ho's *Les Enseignements Trebor* (ed. M.-V. Young; 11. 955–90, giving 13 (+ 1) *Folies*). For two copies of the *Folies* in the library at Dover, see M. R. James, *The Ancient Libraries of Canterbury and Dover* (Cambridge, 1903), pp. 461 (170.7 Stulticie mundi principales in gallicis. Inc. fo. 164b *Qui nul bien ne soyt*) and 491 (414. Fatuitates seculi 37 [in gallicis] 36a *Qui nul byen*).

[16] There are a number of other instances where it seems likely that the hand is not that of the scribe, e.g. 1. 543.

[17] See Arnould, *op. cit.*, pp. 1–59.

of the twelfth century in this direction,[18] and Pierre Michaud-Quantin pursued their influence in compendia or *summae* from the thirteenth to the sixteenth century.[19] The publication of an early-thirteenth-century *Liber poenitentialis* by Robert of Flamborough[20] at last enables us to examine one of the many penitentials which pullulate at the beginning of the thirteenth century and most of which remain in manuscript. The shift of emphasis from the austerity of tariffs and penances to the value of contrition and confession, in all their psychological, moral and theological aspects,[21] brought with it the need for new practical guidelines, not only for compliance with the requirements of canon law, but also for the treatment of specific *casus*. The casuistry of Robert of Flamborough's treatise, as of Thomas Chobham's *Summa confessorum*, marks a striking advance on the old-fashioned *Poenitentiale* of Bartholomew of Exeter.[22] The works of William de Montibus are also testimony to the practical needs created by the Fourth Lateran Council.[23] In 1215 the bull *Omnis utriusque sexus* enjoined on all Christians who had reached the age of discretion to confess their sins at least once a year to their own priests. Within five years we have the activities of Raymond of Peñafort who begins the first version of his *Summa de casibus poenitentiae* which was later to receive a gloss from William of Rennes. The four books of Raymond's *Summa* cover all the major kinds of sin and acted

---

[18] See P. Anciaux, *La Théologie du sacrement de pénitence au XIIe siècle* (Louvain/Gembloux, 1949).

[19] See P. Michaud-Quantin, *Sommes de casuistique et manuels de confession au moyen âge (XIIe—XVIe siècles)* (Louvain, 1962).

[20] J. J. Francis Firth (ed.), *Robert of Flamborough . . . Liber Poenitentialis* (Toronto, 1971). The Deadly Sins are treated on pp. 179—99.

[21] See A. Teetaert, *La Confession aux laïques dans l'Eglise latine depuis le VIIIe jusqu'au XIVe siècle* (Bruges/Paris, 1926).

[22] See Adrian Morey, *Bartholomew of Exeter, Bishop and Canonist: A Study in the Twelfth Century with the Text of Bartholomew's Penitential from the Cotton MS Vitellius A XII* (Cambridge, 1937).

[23] See H. Mackinnon, 'William de Montibus, a Medieval Teacher' in T. A. Sandquist & M. R. Powicke (eds.), *Essays in Medieval History Presented to Bertie Wilkinson* (Toronto, 1969), pp. 32—45.

as a guide for further developments.[24] A confessor's manual attributed to a magister Serlo and written *c.* 1234 constructs the bulk of its text on a discussion of the Seven Deadly Sins.[25] Wenzel is right to declare: "In the two centuries following the Fourth Lateran Council the capital vices or 'deadly sins' were the most widely used scheme according to which a priest was taught to ask about the sins of his penitent, or a Christian, to examine his conscience. At the same time, the Seven Deadly Sins became one of the standard pieces of catechetical teaching which all pastors of souls were required to give at regular intervals".[26]

There are many treatises on the Seven Deadly Sins in continental French and Anglo-Norman which remain to be identified and studied.[27] We now have an edition of the *Mirour de Seinte Eglyse*,[28] which contains a discussion of the sins, and there is the notable Anglo-Norman *Compileison* in MS Cambridge Trinity College R.14.7 (s. xiii/xiv), ff. 1r—154v.[29] This work,

[24] On the character of the *summae*, see Thomas N. Tentler, 'The Summa for Confessors as an Instrument of Social Control' in C. Trinkaus & H. O. Oberman (eds.), *The Pursuit of Holiness in Late Medieval and Renaissance Religion* (Leiden, 1974), pp. 103—27, and L. Boyle, 'The Summa for Confessors as a Genre and its Religious Intent', *ibid.*, pp. 126—30.

[25] See J. Goering, 'The *Summa de Penitentia* of Magister Serlo' in *Mediaeval Studies*, XXXVIII (1976), 1—53, and *id.*, 'The *Summa* of Master Serlo and Thirteenth-Century Penitential Literature', *ibid.*, 290—311. The treatise displays an anachronistic concentration on the forms and legal aspects of satisfaction rather than on contrition.

[26] S. Wenzel, 'The Seven Deadly Sins: Some Problems of Research' in *Speculum*, XLIII (1968), 1—22, esp. 13. Particularly elaborate treatment comes to be given to Luxuria and Avaritia; see L. K. Little, 'Pride goes before Avarice: Social Change and the Vices in Latin Christendom' in *American Historical Review*, LXXVI (1971), 16—49.

[27] For the vast range of literature in Latin, see the 6553 entries in M. W. Bloomfield, B.-G. Guyot, D. R. Howard & T. B. Kabealo, *Incipits of Latin Works on the Virtues and Vices 1100—1500 AD* (Cambr., Mass., 1979). See also M. W. Bloomfield, *The Seven Deadly Sins: An Introduction to the History of a Religious Concept, with special Reference to Mediaeval English Literature* (Ann Arbor, 1952).

[28] A. D. Wilshere (ed.), *Mirour de Seinte Eglyse*, ANTS 40 (London, 1982), pp. 22—25. The fragment of a treatise on the Deadly Sins in MS Oxford Bodleian Library Laud Misc. 79, ff. 89—90, has been identified by Dr Ian Short as belonging to the *Mirour*.

[29] See G. Dempster, 'The Parson's Tale' in W. F. Bryan & G. Dempster (eds.), *Sources and Analogues of Chaucer's Canterbury Tales* (Chicago, 1941), pp. 721—60, esp. 726—28, 745—58.

consisting of a series of five treatises, forms a manual for
religious living and contains within it a French text of the
Ancrene Riwle.[30] It was prepared as a manual on preparation
for confession for both lay and religious. The treatise which it
contains on the Seven Deadly Sins closely resembles a 'short
version' which I have noticed in the following MSS:[31]

Edinburgh University Library 107 (s. xiii/xiv) ff. 126va–
129vb; London BL Cotton Vespasian D III (s. xiii) ff. 208ra–
210rb; Oxford Bodleian Library Bodley 82 (s. xiv med)
ff. 50r–57v; Digby 20 (s. xiii) ff. 162r–164r; Digby 86
(s. xiii[2]) (incomplete) ff. 1r–3r; Rawlinson C 46 (s. xiii)
ff. 300ra–vb/322vb.

The originality of the treatise edited below is that it is in
verse and that it relies uniquely on Biblical illustrations to
describe the sins. No less an authority than Peter the Chanter
had declared: "Ad sugillanda vitia commendandasque virtutes
pleraque in seminarium praedicationis, de hortulis sacrae
Scripturae collegimus, et excerpsimus".[32] Peter is cited in an
interesting list of authorities at the beginning of a confessional
manual in MS Oxford Bodleian Library Douce 282 (s. xiii)
ff. 56r–62v:

> Ici comence la confessiun de pechez geir pur aver perdun. [T]uz icez
> ki cest escrit orrunt u lirrunt, k'il le aient le plus en auctorité e plus
> cher sacent il de veir k'il est escepé des escriz de bons clers. Ices sunt
> saint Gregorie la pape, saint Aunsaume le arceveske, saint Augustin le
> eveske, saint Johan le eveske 'Buche d'Or', Bartholomeu le eveske, saint
> Bede le prestre, li abbés Ailred, li prior Clement, li prior Alisandre, li
> prior Ricard, Peres li Lumbard, Pere li Chantre de Paris, maistre Escice,
> maistre Robert de Flemesbroc e plusurs autres. [f. 56r]

It seems clear that our 'petite sume' was written sometime in
the thirteenth century, but the linguistic evidence permits very
little precision. Many of the stock Anglo-Norman features are
attested early: the reduction of *ie* to *e*, so that *e*<tonic free
a rhymes with *ie*<-ariu, -eriu (*lesser*:*mestier*; *acustumer*:*sauter*;
laburer:*dangier*; Pope § 1155); reduction of *iu* to *u* (*luz*;

---

[30] W. H. Trethewey (ed.), *The French Text of the Ancrene Riwle*, EETS O.S.
240 (London, 1958), esp. pp. xviii ff.
[31] I have not seen the treatise on the Seven Deadly Sins in MS Oxford St John's
College 75 (s. xiv in), f. 132v.
[32] *Verbum Abbreviatum* c. cxli, *PL*, 205, 338C.

Pope § 1166); depalatalisation of [ɲ] (*baraigne:plaine*; Pope § 1182); reduction of *ui* to *u* (*celui:receu*; *lui:feru*; Pope § 1160); instability of interconsonantal *e* shown by svarabhaktic forms (*avera*; Pope § 1173) and contracted future and conditional forms (*fra, reguerdunra*; Pope § 1290); velarisation of [ã] (*saunz, grauntera, daunz*; Pope § 1152). More indicative of the second half of the thirteenth century might be: raising of countertonic *e* to *i* in *benison* 11, the spelling *ui* for *u* in *suis* 251 (the preference for first pers. pl. endings in *-um* does not encourage us to go far beyond 1300); the almost universal effacement of final post-consonantal *e* (*afer, comand, empens, fest, gard* etc.), but many such features are merely scribal and there seems little possibility, in the absence of external criteria, of dating our poem more precisely than to the second half of the thirteenth century. It is worth drawing attention to the following rhymes: *returnir:fabler* 35–36; *aparust:mist* 269–70; *ocist:murust* 325–26; *mentirent:mururent* 519–20. The vocabulary is unremarkable, save for the following items: *avanceur* 133, *fraterne* 224, *fausin* 251, *deneruses* 638, *viairesce* 653, *obstinat* 669, *acouper* 723, *nundrait* 737.

The scribe regularly uses accents over vowels in hiatus:[33] *lees* 32, *veez* 104, *proom* 204, (*soot* 507, *Pool* 539), *purseez* 541, *veez* 544, *see* 554, *sees* 555, *peer* 557, *seez* 643, *poom* 676, *Bersabee* 688, *poom* 722. There are paragraph marks in the MS at ll. 27, 67, 81, 213, 277, 367, 649 and 785, and all these, save the second, have been observed in the text. For the sake of clarity I have occasionally interfered with the scribe's somewhat indiscriminate use of *c* and *t*, and I have capitalised each of the Seven Deadly Sins for ease of reference (reverting to lower case where they appear as moral attributes rather than as *abstracta agentia*). Textual emendation has been kept to a strict minimum.[34] The usual editorial conventions have been observed, except that diaeresis has not been used in view of the difficulty of distinguishing consistently between scribal practice and authorial intention as regards syllable-count.

[33] Cf. K. Lincke, *Die Accente im Oxforder und im Cambridger Psalter sowie in andern altfranzösischen Handschriften* (Erlangen, 1886); Ulrich Mölk in *Zeitschrift für französische Sprache und Literatur*, LXXXVII (1977), 300–1; J. Grant (ed.), *La Passiun de Seint Edmund*, ANTS 36 (London, 1978), p. 59.

[34] Rejected MS readings: 16 *des espines*; 81 *men amis*; 469 *Li Constantin*.

Ci comence une petite sume de les set pechez morteus

f. 99va

De bien fere e le mal lesser
Nus en avum tuz mestier.
Dunt pur nus acustumer
4   Ceo dit David en le sauter:
'Declinez del mal e bien facez,
Querez peis e la suez'.
E saint Pol li apostle dit
8   En une epistel ke il escrit:
'Ki ke seme escharsement,
Al sier le meins il prent,
E ki ke seme en benison,
12   De bon semail avera guerdun'.
Ceo est la joie pardurable,
Si son semail sait profitable,
Mais ceste tere est si baraigne,
16   De runces e d'espines plaine,
Nostre jument laburer
Ne se deigne sanz dangier.
Envogel se fet e veer poet,
20   La draite vaie aler ne voet;
Quant ele est en draite chemine,
Tut jurs va a decline;
En vaie ke ne dust aler
24   Tut jurs volait sujurner.
Tel est men aver a daunter,
Ke tot me veut por li chasser.
De les voyes ke nomé ai,
28   S'il vus plest, un poi dirrai:
Mult est estrait, çoe dit l'estoire,
Icele voye ke mein a gloire;
L'aultre est large, lunge e lié,
32   Ki cele voit tut ert gabé.
En cele voye sunt portes set,
Lees e larges e fortes fet.
Ki en els enter sanz returnir,
36   Dampné serra saunz fabler.
Uncor entendez a mai

E quei ai dit vus declarai:
La tere nus memes signifie,
40 Kar nus la portoms a l'asaye.
Le semail, ceo sunt vertuz
Ki semé sunt en poi de luz.
La jument nostre char est dit,
44 Ke trop parmaint en fol delit.
Des espines e runces replenie,   *f. 99vb*
Çoe est de vices nostre vie.
La voye ke tant est estrait,
48 Bon over est, par resun drait;
Estrait est e cuntermunt
E par tant mut poi i vunt.
Icele voy pot ester dit
52 Noster Seingnur Jhesu Crist.
'Je sui', çoe dit li Bonuré,
'Vie e voye e verité'.
Icele voye il nus revele
56 Par sa doctrine e apele.
Il nus apele, a li alum,
La voye large si lessum.
La voye estrait vait a destre
60 E la large a senestre.
En cele vunt clers e prestres,
Frans e serfs, diciples e mestres,
Ducs e rais e chevalers,
64 Dames, damoiseles, esquiers,
Pur veirs, si mentir ne dai,
Tuz ceus e plus, ceo crai.
De cele voye l'entré
68 Comence a proper volenté.
Or a mai entendez,
Ki proper volunté amez.
Ne vus pais si je le vus die,
72 De ceo vient Orguil e Glutunie,
Ire, Peresce e Envie,
Avarice e Lecherie.
Ces sunt le set portes posez
76 En cele voie ke tant est lez.

Ki ke enter e sait enclos,
Ja ne estut turner le dos.
Si il la einz fine sa vie,
80   Tart ert de requer aie.
     Or escutez, men amis,
De Orgoil dirrai mes avis.
Orgoil sur tuz maus est mal,
84   De tutes vices principal.
Orgoil hunist Lucifer,
Ke tant estait nobles e cler.
En ciel des angles ne out il per,
88   Orgoil le fit asoter.
Orgoil estait ki le fesait   *f. 100ra*
Ke il son seignur guerrait.
Sun dit nus muster Ysaye,
92   Disant en sa prophecie:
'Sur les estailes ascenderai,
Men scé en le firmament mettrai,
El munt de testament serrai,
96   Semblabel al plus haut me frai'.
Mes Orgoil trop se leva haut
E tost fist un merveilus saut,
Kar nus truvun ke en un moment
100   En enfern chai de le firmament.
E tuz ke a lui cunsentirent
Ensement ove li chaierent.
Or veez a quel dolur
104   Orgoil rent sun possessur.
Orgoil a tuz est enemi.
Çoe sout le primat de Surie,
Kar par Orgoil, mes amis,
108   De forte gent estait ocis.
Li rois Nabugodonosor,
Ki tant fu riches de tresor,
Par Orgoil estait exilé
112   De sun regne e anenté;
E tant Deu se humilia,
Ke pur delices fain manga!
Orgoil Goli abati,

116 Aman Orgoil suspendi,
     Nicanorem Orgoil ocist,
     E Antiochus ausi fist,
     Faraon en mer naia,
120 Sennacherib Orgoil tua.
     La tur de Babel Orgoil leva,
     Mes Deu de ciel la cravanta
     E quanque furent al lever,
124 Deu lur lange fit turner.
     Dunt a chascun naciun
     Diverses langages parlent chesun.
     Simon Magus fit voler
128 Orgoil e puis le col briser.
     Or veez coment rent
     Sun servise ke Orgoil prent.
     Ja ne verrez orgoilus
132 Ke il ne seit dedeingnus,   *f. 100 rb*
     Avanceur, malicius,
     Medisant e envius,
     Trop parlant e coveitus,
136 De ester prisé familuse;
     A nul ne deigne acorder,
     Cumpaignun ne vout aver,
     A la gent ne vot parler,
140 Mes tuz le deivent encliner;
     Quancque il dit sustendra,
     Ainz ke il ait oi respundra;
     Si il de nul sait repris,
144 Pur un mot vus dirra dis.
     Ces sunt vices esprové
     Ke sunt en orgoulus trové.
     Mes or oyez de tele gent
148 Ke dit saint Job le pacient:
     'Si Orgoil poait al ciel voler,
     La nue de sun chief tucher,
     Perdu serrait a la fin
152 E cum fens irrait a declin'.
     Or ki est de Orgoil naffré
     E desir sa sauveté,

Encuntre Orgoil humilité
156 Aprenge e tost serra sané.
Ensampel nus duna Jhesu Crist
Quant il del ciel descendist
E il char de la Virge prist,
160 Trent anz e plus en tere remist.
Ki tutes choses fit e furma,
De la Virge neister deigna.
Ausitost cum il fu né,
164 En une creche fu posé,
Circumcis e presenté
Al temple e puis baptizé,
E pur nus example doner
168 Quarant jurs deigna juner.
Tot aprés ke il out juné
Del diable estait tempté,
Des Jués sovent reprové,
172 Ke tant estoint maleuré.
Devant Pilat estoit jugé
E od larruns condempné,
A un piler fort lié,
176 Des escurges flaelé,
Ses mains, ses pez des clous percé,   *f. 100va*
E en la face escraché,
E en sun duz vis bufeté,
180 La lance mis en son duz costé
E des espines coruné
Pur nus pechurs, pur verité.
A son seif estancher
184 Aisil e fel firent meller.
En son saint cors fu nul liu
U le sanc ne fust issu.
Itel estait pur nus pené
188 Ke unkis ne fist peché.
Mort suffrit a deshonur
Pur nus reinder de dolur.
Or escutez, ceo vus pri,
192 Quei saint Pier dit de li:
'Crist si est peiné pur nus,

Example relessant a vus,
Ke vus ses tracis ensivez',
196   Ceus ke or oi avez.
Mes ki ke volt lui ensure,
Primes covient peché eschure,
Ester humble e pacient,
200   Kar tel estait il verraiment,
Deboner e obedient,
Cum il estait pur la gent,
E li amer cum creatour,
204   Son proom pur la sue amur,
De lui sovent mediter,
Sa proper volunté lesser.
Eissi purra engetter
208   Orgoil loinz de sun quer
E la joie lui durra,
Ke ja fin ne avera,
Laquele nus doint li fiz Marie,
212   Ki ciel e tere guarde e guie!
     Unkore escutez a mai
E de Envie vus dirrai.
Si nus comand saint Piere
216   Tutes malices oster
E faintise e tricherie,
Detractiun e envie.
E Salomon li sage bier
220   Vus defent od les envius mangier,
Kar a mangier vus priera   *f. 100vb*
E loinz de vus sun quer serra.
Ou est Envie, ceo dit li mestre,
224   Amur fraterne ne poet estre.
Il est envious verraiment
Pur autri pru ki est dolent,
Mes cel vice al diable apent,
228   Ne mi a cristiene gent.
Envie est membre al malfé
Dunt mort el mund est entré,
Kar par le envie de l'enemi
232   Adam deprimes estoit trahi.

Tost aprés Chaim le fel
Par envie ocist Abel.
Esau taunt cum pout
236 Vers Jacob envie out.
Les fiz Jacob par hatie
Joseph vendirent e envie
E Saul David ausi
240 En tut sun tens pursui.
Les Jeus Jhesum condempnerent
Par envie e crucifierent.
Dunt David dit: 'Ne enviez mie
244 Iceus ke funt felonie'.
De envie des traiturs
Venent sovent les robbeurs,
Mesdisaunz e hasardurs.
248 La vie perdre fet plusurs,
El fet cez clers desputer,
Les uns le faus sustenir,
Kar ki le fausin sustent suis
252 De ciel lasuis charra jus.
Envie fet les chevaliers turnaier
E maint hardi coup duner,
Les esquiers burdaier,
256 Des uns les autres fet tuer.
Envie fet plusurs larruns
E dames perder lur baruns.
Maint gentil home de lin
260 Envie ad fet orphanin.
En ki Envie est entré
Regner ne poet en charité.
E sanz charité nuli
264 Ne ert sauvé, ben le vus di.
Saint Johan li apostle escrit   *f. 101ra*
Ke Deus est charité e dit:
'En charité ki maint, celi
268 En Deu maint e Deus en li'.
Sa charité en nus aparust
Quant il sa alme pur nus mist,
Par quei devum, ceo dit la lettre,

272 Nos almes pur noz freres mettre.
Pur lur bien devum aver
Joie, e pur lur mal doler.
Issi purrum nus Deu paier,
276 Ki tant nus tuz achata cher.
    De Envie avez oi,
De Ire escutez, ceo vus pri.
Cele est plein de deverie,
280 De manace e de hatie,
De deceivance e felonie,
De male art e de reverie.
Tut est pleine sa meisun
284 De trespas, haunge e tensun,
De esclandes, reproces e rancur,
De amertume e de clamur;
Corrupciun est de saunté
288 E enoytement de enfermeté.
Ele est pleine de cruelté,
Maint est par li a mort liveré.
Noster Seignur crucifié
292 E seint Estevene lapidé,
Saint Pier, saint Pol e saint Andreu,
Sain Luk, saint Marc, saint Matheu,,
Saint Johan le Baptist decolé,
296 Saint Jorge la teste coupé,
Saint Thomas nostre avoué
De Engeltere encervelé,
Saint Agate e sainte Katerine,
300 Sainte Cecile e sainte Cristine,
E Margarete la Deu amie
E la virge sainte Lucie;
De male ceus par Ire
304 E mut plus suffrirent martire.
Çoe fit le diable par Envie
Ki tant est plein de tricherie.
Il fit les rois e emperours
308 Cruels tirauns e turmenturs,
Cum fu Cesar le felun   *f. 101rb*
E Pilat e Nerun,

Herode ou Estasie
312 Ou li emperur Julie,
Quincian e Constantine,
Dacian e Anoline,
Li emperur Maximian
316 Ou celui Dioclician.
Iceus firent plusors pener
Pur Deu amur e martirizer.
Or ou sunt devenuz
320 Les tiranz, les malestruz?
Lur cors sunt tut anenti;
Les almes ou unt deservi?
Plus sunt pur lur mavaitez
324 Ke pur lur pruesce renumez.
Herodes sei memes ocist
E Neron de male mort murust.
Issi par ire e coruce
328 A male fin devindrent tuz.
Li irus tant fet lever,
Le paciente le fet aswager,
Mole respuns li refreint,
332 Bele parole coruz veint.
E de l'irus sanz fable
Oreisun est abhominable;
Ou est Ire e Envie
336 Poi vaut chaunt ne spalmodie.
Quer penser ne lange dire
Ne poet les maus ke vient de Ire.
Encunter Ire medicine
340 Nus aprent la voye divine:
'Les pacient sunt benurez,
Kar les fiz Deu sunt apelez'.
Ki Ire voudra aswager,
344 Pacience estuet aver.
'La pacience del pover ja',
Ceo dit David, 'ne perira'.
A l'irus respunder u parler
348 Est cum lungaine mover;
Tant cum est mu plus,

Plus mettra de la puur sus.
Si fet le irous emmu,
352 Ja par parole ne ert vencu,
Tant cum il ait of ki tencer,   *f. 101va*
Pes jamés ne set aver.
Dunt mal est acumpaigner
356 A tele gent u aprocher.
Or vus avera cher e dru,
Mes cel amur ert tost perdu.
Or vus aime, or vus het,
360 Lealment amer ne set.
Dunt mielz vaut de li retrer,
Ke trop charger sun afer,
E en pacience parmaindre,
364 Si purra li irrus vaindre,
Ambur li e son vice,
Kar pacience vaint malice.
    Or escutez de une vice
368 Ki est apelé Avarice.
Li avers sanz coveitise
Ne set ester en nule guise.
Mes coveitise poi profite
372 Ke de tuz maus racin est dite.
De trais chosis vus sai dire
Ke tut le mund prés desire:
Delit, richeises e honurs,
376 Ceo treis desirent plusors.
De richesces Avarice crest
E covaitise of li est.
De fol delit vient glotonie
380 E li ensuit lecherie.
Ki desir richeces e dons,
Il charra en temptaciuns.
De coveitise vent lecherie
384 E faus serment e simonie.
Ele fet les seculers
— Ces marchanz e cez drapers,
Vineters e especers,
388 Orfevers e les mercers,

Tailurs e les parmenters,
Tanurs, suurs e corveisiers —
De nuit e jur, par tere e mer,
392　Forment lur cors travailer.
Quancque funt del jur, par songe
La nuit lur vendra tut a runge.
Kar ceo dit Nostre Seignur:
396　'Tun quer ert u est tun tresor'.
Mut par sai levent matin,　　　　　　　　　　*f. 101vb*
Vers le marché tenent lur chemin.
Ilok irunt e mal dirrunt
400　E mut suvent parjurs serrunt
Pur lur prome enginer
E pur l'amur de Danz Dener.
Si eus par cas oient suner
404　A la messe e al muster,
Pur ester veu iloc vunt,
Mes poi ilokes demurrunt.
Si il i ait predicaciun,
408　Tost se muster le talun.
Ilokes ne volt demurer,
Al marché l'estot turner,
E tut fussent demurré,
412　Lur quers serraint en le marché.
De cels Deus le Tutpuissant
Par le profet [va] disant:
'Icest pople ki me honurent,
416　De lur lievers en vain laburent,
Kar lur quers loinz sunt de mai'.
Si purrunt dire, ceo je crai,
Ke il lesent pur lur marchandise
420　Deu de ciel e sun servise.
Ne di pas ke tuz seient iteus,
Mes de tels i ad, e jofnes e veuz,
E ke lessent la draite voy
424　Pur l'amur de la monay.
De cez dit li rai Davi:
'Tresor funt, ne sevent a ki',
Kar tel vendra, si poet estre,

428 Ki se fra seignur e mestre
E despendra largement
La chose ke li ne custa nent.
De ses biens fra il sa fest:
432 La robe avera de escarlet,
Palefrai avera gras e gros,
Le riche avera purri les os,
Plenté avera de or e argent
436 E li autre girra pudlent,
En une haire gist envolupé,
Li autre se fra tut envaysé.
Cusu avera les gaunz de saie,
440 Kar 'de autri quir large curaye',
E la feste tendra en sa meisun   f. 102ra
Ov karole e grant channçon
En ces harpes e ceus vieles
444 E ces serjanz e ces anceles,
Je quid ke ja n'ert nomé
Celi qui tut out purchacé.
Il empens mut petit
448 En le anfer sun obit,
Tant en avera en despit
Celi qui tut conquist.
Dunt n'est pas sen ne saver
452 En autre trop afier.
Mielz vaut un poi duné avaunt
Ke aprés dis itant.
Uncore vus dirrai de Avarice,
456 Tant repleni de malice:
Ele met sun conquerur
En purchasant e en labur,
En grant dute, en grant pour,
460 En pert e en grant dolur.
Li avers duns vus promettra,
Mes poi u nient vus durra.
A nent fet les povers raindre
464 Pur sa sale bel depeindre.
Le rai Charles fet purtrayer,
Od li Rolland e Oliver,

Tuz les duz pieres i sunt,
468 Od les quatre fiz Eamund.
Constantin le ray i est
E sa raine od li contret.
Ilok fet les beus chevaus,
472 Les chevalers e les vassaus.
E le pover vait en la rue
Nu pé e la jambe nue,
Pur deprier pur le aumon,
476 Mes il ne trove ki li dune.
La parrai ert de or cuché,
Le pover fiebel e mesesé.
Iluk fet chastels e turs,
480 Cerfs e chens e venurs.
Tut ceo fet en la paraie
E son proom murt en la vaye
De faim e frait, pluvie e vent,
484 E cil ja gard de li ne prent;
Pur quei a le jur de juise
Je dout ke Deus em fra justise,
Kar a estrange e a privee
488 Est il sanz humanité.
Il fet malement doner
E ses aumones recouper.
Ja nul hospitalté
492 Ert en sa meson truvé.
Si nul li pri a mangier,
De ses deniers esparnier
De bon quer grauntera,
496 Mes ja li ne reguerdunra.
De duner la main clorra,
Mes a receiver uvert serra.
Sanz pessun serra la mer
500 Einz ke il ces cuvayter.
Plusurs en le secle sunt deceu
Par cuveytise e perdu.
Balaam, ke profet fu,
504 Par duns estait il corumpu.
Par coveitise de argent e or

f. 102rb

Lapidé esteit Achor.
Covaytise fet maint soot,
508 Ele fit Achab ocir Naboth.
Gyezi fu par lui
Vilement de leper feru.
Ele fit a deshonur
512 Judas vendre sun seignur,
E Julia Apostata
Pur coveitise Deu nia,
Ke primes estait cum heremite,
516 Puis devint tirant e herite.
Ananie par covaiter
E Saphir sa mulier
A Saint Espirit iceus mentirent,
520 Dunt de mort subit mururent.
Dives, dunt hum parolt tant,
Fu riches hum e manaunt,
Ki tutdis en delices fu,
524 De purpir e de cheisil vestu.
Sitost cum il estait devié,
Sa alme al diable fu liveré.
E Lazer, ki estait e pover e nu,
528 De frait e de faim vencu,
Sitost cum mort fu celui,
Sa alme en repos fu receu.
Dunt meuz vaut poverte e mesure
532 Ke trop richeise e suffretur.
Ben le sout celi ki dit
Salomon ke Deu requit
Ke trop richeise ne povert
536 Li dunast par sa desert,
Mes li dunast si li plust
Ke a sa sustenance suffir pust.
Çoe dit sain Pool, oyum avant,
540 Tute gent amonestant:
'Tutes choses purseez,
E seez cum rien ne eussez'.
E saint Pere dit a Jhesum:
544 'Sire, veez! nus lessum

f. 102va

Tutes choses e vus suum,
Quel guerdun averum?'
E Jhesus a li respundi:
548　'Verreyment, pur veir vus di,
Vus ke tut lessé avez
Pur mai e me ensuez,
Ceo serra voster guerdun;
552　En la regeneraciun,
Kant le fiz de hum serra
En le see de majesté e jugera,
Su ceus sees vus serrez
556　E le pople od Deu jugerez.
E ki let peer u mere
En ceste vie u suor u frer,
Femme, emfant u meisun,
560　Ou sa tere pur men nun,
Cent duble avera sanz fable
E la joie pardurable'.
Jadis un juvencel estait
564　Ki parfit ester volait,
De Noster Seignur requist
E il li respundi e dit:
'Va vendre quant que avez
568　E as povers le donez,
E puis ensuyer me venez
E tresor en ciel averez'.
Or seignurs, empensez,
572　La comparisun veez:
Donez vus e Il durra　　　　　　　*f. 102vb*
Tresor ke ja ne finera,
Ou robeur ne poet entrer
576　Ne larrun ne poet embler,
Ou ami ne poet issir
Ne nul enemi venir.
Ilok est joie e duceur,
580　Buntez e lel amur,
Solaz e bon confort;
Ja ne murra nul de mort,
Tant pardurable ert la vie,

584   Tant cum Deus est n'ert finie.
      Le cors de li ki ert sauvé
      Tut ert repleni de belté,
      Fort ert, fraunk e ignel,
588   Saint, delitable e nunmortel.
      Sa alme ert aurné
      De saver e de amisté,
      De concorde e de aseureté,
592   De honur e de joie avera plenté.
      Nul angel de ciel verra
      Sun creatour si cum il fra.
      Il verra Deu en Trinité,
596   En sa char glorifié,
      E la noster humanité
      Sus les angles enhaucé.
      Bor unkis nasqui en tere
600   Ki tel tresor poet conquere,
      Bor esteit engendré
      Ki son tresor ad la fermé.
      Pover dunc ici seum
604   E riches la ester purrum,
      E ke dire pussum ausi
      Cum David, ki fu le Deu ami:
      'Pover sui e en labur
608   De ma juvent a icest jur,
      Enhaucé e humilié
      E mut suvent desturbé'.
      Kant Davit pover se fesait,
612   Ki est dunc ki pover ne sait?
      Dunt sumes venuz engardum,
      Ou sumes e quei devendrum.
      Povers adés, si ne mentum,
616   Chaitifs nus nus truverum,
      Rien ne portames al primur,   *f. 103ra*
      Ici avum travail e dolur,
      E si tut le mund ussum,
620   De ci ren ne porterum;
      Nos os en tere purrirunt
      E verms la char mangerunt.

La mesun serra mesuré
624 Ou nus serrum herbegé;
De set piez ert la longure,
De treis a pain la leure,
E la cumble de la mesun
628 Tuchera pres le mentun.
Ilok le cors sarra
E a poudre devendra.
Ki ben ad fet le truvera
632 E ki le mal ausi le fra.
Dunt Salomon mut sagement
En sa doctrine sun fiz aprent:
'Beu fiz, ta fin remembrez,
636 E jammés ne pecherez'.
De çoe pensez vus covaytuses,
Vus usereres e deneruses,
Ostez voster iniquité
640 E voster tresor sait entamé.
En cele mettez voster pensé,
Kar tut le mund est vanité.
Seez large almuner
644 Pur Deu e si poez changer
Pur voster tresor deceivable
Tresor ke tuz jurs est estable.
Ceo est la joie ke ai nomé,
648 Laquele nus doint Dampnedé!
  De Avarice oi avez,
De Peresce or escutez,
Ke plain est de confusiun,
652 Pur ceo ad Peresce a nun.
De lachesce est viairesce,
Tutdis desire uduiesce.
De ben fer ne ad le quer,
656 Encunter Deu volt murmurer;
Encunter les Deu comandemenz
Ele fet mutes de negligenz;
Ele met hom en pensé
660 A deliter en vanité;
Ele fet hum suvent targer

f. 103rb

De ses pechez espurger,
E sai fetement confesser
664 E de ses pechez escuser;
Ele fet son confessur changer,
A l'un dir, a l'autre celer;
Ele met hum en obliance,
668 Si li fet frainder sa penance,
Impacient e obstinat
Encunter Deu e son prelat;
Ele fet les uns veiller
672 En lur lit e mediter
De vanité, e puis al muster
Dormir cuvient e somoiller.
E ausi fet ele sovent
676 Ke laschement sun servise rent.
Ele est a l'alm enemi
E noriz de lecherie.
Çoe vus poom ben prover,
680 Si il le vus plest a escoter,
Ke ne sai tenu mensunger.
Le rai David mettrai primer:
Tant cum fust en batayle
684 De rien tempté ne fu saunz faile,
Mes sitost cum cessa a guerrayer
E vint a l'ostel sujurner,
Tost aprés fit la folie
688 Of Bersabee la femme Urie.
Tant cum en bataile estait,
Sampson de nul pour avait,
Mes sitost cum sojorna
692 Of sa amie Dalida,
Tanttost par li fu deceu
Ki unkis avant ne fu vencu.
Salomon tant cum estait
696 Entur le temple que il fesait,
Ja ne estait a cele fiez
De nule lecherie temptez,
Mes sitost cum le labur lessa,
700 Lecherie li encumbra.

Dunt mut vaut par resun
Estre en bone occupaciun,
Mes Peresce ne vout suffrir,
704 Ou ke ele sait fra sun desir.
Ele fet hume returner   *f. 103va*
A son peché e pis pecher,
E pur li le plus engigner,
708 A la fin le fet deseserer.
Ele li met en memes le cas
Ke le diable fit Judas,
Ki reconut sun trespas,
712 Mes merci ne cria pas.
E si il requis eust merci,
Il [l'] eust eu, pur veir vus di.
Encunter cez pechez notables
716 Trais choses sunt profitables:
De quer verrai contriciun,
De buche verrai confessiun,
De over satisfaction,
720 E Deu dunc i mettra pardon.
Example pur nus conforter
Poom prender de saint Per.
Une meschine li acoupa
724 Par quei il sun seignur nia.
Puis plurout e fu contrit,
E Deus li pardona le dit.
Li lers ki estait pendu
728 E tost cum il out recunu
Ses pechez e Deu merci requit,
Ceo li respunt Jhesu Crist:
'Icest jour serrez od mai
732 En parais ou serrai'.
Daunz Zacheu ne dai passer,
Ki tant fu noble almoner;
La maité del seon volait
736 As povers doner, e si il ren avait
De nuli pris a nundrait,
Quater duble le rendrait,
Pur quai ke Jhesu mut le loa

740 Le jour ke od li sojorna.
De le publican ne dai lesser
Cum en le temple ala urer.
Il ura par humilité
744 E [fu] del tut justifié.
Quai dirrum de la Magdalaine
Ke tant estait de vices plaine?
Deus ses pechez li parduna
748 Pur ceo ke tant li ama.
Dunt ove saint Per contriciun,   *f. 103vb*
E ove le larrum confessiun,
E ove Zacheu le bon barun
752 Fesum satisfactiun,
Ove le publican merci crium
E ove Marie Deu amum.
De ceo fere seum prest
756 E sauvé serrum, si Deu plest.
E pur tut ceo confermer
Un temple estot edifier,
Tant cum avum le poer,
760 En quei pussum herberger.
Je vus dirrai le fundement
E les paraies ensement,
E puis vus dirrai la coverture
764 Ke mut profit tant cum dure.
Le fundement la fai serra,
Si ele est verrai, ja ne faudra,
E les parraies tut entur
768 Fetes serrunt de duble amur.
La cuverture de la mesun
Esperance avera a nun.
Iceste meson dunc fesum
772 E dedenz herbergom,
Kar en li ki voudra mainder
Tuz ses enemis purra vainder
E de ciel aver la joie,
776 Laquel Deu nus ottraye
Ki nus tuz furma e fit,
Noster Seignur Jhesu Crist,

Ki ov le Deu Pere rengnist
780 ´ E ov le Sainz Espirit,
Treis persons en trinité,
Un Deu verrai en unité,
Par tut le mund dit e preché.
784 Amen dium chescun pé.
Or oez de Glotunie
Ke tant est de mort replenie.
Maint home par li perd la vie
788 E mainte femme est huni.
Ele fet Deu reneyer
E son saint nun parjurer,
Le jur de Sabat violer,
792 Le fiz le per deshonurer
. . .

Notes to the Text

3. For *acustumer*, which is not given in *AND*, see *FEW*, II, 1091b ('amener qn à la pratique de qch.'). **4.** *Ps.* 33, 15. **7.** 2 *Cor.* 9, 6. **10.** The verb *soiier* has a wide variety of forms in Old French as well as Anglo-Norman. **18.** *sanz dangier* 'without compulsion, duress'. **19.** On the form *envogel* with change of prefix, see *FEW*, I, 7a. **25.** The scribe wrote *aver* which was then corrected by the addition of a superscript *n* and the insertion of *an* in the right-hand margin, without expunction of the final *r*. I assume that the image is still that of the *jument/ane*, both of which symbolised the flesh, and I therefore retain *aver*. **26.** MS *me me deut* (with superscript *e*). The *d* has been expuncted and the letter *v* written in the left-hand margin. The line is very obscure and seems corrupt; understand: "It [the *jument/aver*] wants to drive me just as it likes"? **29.** *Matth.* 7, 14. **31.** *ibid.* 7, 13. **33.** On doors as symbols of 'actiones/cogitationes pravae', see *Gregorianum*, *PL*, 193, 404BC, and Rabanus Maurus, *PL*, 112, 1031BC. **39.** On *terra* as a symbol of the flesh, see *Gregorianum*, *PL*, 193, 243D/ 244A; *Allegoriae in Sacram Scripturam*, *PL*, 112, 1031C. Rabanus Maurus, *PL*, 112, 1065D, gives 'corpus nostrum' and 1066A 'mens prava, infirma actio'. **40.** *asaye* is presumably a form of *assai* (cf. *AND*, 42) and the sense 'at the test, in temptation', though this scarcely provides a satisfactory explanation of the earth-image. **41.** See *Gregorianum*, *PL*, 193, 85D: 'Jumentorum nomine carnales homines designantur'. **45.** See *Gregorianum*, *PL*, 193, 339C. **47.** See *Allegoriae*, *PL*, 112, 1077B. **53.** *John* 14,6. **59.** See W. Harms, *Homo viator in bivio. Studien zur Bildlichkeit des Weges*, Medium Aevum Philologische Studien, 21 (München, 1970), esp. pp. 158ff. & 264ff., and U. Deitmaring, 'Die Bedeutung von Rechts und Links in theologischen und literarischen Texten bis um 1200' in *Zeitschrift für deutsches Altertum*, LXXX (1969), 265—92. Cf. Rutebeuf, *La voie de paradis*, 11. 35ff. in *Oeuvres complètes* ed. E. Faral & J. Bastin, I (Paris, 1959), 342ff. **61.** MS *celes* with *s* expuncted. Cf. *Aucassin et Nicolette* ed. Bourdillon, 6, 24ff. **75.** *Sunt* is inserted on the right of the line. **76.** MS *liez* with *i* expuncted. **91.** *Isaiah* 14, 13—14. **106.** Is this Seron 'princeps exercitus Syriae' (I *Macch.* 3, 13)? See Rabanus Maurus, *PL*, 109, 1150B ('significatur potentatus istius mundi . . . Syria interpretatur sublimus . . . quia mundus iste superbia excolitur'). **109.** The link with Pride is clearly indicated in *Daniel* 4, 34 and is reflected in Jerome, *PL*, 25, 541D ('idcirco se humiliatum, quia contra Deum superbierit'), and many writers up to Bozon, *Contes moralisés* ed. L. J. Smith & P. Meyer (Paris, 1889), p. 18 ('par orgoill fust destruit . . . richesse en Nabugodonosor'). The association with 'orguoilz et vainne gloire' is also found in the *Roman des trois ennemis de l'homme* ed. P. Meyer in *Romania*, XVI (1867), 16, 11. 775—80. **115.** See Rabanus Maurus, *PL*, 109, 52BC ('diaboli superbiam', 'provocavit superbia humilitatem'), and *ibid.*, 53C ('hereticorum superbiam signans'). See also Bernard of Clairvaux, *PL*, 183, 334D ('credo enim non incongrue in superbo homine superbiae vitium designari'). **116.** See Rabanus Maurus, *PL*, 109, 652B ('Quid per Aman superbum, nisi fastus potentum huius saeculi exprimitur?'). **117.** II *Macch.* 15, 6: 'Nicanor quidem cum summa superbia erectus'. **118.** See I *Macch.* 1, 11: 'Et exiit radix peccatrix [var. peccati] Antiochus illustris'. See Rabanus Maurus, *PL*, 109, 1134C ('Antiochus . . . qui intravit in terram sanctam cum superbia . . . typum tenet Antichristi') and Godfrey of Admont, *PL*, 174, 1132D—1133A. **119.** See Adam Scotus, *PL*, 198, 332D—333A ('elatio' and 'appetitum vanae gloriae'). **120.** *Sennacherib* rased the city of Babylon to the ground in 689BC and was assassinated by his sons. See Rupert of Deutz, *PL*, 169, 1339C ('propter magnitudinem superbae potentiae vel potentis superbiae'). **121.** On the association of the Tower of Babel with the proud, see Adam Scotus, *PL*, 198, 813D—814A. **124.** For *turner sa langue* 'eine fremde Sprache sprechen', see *TL*, X, 429. **125.** The apocryphal legend of the flight of Simon Magus is found in The Acts of Peter, written *c.* 200 AD in Asia Minor; see M. R. James, *The Apocryphal New Testament* (Oxford, 1924), pp. 331ff, and subsequently in the Ps. Clementine Recognitions, an OF verse translation of which exists in MS Cambridge Trinity College R.3.46 (s. xiii), ff. 122r-357. For further refs. to the story of Simon Magus, see *PL*, 85, 769 note b, and Flodoard of Rheims, *PL*, 135, 597ff. See also Ambrose in *PL*, 15, 2068ff. **130.** In the left-hand margin there is a pointing finger and the word *nota*. **133.** *Avanceur/avanteur* 'boastful' is rare. Godefroy, I, 511a gives a single example from Thomas of Kent's *Roman d'Alexandre* in MS Paris BN f.fr. 24364, f. 85r. This is actually an interpolation from the *Roman d'Alexandre* Branch IV and is not included in the standard edition of Brian Foster and Ian Short, *The Anglo-Norman Alexander*, ANTS 32—33 (London, 1977). *FEW*, XIV, 156a gives " 'avanteur' (*ca.* 1240)" without specifying a source. **144.** MS *durra* with second minim expuncted. **149.** *Job* 20, 6—7. **154.**

sa inserted in right-hand margin. **156.** MS *saune* with *u* expuncted. **160.** *re-* has been inserted as a correction. **163.** *il* is a superscript insertion. **180.** *duz* inserted in right-hand margin. **192.** I *Peter* 2, 21. **196.** See 11. 157ff. above. **215.** I *Peter* 2, 1. **219.** *Proverbs* 23, 6–8. **224.** *fraterne* is rare and attested relatively late in both OF and ME. Of the three recorded instances only one is of the 14th century, the others are later. **229.** *Wisdom* 2, 24. **234.** See Rabanus Maurus, *PL*, 107, 502C ('invidiae in fratrem livore cruciatus'). **236.** See Rabanus, *PL*, 107, 590D ('invidiae stimulis concitatus'). **237.** See Rabanus, *PL*, 107, 623A ('invidebant ei'). **238.** See Rabanus, *PL*, 109, 54C ('invidia Saulis'). **243.** *Psalm* 36, 1, and cf. *Proverbs* 24, 1 & 19. **262.** *en* added in right-hand margin. **265.** I *John* 4, 16. **269.** I *John* 3, 16. **283.** *tut* appears over expuncted *trop*. **295.** MS *de Baptiste*. **297.** *avoué* 'patron' suggests the English provenance of the treatise. **311.** St Polycarp was martyred in Smyrna under Herod at the time when Statius Quadratus was governor; see H. Musurillo (ed. & transl.), *The Acts of the Christian Martyrs* (Oxford, 1972), esp. p. 19. **312.** Cf. *infra* 11. 513ff. On Julian the Apostate, see A. H. M. Jones in *The Oxford Classical Dictionary* (Oxford, 1972), pp. 567ff. **313.** The reference to Quintian is obscure. For an Aurelius Quintianus, *Praeses Numidiae* (303), see A. H. M. Jones, J. R. Martindale & J. Morris, *The Prosopography of the Later Roman Empire*, I, A.D. 260–395 (Cambridge, 1971), 758. **314.** For 'P. Datianus', see *The Prosopography* . . ., I, 244. *Praeses* under Diocletian and Maximian, he is mentioned as the executioner of the martyr Eulalia of Merida (died *c.* 304). On his role as persecutor of St George (died *c.* 303), see J. E. Matzke in *PMLA*, XVII (1902), 464–535, and XVIII (1903), 99–171, and cf. *Chanson de Sainte Foi d'Agen* ed. A. Thomas (Paris, 1925), 11. 327ff. There is some confusion with the Emperor Decius (see var. in Matzke's edition of the St George legend). For C. Annius Anullinus, see *The Prosopography*. . ., I, 79. **315.** For Maximian, see *The Prosopography*. . ., I, 573ff., and for Diocletian *ibid.*, 253ff. **325.** *s'ocire* here probably has the sense 'to be beside oneself'; On the medieval image of the raging Herod, see R. E. Parker, 'The Reputation of Herod in Early English Literature' in *Speculum*, VIII (1933), 59–67. **329.** *Proverbs* 15, 18. Cf. *Ecclesiasticus* 28, 11. **331.** *Proverbs* 15, 1. *Respuns* here shows loss of final postconsonantal *e*. **341.** *Matthew* 5, 9. **345.** *Psalm* 9, 19 (A.V. 18). **347.** See *Li Proverbe au vilain* ed. A. Tobler (Leipzig, 1895) no. 240: "Quant plus remuet en la merde, et ele plus put"; *Li Respit del curteis et del vilain* ed. E. Stengel in ZfSL, XIV (1892), 157 n. 36: "Cum l'en plus fule la merde, plus pu[e] "; *Proverbes français antérieurs au XVe siècle* ed. J. Morawski (Paris, 1925) n. 410: "Con plus esmuet [on] la merde, e ele plus pu(e)t", and 1757: "Quant plus muet len la boë, et ele plus put". **389.** MS *tailuis* with superscript *r* over expuncted *i*. **394.** *venir a ronge/en ronge* 'cause remorse', 'prick the conscience'. **396.** *Matthew* 6, 21; *Luke* 12, 34. **401.** See *Li Proverbe au vilain* ed. Tobler, p. 31, no. 69: "Deniers va en touz lieus;/les terres et les fieus/achate danz Deniers;/l'un lasche, l'autre apresse,/les orgoilleus abaisse,/et les unbles fait fiers". For the 13th-century Continental poem 'De dan Denier', see T. Wright (ed.), *The Latin Poems commonly attributed to Walter Mapes*, Camden Society, 16 (London, 1841), pp. 357–59 (later English and Scottish poems on the same theme on pp. 359–62). **408.** Godefroy, X (Suppl.), 741a gives one (later) example, whilst *FEW*, XIII, i, 58a gives "*montrer les talons* 's'en aller, s'enfuir' (seit *ca.* 1330)". **415.** *Matthew* 15, 8; *Mark* 7, 6. **426.** *Psalm* 38, 7 (A.V. 39, 6). **439.** MS *gañz*. **440.** See *Li Proverbe au vilain* ed. Tobler, p. 56, no. 131, and pp. 98–99, no. 238; Morawski, *Proverbes français* 453; *TL*, II, 882. Cf. the similar development of ideas in *Li Proverbe au vilain, ed. cit.*, p. 26, no. 58: "Mainz hon est d'autrui chose/ larges et doner l'ose,/ne li chaut ou l'espande;/le suen garde et estraint,/si se demente et plaint,/quant nus rien li demande". Cf. also Serlon de Wilton, *Poèmes latins* ed. J. Oberg (Stockholm, 1965), p. 117, no. 61. **447.** MS *il le ne pas petit* with central three words expuncted and *empens mut petit* written in right-hand margin. **453.** *un poi* inserted in right-hand margin. **468.** *fiz* inserted in right-hand margin. The dispute between Charlemagne and the four sons of one of his vassals, Aymes de Dordonne, is the subject of a late-12th-century *chanson de geste, Renaut de Montauban (Les Quatre Fils Aymon).* **469.** *le ray* is inserted in the right-hand-margin. **470.** *raine* is written out in the left-hand margin as well as appearing in the text. On the legend of the Empress's liaison with a dwarf, see A. Tobler, 'Kaiser Constantinus als betrogener Ehemann' in *Jbch. f. rom. u. engl. Lit.*, XIII (1874), 104–8. **482.** *proom* is entered in the left-hand margin and as a superscript insertion in the text. **494.** The *s* of *esparnier* (written out again in the right-hand margin) is a superscript insertion. **500.** *ces* for *cesse*. **504.** *Numbers* 22, 17–8. Cf. Rabanus Maurus, *PL*, 108, 729B ('cupiditas pecuniae'). **506.** Achor is in fact the name of the valley where Achan, having stolen booty at the sack of Jericho, was stoned; see *Joshua* 7, 24–6 and Rabanus Maurus, *PL*, 111, 54C. **508.** The story of Ahab's participation in the false accusations against Naboth is related in 3 *Kings* 21, 1–29. Cf. Rabanus Maurus, *PL*, 111, 60D, 64D. **509.** See 4 *Kings* 5, 20–7, and Rabanus, *PL* 109, 233B ('cupiditas'). **517.** See *Acts* 5, 1–11. **519.** *esprit* is inserted in darker ink in the left-hand margin. **521.** For Dives, see *Luke* 16, 19–31, and Rabanus, *PL*, 111, 80B–81C. **524.** *Luke* 16, 19. **527.** *Luke* 16, 20–31. **532.** *suffretur* corrected from *sussaillur* in a different hand in the left-hand margin. **533.** *Proverbs* 30, 8. **534.** The last letter of *Deu* is a super-script insertion. **541.** 2 *Cor.* 6, 10. **543.** *Pere* inserted in left-hand margin in a different hand. **544.** *Matthew* 19, 27. **547.** *Matthew* 19, 28. **552.** *re-* is a superscript insertion. **557.** *Matthew* 19, 29. **563.** *Matthew* 19, 28. **565.** *seigneur* is inserted in the right-hand margin in the hand of the text; *requist* is a superscript insertion over expuncted *estait*, also in the hand of the text. **602.** *fermé* 'secured'. **607.** *Psalm* 87, 16 (A.V. 88, 15). **623.** Cf. the description in the treatise made up of sermons on the Seven Deadly Sins in MS Oxford Bodleian Library Bodley 90, f. 9r [on pride]: "De la mesoun au morz. Pensez de autre part come estreite serra donke vostre meson. Issi ele serra estreite: lors ke

vous ne purriez herberger ove vus nul [f. 9v] autre home e si basse serra
ke li fest vus serra ferm au nees e au mentoun. Mout serreit fol ki sei
enorgoillereit de une tele mansion". **635.** *Ecclesiasticus* 7, 40. **638.**
deneruse is a hapax. Cf. *FEW*, III, 39b (in Mistral, *deneirous* 'pécunieux').
653. *viairesce* 'instability, inconstancy' is a hapax. **687.** 2 *Kings* 11,
2–5. **691.** *Judges* 16, 4–31. **692.** *Dalida* is the form most commonly
found in the *Roman de la Rose*. **698.** *nule* and *lecherie* are interverted
in the MS and accompanied by signs to indicate the correct order.
703. In *suffrir* the final *i* is a superscript insertion over an expuncted *e*.
723. *Matthew* 26, 69–75; *Luke* 22, 56–62. **726.** The final *a* of *pardona*
is written over an expuncted *e* and also inserted in the left-hand margin.
730. *Luke* 23, 43. **733.** *Luke* 19, 8. **735.** MS *soen*, which has been
corrected in the left-hand margin to *seon*. **737.** MS *pris a nundrait de
nuli* with signs to indicate the correct order. *Nundrait* appears to be a
hapax. *Nondreiturier* is given as a hapax in *FEW*, III, 89b. **741.** *Luke*
18, 10–14. **745.** The picture of Mary Magdalen as the type of the
penitent sinner derives from the identification of her with the sinful
woman of *Luke* 7, 36–50, flimsy though this be. See H. M. Garth, *Saint
Mary Magdalene in Mediaeval Literature* (Baltimore, 1950). **749.** *Per* is
a superscript addition in black ink. **756.** The second letter of *si* is a
superscript addition.

THE DISCOVERY IN OLD FRENCH PHONOLOGY OF THE *niece, piece, tierç, cierge* TYPE

YAKOV MALKIEL_____

The present paper is, essentially, a sketch of a key chapter in a future history of Romance linguistics: the gradual discovery of the process which underlies the formation of OF *niece, piece, tierç, cierge,* and the like.[1] At the risk of slightly diluting or distorting my self-imposed assignment of merely chronicling and criticizing certain scholarly pronouncements and verdicts, I have here and there tried to come to grips with the phenomenon at issue itself.

The realization of what was actually involved in the transmutation of, say, **nĕptia** (for Class. **nĕptis**) 'niece', ***pĕttia** (Celto-Lat.) 'piece', and **tĕrtiu** 'third' into OF *niece, piece, tierç* (to confine myself to the arbitrary choice of these three examples) came fairly late to scholars; it would seem, for instance, that Diez, the founding father of the discipline, never grappled with this issue, at least not in the successive editions of his tonesetting comparative grammar and etymological dictionary (for details see below). The initial break-through came in the 1870s, but the earliest findings were still haphazard and hazy, and had to undergo several consecutive revisions before serious attempts could be made to integrate them with, and absorb them into, general accounts of Old French phonology.

One facet of organized scholarship's slow triumph over the obstacle involved was the protracted terminological imbroglio. Unquestionably, on the descriptive plane, what we are faced with in words structured like *niece, piece, tierç* (mod. *tiers*), all three preserved to this day, is a rising diphthong /je/ or

---

[1] *Cierge* (f.) here refers to the zoonym 'hind', not to its masculine homonym for 'wax candle', from **cēreu**, unless expressly so marked.

/jɛ/.[2] Paradoxically, however, the diachronic process that gives rise to a diphthong, generating it from a monophthong, is not necessarily, under any set of circumstances, straight diphthongization.

The earliest scholars who dealt felicitously with *niece, piece, tierç* (or, for that matter, with *cierge* *cĕrvia 'hind', learning to contrast it with *cerf* cĕrvu 'stag') described their findings with increasing accuracy and strove honestly to expand their corpus of supporting examples, but had no label yet to attach to the shift of parental ĕ in a checked stressed syllable to *ie*; as a result, they operated with all sorts of lame, lengthy paraphrases. At later stages of the discussion, it became customary to use the tag 'conditioned diphthongization' and to oppose it to 'spontaneous diphthongization' as in fĕru > *fier* or in cŏr(e) > *cuer* (mod. *cœur*), and this terminological preference is still very widely favoured.[3] However, the qualifiers chosen to bring home the difference between the trajectories of *niece* and *tierç*, on the one hand, and of *fier* and *cuer*, on the other, do not carry conviction. Over against the assumption of genuine spontaneity one can place, in a case history like fĕru *fier*, certain conditions (e.g., the occurrence of the change under observation in a syllable both free and stressed), which make the implied typological contrast to truly conditioned change, as a nĕptia *niece*, very dubious — to say the least. What those philological linguists who coined the respective terms actually meant was the fact that in *fier(s), fiere(s)* no other segmental phoneme of the prototype intervened and co-determined the direction of the change, whereas in *cĕrvia, nĕptia, *pĕttia and tĕrtiu an interplay of two internal conditions (checked, stressed syllable) and of one external condition (namely the ĭ more and more pro-

---

[2] I deliberately disregard here the school of thought that operated with the assumption of a large-scale stress of *ie* on its first component.

[3] For one example among many, see the excellent review article ('Orientations actuelles en linguistique historique') by Otto Gsell in *RPh*, XXXVI (1983), 428–42, at 439, plus the apparently very weighty book to which it is devoted: Jakob Wüest, *La Dialectalisation de la Gallo-Romania; problèmes phonologiques*, Rom. Helv., XCI (Bern, 1979). For a mid-20th-century check on one dialectalism discussed in this paper, see C. T. Gossen, *Petite grammaire de l'ancien picard* (Paris, 1951), § 11, who records many doublets and reckons, in the wake of H. Morf, with ecclesiastic border-lines.

nounced as /j/ in the following syllable) triggered the crystallization of the rising diphthong *ie* /je/. Perhaps it would be most
effective to oppose, in this context, endogenous to exogenous
conditioning.

What the pioneering scholars apparently failed to grasp is the
abyss that separates the processes themselves from the results
of processes. Starting with the latter, OF *ie* /je/, regardless of
its varying provenience (alongside *fier* and *tierç* one can cite,
for the sake of variety of sources, the familiar instance of
carri-cāre *chargier* 'to load'), was first and foremost a rising
diphthong; more specifically, a newly-produced rising diphthong
and, to that extent, legitimately comparable to the *ui* of *muir*
'I am dying', *tuit* 'all', and the *ue* of *cuer* 'heart', etc. By the
same token, it was sharply contrastable, within the chosen
perspective, with the monophthongs arrived at through raising
under the impact of metaphony, i.e. through anticipation of a
following high vowel, as in **vēnī** *vin* (mod. *vins*) 'I came'.

But if one reverses the procedure by placing emphasis entirely
on the process, at the heavy cost of minimizing the importance
of the effects thus achieved, then **vēnī** *vin* and **nĕptia** *niece*
immediately become two subcategories of a single sort of change
metaphonically induced. The five characteristics of **vēnī** *vin*
are: (a) pre-existence of word-final unstressed -ī /iː/ in a word
whose stressed syllable (b) was free and (c) contained, as its
nuclear vowel, /e/ from earlier /eː/, the product being (d) /i/
or, as in this instance, /ĩ/, coincident with (e) the loss of the
final vowel which had started the chain reaction. The parallel
set of characteristics for the other subcategory exemplified by
tĕrtiu *tierç* is as follows: (a) availability of a near-final /j/, apt
to exert its influence on (b) /ɛ/ (from earlier ĕ), provided the
syllable at issue (c) is checked, the net gain being (d) the formation of a rising diphthong. From the record of **tĕrtiu** *tierç* one
is tempted to infer, as the fifth mandatory characteristic, (e)
the eventual disappearance of /j/ — once more the ultimate
cause of the whole chain reaction — through merger with the
preceding dental occlusive: tĭ > ç /ts/, but an important alternative exists: *cĕrvia* *cierge* shows hardening of /j/ to /dʒ/
(eventually /ʒ/), and concomitant loss of the central part of
a 'heavy' medial consonantal cluster: */rvdʒ/.

Had the pioneers encountered solely metaphonic diphthongs divergent in kind from what their immediate successors called 'spontaneous' diphthongs, as is true of the *ui* /yi/ or /wi/ underlying *muir* mŏrio(r) and *tuit* tōt(t)ī (with expressive gemination of the pillar consonant), they might have run into distinctly fewer difficulties. Their misfortune stemmed from the need to deal simultaneously with the *ie* of *fier* and the *ie* of *tierç*, identical in one respect, yet totally different in another. Another handicap was the early experts' (in Old French) scant familiarity with the phonology of southern Italian dialects (to say nothing of Rumanian), that is with varieties of Romance folk speech in which diphthongization is typically conditioned by the codae of the respective words. Next, for pedagogical reasons, it seems safer and simpler, in initiating beginners into French (or, for that matter, into Spanish) historical grammar, to dramatize the contrast between metaphony and diphthongization by concentrating on the pure raising effects of the former (as in *vin* or *vine* 'I came'), to the temporary exclusion of the hybrid-looking process (diphthong-ization through metaphony, as in *niece*), except perhaps in the privileged instances of *muir, tuit*. Finally, the pathfinders found it puzzling that the front-vowel series *niece, piece*, etc. should be lacking a counterpart among words clustering around a back vowel, much as *fier* fĕru parallels *cuer* cŏr(e), to the point of virtually perfect symmetry.

It can be stated categorically that Diez, as a practitioner of both historical grammar and lexicographically slanted ety-mology, was to the last totally unaware of the problem under discussion, so far as can be inferred from the record of his publications, including spells of eloquent silence. This follows clearly from the analysis of his concluding studies.

In the late 1860s, when Diez himself was in his mid seventies,[4]

[4] The original edition of Diez's grammar, in three volumes, appeared in Bonn, between 1836 and 1844; the 2nd, revised ed., between 1856 and 1860 (this is the version which G. Paris translated into French [Paris, 1863], while C. B. Cayley that same year rendered the introductory part of Vol. I into English [London and Edinburgh: Williams & Norgate]); the 3rd ed. dates from 1870–72, and was later twice reprinted.

he was busy revising for the last time the work that had
propelled him to fame, namely his historico-comparative
Romance grammar; specifically, the opening volume, devoted
in large part to phonology and spelling viewed in diachronic
projection. As has been independently established,[5] Diez, in
the second and the third editions of that work, offered his
readers a bi-directional vista of the major processes by studying
the given transmutations in Section I ("Buchstaben der Quel-
lensprachen", pp. 144—331) in a Latin-Romance perspective,
and by later re-examining them afresh, where such a shift of
angle of observation was at all possible, in the opposite direction (Section II, "Romanische Buchstaben", pp. 331—485).
Let us observe closely how he took these two steps.

In Section I, he broke down his material according to the
source language involved, pitting Latin (pp. 144—305) against
far more meagrely represented Germanic (pp. 305—27) and
Arabic (pp. 327—31); and in the lengthy chapter on Latin-
Romance relationship, he granted pride of place to vowels
(pp. 146—202), starting out with those collocated in stressed
syllables (pp. 146—72). Here we come across the vernacular
reflexes of parental e (pp. 150—54), in three subdivisions, of
which the first and the second each boast two paragraphs. This
total of five consecutive paragraphs constitutes our principal
source of information on Diez's thinking; in summarizing and
paraphrasing his ideas, we shall, for obvious reasons, consistently
give prominence to slices of Gallo-Romance material.

For primary or secondary *e* we must reckon, basically, with
the retention of the ancestral vowel; here and there, with its
change into a falling diphthong (mostly *ei*, in French occasionally *ai*), while the situation in Wallachian (i.e. Rumanian)
remained relatively obscure on account of two conflicting
currents.[6] The few instances of the appearance of the cor-

---

[5] For any analysis of the 'tactical arrangement' of the section on phonology see
§§ 4.0 — 4.2 of my paper 'A Tentative Typology of Romance Historical Grammars'
in *Lingua*, IX (1960), 321—416; reprinted, with slight improvements, in my *Essays
on Linguistic Themes* (Oxford, 1968), pp. 71—164.

[6] Without going into the details of Diez's treatment of "Wallachian", let me
remark that he transliterated a Cyrillic letter as -ę, which stands for today's -ă. For
Diez's *eapę* 'mare' read with S. Puşcariu, *Etymologisches Wörterbuch der rumänischen*

responding rising diphthong (typically *ie*) testify to the confusion of ē and ĕ at the chronological level of Latin. In this
context French stands out on account of its uniquely lively
development, with *oi* emerging as the terminal stage. Diez,
thus, correctly sets apart *avoir, avoine, coi, courtois, crois,
dois, espoir,* obs. *hoir, moi, mois, poids, soir, soie, toile, trois,
voile, voir* as the nuclear group, when viewed against the background of **habēre, habēna, qu(i)ētu, *cortē(n)se, crēdō, dēbō,
spēr-, herēde, mē, mē(n)se, pē(n)su, sēru, sēta, tēla, trēs, vēlu,
vēru,** and he grants the rank of a side-line to *cannaie* (**cannētum**),
craie (**crēta**), and *taie* (**thēca**), isolating the following nasal as
the factor behind the failure of *ei* to join the broad-gauged
ei > oi movement: *frein, haleine, plein, veine* (*avoine* thus
remains isolated and unexplained). So far so good; but since
Diez has not yet learned to operate with the concept of learned
transmission, he now makes his first fatal mistake by postulating another evolutionary side-line — a gambit immediately
recognizable to us as false —, namely plain retention of *e*,
especially before *l*, citing as evidence words like *blasphème,
cantele, carême, cède, complet, fidèle, règle*, to say nothing of
his mind's or ear's apparent imperviousness to the effect of a
nasal (*étrenne, femme, sème*).

Diez next parades before his readers' eyes a procession of
words exemplifying the raising of *e* to *i* highly characteristic
of, though by no means exclusive to, Old Provençal (*berbitz,
pouzi, razim, sarrazi*) and, especially, to French (*brebis, cire,
marquis, merci, pais* [= *pays*], *pris, poussin, raison, tapis, venin*),
announcing his discovery of a similar trend in Old High German,
but neglecting to point out the special conditioning factors that
must, individually or concurrently, have prevailed in Gallo-
Romance.

Diez now invites his readers to join him on a promenade

Sprache, I: *Lateinisches Element* (Heidelberg, 1905), *iapă*; of the two forms Diez
supplied for 'gall' (**fel**), *fiere* prevailed in the new standard over *feare*; similarly,
miere 'honey' (**mel**), rather than *meare*, entrenched itself, even though *(m)njari*
has been recorded in Meglenitic, a dialect spoken near Mount Olympus. The remaining items lend themselves to this re-interpretation: *mierlă, miez, peadecă*, and *piatră*.
One must reckon, then, with as many as three — and not just two — diphthongal
outcomes: *ea, ia,* and *ie*.

through the domain of stressed ĕ. French, for a change, acts typically, i.e. as a member of a sharply profiled majority group of sister languages which will allow that monophthong to change into a rising diphthong:

> *bien, brief* [witness mod. *brièvement*], *dieu, fiel, fier, fièvre, hièble, hier, liège, lierre, lièvre, miel, mieux* [as once pronounced with /jєw/], *pied, piège, relief, sied, tiède, tient, vient*

are excellent examples indeed; so are OF *criembre* trĕmĕre, *espiegle* spĕculu, *fiert* fĕrit, *ieque* ĕqua, *miege* mĕdicu, *mier* mĕru, whose citation, however, might have profited from a succinct commentary on certain idiosyncrasies; thus, the asymmetry of *ueil* ŏculu and *espiegle* spĕculu should not have been overlooked, and *iue* should have been parenthetically referred to as the most common descendant of ĕqua. Old Provençal counterparts are also adduced (*brieu, dieu, ieu, fier, hier, lieu, mielhs, mier, mestier, mieu, siec, vielh*) — yet here Diez neglects to make it clear to his readers that (unlike the state of affairs in Oïl) diphthongization in Oc was consistently optional rather than, practically, obligatory. Worse, the uninitiated peruser of these pages will hardly learn from the inventory of Spanish illustrations, including *viernes* 'Friday' as against Fr. *vendre-di* Vĕn(e)ris diēs,[7] that the configuration of the syllable (checked vs. free) was a major factor in one provincial variety of colloquial Latin, namely that which was on its way to evolving into Old French, without necessarily being a prime determinant in another, which one dimly recognizes as underlying Old Spanish. Diez's indifference to this crucial divergence explains why such startling trajectories as VL *cĕrvia *cierge*, nĕptia *niece*, *pĕttia *piece*, tĕrtiu *tierç* fell short of stirring his thoughts along the arresting line which his successors before long were to follow.

At this juncture of his presentation, Diez goes off on a tangent,

---

[7] Extra-early syncope of the second ĕ in Ven(e)ris could have been provoked by pressure from **Martis** and **Iovis** within the same series of pagan names for weekdays, much as **Lūnae** (diēs) yielded ground to *Lūnis, cf. Sp. *lunes* 'Monday'. But even if one hesitates to espouse this hypothesis, the model of Fr. *tendre* tĕnĕru shows how a somewhat later syncope could have given rise to a secondarily checked stressed syllable resistant to diphthongization.

committing his possibly most grievous error. He is quick to recognize that all too often a Romance diphthong, counter to expectation, failed in the end to jell. Here the alarmed author hastily lumps together several visibly disparate processes, for example the wavering in Italian (a language, as we know, characterized by a weak degree of diphthongization) between *pedica, tepido* and *piedica, tiepido* [what about *tiepolo*, one is tempted to interject?] ; the behaviour of such, as we realize, out-and-out 'cultismos' as *edera, genere, lepido, medico, merito* in the same language, which had such a strong impact on Diez's thinking, and of certain Spanish congeners as well, equally and for the same reason geared to the monophthong; plus the sporadic emergence in Portuguese of isolated instances of the 'reverse diphthong' *ei* (as in *ideia, queimo*), which moderns unanimously prefer to keep out of the picture completely. Because Diez throughout remains blissfully unaware of the separate existence and autonomous status of a learned lexical stratum in the Romance vernaculars, he hastens to assign most cases of erratic retention of the monophthong to a special pattern of retarded behaviour allegedly observable in antepenultimate syllables, thus introducing a syllabico-accentual category almost entirely alien to Spanish sound shifts, if probably operative in Italian.[8] The importance of — to us, wholly transparent — borrowings among the lexical items cited (Sp. *menester*, for one) and of blends (Ptg. *queimo*, a Graeco-Latin hybrid) is nowhere correctly gauged. Fr. *dix* and *dîme* are also thrown in for good measure, without any clear realization, one gathers, on the author's part of the role that the following velar consonant is at present known to have played in the transmutation

---

[8] As the example of OSp. *piértega* > mod. *pértiga* 'pole, rod, staff' (from *pĕrtica*) shows, there was a tendency, under certain conditions, to monophthongize rising diphthongs in proparoxytonic syllables; a sequel to my earlier paper which started attacking this problem ('Latin **pedica**, **pēnsum*, and **pertica** in Hispano-Romance' in *Etudes romanes de Lund*, XVIII, 130–50) is in preparation. For one variety of consonant gemination in Tuscan, proparoxytonic structure of the given word is a crucial condition. In general, however, what matters most in Romance is the distance of the syllable at issue from the word's accentual peak, not from its coda.

of ĕ into *i*; then, too, a few finer points of the development into Old Provençal belatedly come up for mention.[9]

The concluding paragraph serves, far too late, to set apart the evolution in a checked syllable ("in der Position"), citing Spanish, Rumanian, plus the Walloon dialect of French, alongside Western Raeto-Romance (*'Churwälsch'*, i.e. Romaunsch) as four varieties of vernacular speech which at no time have barred the spread of rising diphthongs, such as *ie* and *ea* and *ia*, to checked syllables. This point is well taken; but the picture is, once more, blurred when Diez, in reference to French, tosses in the following remark: "Die franz[ösische] Sprache enthält sich des Diphthonges. Nur bei den Alten kommt er als mundartliche Eigenheit häufig vor: so *biel* (**bĕllus**), *bieste, ciert, cierve, confiesse, iestre* (**ĕsse**), *tierme* (**tĕrmĭnus**), *viespre*". One is left wondering whether, in the case of *biel, ciert, confiesse, iestre, tierme, viespre* there exists some temporal, territorial, or causal connection with ancient and modern Walloon usage, which Diez describes separately, while *bieste* (**bēstia**) and *cierve* (***cĕrva**), even more intriguingly, could very well come close to hinting at the very same evolutionary curve we have been plotting here;[10] note, however, Diez's concern with *cierve* rather than *cierge*.

[9] Noteworthy is the fact that, in discussing the overwhelming preference that Old Provençal granted the monophthong *e* over *ie* before *-n* and *-l* as well as in absolute word-final position, Diez, whom nobody has yet suspected of being a camouflaged Neogrammarian, let alone a precursor of that school, invoked a "*Gesetz*": clearly, by 1870 a vision of 'sound laws' was in the air, at Bonn no less than in Leipzig. Arresting is also Diez's feeling for symmetry in sound development, as when he parenthetically remarks on the parallelism of the vicissitudes of ancestral ĕ and ŏ in Old Provençal.

[10] While Diez's grammar, through its consecutive elaborations, remained a source of disappointment, its companion piece, the etymological dictionary, from the start contained valuable bricks for the future edifice. Already the original edition of the *Etymologisches Wörterbuch der romanischen Sprachen* (Bonn, 1853), pp. 243ff., contained a substantial, ingeniously devised entry on It. *pezz-a -o*, Sp. *pieza*, etc., with an Albanian reflex included (*pjesę*), with references to three Celtic languages as aids to reconstruction, and with two 8th-century Barbaric Latin records extracted from L. A. Muratori's *Antiquitates Italicae Medii Aevi*, 6 vols. (Mediolani, 1738—42), plus alternatives in derivation allowed for, in a liberal climate of opinion. From the revised 3rd (i.e. the definitive) edition, I would select the entry on *nièce* as a fine sample of Diezian scholarship at its best: "Keine der romanischen Sprachen hat sich mit lat. **neptis** begnügt, welches it. [*]*nette*, fr. [*]*net* hätte geben müssen. Man bog es, vielleicht um seine weibliche Bedeutung besser fühlen zu lassen, in die erste

Diez's conspicuously weak performance — unsatisfactory even if measured by the standards of its own time — will cause less dissappointment and appear more venial once we remind ourselves that he tended all along to view Old French through the prism of its sister languages. A quick glance at the record of his publications and at the skewed organization of his dictionary suffices to show immediately that he concerned himself, monographically, above all with Old Spanish and Old Provençal, in this chronological order; while, as a comparatist, he tended to place the evidence of Italian on a pedestal.[11] Small wonder that where the course of events forced him to return verdicts on strictly local developments of Old French, such as the shift ĕ > i in dĕcem *dix*, dĕcimu *dîme*, he felt uncomfortable and insecure, judging from his rambling analyses. As regards bēstia, it is worth observing that the vowel of the standard form disqualifies that word from any further discussion in this context, unless persuasive evidence is offered of the coexistence of such variants as *bĕst(i)a, a step Diez failed to take, even though the possibility cannot categorically be ruled out.[12] Finally, the time had not yet arrived for a firm

---

Deklination um, *nepta*, das im früheren M[ittel]latein begegnet, pr[ov.] *nepta*, sp. *nieta*, pg. cat. *neta*. Der Franzose verschaffte sich mit Hilfe des ablautenden *i* in *nept-i-s* die ganz ungewöhnliche Form *neptia*, *nièce*, pr. *netsa* (it. *nezza* wenig üblich). Aber auch dem Masc. **nepos** entlockte man ein unmittelbares Femininum **nepota** pr. cat. *neboda*, wal. [= rum.] *nepoatę* [i.e., *nepoată*]".

[11] The closest that Diez ever came to granting pride of place to Old French for its own sake, so to speak, was in the following triptych of exegetic studies, all three issued in Bonn, the earliest of which appeared when he was past fifty: *Altromanische Sprachdenkmale berichtigt und erklärt* (1846); *Zwei altromanische Gedichte berichtigt und erklärt* (1852); *Altromanische Glossare berichtigt und erklärt* (1865).

[12] The by-form **bĕsta** is attested in Late Gallo-Latin (Venantius Fortunatus) and receives collateral support from the dimin. **bĕstula**; OF *beste*, confirmed by the *Song of Roland*, is thus accounted for and *bieste* as an Old Walloon var. would be understandable (see Dauzat-Dubois-Mitterand, *NDEH*, s.v.). To justify OF *bisse*, *biche* 'hind', however, as well as its offshoot *bichette*, French etymologists have recourse to acrobatics, positing some such fancy base as *bīstia. OSp. *bestia* exhibits **bestia** in learned transmission, whereas *bicho*, of fairly late appearance, is explained by J. Corominas, *BDE*, 2nd, rev. ed. (Madrid, 1967), p. 95a, as a borrowing from Old Galician-Portuguese, where its counterpart (of older coinage) perpetuates Low Lat. **bēstius**. The purpose of the borrowing remains unexplained, as does the seemingly learned transmission of *bestia*. Could the learned conduit upon occasion have been chosen to avoid complications which transmission by word of mouth might have

grasp of the -ia series of the designations of females (animals and humans, including a scattering of kinship terms).[13]

Through an astounding coincidence, the discussion started moving ahead with the appearance of Adolf Tobler's meticulously annotated edition of *Li dis dou vrai aniel*, an Old French text given away as being Artesien by its very title (*aniel* 'ring' in lieu of Francien *anel*, mod. *anneau*) and the circumstances of its composition. It is no mere coincidence, however, that the debate picked up momentum so rapidly. Throughout the so-called *Gründerjahre*, the years immediately following upon the Franco-Prussian War of 1870–71, the study of Old French language and literature began to develop by leaps and bounds in Germany and the adjoining countries, even threatening to eclipse inquiries into sister cultures. Within the framework of Romance philology — in sharp contrast to the earlier practice and theoretical preference of Diez —, the most active minds of the period, such Central European scholars as Tobler, Mussafia, Gröber, Neumann, and Horning, had something to say on the

---

entailed? Some of the intricacies of the Italian record can be inferred from W. Meyer-Lübke's *REW*, 3rd, rev. ed. (Heidelberg, 1930–35), § § 1061, 1063. The semantics and (semilearned) phonology of ONav. *bestiglo*, OPtg. *bestigoo* 'monster' raise further issues.

[13] Innovative **nĕptia** incontrovertibly echoes **avia** 'grandmother', beside **avus** 'grandfather'. At a later stage, the outgrowth of avia, namely *aya* 'governess', cast off *ayo* 'mentor', unless one prefers to project the mintage of *avius onto the level of Vulgar Latin, with proper allowance for the separate development of OSp. *avuelo, -a* (mod. *ab-*) 'grandfather, grandmother', as against Fr. *aïeul*, pl. *aïeux* 'greatgrand-parents, ancestors'. On this imbroglio see my article, to appear in *Medioevo romanzo*, 'El prototipo latino de (esp. ant.) *avuelo-avuela*, *ayo-aya*, (port. ant.) *avoo-avoa*, (francés) *aïeul(e)*'. As an extension of avia and neptia, one is free to posit *nŏvia 'bride' on the strength of Sp. *novia*, Ptg. *noiva*, with the proviso that *novio/noivo* 'fiancé, bridegroom' be then declared analogical innovations. Still further afield leads us the possibility that Ptg. *comborça*, older Sp. *combleza* from still more remote *comblueça, combrueça, combuerça* 'concubine' be traced to *convŏrtia, coined in contradistinction to **dīvŏrtium** 'estrangement, separation, legal divorce', in the last analysis from **vĕrtĕre/vŏrtĕre** 'to turn'. See my contribution to the forthcoming testimonial in honour of Alvaro Galmés de Fuentes (Oviedo). The case of *cervia is not isolated among zoonyms; add the classic example of *can-ia 'bitch' (It. *cagna*, etc.) plus, in all likelihood, *cŭrt-ia as the foundation of OSp. *cor-ço, -ça* (mod. *-zo, -za*) 'roe deer', once more on the plausible assumption that the feminine preceded the masculine.

rapidly emerging problem; they were joined by medievalists and comparatists from neighboring countries (for example, by Ascoli and G. Paris) who, by background, training, or intellectual affinity, were leaning toward the German tradition of Romance scholarship, in those years undeniably the main-stream tradition. With the notable exception of H. Suchier,[14] almost everyone had something noteworthy to offer on the subject, and a few participants in the debate spoke up more than once.

Characteristic of the period (and distinctly alien to our own taste) was the fact that textual criticism, exegetic anno-tation, phonology (in addition to morphology and syntax), and even palaeo-dialectology were all inextricably enmeshed in the *fin de siècle* style of philological research. Consequently, one must not be surprised to discover that the issue of the diphthong *ie* in *niece, piece, tierç*, etc. was thrashed out in critical editions of medieval texts more thoroughly than in formal historical grammars (or than in articles and mono-graphs conducive to them). As a matter of fact, the tradition of the circumstantial book review — once more a genre not particularly favoured by our own times — was so deeply rooted in European erudition of a century or so ago that not a few relevant comments must be traced to critical appraisals by prestigious and conscientious reviewers.[15]

Strictly speaking, Tobler's preface and appended annotations to *Li Dis* (1871; 2nd ed. 1884), which Fritz Neumann — my guide on this cruise through shallow waters[16] — placed at the

---

[14] I am alluding to his apodictically phrased, but enigmatic statement: "Unab-hängig von der Dehnung der Tonvokale hat die Diphthongierung von *ǫ* und *ę* vor mouillierten Lauten stattgefunden" ('Die französische und provenzalische Sprache und ihre Mundarten', in G. Gröber's *Grundriss*, I [Strassburg, 1888], 561—668, § 8), without any helpful hint, cross-reference, or clarification.

[15] Judging from collateral references, the issue is likely to have received exegetic and/or phonological attention in various treatises, editions, and critical reactions unavailable to me at short notice. These lacunae include: Otto Knauer, *Zur altfranzö-sischen Lautlehre* (Leipziger Gymnasialprogramm, 1876), repeatedly cited by Fritz Neumann (see *infra*); an extended review article from the pen of W. Foerster, in the 1874 volume of the *Zeitschrift für österreichische Gymnasien*, 134—62, and a shorter review, by A. Mussafia, in the 1877 volume of the same high-level teachers' journal.

[16] *Zur Laut- und Flexionslehre des Altfranzösischen, hauptsächlisch aus pikardi-schen Urkunden von Vermandois* (Heilbronn, 1878), Introduction. For details, see below.

head of the new trend in dialectologically orchestrated inquiries into the language of Old French texts (preferably those assonanced or rhymed), contains no statement that would directly bear on our narrower problem. Tobler was a firm believer in the (undemonstrated, and, from today's angle, questionable) thesis that any speaker of Old French was governed in his preferences by the norms of a single regional dialect, but that varieties of what to him was *Schriftsprache* and to us is *scripta* could very well represent compromises between two such dialects. Starting from this methodological premiss, he analysed with unprecedented rigour such Old Picard, especially Artesien, peculiarities as, say, /k/ and /w/ for Francien /tʃ/ and /g/, also infinitives in *-eïr* in lieu of *-eoir*.[17] The relation of *terre* to *tierre* and of *guerre* to *guiere, wier(r)e* entered into his purview of suspected regionalisms (p. xxiii); superregional *niece, pièce, tierç*, by definition, were barred. In any event, a technique of microscopic inspection was created by which others could henceforth study comparable material at any later date.

The dramatic effect jointly produced through the launching of the journal *Romania* in 1872 by G. Paris and P. Meyer, and through the publication, that same year, of a major monograph on the successive versions of the *Vie de saint Alexis*, again by G. Paris, this time in collaboration with his short-lived friend L. Pannier, cannot be exaggerated. Apropos of the phonological sketch attached to the edition of a rhymed 13th-century derivative version,[18] one finds a penetrating discussion of such forms, aberrant from the Francien standard, as *biele, mesiele, priestre, puciele, siers, tiere* with sustained attention to the varying predilections of writers who hailed from such sections of the Northeast as Artois, Tournaisis, and Lillois. *Niece* etc. still remain waiting in the wings, but a helpful line of demarca-

---

[17] '*Li Dis du vrai aniel*'; *die Parabel von dem echten Ringe; französische Dichtung des dreizehnten Jahrhunderts* . . . (Leipzig, 1871; 2nd ed. 1884), pp. xix–xxxiv. (I have had access solely to the 2nd ed., slightly revised and expanded.)

[18] '*La Vie de Saint Alexis*', *poème du XIe siècle et renouvellements des XIIe, XIIIe et XIVe siècles, publiés avec préfaces. . .et glossaire*, Bibl. de l'Ec. H. Et., VII; see pp. 267–74. There is no need here to expatiate on the merits of the author's bizarre hypothesis (pp. 268ff.) that *puciele* etc. contained a *iè* contrastable with the ordinary *ié*.

tion is henceforth easily drawn between strictly regional and
general Old French usage.

Just one year later, E. Mall, an intellectual protégé (and,
possibly, former student) of Tobler's, finally succeeded — after
repeated setbacks — in publishing his elaborate edition of
Philippe de Thaun's *Cumpoz*, for once a North-Western text.
The phonological analysis — which enters into the scrupulously
detailed introduction (pp. 1—111), magisterial if measured by
the standards of its time — contains a circumstantial break-
down of the sources of the OF diphthong *ie*.[19] Among the more
conspicuous individual cases, the author singles out, in this
context, *tierz, -ce*, which he correctly etymologizes and likens
to It. *terzo, -a*.[20]

W. Förster's expertise qua learned editor of medieval texts
carried particular weight in the 1870s, because in those years
he was at work polishing his monograph-length article on
Romance metaphony,[21] doubtless his most ambitious venture
into historical linguistics. To that extent the introduction to
his edition of *Richars li Biaus*, written in the same vein as
Tobler's and Paris's aforementioned studies, comes as a disappointment. The author of the romance, Förster argued, was
a Burgundian, while the copyist, a Picard, hailed from the
Flanders-Artois-Hainaut area, a conclusion reached mainly on
the basis of the widespread use of *ie* for Francien *e*.[22] Dis-
cernibly more circumstantial is the apparatus supporting and
surrounding Förster's somewhat later edition of *Li Chevaliers*

---

[19] *Der 'Computus' des Philipp von Thaun, mit einer Einleitung über die Sprache
des Autors* (Strassburg, 1873).

[20] Other noteworthy cases are *cirge* 'candle' (m.) and *virgene* 'maiden', still
monophthongal before their eventual transmutation into *cierge* and *vierge*; and
fieble 'weak', as against the more common var. *foible*. (Here a brief remark on E.
feeble as against *foible* would have been most welcome.) Like everyone else, Mall
traced both variants to flēbilis 'lamentable' without implicating fēbrīlis 'sick, feverish'
and/or dēbilis 'weak'. See my forthcoming note to this effect in *RPh*.

[21] 'Beiträge zur romanischen Lautlehre: Umlaut (eigentlich Vokalsteigerung)
im Romanischen' in *ZrPh*, III (1879), 481—517. H. Schuchardt stated his counter-
view in the same journal the following year (IV, 113—23), and G. Paris reacted to
both papers, with reservations aimed at the first, in *Rom.*, IX (1880), 330—32, 479.

[22] Ed. *Richars li Biaus* (Wien, 1874), p. viii. The only innovative statement was
the demonstration that the monophthong *e* and the variety of *ie* peculiar to the NE
occasionally did rhyme, e.g. *damoisielle : vermeille, bielle : pareille*.

as deus espees.[23] *Piece* was definitely one word that held
Förster's attention on that occasion, but only on the phraseo-
logical side: *a, por, de por, de grant piece* (see p. 428*b*). Through
a strange coincidence, the scribe of the MS hailed, once more,
from the region (NE) favouring *foreist* and *tieste* over *forest*
and *teste*, an idiosyncrasy which, as Förster was probably the
first to point out, spread to the pretonic syllable in the chosen
text and in others phonologically akin to it (p. xxxviii: *arriester,
apieler*). While the editor discussed creditably divers side-issues,
the one of principal concern to us was not included in their
number. This omission need not be entirely coincidental. Since
for Förster 'metaphony' meant solely 'Vokalsteigerung', i.e.
'vowel raising', such as $e > i$, $o > u$, metaphonic diphthongization might have been to him tantamount to a paradox or
oxymoron (*contradictio in adiecto*).

On balance, it was the temporary preoccupation with Old
Flandric texts, characterized by a superficially similar rule
for the conversion of ancestral ĕ into *ie*, that prevented scholars
of the calibre of Tobler, Paris (in association with Pannier),
and Förster from recognizing the separate issue posed by *niece*,
etc. Characteristically, Mall, who for once had turned his
attention to the NW, clearly identified the related problem
raised by *tierz* without, it is true, managing to solve it. We
owe perhaps the first forceful formulation of the actual state of
affairs to A. Mussafia, who in reviewing in a newly-founded,
immediately prestigious journal, K. Hofmann and K. Vollmöller's
joint edition of the rhymed Munich Old French *Brut* (1877),[24]
skillfully bracketed *tierz, tierce* — already recognized as a case
of intrusion of /je/ upon a checked syllable — with *cierge* 'hind'
and *niece*, and unequivocally stated the condition governing
the rise of the diphthong: "Zu *ie* aus Pos[ition] *e*. . .war das
Vorhandensein des Hiatus *-i* in der folgenden Silbe zu bemer-

---

[23] Ed. *'Li Chevaliers as deus espees', altfranzösischer Abenteuerroman* (Halle,
1877).
[24] See *ZrPh*, I (1876[-77]), 402—14, at 410. The only minor infelicity which
one detects was Mussafia's attempt to lump together the evolutionary curves of
cierge *cĕrvia and of *cierge* cēreu. As Mall had shown in 1873 (p. 70), the more
archaic Old French texts still used *cirge* for 'candle' (and *virgine* alongside *virge*);
see above.

ken". Particularly brilliant was Mussafia's ability to contrast, within the same textual tradition, diphthongal *cierge* 'hind' ("gleichsam **cervia**", i.e. **cĕrvia*) with monophthongal *cers* < **cervōs** 'stags'. What helped the critic to hit upon the right answer was doubtless his superb native command of Italian; he himself adduced *cervia, cerbia* by way of corroboration. Incidentally, Meyer-Lübke later (*HGFS*, I, § 51) credited the discovery of the **vēnī** *vin* type of metaphony also to Mussafia's intuition, as early as 1865.

One younger scholar who, at one blow, succeeded in reconciling Mussafia's sharp thinking (and, by implication, also the less cogently phrased previous statements by Mall and by the Hofmann-Vollmöller team concerning *tierz*) with the findings by the three Flanders-oriented scholars was F. Neumann, in his already praised trail-blazing 1878 monograph (p. 62). Even though his own starting point had been the edition, by the archivist-palaeographer F. Le Proux, of the *Chartes françaises du Vermandois* (1218–50),[25] he went far beyond his immediate goal and distinguished accurately between "gemeinfranzösisch" *niece* and *tierce*, whose crystallization hinged on certain conditions established by Mussafia, and Picard-Walloon *apriest, bielle, foriest, tiest*, totally independent of any hiatus vowel, i.e., of /j/: ". . . die hierher zu gehören scheinen, unterliegen anderen Gesichtspunkten". Thus the discovery of the phenomenon with which we are concerned was actually made around 1876–78, through the felicitously convergent observations made by at least four scholars.

In dramatic contrast to C. Verner's celebrated 'law', formulated in those same years, which met with instantaneous success in the headquarters of Indo-Europeanists, Mussafia's conjecture, despite its prompt endorsement by Neumann, produced no sensation, let alone euphoria, among Romanists, because its wedge-driving potentialities for the re-drawing of the demarcation line between 'spontaneous' diphthongization and metaphony were not immediately recognized for what

---

[25] See *Bibl. de l'Ecole des Chartes*, XXXV (1874), 437ff. The charters were issued chiefly in the present-day arrondissement of Saint Quentin, where a southern variety of the Picard dialect was in use.

they were worth. To be sure, by dint of searching one finds scattered and succinct references to the nĕptia *niece* type of diphthongization from the pens of Ascoli, Gröber, Horning, and other leading figures;[26] but the evasive attitude of H.

[26] The start of the second, and less friendly, round of the discussion can be associated with the appearance of A. Horning's influential monograph: *Zur Geschichte des lateinischen "C" vor "E" und "I" im Romanischen* (Halle, 1883). By way of prelude let me cite two comments by G. I. Ascoli on medieval North Italian descendants of nĕptia: one on OGen. *neça* ('Del posto che spetta al ligure nel sistema dei dialetti italiani' in *AGI*, II [1876], 111—60, at 121, note 1); the other on OVen. (f.) *neza* beside (m.) *nievo* nĕpōs ('Annotazioni dialettologiche a una cronica veneziana [*Cronica deli Imperadori Romani*]', *ibid.*, III [1878], 244—84, at 281), with a reference to § 35 of the preceding grammatical prospectus for the erratic preservation of the nominative case (as in *statio* and *dessensio*), also to G. Boerio's *Dizionario del dialetto veneziano*, 2nd rev. ed. (Venezia, 1856); and, as regards the feminine (preserved in actual use to Ascoli's own days), to the 'Additamenta duo ad *Chronicon Cortusiorum*', 84, included in L. A. Muratori's *Rerum Italicarum Scriptores*, 25 vols. (Mediolani, 1723—51), XII, 959—88. As Ascoli, stimulatingly enough, observed, nĕptia, in lieu of Class. nĕptis, had been deftly reconstructed by Romanists even before T. Mommsen's *Corpus Inscriptionum Latinarum* (Berolini, 1863 —), V, 1208, produced the tangible evidence of the neologism's occurrence in two Roman epigraphs.

Horning (*op. cit.*, p. 22) sharpened the formulation of his predecessors, arguing that the presence of a diphthong in checked syllable could have been provoked only by the following /j/, so that, all told, a case of 'attraction' of the semi-consonant into the radical was involved; his critics did not applaud this analysis. Gröber, for one, in 1887 felt that diphthongization so conditioned was alien to the prehistory of French and, moreover, that any 'attracted' /j/ could, at the very least, have tended to follow upon, rather than to precede, the stressed vowel (*ZrPh*, XI, 287ff.). Three years later, Meyer-Lübke castigated Horning (and Ascoli as well; see below) for the superficiality of their explanation and for the older scholars' failure to account for the lack of any parallelism as between ĕ and ŏ: ". . . den Diphthongen in *nièce, pièce, tiers* dem Einfluss des *i* zuschreibt, ohne sich über die Art zu äussern, wie dieser Einfluß zu verstehen sei, noch auch die Verschiedenheit in der Behandlung von *neptia* und *noptia* zu erklären" (*Romanische Lautlehre*, § 154).

Strictly speaking, the next step after Horning's book was Gröber's contribution ('Etymologien', pp. 39—49) to the famous volume memorializing Napoleone Caix and Ugo Angelo Canello (*Miscellanea di Filologia e Linguistica*, edd. G. I. Ascoli et al. [Firenze, 1886]); the relevant passage is found on p. 46. Small wonder that Ascoli, who piloted the venture, made a point of reading Gröber's arguments carefully. . . and, briefly holding back his anger, criticized them mercilessly in the August 1886 post-script to his polemic epistle, 'Die Neogrammatici; Lettera al prof. Pietro Merlo' in *AGI*, X (1886—88), 18—105; see p. 84, note 1. Gröber saw in the rise of the diphthong *ie* mainly a lexico-analogical process, namely the transfer of /j/ from *nies* nĕpōs 'nephew' to its referential and semantic counterpart *niece* 'niece', while Ascoli sided with Horning's phonological interpretation, expatiating for good measure on the related if not identical cases of *vieil* and *œil*. In the end, Ascoli bracketed with *niece* etc. those lexical trajectories which, at a certain point of the prehistory, included triphthongs ultimately simplified, such as dĕcĕm 'ten' > *dieiç > dix.

Foreseeably, Gröber rose to the occasion, discretely appending his rebuttal in

Suchier, as late as 1888, has already been pointed out, and
even young Meyer-Lübke's 1890 volume on comparative
Romance phonology marked no break-through.[27]

As a matter of fact, Meyer-Lübke's performance in 1890,
so far as the problem at issue is concerned, was distinctly less
than impressive. He found it difficult ("schwer zu erklären
sind. . .", § 154) to justify *niece, piece, tiers*, but actually
himself complicated his task by placing these words (oblivious
of *cierge*, as he was also of Mussafia's share in the early stage of
the debate) in the immediate vicinity of OF *nice* **nĕ-scia**, *espice*
spĕcie, and *Grice* **Graecia**, even though at the end he extricated
himself from his predicament by recognizing that in *nice* etc.
the **c** may have generated a /j/ of its own (and the ensuing
triphthong *iei* could ultimately have been reduced to *i*, if I
correctly interpret his hermetically syncopated thinking).
Meyer-Lübke was particularly annoyed by the asymmetry in
the development of **ĕ** and **ŏ**, even though at present even a
tyro realizes that the front vowels often not only precede the
back vowels in a given development, but are also apt to advance
much faster, leaving their partners far behind.[28] The doubt
gnawing the author caused him to espouse the hypothesis
(traceable to Ascoli) that *niece* may have been cast in the mould
of its masculine counterpart *nies* **nĕpōs**, with *tierç* apparently
following suit. By operating with **nĕscia** rather than **nĕ-scia**,
and by accepting the reconstruction (left unstarred) **pĕtia**
rather than **pĕttia*, the author needlessly blurred the role
of the favored configuration of the stressed syllable. To sum
up: after a minor break-through achieved in the mid 1870s,

ZrPh, XI (1887), 287ff. to W. Meyer-[Lübke]'s digest of Vol. X of the *AGI*. We
have already ourselves concisely hinted (see supra) at the substance of his disagreement with the Horning-Ascoli thesis. All in all, the progress achieved in the 1883—90
interlude was disappointingly modest.

[27] *Grammatik der romanischen Sprachen*, I: *Romanische Lautlehre* (Leipzig,
1890), 141—66 (= §§ 150—82): "Vulgärlat. **e** = Schriftlat. **e**"; see § 154. Meyer-
Lübke unmistakably shows his eagerness to keep out of the Gröber-Ascoli duel.

[28] Thus, the shift **ī** > /e/, at present believed to have been started in the Lyon-Milan-
Cologne area, reached far-off Dacia on a massive scale (witness **nĭgru** > Rum. *negru*
etc.), whereas the parallel but obviously retarded shift **ŭ** > /o/, with negligible exceptions, never came close to hitting the Black Sea coast (hence, **lŭpu** > Rum. *lup*).
Similarly, the final step of the Spanish **ĕ** > *ie* > *i set* measurably preceded its counterpart in the **ŏ** > *ue* > *e* set by a margin of centuries; contrast *ari(e)sta* with *fr(u)ente*.

further progress along a tortuous path remained almost consistently blocked through the anticlimactic '80s.

Meyer-Lübke's obvious dissatisfaction with his own analysis prompted him to revert to the recalcitrant problem, first in a contribution to a journal,[29] and next in § 58 of his easily most mature work, namely Part I ("Laut- und Flexionslehre") of his historical grammar of French.[30] This time he caught, at long last, OF *cierge* in his dragnet and added to the older inventory of forms OF *fierge* 'iron fetter' fĕrrea (i.e., let me add on my own, /fɛrja/), OF *tenierge* 'darkness' tenĕbricu (conceivably on the understanding that the word was pronounced /tɛnɛ-(b)rju/),[31] a molecule of forms which, one gathers, also attracted *liège* 'cork' *lĕviu. Meyer-Lübke's score-card, at the height of his career, would have been even better had he agreed to substitute for tĕnĕbricu and *lĕviu the corresponding feminines, as surely nothing hindered him from doing.[32] He would then have come up with a more homogeneously structured series, on the temporal levels of both Old French (*cierge, fierge, liege, niece, pièce, tenierge, tierce*) and of Latin (*cĕrvia, fĕrrea /fɛrja/, *lĕvia, nĕptia, *pĕttia, tĕnĕ(b)ri(c)a, tĕrtia), with the two almost pervasively characteristic features of the entire development being: (a) stressed ĕ in checked syllable, and (b) -ia /ja/ as the coda, coincident with a marked preference for the feminine gender.[33] Such degree of rigour in the postulation of conditions would also, almost automatically, have accounted for the otherwise shocking discrepancy between *neis* nĕsciu vs. *nice* (via *nieice*) nĕscia. The only residual exception would then have been *lĕ-viu; but as Ernout-Meillet's *DELL*, 4th ed.,

---

[29] Unfortunately, the author's bibliographic reference to his own paper (*ZfSL*, X, 65) contained a false lead.

[30] *Historische Grammatik der französischen Sprach*, I, 2nd and 3rd, rev. eds., (1913). The original ed. appeared in 1908.

[31] In Latin, the adjective in -ĭcu tended to be replaced by one in -ōsu; cf. the learned borrowing into French, *ténébreux*. An overlap of the two offshoots (even Cicero stooped to the use of tenebricōsus) led to OSp. *tenebregoso*, on which *negregoso* 'blackish', in turn, was patterned, with *negregura* 'blackness', in lieu of more common *negrura* (an indirect echo of nĭgrōre), attached to it as a companion. Add Ptg. *negregar* = Sp. *negreguear* 'to blacken'.

[32] Unless it was the suspicion that the spirantized velar element may have lingered on longer in -ĭca than in -ĭ(c)u, giving rise to -che at the level of Old French.

[33] Except, of course, that *tierç, tierz* tĕrtiu followed in the wake of *tierce* tĕrtia.

s.v. **levis**, opportunely makes clear, this elaboration crystallized via a detour, branching off from (**ad-, sub-**)**leviāre** (cf. Fr. *alléger*, Sp. *aliviar*, also *soliviantar* 'to rouse, stir up'), and thus must not be allowed to count heavily.

Although Meyer-Lübke in the end detected isolated dialectal traces of *nœces* beside *noces* **nŭptĭas** 'wedding' and of *terst* **tŏrq(u)et** 'twists', which may or may not belong here, he never, not even at the summit of his career, ceased to marvel at the lack of parallelism between the vicissitudes of ĕ and ŏ and found the forms which he had ultimately managed to assemble "merkwürdig", concluding his exploration with a lapidary confession of defeat: "Eine befriedigende Erklärung fehlt".

This sort of honesty on his part prepared the next generations of Romanists for better-planned strategies of attacks on a singularly rebellious question.

TEXTUAL TRANSMISSION AND COMPLEX MUSICO-METRICAL FORM IN THE OLD FRENCH LYRIC

J. H. MARSHALL_____

Our conception of the metrical form of an Old French lyric song is derived from the text as transmitted by one or more MSS, mediated through the work of one or more modern textual (in some cases also musical) scholars. It is customary for editors to make various — usually unstated — assumptions concerning the desirable degree of metrical regularity (in rhyme, syllable-count, strophic structure, and so on) which the edited text ought to display. In the majority of strophic pieces — *chansons, jeux-partis* and the like — these normative presuppositions will lead to an acceptably neat printed presentation of a metrically regular text. And the metrical regularity of the end-product will, as it were, receive a kind of consecration by its inclusion, in schematic form, in the *Répertoire métrique* of Mölk and Wolfzettel.[1] The establishment of the metrical form of texts for which no music has come down to us must evidently depend on the results of purcly philological investigation, though this needs to be informed by an awareness of results obtained from the study of songs whose music is extant. The collaboration of musicology with textual scholarship is central to the study of those lyric pieces for which music has been preserved. Indeed, in a number of cases it is the form of the music which provides the key to an understanding of the metrical shape of the text.

My object in the present article is not to call into question the general validity of editorial assumptions about metrical

[1] U. Mölk and F. Wolfzettel, *Répertoire métrique de la poésie lyrique française des origines à 1350* (Munich, 1972). References to the metrical schemes are given in the form "MW 116:1". It should be stated here once for all that these schemes are only as reliable as the — often totally misleading — editions on which they are based.

regularity. I am concerned here with a small group of pieces whose peculiarity is that they are neither conventionally iso-trophic like a *chanson* nor straightforwardly heterostrophic like a *descort*. Application of the editorial assumptions referred to above has led to fundamental misinterpretations of such pieces; this in its turn illustrates the limitations and pitfalls of normative editing when misguidedly applied to complex musico-metrical structures.

The pieces examined here have nothing in common in their textual content, in their authorship (most are anonymous) or in their chronology (except that all date from the thirteenth century). Nor do they show any obvious outward similarities in melodic line or metrical shape. Their peculiarity resides in the fact that, although each is strophic in the sense that the tune of the first stanza provides the music to which the rest of the text is sung, the second and subsequent stanzas are not identical with the first in size and shape: they can be made to appear so only by the editorial introduction of lines of dots signifying supposed lacunas deriving from faulty scribal transmission. What is more, in the instances in which two textually different versions of the same piece are preserved, divergences of metrical shape are also found to occur between one MS or MS-family and the other: these have encouraged some editors to conflate MS readings as a procedure for attaining metrical regularity. The present paper contends that neither the postulation of lacunas nor the conflation of readings is a legitimate editorial procedure here, and that the elimination of irregularities by one or both of these means has hitherto masked the real musico-metrical struc-ture of the pieces in question. The rather special case of the *Note Martinet* (RS 474), the only piece of this kind for which (in one MS) the tune is notated throughout the text, is left aside altogether, since its problems merit a separate investigation. The case made out here is based on *Quant voi nee* (RS 534), an anonymous *pastourelle*; a number of other Old French songs presenting analogous features are then submitted to a briefer and more schematic examination.

The anonymous *pastourelle Quant voi nee* (RS 534) is preserved in two versions[2] by *chansonnier C* and *chansonniers K* and *N* respectively:

C, f. 114r-v, four stanzas without music (empty staves above stanza I). Diplomatic edition: *ASNS*, XLII (1868), p. 356 (J. Brakelmann). Collation of this text with MS in *ZrPh*, III (1878), 52, no. ccliv (G. Gröber and C. von Lebinski).

K, pp. 306—7, five stanzas, with music for stanza I. Facsimile edition: P. Aubry and A. Jeanroy, *Le Chansonnier de l'Arsenal* (Paris, 1912).

N, ff. 145v—146r, five stanzas, with music for stanza I.

Three critical editions of the piece exist:

C. Bartsch, *Altfranzösische Romanzen und Pastourellen* (Leipzig, 1870), pp. 109—10 (text).

H. Spanke, *Eine altfranzösische Liedersammlung, der anonyme Teil der Liederhandschriften KNPX*, Romanische Bibliothek, XXII (Halle, 1925), pp. 9—12 (text), 414—15 (music).

J.-C. Rivière, *Pastourelles*, 3 vols. (Geneva, 1974—76), II, 22—25 (text).

The music is also printed (with the text of stanza I) in F. Gennrich, *Die Kontrafaktur im Liedschaffen des Mittelalters* (Langen bei Frankfurt, 1965), pp. 229—30, together with that of the Latin *conductus Ortum floris*, which shares the same tune. The same material was already printed in Gennrich's *Lateinische Liedkontrafaktur* (Darmstadt, 1956), pt. 1, p. 18 (French),[3] and pt. 2, p. 19 (Latin). In the same author's *Der musikalische Nachlass der Troubadours, III: Prolegomena* (Langen bei Frankfurt, 1965), pp. 26—27, the music of stanza I is printed, this time in modern notation, to illustrate the structural principle of the *Strophenlai*. (It is extraordinary that even in this context Gennrich continued

---

[2] I leave aside, since it is irrelevant to present purposes, the Occitanised text of the first stanza (lines 1—23 in a version showing a number of substantial divergences from *C* and from *KN*) copied without music on the last fly-leaf of the Old Provençal *chansonnier G*, f. 143r (diplomatic edition in G. Bertoni, *Il Canzoniere provenzale della Biblioteca Ambrosiana R. 71. Sup.*, Dresden, 1912, p. xxii; see also *id.*, 'Sur une pièce française copiée dans un manuscrit provençal' in *Annales du Midi*, XXI, 1909, 59—60). All line-references in the present section, unless the contrary is specifically stated, refer to the texts printed below.

[3] Here Gennrich's text and tune follow MS *N* and include the erroneous readings noted below, p. 128, n. 12.

to assume without question that *Quant voi nee* consisted of four regularly isostrophic stanzas.)

The music for lines 1–17 of the Old French piece is identical with that of *Ortum floris*:[4] if the tune of the *pastourelle* may be represented schematically as ABAB CDCE FFGG BCDCE'* HII JKLK,[5] that of *Ortum floris* ends at the point marked with an asterisk. The relationship between the two pieces was first pointed out by Spanke,[6] who maintained the priority of the Latin text, from which the anonymous *trouvère* had in his view borrowed and extended the tune. This conception of the link between the texts was rejected by Gennrich,[7] who argued on convincing grounds in favour of the priority of the Old French piece, from which the Latin poet took over, though with structural modification, the metrical shape and the tune.

Spanke and Gennrich agree in classing the Old French text as a *Strophenlai*, i.e. a composition in which the structural principle of the *lai* or sequence is the basis of a tune which is then repeated strophically to fit the second and subsequent stanzas of the text. This is evidently true: the sequence-structure is brought out most clearly in Gennrich's analytical scheme.[8] In my view, however, all editors, both textual and musical, make a false assumption in considering the Old French song to have been *perfectly* isostrophic, i.e. in supposing that it consisted of four stanzas of which the second, third and fourth were exact and complete replicas of the sequence-structure of stanza I. This

---

[4] Text ed. Dreves in *Analecta hymnica*, XX (1895), 51–52, and XLVb (1904), 23–24.

[5] This schematic representation does not altogether do justice to the subtlety of the melodic construction. B and C begin with the same three-note phrase (G–F–G); B ends with the same cadential figure as E and E' (A–G–G); E begins with a transposition of the three-note phrase which also opens D (respectively B♭ –A–G and A–G–F); and E' begins in the same way as D (A–G–F) but ends, as we have seen, with the same phrase as E. Readers are referred to the edition of the tune given below, p. 132.

[6] 'Das öftere Auftreten von Strophenformen und Melodien in der altfranzösischen Lyrik' in *ZfSL*, LI (1928), 73–117, at 113–16. The same view is repeated in his *Beziehungen zwischen romanischer und mittellateinischer Lyrik* (Berlin, 1936), pp. 90 and 92, in the course of a survey of Latin and Old French *Strophenlais*.

[7] *Kontrafaktur*, pp. 76–78. H.-H. S. Räkel, *Die musikalische Erscheinungsform der Trouvèrepoesie* (Bern, 1977), pp. 83, 106, still accepts Spanke's viewpoint, though without attempting to counter Gennrich's arguments.

[8] *Kontrafaktur*, p. 76.

unexamined assumption has had significant repercussions on the editorial process, for it can be sustained only by postulating extensive lacunas in the MSS and by rejecting out of hand the fifth stanza given by *KN* (cf. Rivière, *ed. cit.*, p. 27: "quant aux éléments de cinquième strophe, donnés par KN, ils ne sont pas indispensables au sens général, comme le reconnaît Spanke, et sont trop mutilés pour offrir un réel intérêt").

To pursue these matters, we must turn to an examination of the editions and their relation to the MSS. The eye is immediately struck by differences in the printed shape of the text. The Bartsch and Spanke editions present stanzas of 16 lines each, with sporadic internal rhymes, whereas Rivière's text shows 25 lines to the stanza. The various metrical analyses of the piece do not greatly clarify matters and differ significantly from one another.[9] Nor are the printed texts any less divergent in substance than in form. Bartsch prints an eclectic text drawing quite heavily on *C*, Spanke an eclectic text based largely on *KN*. Rivière rejects eclecticism and adheres (with only one small correction) to *C*, on the grounds that this MS preserves 85 of the 100 lines required by the four stanzas whereas *KN* have only 81. But the assumption of perfect metrical regularity in the original leads Rivière to postulate within the text of MS *C* a large lacuna in st. II (lines 34—42 in his numbering), another in st. III (68—73), plus two small lacunas in st. IV (end of 85, 87). Like Bartsch and Spanke, he rejects st. V. The German editors show a lacuna in st. II only (lines 21—24 in their numbering, i.e. the lines absent from all MSS). They make up the remainder of this second stanza by using lines peculiar to *C* (19—20 in their numbering) and lines found only in *KN* (25—26). Similarly Spanke confects a complete third stanza by using the lines given by *KN* but not *C* (his 43—46), and those present in *C* but not *KN* (his 47—48). Bartsch had already proposed a similar solution in his notes (*ed. cit.*, p. 360). And both editors conflate the two versions of st. IV in order to arrive at a metrically complete structure.

It is worth considering in more detail the nature of the postulated lacunas and textual conflations. In st. II no MS has the

---

[9] See MW 116:1, 114:1 and 115:1, which follow Bartsch's text; Rivière, *ed. cit.*, pp. 28—29; Gennrich, *Kontrafaktur*, p. 76.

shape (and the extent of postulated lacuna) given by Bartsch and Spanke. The latter maintains (*ed. cit.*, p. 355, note to 21—24) that the sense reveals the transmitted texts to be defective and that the supposedly missing lines must have included the knight's proposal of marriage to the shepherdess. This opinion is echoed by Rivière (*ed. cit.*, p. 28). But such a view ignores the cynical humour of the text, which, in either version, makes perfect sense as it stands, with the knight attempting to seduce the shepherdess with fulsome courtly phrases. It is in this sense, and not as a result of any supposed proposal of marriage, that the girl has been "flatee, guilee" (*KN*) or "mokee, chiflee, bobee"(*C*). Neither the sense of the stanza nor, as we shall see, its metrical form requires us to suppose any lines omitted through scribal inattention.

Such a supposition is equally unjustified in stanzas III and IV, where it is possible to obtain (as in the editions of Spanke and, less consistently, Bartsch) a 'complete' stanza by conflating into a single text lines peculiar to one or other of the two versions. Each version, however, makes perfectly good sense in itself, though one may feel that two lines peculiar to *C* (III 24—25 in my text) have all the air of a crude improvisation reflecting a rather different level of literary taste. It is worth adding that the apparent lacuna of two lines at the end of st. III in *KN*'s version is exactly paralleled at the corresponding point in their version of st. IV. The fact that the same irregularity occurs twice strongly suggests that we are not dealing here with mere accidental omissions.

What, then, of stanza V, peculiar to *KN*, rejected as inauthentic by all editors, and printed separately by Rivière (*ed. cit.*, pp. 25—26) as a 25-line stanza ("très mutilée") in which no fewer than 15 of the lines consist entirely or partly of dots? What bizarre scribal butchery, one wonders, could have produced such a torso? How remarkable that so defective a text should (apart from a small omission in lines 3—4) make perfectly good sense! Indeed, the *pastourelle* is better rounded off with this fifth stanza than is the case in the four-stanza version of *C*. But are these lines (allowing for the defect already mentioned) metrically acceptable?

This question raises in its most acute form the same issue of musical viability which presents itself for stanzas II, III and IV. In what way are the four short-weight stanzas singable to the tune notated above the text of stanza I? The reader will have noted from the schematic presentation of the melodic form given above that the tune includes a number of exact or slightly modified repeats, so that, for example, lines 3—4 are sung to the same music as lines 1—2, lines 13—17 to a slightly modified version of the music of lines 4—8, and so on. We must assume that the incidence of these repeats was varied from stanza to stanza by the anonymous *trouvère*, in such a way that the full range of melodic repetition found in the first stanza does not recur in any of the subsequent ones and is in fact reduced to a minimum in the concluding section of the text. It is this feature (not, as we shall see, limited to this particular piece) which explains the differing dimensions of the stanzas and provides the key to the paradox of apparently defective metrical units which nevertheless seem to lack nothing from the point of view of their content. Despite the degree of formal diversity between one stanza and another, it is striking that most of the musical 'irregularities' postulated here occur twice: the non-repetition of F (after III 9 and V 9) and of I (after II 19 and IV 19), the omission of LK (after III 23 and IV 23) and of CD (after IV 13 and V 4). And the 'truncation' of the tune in st. V, so that CDCE' forms its final phrase, is exactly paralleled in all stanzas of *Ortum floris*.

The musico-metrical scheme below (p. 127) will, if read in conjunction with the texts, sufficiently indicate the remarkable subtlety of these procedures. My presentation of the text, however, demands some further observations on the versification in order to justify my printing of a full stanza (i.e. st. I) of 15 lines where earlier editions have, as already mentioned, 16 (Bartsch, Spanke) or 25 (Rivière). The French editor greatly exaggerates the metrical irregularity (as well as the textual deficiencies) of the piece: "Les textes offerts par chacune des deux familles sont aussi peu satisfaisants les uns que les autres; très délabrés, ils présentent des lacunes et de nombreux vers faux. [. . .] Malgré tout, le schéma métrique du texte donné par C est très difficile à établir. [. . .] Le texte de C est loin d'être satisfaisant, tant pour la mesure que pour la rime. [. . .] Ces faits [i.e. the irregularities of rhyme and syllable-count] ne sont pas imputables à l'archaïsme de la pièce ou à la liberté relative conservée dans la pastourelle, mais bien au délabrement de la tradition manuscrite dans les deux familles" (*ed. cit.*, pp. 26, 27, 28). In all these strictures on the crass carelessness of poet and scribes alike, there is not one single reference to the tune, nor, it would seem, much recognition that the versification of an anonymous *pastourelle* is not subject to the same strict conventions as that of a courtly *chanson* on the troubadour model. In particular, the placing of internal rhymes is sporadic, their gender may fluctuate and, in the case of feminine rhymes, they may show rhyme-elision, so that (for example) $7' + 5'$ and $13'$ and $7 + 6'$ (respectively I 5–6, III 5–6 and IV 5–6 in *KN*'s text) are equivalent (and are singable to the same notes), and the same is true of $5' + 2' + 2'$ and $5(') + 6'$ (I 18–20 and III 18–20). Indeed, it is precisely these licences which allow us to distinguish here, with a fair degree of certainty, between internal and end-rhymes,[10] i.e. between rhymes which fall within the musical phrase and those which mark its end. The latter are in fact remarkably consistent. How much these metrical liberties are a matter of ingenuity rather than carelessness may be suggested by one small detail: this is the 'extra' internal rhyme at V 7–8 echoed in V 16–17, so that in these two lines (and in these two lines alone,[11] V 16–17 being the final words of the text) the expected $7' + 5'$ or $7 + 6'$ becomes $3 + 4 + 6'$. Chance does not produce such effects.

It remains to mention certain irregularities of syllable-count which are not open to this kind of explanation. The most striking is found in lines 2, 4 and 13 of the stanza (i.e. the elements corresponding to B in the melodic scheme), which show $5'$ syllables in st. I, as do the equivalent lines throughout *Ortum floris*, but $6'$ syllables on their nine occurrences elsewhere in the text. Except for *C*'s reading in III 13, the MSS do not

---

[10] This was also the opinion of M. Burger, *Recherches sur la structure et l'origine des vers romans* (Geneva, 1957), pp. 56–57.

[11] Possibly a similar internal rhyme was intended in IV 10 (*Non ferai,/par saint Liefroi*).

QUANT VOI NEE: MUSICO-METRICAL SCHEME

Line:	1	2	3	4	5	6	7	8	9	10	11	12	13	14	15	16	17	18	19	20	21–22	23	24	25	
Tune:	A	B	A	B	C	D	C	E	F	F	G	G	B	C	D	C	E′	H	I	I	J	K	L	K	
K, I	a′3	a′5	a′3	a′5	b′7	a′5	b′7	a′5	c7	c7	c4	c4	a′5	b′7	a′5	b′7	a′5	a′5	a′2	a′2	dddd 2222	a′6	a′6	a′6	ee, oie, ot (ost, oz), in
II	a′3	a′6	a′3	a′6					b7	b7	b4	b4	a′6	b7	a′6	b7	a′6	a′5	a′2		b 4	a′6	a′6	a′6	ee, is (uis, i, it)
III	a′3	a′6	a′3	a′6					b7	b7	x4	b4	a′6	b7		b7	a′6	a′5(′)	x3	a′3	b 8	a′6			ee, is (uis, i)
IV	a′3	a′6	a′3	a′6		a′6		b,b,a 3 4 6	b7	b7	b4	b4	a′6	b8		b,b,a 3 4 6	a′6	a′6(′)	a′3	a′3	b 8	a′6			ee, oi
V	a′3	a′6	a′3	a′6	x7		b7		b7		b4		a′6	b8	a′6	b,b,a 3 4 6	a′6					a′6			ee, i
C, I	a′3	a′5	a′3	a′5	b′6	a′5	b′7	a′5	c7		c4	c4	a′5	b′7	a′5	b′7	a′5	a′5	a′2	a′2	dddd 2222	a′6	a′6	a′6	ee, oie, ot (ost, os), ins (is)
II	a′3	a′6	a′3	a′6		a′6			b7		b3	b4	a′5	b7	a′5	b 7(′)	a′5	a′5	a′2	a′2	c 4	a′6	a′6	a′6	ee, oie, ist
III	a′3	a′6	a′3	a′6		a′6	b7		b7	b7	b4	b4	a′6	b7	a′6	x7	a′6		a′3		c 4	a′6	a′6	a′6	ee, is (i, ist, uis)
IV	a′3	a′6	a′3	a′6	b7	a′6	x7		b7	b7	b4	b4	a′6	x 7(′)	a′6	b7	a′6	a′5(′)	3(′)	a′3	c 4	a′6	a′6	a′6	ee, oi (ois, oit), ai

diverge in this matter.[12] The most likely explanation of the irregularity or licence is that an up-beat (to use the modern term) gave the extra note. And this may also be the case for two other lines which are hypermetric by one syllable, namely IV 18 (in *KN*) and V 14. It will be noted that in each instance the expected odd-numbered syllable-count is increased by one, a phenomenon easily explicable in a first-mode tune (in modern notation, ♩|♩♩|♩♩|♩ instead of 𝄾|♩♩|♩♩|♩). Here too, therefore, metrical irregularity is open to musical explanation.

The musico-metrical schemes on p. 127, based respectively on the versions of *K* and of *C*, reflect my conception of how the complete text could be sung to the transmitted tune. Somewhat arbitrarily but, it is hoped, conveniently, it takes over the 25-unit division employed by Rivière. My edition of the two versions of *Quant voi nee*, though laid out in a fashion better suited to the metrical realities of the text, also includes this same numbering and carries it through stanza by stanza in place of the more usual continuous numbering of lines. Elision of feminine rhymes is indicated in the scheme by "(')"; in the text the same phenomenon is noted with brackets around the elided -*e*.

Version of *KN* (graphy of *K*, pp. 306−7)

I.	1−2	Quant voi nee	la flor en la pree,	AB
	3−4	Plus m'agree	que noif ne gelee.	AB
	5−6	A ce douz tens chevauchoie	par une ainzjornee,	CD
	7−8	Toute seule en mi ma voie	pastore ai trouvee.	CE
	9	Je la saluai tantost,		F
	10	El me respont a briés moz		F
	11−12	Du melz qu'el sot	qu'a fere l'ot:	GG
	13	'Sire, que vos gree?		B

Variants: I 1 voi *added above in N*   4 ne que gelee *N*   6 par] a *N*   7 Tote *N*
          10 Ele *N*; briez *K*   11 meuz *N*; seut *K*

[12] MS *N* in fact shows 6′ syllables in I 4, where the text *que noif ne que gelee* is set to the notes G F G A A G G. The scribe simply repeated one note (A) in order to accommodate the (incorrect) extra syllable, just as he did in I 10: here the hypermetric reading *Ele me respont* is set to the notes G D D D D, with the four-fold instead of three-fold repetition of D serving to fit the tune to the supernumerary syllable). Clearly these phenomena, in which *N* diverges from *K*, are purely scribal in origin.

	14—15	Por ce qu'en mi ceste voie m'avez encontree,	CD
	16—17	Ne cuit pas que par vos soie gueres loig menee.'	CE'
	18—20	Lors s'est escriee: 'Valee, susee!	HII
	21—22	Perrin, Martin, Guerin, Robin,	J
	23	Trop m'avez oubliee.'	K
	24	Quant la vi esfr[ë]ee,	L
	25	Si l'ai reconfortee:	K

II.	1—2	'Bele nee, ne soiez esfr[ë]ee,	[AB
	3—4	Qu'enamee vos ai en ma pensee;	AB
	14—15	Et s'en vous merci ne truis, douce dame honoree,	CD
	16—17	Por vos morra vostre ami sanz nule demoree.'	CE'
	18—19	Lors l'ai tant flatee, guilee,	HI
	21—22	Qu'ele m'a ris et si m'a dit:	J
	23	'Or m'avez vos gabee;	K
	24	Ne sui pas acesmee	L
	25	Por estre bien amee.'	K

III.	1—2	En la pree descent sanz demoree,	AB
	3—4	Acolee l'ai et vers moi serree.	AB
	5—6	Quant el vit que je la ting, mult en fu esfr[ë]ee;	CD
	7—8	De honte li monte el vis color enluminee.	CE
	9	Seur l'erbe fresche l'assis,	F
	11—12	Lors si en fis quanque g'en quis	GG
	13	Et quanque moi agree.	B
	14—15	Autresi plesant la truis et ausi savoree	CD
	16—17	Com s'el fust fille au marchis de sa fame espousee.	CE'
	18—20	Une grant loe(e) et demie a duree	HII
	21—22	La joie de moi et de li,	J
	23	Ainz qu'ele fust finee.	K

IV.	1—2	Recenglee ai ma sele doree.	AB
	3—4	Pou senee s'en est en piez levee;	AB
	5—6	Si a pris mon palefroi par la rene noee,	CD
	7—8	Puis a dit: 'Estés, estés, avez me vos guilee?'	CE
	9	'Nenil, bele, par ma foi,	F
	10	Ainz monterez devant moi,	F
	11—12	Si en vendrez avecques moi	GG
	13	En la moie contree.'	B
	16—17	'Non ferai, par saint Liefroi, ainz m'avroiz espousee.'	CE'
	18—19	Et quant j'oi sa pense(e) escoutee,	HI

I 24 eśfree *KN* (*but with four notes in both MSS*)

II 2 esfree *KN*   3 Bien amee *K*   14 Et *om. N*; vos *N*

III 4 lai uers moi et s. *K*   6 esfree *KN*   9 Sor *N*

IV 2 do/doree *over two lines N*   3 Poi *N*   6 resne *N*   7 estez estez *N*
   11 uendroiez *N*   12 auequ*es N*   16 liefrai *N*   17 maurez *N*

	21–22	Lors montai sus mon palefroi,	J
	23	A Dieu l'ai conmandee.	K
V.	1–2	Esploree remest, eschevelee:	AB
	3–4	[Forsenee, tot en mi] la valee	AB
	7–8	A choisi le sien ami, Robin qui l'a amee.	CE
	9	Lors li dist: 'Pour Dieu, ami,	F
	11	Merci te pri,	G
	14–15	Q'un chevalier s'en va par ci qui m'a despucelee;	CD
	16–17	Si te pri, biau douz ami, que n'i soie encusee.'	CE']

IV 22 palefoi *N*   23 deu *N*

V 7 sian *N*   8 Robin *om. N*   9 deu *N*   14 par] de *N*   16 doz *N*

Version of *C*, f. 114 r–v

I.	1–2	Kant voi nee la flour en la pree,	[AB
	3–4	Plux m'agree ke noif ne jalee.	AB
	5–6	L'autrier m'en chevachoie per une anjornee,	CD
	7–8	Trestout droit en mi ma voie pastoure ai trovee.	CE
	9	Je la salue a briés mos,	F
	10	Elle me respont tantost	F
	11–12	A muels ke sout, plux bel ke pout:	GG
	13	'Sire, ke vos gree?	B
	14–15	Por tant s'en mi ceste voie m'aveis si trovee,	CD
	16–17	Ne cuit pais ke per vos soie gaires loing monee.'	CE'
	18–20	Lors c'est escriee: 'Sussee, valee!	HII
	21–22	Robins, Perrins, Thieris, Abris,	J
	23	Aveis moy obliee?'	K
	24	Quant la vi effrahiee,	L
	25	Si l'ai resconfortee:	K
II.	1–2	'Belle nee, ne soiés effraihee:	AB
	3–4	Enamee vos ai et desiree;	AB
	14–15	Et saichiez, ou ke je soie, toute ma pensee	CD
	16–17	Est en vos, toute autre joi(e) en ai entreobliee.'	CE'
	18–20	Quant l'o tant mokee, chiflee, bobee,	HII
	21–22	Elle me rist, puez si me dist:	J
	23	'Sire, or m'aveis gabee;	K
	24	Ne seux pais asemee	L
	25	Por estre bien amee.'	K
III.	1–2	En la pree descent sens demoree,	AB
	3–4	Acollee l'ai, a mes brais serree.	AB
	5–6	Et quant vit ke je la ting, molt en fut effraihee;	CD
	7–8	De honte li monte el vis color enluminee.	CE

Rejected Reading: II 4 vos] nos

9		Entre mes biaus brais la prix,	F
10		Sors la frexe herbe l'aisis,	F
11—12		Pues en fi kanke moy cist,	GG
13		Toute ma pensee.	B
14—15	Toute asi plaixant la truis	et asi savoree	CD
16—17	Comme se fust fille a duc de sa femme espousee.		CE$'$
24		Quant l'o despucelee,	L
25		Molt en fut effraihee.	K
IV. 1—2	Recinglee	ai ma celle doree.	AB
3—4	Pouc senee	s'en est en piés levee;	AB
5—6	Si saixit mon palefroi	per la regne noee,	CD
7—8	Pues ait dit: 'Esteis arier, aveis me vos guillee?'		CE
9		'Nenil, belle, per ma foy,	F
11—12		Ains monterois, si en venrois	GG
13		En la moie contree.	B
14—15	Lai sereis vos bien vestue et richement pairee.'		CD
16—17	'Non ferai, per saint Liefroit,	ainz m'avrois espousee.'	CE$'$
18—20	Quant j'o sa pence(e)	escoute(e), a coi bee,	HII
21—22	Lors me montai,	si m'en alai.	J
23		A Deu l'ai comendee,	K
24		Dolente et esgairee	L
25		La laissai en la pree.	K]

The two versions of *Quant voi nee*, though far from identical, share one striking formal characteristic: both consist of one 'complete' and three or four more or less 'incomplete' stanzas. The lines present in the two versions are not the same, nor are those which are seemingly omitted. A defective common archetype is therefore not a possible hypothesis. If a purely scribal explanation were to be sought, it would involve the supposition that two copyists (or series of copyists) were guilty, not of the same errors, but of the same *kind* of errors, and what is more that they erred repeatedly. The inherent improbability of such a supposition has led me to propose a different type of explanation, one which allows us to accept far more of what the MSS actually transmit. This does not mean that either of the extant versions is necessarily to be thought of as identical with the original. As Rychner found in comparing different versions of the same *fabliau*,[13] the *KN* and the *C* texts differ in 'quality', *C*

---

[13] See J. Rychner, *Contribution à l'étude des fabliaux* (Geneva, 1960).

being distinctly cruder in its literary effects as well as somewhat less unconventional in its versification.[14] As with differing versions of the *fabliaux*, it is reasonable to suppose that we are dealing here with different 'realisations' of the same song, in the sense that each version transmits in written form one of the ways in which the piece might be realised in performance. The fact that each makes musical as well as linguistic sense argues strongly in favour of this hypothesis.

The pieces which we shall now proceed to examine all share one feature with *Quant voi nee*: each consists of a series of stanzas of different dimensions. Nevertheless they are clearly not heterostrophic in the fashion of a *lai* or a *descort*; and they can be made to appear perfectly isostrophic only by editorial insertion of lines of dots and/or excision of supernumerary lines. They are strophic, but imperfectly so. In the hypothesis advanced here, the divergent sizes of stanza are accounted for by the variable presence or absence of melodic repetitions in successive deployments of the same tune. Since this phenomenon has not been examined previously, there is no ready-made term to describe it. I propose therefore to use the adjective 'heteromorphic' to designate such pieces.[15]

The first case is the well-known song *Il me covient renvoisier* (RS 1300; unicum in MS *O*, with music for st. I), often attributed to Colin Muset (ed. Bédier, 2nd ed., 1938, p. 30; earlier editions by Jeanroy, *Les Origines de la poésie lyrique en France au moyen âge*, 3rd ed., Paris, 1925, pp. 504–5, and Jeanroy and Långfors, *Chansons satiriques et bachiques du XIIIe siècle*, 2nd ed., Paris, 1965, pp. 76–77; text and music in Beck, *Le Chansonnier Cangé*, II, Paris, 1927, 159). The three stanzas

---

[14] *C* avoids the non-repetition of I at II 20 and IV 20, that of F at III 9–10, that of CD at IV 14–15, and contrives to end all stanzas with LK (III 24–25 and IV 24–25).

[15] The examples cited are not intended to be exhaustive; a notable case not discussed here is the *Tournoiement des Dames* of Huon d'Oisy (RS 1924a). In general I have avoided citing instances involving relatively small 'omissions' (which could be explained as scribal slips due to homoeoteleuton) or 'additions' (like the pieces cited in n. 17 below).

have different dimensions and can be made to look 'regular'
only if one suppresses part of the text of st. II and prints lines
of dots at the end of st. III. These normative corrections by
Jeanroy were rightly rejected by Bédier (*ed. cit.*, pp. 59–60),
whose text is the basis for Mölk's analysis (MW 981:1). Although
Bédier's division of the lines of the text is misleading, he nevertheless saw intuitively that the three stanzas needed no textual
modifications to make them singable.[16] If the musico-metrical
structure is correctly analysed, it is immediately apparent how
the tune notated for st. I can be used for the rest of the text.

	A	B	A	B		C	D	E			C	D	E	
I	a	b	a	b		b	x	b			b	x	b	ier, é (er)
	7	4	7	4		3	7	4			3	7	4	

	[A	B	A	B		C	D	E		C	D		C	D	E]	
II	a	b	a	b		b	x	b		b	b		b	a	b	eaus, on(s)
	7	4	7	4		3	7	4		3	7		3	7	4	

	[A	B	A	B		C	D	E]	
III	a	b	a	b		b	a	b	ier, é (er)
	7	4	7	4		3	7	4	

The procedure whereby the perfect symmetry of the tune is
rendered asymmetrical by extension in st. II, by contraction in
st. III, is particularly subtle.[17]

The best-known of all Old French *reverdies* (*En avril au tens
pascour*, RS 2006) offers some similarity to *Quant voi nee* in
that it is preserved in two textually very different versions, one
with music and one without (MSS *K*, with music for st. I, and
U, with space left for staves above st. I). Only the editions of

---

[16] Bédier's explanation — "La mélodie autorise l'exécutant à répéter deux fois,
ou trois ou quatre, les mesures sur lesquelles il chante le dernier vers" (*ed. cit.*, p. 60)
— is not quite correct, since it is not the final hendecasyllable (DE in my melodic
scheme) which is repeated. Nevertheless, the observation indicates that Bédier (and
he alone, unless I am mistaken) had an instinctive understanding of what I have here
baptised heteromorphic songs.

[17] Three other pieces by Colin Muset show 'extra' lines in the final stanza and
should probably be classed as heteromorphic: on V and XIV, cf. *ed. cit.*, p. xix; the
third case is IX, where lines 58–59 are supernumerary but evidently authentic.

Gennrich, Tyssens, and Rosenberg and Tischler,[18] all of them with music, require consideration here, since they alone take account of the totality of the material transmitted by U. In fact all three present the text of K, which, with some degree of emendation, furnishes two isostrophic stanzas. U's readings are relegated to the variants or (in Gennrich) partially printed in parallel with K. The latter, if one introduces one emendation,[19] offers the following structure:

	1	2	3	4	5	6	7	8	9	10	11	12	13	14	15	16		17	18	19	20	
	A	B	A	B	C	D	C	D'	E	F	E	F'	G	H	G	I	R	K	L	M	N	
I	a	a	a	a	b	c	b	c	x	d	x	d	e	e	e	e		x	e	x	e	our, el, in, ure, on
	7	7	7	7	8	8	8	8	7	7'	7	7'	5	5	5	5	1	7	8	7'	7	
II	x	a	a	a	b	c	b	c	x	c	c	d	e	e	f	f		d	g	d	g	our, el, ier(s), i(r)e, oit, ors, ai
	7	8	7	7	8	8	8	8	7	7	7	7'	5	5	5	5	1	7'	7	7'	7	

('R' stands here for the monosyllabic refrain-word *Deus!*)

The small fluctuations in syllable-count and the fluidity of rhyming are features found in other songs cited in this article. These licences apart, K's version is regularly isostrophic.

MS U offers a longer version of the song. The lines peculiar to this MS (II 9—20 in the text printed below, pp. 137—38) were laconically dismissed by Gennrich with the words "gehört offenbar [!] nicht dem Lied; oder ist verderbt" and are presented by Rosenberg as merely "an apocryphal version of ll. 9—17" [= I 9—20 in the scheme above]. Spanke (*op. cit.*, p. 406) was already no less dismissive, rejecting these lines because they lacked the allegorical element found in the rest of the piece and because they did not conform to its metrical structure. And yet the passage in question makes sense and is (as I hope to show) singable. Editors may have been unduly influenced by the seemingly disordered fashion in which MS U presents the text,

---

[18] F. Gennrich, *Altfranzösische Lieder (1. Teil)* (Tübingen, 1955), pp. 47—49; M. Tyssens, 'An avril au tens pascour' in *Mélanges Boutière* (Liège, [1971]), I, 589—603; S. N. Rosenberg and H. Tischler, *Chanter m'estuet* (London, 1981), pp. 32—34. The metrical schemes given by Mölk (MW 93:1 and 524:1 for K, 90:1 and 1207:1 for U), being based on Bartsch's edition, are worthless.

[19] II 1—2 are placed after II 20 in the MS; all three editors make the correction. On the other hand, I have disregarded the normative emendations of I 13—14 (where all three editors alter the rhyme-words *orion* and *rosignon* to give forms in *-ou* or *-or*), of II 9—12 (Tyssens and Rosenberg both substitute U's reading for that of K), of II 1 (Tyssens and Rosenberg both correct *son* to *tor*, against both MSS) and of II 2 (all three editors follow U in suppressing *Onc*, thus reducing the line to seven syllables).

for the copyist interrupted his work, returning to complete it in
a different ink with a different pen and then continuing on to a
supplementary half-sheet of parchment, a state of affairs found
elsewhere in this part of the MS.[20] Evidently this is not in itself
an argument against the authenticity of the text, whose metrical
structure is set out below. To enable comparison to be made,
the scheme uses the same numbering and lettering of the elements
of the tune as were employed for K's version. This highlights
the fact that U's text, if accepted as it stands, has an absolutely
different structure. Editors have universally assumed that the
six lines which open III are simply misplaced from the middle
of st. I (which is where four of them occur in K) and that the
copyist of U was merely trying to make good his own earlier
omission of them. This immediately identifies the scribe as
inept and inherently worthy of distrust. It is only a small step
to summarily condemning as inauthentic the whole passage
peculiar to U; as we saw above, trumped-up charges have easily
been found by successive editors, who have unanimously assumed
the 'superfluous' dozen lines to have been intended as a *final*
stanza. But there is no indication that U's scribe intended the
passage to go elsewhere than where he placed it. Admittedly, he
could have made the structure clearer to the eye by using a
large capital to mark the beginning of III and of IV. But perhaps
he was right to consider these divisions as something other than
stanzas. The overall structure of U's text, which may be
represented as ABCD ECD EAB ECD, is not genuinely strophic
but rather resembles (though on a smaller scale) the unpredictable patterns of recurrence found in some of the more complex
lais.[21]

The edition of U which follows the metrical scheme will, it is
hoped, give form and substance to these abstract considerations.
It makes only one metrical correction (IV 11) and leaves the

[20] For a clear and detailed explanation of the state of the MS, see Tyssens,
art. cit., pp. 595—97, in conjunction with the facsimiles of ff. 152r and 151r in
P. Meyer and G. Raynaud, *Le Chansonnier français de Saint-Germain-des-Prés* (Paris,
1892).
[21] See Spanke's analyses of RS 900, 1012, 635, 1017 and 1642 in 'Sequenz und
Lai' in *Studi medievali*, XI (1938), 12—68, at 56—63 [reprinted in his *Studien zu
Sequenz, Lai und Leich*, Darmstadt, 1977, pp. 146—202, at 190—97].

Lorrain graphies unretouched. Letters cut off by the binder on f. 151r are restored between <>.

EN AVRIL AU TENS PASCOUR: MUSICO-METRICAL SCHEME

Line:	9'	10'	9	10	11	12	1	2	3	4	5	6	7	8	13	14	15	16	17	18	19	20	
Tune:	[E	F	E	F	E	F'	A	B	A	B	C	D	C	D'	G	H	G	I	R	K	L	M	N]
I							a	a	a	a	b	c	b	c	a	a	d	d	d	d	x	d	or, el,
							7	7	7	7	8	8	8	8	5	5	5	5	8	8	7'	7	in, on(s)
II			x	a	x	a									b	b	x	b	x	b	x	b	oie(nt),
			7'	7'	7	7'									5	5	5	5	7	8	7'	7	or
III	a	b	a	b	a	b	x	c	c	c	d	e	d	e									ant, ure,
	7	7'	7	7'	7	7'	7	7	7	7	8	8	8	8									or(s), el, ier
IV			x	a	x	a									b	b	c	c	a	d	a	d	i(s)e, oit,
			7'	7'	7	7'									5	5	5	5	1	7'	7'	7' 7	ors, ai

I. 1   An avril a tans pakour   *U, f. 152r*
   2   Ke nest la fuielle et la flour,
   3   L'aluete a point dou jor
   4   Chante et loie son signor,
   5   Por la dousour dou tans novel
   6   Si m'en antra an ·i· jardin,
   7   S'oï chanteir sor l'arbrexel
   8   Les ozelés an lour latin.
 13   Je vi l'oriour
 14   Et lou rosignor,
 15   Se vi lou pinson
 16   Et l'esmerillon,
 17   Et tant des atres ozillons
 18   Dont je ne sai dire lou non,
 19   Ke desor l'arbre s'asisent:
 20   Chacuns chantait sa chanson.

II. 9   Un petit me trais arriere,
 10   Ke corresier nes osoie,
 11   Et ses pris a regardeir,
 12   La joe ke il movoient:
 13   Vi lou roisignor
 14   Demeneir badour;

Rejected Readings: I 1 aurit; tant   1—2 En aurj a tens paskor que nest la fuelle
            Index (f. 2v)   6 si *added above the line*
        II 12 mouoient *rather than* monoient

	15	Tut sont antor lui
	16	Et grant et menour,
	17	Et chantent tut antor lui
	18	Et demoinnent feste grignor,
	19	Ke d'une grande luée
	20	Puet on oïr la tantour.

III.   9′   Un petit me tras avant,   *f. 151r*

```
III.   9'    Un petit me tras avant,                    f. 151r
      10'    Ke veoir voi[l] lor faiture.
       9     Ne soi mot ca<nt> de lor gent
      10     Vis venir a demesure:
      11     Il an i ot plus de ·c·
      12     Toz de dive<rse> faiture.
       1     Tut conmansent a un son,
       2     N'i ot atre juglëor.
       3     Je m'an alai <a> la tor
       4     Por oïr joie d'amors,
       5  Se regarda par ·i· prael,
       6  Lou duc d'amo<r> viz chevachier.
       7  Je m'an alai a son apel,
       8  De moi ait fait son escuei<r>.

IV.    9     Ces chevals fut de deport,
      10     Sa celle de signorie,
      11     Ces frains [fut] de son d<an>gier,
      12     Ceu estrier de fil de sie,
      13         Ces habers estoit
      14         D'acoleir estroit,
      15         C<es> hiames de flors
      16         De divers colors.
                     Deus!
      17     Lance avoit de cortosie,
      18     Espee ot de fuel de glai,
      19     S'ot chaces de mignotise,
      20     Esperon de bec de jai.
```

III 9 soi] sot   10 a] *et*

My defence of *U*'s text of this piece necessarily carries with it various implications. To defend *U* simply by condemning *K* would imply that the scribe of *K*, or one of his predecessors, carried out a regularising operation on the written text in such a way as to produce two neatly isostrophic stanzas. This seems to me unlikely. But that one and the same text (and one and the same tune) could exist in two structurally different versions, each

performable, is a much more reasonable hypothesis. This pre-
supposes that the tune was not an unalterable entity with proportions and constituents fixed once for all, but was altogether
more protean. An interesting sidelight on this matter is cast by
RS 1254, an anonymous *pastourelle* whose similarity to our
reverdie did not escape Tyssens (*art. cit.*, p. 601). This text
(ed. Rivière, *op. cit.*, I, 116—17), whose music is unfortunately
not extant, consists of five stanzas with the shape

$$\begin{array}{cccccccccc}
a & b & a & b & c & c & R & d & c & d & c \\
7 & 7' & 7 & 7' & 5 & 5 & 1 & 7' & 5 & 7' & 7
\end{array}$$

(The monosyllabic refrain is *Deus*. The *d*-rhyme is absent from
all stanzas but the first and third.) The form is, of course, not
identical with that of st. IV of the *reverdie* in *U*'s version. But
the similarities are of such a kind as to rule out mere coincidence
and to suggest therefore that an incomplete and somewhat
modified version of the tune of RS 2006 could form a viable
basis for a new isostrophic piece. The case is, after all, not more
strange than that of *Quant voi nee* and *Ortum floris*.

Yet another anonymous *pastourelle*, namely *L'autrier tout
seus chevauchoie* (RS 1709; MSS *K* and *X*, both with music for
st. I), presents metrical problems which have teased modern
editors. Both Spanke (*op. cit.,* pp. 164—65, with tune,
pp. 426—27) and Rivière (*op. cit.*, II, 118—19) rightly prefer
the text given by *K*, but both confess themselves puzzled by the
multiple irregularities of its metrical form. Spanke (p. 388)
thought it the work of an unskilled versifier attempting to put
words to a pre-existent tune. Rivière observes (p. 120): "Le
poème ne peut être analysé d'un point de vue formel. [. . .] il
n'y a pas trace d'une régularité quelconque." Jean-Marie d'Heur[22]
has recently attempted, with some conflation of the readings of
the two MSS, to arrive at a more exact notion of its verse-form.
It is unnecessary to go over d'Heur's work again, beyond observing that its tentative conclusions do not contradict mine, but
that it suffers from a total absence of any reference to the music
of the piece, as well as from a curious notion of metrical arith-
metic. The oddities of the text's versification are in fact not so

---

[22] 'Pour le texte des pastourelles anonymes en langue d'Oïl' in *Mélanges Pierre
Jonin* (Aix-en-Provence, 1979), pp. 305—33, at 322—27.

much unusual (at least in *pastourelles*) as unusually numerous. The musico-metrical scheme given below is based on MS *K* without any textual corrections, not even the two small modifications (8 *aim plus* for *aim je plus*, 36 *con* for *conme*) proposed by d'Heur and already introduced by Spanke: since the scribe gave a note for each of the 9' syllables of the text, it is possible to make a textual emendation only by also introducing (as Spanke did) a musical alteration of doubtful validity.

	A	B	A	B	C	C	C	D	E[23]	D	E	
I	x / 7'	a / 7'	x / 7	a / 7'	a / 8'	a / 8'		x / 8'	a / 9'			(i)ere
II	x / 7'	a / 7	x / 7	a / 8	a / 8			x / 8'	a / 8	x / 8'	a / 8	al
III	a / 7	a / 7	x / 7'	a / 8	b / 7	b / 7	a / 7	c / 8'	a / 8	c / 8'	a / 8	or(s), on, ete
IV	x / 7'	a / 7	a / 8	a / 8	b / 8	b / 8		x / 8'	b / 9	x / 8'	b / 8	i(r), a(rt)

The diagrammatic lay-out adopted readily suggests the explanation of the varying dimensions of the stanzas: in st. II C was sung only once but in st. III it appeared three times; and DE was sung twice in all stanzas after the first. For the rest, it is clear that the anonymous poetaster was content to set masculine endings to the two notes appropriate to a feminine ending (as already in line 3) and to add or suppress an upbeat (as the tune very readily allowed; cf. n. 23) in order to accommodate the same musical phrase indifferently to a heptasyllabic or an octosyllabic line. That he was unskilfully fitting new words to an old tune, as Spanke suggested, seems very probable. The similarity of the tune to that of another anonymous *pastourelle* with a similar opening line (*L'autrier quant je chevauchoie*, RS 1698a; most recent edition, with music, in Rosenberg and Tischler, *op. cit.*, pp. 41—42) was already pointed out by Gérold.[24] The tunes, though not identical, have an unmistake-

---

[23] The melodic structure is much subtler than this formula would suggest. Both A and B begin with the same rising three-note figure (B-C-D) which, transposed and provided with an upbeat, opens both C and D (respectively A-G-A-B and D-C-D-E). And B and C end with the same six-note phrase, which in a slightly modified form also concludes E. The text may be shoddy stuff, but the tune has quality.

[24] Th. Gérold, *La Musique au moyen âge* (Paris, 1932), p. 199.

able family resemblance, that of RS 1698a having the structure ABABCDE and being fitted to heptasyllabic lines of which the first, third and sixth (= A, A and D in the tune) are indifferently of 7 or 7' syllables, normally without rhyme. Metrically, therefore, RS 1698a is much more regular, and it is not heteromorphic: like RS 1709, it exploits the archaic fifteen-syllable line, with caesura but without internal rhyme (7' + 7 or 7 + 7), studied by Jeanroy, *Origines*, pp. 345—49, and by M. Burger, *op. cit.*, pp. 63—64. If it was indeed the model for RS 1709, as I am inclined to believe, then this would furnish another instance (in addition to RS 308a, discussed below) of a heteromorphic piece based on an isostrophic model.

The metrical form of *Un motet vous voudrai chanter* (RS 836), a devotional piece preserved with its tune in a single copy (MS *i*), is not easy to represent schematically. The three complete editions of the text differ considerably. That of Jeanroy (*Mélanges Wilmotte*, Paris, 1910, pp. 258—61) regularises rhyme and scansion in a quite excessive degree, while that by Järnström and Långfors (*Recueil de chansons pieuses du 13e siècle*, II, Helsinki, 1927, 185—89), like the *editio princeps* by Stengel (in F. Noack, *Der Strophenausgang in seinem Verhältnis zum Refrain und Strophengrundstock in der refrainhaltigen altfranzösischen Lyrik*, Marburg, 1899, pp. 151—52), leaves the MS readings virtually unaltered. Mölk (MW 844:1 and 830:1) follows the 1927 edition but is very misleading in the matter of syllable-count. The basic shape may be represented as follows:

A	B	A	B	C	D	E	
a	b	a	b	x	c	d	+ refrain[25]
8	8	8	8	6'	6	5' *or* 6'	

The rhyming and syllable-count of the fifth, sixth and seventh elements in the scheme show much variation. Even the octosyllables, which scan regularly, do not consistently show the *a*-rhyme. And assonance does duty for rhyme in many places. The reason for mentioning the piece here, however, is that five

---

[25] The textual and musical shape of the refrain, which is given in full only once, at the beginning of the piece, is unclear because of material damage to the MS. For this and as much as can be made out of the tune, see F. Gennrich, *Musikwissenschaft und romanische Philologie* (Halle, 1918), pp. 50—52 (= *ZrPh*, XXXIX, 1919, 357—59).

stanzas out of nine (II, IV, V, VII, IX) present the *ab*-element, not twice, but three times. Thus the stanzas, in addition to the metrical licences already mentioned, are heteromorphic.

The next example may serve to show how a regularly isostrophic model could form the basis of a heteromorphic *contrafactum*. Pierre de Corbie's *pastourelle Par un ajournant* (RS 291; ed. Bartsch, *op. cit.*, pp. 281—82) is constructed as follows:

A	B	A	B		A	B	A	B		C	D	D′		C	D	D′
a	b	a	b		c	b	c	b		d	d	b		d	d	b
5	5	5	5		5	5	5	5		5′	5′	5		5′	5′	5

(MW 1135:1; in st. I—II, rhymes *a* and *c* are identical.) The anonymous religious piece *Prion en chantant* (RS 323; ed. Järnström and Långfors, *op. cit.*, pp. 125—127, and, with music, F. Gennrich, *Cantilenae Piae*, Langen bei Frankfurt, 1966, p. 10) takes over the tune of the *pastourelle* and, with some small degree of modification, its metrical form (MW 761:1). Both these pieces are isostrophic. But it is a second *contrafactum* of Pierre de Corbie's piece, the anonymous *reverdie A un ajournant por oïr le chant* (RS 308a; unicum in MS *C*, without music; ed. Bartsch, *op. cit.*, p. 104), which is relevant here. The first and third of its four stanzas display the metrical shape

x	a	x	a		x	a	x	a		b	b	a		b	b	a
5	5	5	5		5	5	5	5		5′	5′	5		5′	5′	5

(MW 127:1; some lines show $\frac{x}{5'}\ \frac{a}{5}$). But in st. II the *bba*-element occurs once only, in st. IV the *xa*-element comes once instead of four times. Despite the supposition of a lacuna in st. II by Bartsch or of lacunas in both passages by Mölk and by Tyssens (*art. cit.*, *Mélanges Boutière*, pp. 590, note 5, and 592), the apparently defective stanzas reveal themselves to be easily singable when one takes note of the melodic structure of the model; they also make perfectly good sense. The case of RS 308a is particularly interesting. Its status as a *contrafactum* of RS 291 is guaranteed by the near-identity of the incipits. Comparison of the two texts demonstrates the ease with which a heteromorphic piece could be based on a pre-existent tune which itself had regular repeats and was originally designed for a regular isostrophic text.

If this last instance illustrates the possibility of detecting heteromorphic structure in a text transmitted without music but manifestly a *contrafactum* of a piece whose tune is known, our last example involves a text whose music is not known from any source. The anonymous *pastourelle* RS 1990 is transmitted without music in two very different versions by MSS *C* (*L'autrier levai ains jour*) and *U* (*L'autrier me levai au jour*). Bartsch's edition (*op. cit.*, pp. 118—20) gives a series of nine regular eleven-line stanzas (only the first and second have 12 and 10 lines respectively) derived from *C* with some conflation of readings from *U*; that of Rivière (*op. cit.*, II, 43—49) prints *C* virtually without change, indicating no fewer than eighteen 'missing' lines (as well as a few shorter lacunas) by means of dots.[26] (Mölk's metrical scheme, MW 56:1, derives from Bartsch.) The form of the six stanzas given by *U* may be represented as follows:

a	a		a	a	a...		b	b	b	b		c	c	c	c	c
7	7		6	6	6		5	2	4	8		4	2	4	8	8

(The second line is textually identical with the first in each stanza. Each of the two-syllable lines is an onomatopoeic echo-rhyme.) A striking peculiarity, indicated above by the dots after line 5, is that the number of six-syllable lines is variable from stanza to stanza: respectively six, three, four, six, two and four. There is no evident lacuna of sense in any of the stanzas. It seems very probable that each of the hexasyllables was sung to the same melodic phrase and that the number of musical repetitions varied freely from stanza to stanza. The structure of the nine-stanza version of the piece found in MS *C* bears this out. Although *C* differs from *U* in presenting six-, not seven-syllable lines at the opening of all stanzas and in lacking the textual repetition in two of them (II and IX — probably a simple scribal error), it shares with *U* the characteristic variability in the number of

---

[26] This piece is one of three anonymous *pastourelles* for which Rivière (*op. cit.*, I, 20) considers it impossible to establish a metrical scheme, the others being *Quant voi nee* and RS 1680 (*ibid.*, II, 162—63). This last piece, not directly relevant here since it is not heteromorphic, is a good example (as is its model, RS 1583) of the musically determined fluidity of syllable-count found in so many of our pieces, as well as of the total impossibility of understanding the structure of such songs without reference to their music (on RS 1680 and 1583 see in particular Gennrich, *Die altfranzösische Rotrouenge* (Halle, 1925), pp. 45—47 and 35—37 respectively).

hexasyllables on the *a*-rhyme (respectively seven, three, five, six, six, five, six, four and eight). It is not possible to attribute to the carelessness of copyists this feature shared by the two, otherwise very different versions of the piece. Nor is scribal error in some distant archetype a possible explanation, for there is a considerable degree of textual divergence between the two versions. Of the total of 25 hexasyllabic lines transmitted by *U*, five are not found in *C* and a number of others diverge considerably. Thus, here as in *Quant voi nee*, the metrical peculiarity is shared even though the textual substance is different. It is clear that the original song was heteromorphic. Certain other irregularities peculiar to MS *C* support this, in that they too are explicable via a variable incidence of musical repetitions. Stanza IX ("particulièrement aberrante du point de vue de la métrique", notes Rivière, p. 49) shows the following metrical shape:

$$
\begin{array}{cccccccc}
a\ a\ a\ a\ a\ a\ a\ a & b\ b\ b\ b\ b\ b & \left[\begin{array}{c}c\\4\end{array}\right] c\ c\ c\ c \\
6\ 6\ 6\ 6\ 6\ 6\ 6\ 6 & 5\ 4\ 4\ 8\ 8\ 8 & \phantom{\left[\begin{array}{c}c\\4\end{array}\right]} 2\ 4\ 8\ 8
\end{array}
$$

Here, in the concluding stanza, the melodic repetitions must have reached their maximum, with $\frac{b}{4}$ twice instead of once, $\frac{b}{8}$ three times instead of once.

In the present case, then, the two extant copies stem from two different realisations of the piece, the shorter version of *U* being, despite its rearranged stanza-order, metrically slightly more consistent than the nine-stanza text furnished by *C*. The text printed below may serve to substantiate my view that the short version of the piece is perfectly viable and is indeed less prolix than *C*'s text.

I.	1	L'autrier me levai au jor,	*U, f. 79v*
	2	L'autrier me levai au jor,	
	3	Trovai en un destor	
	4	Pastore et son pastor,	
	5	En sa main un tabor,	
	6	En l'autre mirëor,	
	7	Se mire sa color	

Rejected Readings: I 1–13 *empty staves above text*

	8	Et chante par amor:
	9	'Dorenleu diva, eya, oi ça oi la.'
	10	Mais en pou d'ore li chanja
	11	Li dorenleus — eyeus — qant uns granz leus,
	12	Gole baée, familleus,
	13	Se fiert entre les floz andeus.
II.	1	Tot ont perdu lor deduit,
	2	Tot ont perdu lor deduit,
	3	Ez vos lo leu q'en fuit
	4	Au bois, cui qu'il ennuit,
	5	Et j'en oï lo bruit.
	9	Cele part m'en vois — eyois, — tot demenois
	10	Me mis entre lui et lo bois
	11	Por detenir — eÿr — en son venir,
	12	Feri lo leu de tel aïr
	13	Que la proie li fis guerpir.
III.	1	Ele commence a huchier,
	2	Ele comence a huchier:
	3	'Ferez, frans chevaliers,
	4	Pensez de l'esploitier,
	5	Car por vostre luier
	6	Avrez un douz baisier.
	9	Revenez par nos — eyous, — Robins iert cous.'
	10	Quant je li oi l'aigniau rescous
	11	N'ai rien perdu — eyu, — joianz en fu.
	12	Robins qui l'avoit entendu
	13	Par felenoie a respondu.
IV.	1	Adonc respondi Robin,
	2	Adon respondi Robin
	3	Qui tint lo chief enclin
	4	Et jure saint Martin
	5	K'ague n'est mie vin
	6	Ne sage perresin
	7	Ne poivres n'est comins
	8	Ne cuers de fem/me fins:
	9	'Fous est qui la croit — eyoit — s'il ne la voit.
	10	Femme fait bien que faire doit
	11	S'ele fait mal — eyal: — por un vassal
	12	Qui par ci passa a cheval,
	13	M'a guerpi cele desloial.'

f.80r (aligned with line IV 8)

I 9 ca   10 ian *struck through after* li

II 12 feri *altered from* ferir

IV 2 Robin] .R.

V. 1   Adon la levai errant,
    2   Adon la levai errant,
    3   Sor mon cheval ferrant.
    4   Ele dist en riant:
    9 'Robin, Deus te saut — eyaut, — plorers que vaut?
   10   Je vois esbanoier el gaut
   11   Por mon delit — eÿt, — n'est pas petiz!
   12   Se tu m'aimes si com tu diz,
   13   Pren te garde de mes berbiz.'

VI. 1   'Dame, tost m'avez guerpi,
    2   Dame, tost m'avez guerpi,
    3   Quant por vostre delit
    4   Avez un home eslit
    5   C'onques mais ne vos vit.
    6   Pou se prise petit
    9 Femme qui son cuer — eyuer — vuet vandre a fuer:
   10   Bien at geté lo sien a fuer
   11   Qui par covent — eyent — son baisier vant,
   12   Qui va derriers ne va devant,
   13   Qui chainge menu et sovent.'

V 9 Robin *altered from* Robins   11 e *of* nest *altered*
VI 11 qui *erased before* son

The versification of the texts examined here does not follow the rigorously isosyllabic and isostrophic patterns of the courtly *chanson*. They are composed within a much looser and more flexible system which we may call 'quasi-popular' in the sense in which Pierre Bec has used the term *popularisant*.[27] It is noticeable that, besides the irregularities of strophic structure with which this article has been principally concerned, these texts also display, in their rhyming and their syllable-count, a number of other licences. If courtly verse strives after smoothness, these pieces can only be called rough-hewn. But their apparent defects become comprehensible (and indeed cease to be defects) when seen in the context of the music to which they were sung. In

---

[27] See in particular *La lyrique française au moyen âge (XIIe et XIIIe siècles). Contribution à une typologie des genres poétiques médiévaux*, 2 vols. (Paris, 1977—78), I, passim. H. Spanke, 'Volkstümliches in der altfranzösischen Lyrik' in *ZrPh*, LIII (1933), 258—86, is concerned with the content and cultural significance of such pieces but not with their metrical peculiarities.

the fitting together of words and music the authors observe fewer restrictions than courtly poets and allow themselves various liberties. It is likely that in many instances, perhaps in all, the words were composed to an already existing tune, whose formal structure could undergo modifications, by extension and by contraction, hand in hand with the quasi-strophic divisions of the text.

In a monument to a scholar who brought to bear on every text that he scrutinised so wide a range of relevant information and whose work so often demonstrated the difference between blind adherence to, and critical respect for, the work of medieval scribes, it is fitting that the editorial problems presented by heteromorphic lyric texts should have the last word. To edit such pieces as if their structure was totally regular is profoundly misleading. It is unprofitable to judge their MS readings in the inappropriate optic of courtly song; and competing versions of the same piece, so far from meriting condemnation as examples of scribal ineptitude, often deserve to be assessed as equally valid realisations by inventive performers. The understanding of the transmitted texts demands a combination of philological and musicological skills. Those who have ignored this requirement have often imposed a metrical straitjacket on the formal diversity of the songs. Such editorial alterations, even if only amounting to a few lines of dots, have hitherto concealed the existence of an interesting formal type within the Old French lyric. It has long been known that the sequential patterns typical of the heterostrophic *lai* and *descort* could be adapted to the principle of stanza-form by using a miniature sequence-structure as the basis of a single stanza and then repeating it, thus creating an isostrophic *lai* or *descort* (*Strophenlai*).[28] Such structures constituted a perfect compromise between the two musico-metrical types, sequential and strophic. The pieces discussed here (with the possible exception of RS 1990, for which no music survives) reveal an *imperfect* compromise, in the sense that here the unpredictable proportions of sequence-structure are only incompletely subordinated to the principle of strophic

---

[28] See my article 'The isostrophic *descort* in the poetry of the troubadours' in *RPh*, XXXV (1981), 130–57.

recurrence and show through in the lop-sided dimensions of successive stanzas. The frequency with which different copyists attest this type of verse-form is only matched by the misguided zeal with which editors have suppressed the evidence.

TRADITION MANUSCRITE ET EDITION DE TEXTES: LE CAS DES FABLIAUX

P. MÉNARD

On peut estimer le nombre de fabliaux à environ 130.[1] Les manuscrits de fabliaux recensés par Per Nykrog forment une masse apparemment élevée de 36 copies.[2] Mais il faut se garder de croire que la plupart des contes à rire sont conservés par plusieurs manuscrits. Ce serait une illusion. En fait, seul un tiers des textes, approximativement une quarantaine de fabliaux, apparaît dans plusieurs copies: un seul fabliau se rencontre dans 8 mss. (*Auberee*), sept autres fabliaux se trouvent dans au moins 5 mss.,[3] une dizaine dans 4 mss., cinq dans 3 mss., enfin une vingtaine dans 2 mss. Le gros bataillon, c'est-à-dire les deux tiers des oeuvres, ne nous a été transmis que par un seul manuscrit. Il en va ainsi de contes intéressants et importants comme *Estormi*, le *Prestre et Alison*, les *Trois Chanoinesses de Cologne*, les *Trois Dames de Paris*, les *Perdriz*, le *Meunier d'Arleux*, le *Prestre et le Chevalier*, le *Prestre teint*, la *Vescie a prestre*, etc.

Cette situation tient sans doute à des causes diverses sur lesquelles il n'est pas possible ici de s'arrêter. On fera valoir simplement un fait capital: les manuscrits qui nous ont transmis les fabliaux n'ont pas tous la même importance et la même valeur. Sur les 36 copies citées, seuls cinq manuscrits comptent vraiment en raison du nombre de fabliaux qu'ils possèdent. Il s'agit par

---

[1] Cf. la liste de N. van den Boogaard dans *Neophilologus*, LXXI (1977), 242–44, avec les suggestions que j'ai présentées dans mon étude *Les fabliaux, contes à rire du Moyen Age* (Paris, 1983), p. 14, n. 2.

[2] Voir P. Nykrog, *Les fabliaux* (Copenhague, 1957), pp. 310–11. On pourrait ajouter quelques suppléments à cette liste: par exemple des fragments comme le ms. de Paris BN nouv. acq. fr. 934, ou le ms. tardif de la Fondation Bodmer à Genève, 113.

[3] Il s'agit des contes du *Boucher d'Abbeville*, de *Celle qui se fist foutre sur la fosse de son mari*, du *Chevalier qui fist parler les cons* (Version I), de *Constant du Hamel*, de la *Couille noire*, de la *Dame escoillee*, du *Vilain qui conquist Paradis par plait*.

ordre décroissant du ms. *A* (Paris BN fr. 837), du ms. *B* (Berne
Bürgerbibliothek 354), du ms. *C* (Berlin R.D.A. Bibl. nat.
Hamilton 257), du ms. *D* (Paris BN fr. 19152), du ms. *E* (Paris
BN fr. 1593). Pour apprécier le poids respectif de ces collections,
de brèves indications approximatives sont suffisantes: le ms. *A*
contient presque 60 fabliaux, le ms. *B* un peu plus de 40, le ms.
C une trentaine, le ms. *D* un peu moins de trente, le ms. *E* un
peu plus de 20. Si l'on continuait la série décroissante, on tom-
berait vite à des chiffres très bas: le ms. *F* (BN fr. 12603) n'offre
que 12 fabliaux, le ms. *G* (ex Middleton à Wollaton Hall,
aujourd'hui Nottingham Bibl. univ. Mi Lm 6) seulement 8. Tout
le reste des mss. ne présente qu'un très petit nombre d'unités.

Sur ces recueils collectifs, et notamment sur les cinq premiers
manuscrits cités qui représentent l'essentiel des manuscrits de
fabliaux, notre ignorance est grande. Il manque toujours des
études systématiques sur la formation de ces collections (à
l'exception du ms. *B*, dont on trouvera une étude détaillée par
Jean Rychner aux pp. 187–218 de ce volume), sur les habitudes
des copistes et des remanieurs. Les éditeurs de textes seraient
heureux de connaître les types de fautes ou d'innovations, la
nature et l'étendue des réfections, la part faite aux abréviations
et aux amplifications, les défaillances dues à la transmission orale,
à l'inattention, au respect scrupuleux d'un mauvais modèle, à la
fantaisie du copiste qui arrange et déforme à son gré. Des infor-
mations sur les habitudes graphiques des différents scribes
seraient également précieuses et permettraient parfois d'inter-
préter justement des orthographes qui paraissent, à première vue,
singulières.[4] Malheureusement aucune étude d'ensemble (à
l'exception de celle de Jean Rychner sur *B* qui paraît dans ce
volume) n'a été consacrée à l'un ou l'autre de ces recueils pour
tenter de comprendre de l'intérieur la confection et la vie des

---

[4] Par exemple, la graphie *pooist* dans le fabliau des *Tresses* au vv. 6 et 92 de mon
édition ne doit pas être comprise comme un imparfait du subjonctif (il ne convient
pas de mettre un tréma, comme J. Rychner qui imprime *pooïst* dans *Contribution
a l'étude des fabliaux*, II *Textes* (Neuchâtel-Genève, 1960), pp. 136 et 138). Il s'agit
d'un imparfait de l'indicatif avec *s* 'inorganique'. La forme équivaut à *pooit*. Dans son
intéressante édition *Twelve Fabliaux from Ms. fr. 19152 of the Bibliothèque nationale*
(Manchester University Press, 1958), pp. 23 et 25, T. B. W. Reid avait bien inter-
prété cette graphie, sans lui consacrer de note.

textes. Chaque éditeur doit recommencer sur nouveaux frais l'examen des textes qui l'intéressent, sans pouvoir bénéficier, au préalable, d'une vision d'ensemble des manuscrits concernés. Il ne dispose, dans le cas le plus favorable, que des remarques éparses faites par d'autres éditeurs sur d'autres passages des manuscrits. La plupart du temps, il peut seulement constater que les éditeurs antérieurs ont préféré publier le texte du manuscrit *A*, et presque sans changements.

Un premier problème se pose: d'où vient, dans les éditions de fabliaux, cette prédominance du ms. *A* et comment l'expliquer? Plusieurs réponses doivent être apportées.

Il y a, d'abord, une raison de fait. Très souvent le ms. *A* est le seul à nous conserver les textes. Pour les fabliaux il nous donne une vingtaine d'*unica,* qui ne se retrouvent nulle part ailleurs. Ainsi le fabliau d'*Aloul,* les *Trois Bossus, Estormi,* le *Cuvier,* l'*Enfant qui fu remis au soleil,* etc. Les éditeurs étaient obligés en pareil cas de publier le manuscrit unique. Ils ont eu tendance à ne pas changer de manuscrit lorsqu'un texte était conservé par d'autres copies. Une fois que les habitudes sont prises, il est difficile d'innover. Les premiers éditeurs de contes plaisants, Méon et Jubinal, qui ne se piquaient pas de comparer systématiquement les manuscrits et qui se contentaient de transcrire un manuscrit compréhensible, ont commencé par imprimer assez souvent le ms. *A.* Montaiglon et Raynaud, dans leur *Recueil général des fabliaux,* ont publié constamment ce manuscrit. Tout au long des six volumes de leur ouvrage, pour les 40 fabliaux conservés dans plusieurs manuscrits, ils ont donné 38 fois la préférence au ms. *A.* Deux fois seulement, pour le *Mantel mautaillé,* qui n'est, d'ailleurs, pas un fabliau, et pour la *Vieille Truande,* ils font exception à cette règle.[5] Partout ailleurs, qu'il s'agisse des *Trois Aveugles de Compiègne* ou du *Boucher d'Abbeville,* d'*Auberée* ou du *Vilain Mire,* de *Constant du Hamel* ou de *Boivin de Provins,* quels que soient les manuscrits concurrents, ils font toujours le même choix et n'ont cure des mss. *B, C* ou *D.* Ils publient le ms. 837.

Les premiers éditeurs ne nous ont pas donné les raisons de leur choix. Mais on peut les deviner sans peine. Il faut invoquer,

---

[5] Cf. *Recueil général des fabliaux,* III, 1 et 289, et V, 171 et 350.

peut-être, une cause matérielle: l'écriture du ms. 837 est claire, nette, facile à lire. D'un bout à l'autre des 362 folios, les caractères restent très réguliers. Il n'est pas nécessaire d'être un grand expert en paléographie pour lire cette petite écriture gothique, bien formée et soigneusement composée, des dernières années du XIIIe siècle. Les éditeurs de textes apprécient toujours les écritures claires et nettes. Ils ont horreur de peiner sur des caractères écrasés, hérissés, difficiles à déchiffrer. L'écriture du ms. de Berlin, parfois celle de Berne ou du ms. 1593 de la BN, posent des problèmes d'interprétation. En vertu du principe de moindre effort, on comprend que les éditeurs de fabliaux aient été invinciblement attirés par le ms. *A*.

Il faut ajouter que le texte donné par le ms. 837 de la BN est presque toujours correct, élégant, et qu'il peut même paraître excellent si on le compare à ses concurrents. La qualité des autres manuscrits est inégale. Certains textes ont été très maltraités: des fautes graves les déparent. En revanche, le lecteur du ms. 837 avance sur une route dépourvue de fondrières. Si l'on va vite, sans se poser trop de questions, sans ratiociner ou ergoter, on n'est pas arrêté par de grosses difficultés. Point d'erreurs matérielles, de lacunes importantes, de termes obscurs. On glisse au fil de l'aventure, sans verser ou trébucher. La qualité incontestable de ce bon témoin a amené des érudits modernes à le prendre pour base de leur publication. Ainsi a fait G. Gougenheim pour les *Trois Aveugles de Compiègne,* Charles Rostaing pour *Constant du Hamel*, Hans H. Christmann pour *Auberée* et le *Vilain Mire*.[6] Mais les mérites du ms. *A* n'ont pas paru éclatants à tous les éditeurs. Certains se sont demandé si ce manuscrit ne nous donnait pas une version apparemment correcte, mais remaniée, révisée, revue, et donc infidèle. Dans son édition du *Chevalier au barisel*, F. Lecoy déclare: "*A* donne tout à fait l'impression d'une version qui a été soigneusement révisée (d'où sa relative correction), mais à travers laquelle on a sans doute moins de chance de retrouver ce qu'a pu être

---

[6] Cf. Cortebarbe, *Les Trois Aveugles de Compiègne* éd. G. Gougenheim (Paris, 1932), pp. xii–xvi; *Constant du Hamel* éd. C. Rostaing (Aix-en-Provence, 1953), pp. 6–42; *Zwei altfranzösische Fablels (Auberee, Du Vilain Mire)* hrsg. von H. H. Christmann (Tübingen, 1963), pp. 18–19.

l'original".[7] Dans sa publication du fabliau de *Constant du Hamel*, Ch. Rostaing a porté un jugement semblable. Il estime que le ms. *A* "n'est pas le texte original" et "qu'il n'est pas nécessairement le plus proche de cet original", mais ajoute-t-il, "il est de toute évidence le plus soigné, le plus poli".[8]

Plusieurs éditeurs n'ont pas donné la prédominance au ms. *A*. Dans son édition des fabliaux de Jean Bodel, Pierre Nardin a préféré à deux reprises, pour *Gombert et les deux clercs* ainsi que pour *Barat et Haimet*, ne pas imprimer le texte de *A*.[9] L'intéressant recueil de *Fabliaux* 'selected and edited by R. C. Johnston and D. D. R. Owen' avait à choisir pour quatre textes entre le ms. *A* et un autre manuscrit: trois fois le ms. *A* a été écarté.[10] En 1961 Martha Walthers-Gehrig, publiant trois fabliaux, n'a retenu *A* qu'une seule fois.[11] Récemment Jean Rychner s'est livré à un examen approfondi de la tradition manuscrite du *Boucher d'Abbeville* et a conclu que le meilleur manuscrit n'était pas *A*.[12] Dans l'édition de *Fabliaux* que j'ai donnée en 1979, *A* entrait en concurrence avec d'autres manuscrits à quatre reprises. Pour la *Bourgeoise d'Orléans*, où la version du ms. *B* était à exclure en raison de ses erreurs grossières, les mss. *A* et *C* pouvaient être édités avec des corrections. Mais *C* offrant quelques passages difficiles ou impossibles à amender, il convenait de publier le ms. *A*, dont les défaillances ou réfections étaient presque toujours amendables. En ce qui concerne *Boivin de Provins*, les lacunes et fautes du ms. *P* obligeaient sans conteste l'éditeur à retenir le texte de *A*, bien que ce manuscrit commette des remaniements parfois fautifs. Le fabliau du *Vilain Mire* montre que la version *A* présente beaucoup d'innovations individuelles qui s'éloignent de l'original, alors que les mss. *B* et *C*, malgré leurs erreurs, restent plus proches de la version primi-

---

[7] F. Lecoy, *Le Chevalier au barisel* (Paris, 1955), p. xi.
[8] *Op. cit.*, p. 42.
[9] Jean Bodel, *Fabliaux* éd. P. Nardin (Paris, 1965), p. 46—47 et 50—56.
[10] *Fabliaux* ed. R. C. Johnston and D. D. R. Owen (Oxford, 1957), p. 87 (pour *Estula*), p. 102 (pour le *Vilain Mire*), p. 104 (pour *Saint Pierre et le Jongleur*).
[11] *Trois fabliaux* (*Saint Pierre et le Jongleur, De Haimet et de Barat et Travers, Estula*) éd. M. Walters-Gehrig (Tübingen, 1961), pp. 4—6 (pour le premier de ces textes).
[12] Eustache d'Amiens, *Du Bouchier d'Abevile* éd. J. Rychner (Genève, 1975), pp. 10—18.

tive. Le ms. *C* commettant davantage de fautes, dont certaines
sont malaisées à corriger, il a été décidé d'imprimer la rédaction
de *B*, malgré la lacune qui l'entache, car on peut la combler à
l'aide d'un autre manuscrit. Enfin, dans les *Trois Aveugles de
Compiègne*, si le texte de *A* est de loin le plus correct, la rédaction des mss. *E* et *F* paraît plus d'une fois proche de l'original.
Malheureusement de nombreuses petites inexactitudes, des omissions, des fautes de métrique déparent ces deux manuscrits. Il a
fallu se résigner à éditer le ms. *A*, mais en corrigeant les principales erreurs dont il s'est rendu coupable.[13]

Quoi qu'en aient pensé les premiers éditeurs de fabliaux, le
ms. *A* est loin d'être parfait et, à vrai dire, il n'y a pas de manuscrits de fabliaux exempts d'erreurs. Même le ms. *A*, apparemment correct et limpide, ne peut être publié sans corrections.
On peut en apporter diverses preuves et essayer de dégager des
types de fautes.

Il y a, d'abord, des erreurs qui semblent dues à une mauvaise
audition. Dans *Boivin de Provins*, l'héroïne, Mabile, déclare à
Boivin que sa compagne Ysane a été enlevée à sa famille lors
d'un rapt et qu'elle est vierge. Ces paroles sont tenues dans une
maison de prostitution et cherchent à duper Boivin. Mabile se
présente comme l'auteur du rapt. La rédaction du ms. *P* dit:

Lasse! J'en avré grant pechié:
a ces amis la fortrei gié!

Au même endroit, le ms. *A*, qui n'a pas entendu qu'il s'agissait
du verbe *fortraire*, donne un texte erroné:

Oncles, je ai mout fort pechié,
qu'a ses parenz l'ai fort trechié (253—54).

Le verbe *trechier* n'est pas à sa place ici et ne veut rien dire. Le
mot *trichier, trechier* 'tromper, duper' ne convient pas, comme
le montre l'article de l'*Altfranzösisches Wörterbuch* de Tobler-
Lommatzsch (X, 650—51). Nous avons affaire, manifestement,
à une faute de transmission orale. Le copiste n'a pas bien entendu
le mot prononcé, soit que l'erreur se passe dans un atelier de
copiste, soit que la faute remonte plus haut, au moment où le
remanieur a entendu raconter l'histoire lors d'une séance de
récitation publique.

[13] *Fabliaux français du Moyen Age* éd. Ph. Ménard (Genève, 1979), pp. 130—
31, 140, 151—52, 160—61.

On observera, au passage, que la correction effectuée dans mon édition, *l'ai fortrait gié* (v. 252), suit peut-être trop fidèlement le texte du ms. *A*. Compte tenu du fait que normalement le pronom sujet se postpose après l'auxiliaire *avoir* dans les temps composés (par exemple "Voire, fait il, feru t'ai gié" dans le *Perceval* de Chrétien de Troyes, éd. W. Roach, v. 7031) et qu'on attendrait donc ici *fortrait l'ai gié*, il est vraisemblable que la forme composée est également fautive dans le ms. *A* et qu'il conviendrait de corriger en transformant le passé composé en passé simple: *la fortrais gié*. On retrouverait, ce faisant, la leçon du ms. *E*.

Une faute de même nature, mais sans déformation du mot, apparaît dans les *Trois Aveugles de Compiègne* lorsque le clerc voit venir à sa rencontre le groupe des trois aveugles sans conducteur. Le ms. *A* nous dit alors:

si vit que nus ne les menoit;
si pensse que aucuns n'en voie:
comment alaissent il la voie?
Puis dist: 'El cors me fiere goute,
se je ne sai s'il voient goute!' (28–32)

Le texte semble dire que le clerc croit à la cécité des trois aveugles et se demande comment ils peuvent alors cheminer, sans personne pour les aider. En fait, la négation est de trop au vers 29. Les autres mss. nous disent "si pense que aucuns en voie" ('il pense que l'un d'entre eux doit y voir'). Le vers suivant apporte la confirmation: 'Autrement, comment pourraient-ils avancer?'. Georges Gougenheim, généralement mieux avisé, a eu tort d'imprimer le texte de *A* avec un respect aveugle et de publier, ce faisant, une leçon fâcheuse.[14] Ici encore une mauvaise audition du copiste doit être la cause de l'erreur.

Apparaissent aussi dans le même manuscrit des fautes de lecture manifestes. Parfois elles ne sont pas visibles au premier aspect. L'ensemble paraît correct. Mais elles se révèlent dès que l'on compare la version du ms. *A* avec celle des autres mss. Ainsi, dans le fabliau du *Vilain Mire*, le paysan réfléchit à sa situation et décide de frapper sa femme tous les matins afin qu'elle soit en larmes pendant toute la journée: une femme qui

[14] *Op. cit.*, p. 2, v. 29.

pleure, pense-t-il, ne sera pas l'objet des sollicitations amoureuses des galants. Le ms. *A* nous dit:

> Bien sai, tant comme ele plorroit,
> que nus ne la desvoieroit.

Le verbe *desvoier* 'écarter du droit chemin' n'est pas impossible, même s'il surprend un peu. Mais les mss. *B* et *C* ont un texte bien préférable: B parle de *donoier* et dit "que nus ne la donoieroit" (v. 59 de mon éd.). Ce mot *donoier*, classique dans le vocabulaire de la galanterie et de la séduction médiévales, est attesté également par le ms. *C*: il est tout à fait à sa place ici. Sans doute, le copiste de *A* a mal lu, a pris le *n* pour un *v* et a inventé la forme *desvoieroit*.

Les réfections et remaniements de *A* sont nombreux et généralement masqués. Les premiers vers du *Vilain Mire* n'ont rien de scandaleux dans la version donnée par *A*:

> Jadis estoit uns vilains riches,
> qui mout estoit avers et chiches.
> Une charrue adés avoit:
> toz tens par lui la maintenoit
> d'une jument et d'un roncin.
> Assez ot char et pain et vin
> et quanques mestier li estoit. (1—8)

Mais si l'on regarde les mss. *B* et *C*, on découvre que le copiste-remanieur de *A* a procédé à beaucoup de *rifacimenti* et a dégradé le texte. Le ms. *B*, presque toujours suivi par le ms. *C*, donne le texte suivant:

> Jadis ert uns vilains mout riches,
> qui trop avoit, mes mout fu chiches.
> .ii. charrues ot et .viii. bues,
> qui totes erent a son hues,
> et .ii. jumenz et .ii. roncins.
> Assez ot char et blez et vins
> et quanque mestier li estoit. (1—8)

Le style de cette rédaction est meilleur: plus de répétition fâcheuse de *estoit*. Les deux charrues et les huit boeufs mentionnés, voilà de vrais signes extérieurs de richesse. Nous savons par d'autres témoignages que normalement la charrue avait un attelage de quatre boeufs. Un intéressant article de Claude Régnier l'a rappelé à propos d'un passage d'*Aucassin et*

Nicolette.[15] Au XIIIe siècle on commence de temps en temps à attacher des chevaux aux charrues, mais ici la présence d'une *jument* et d'un *roncin* est plus que surprenante. Ce ne sont pas des animaux de trait. Ces bêtes de somme ne sont guère à leur place si l'on suit la version du ms. *A*. Et l'on peut plaindre un historien des techniques, qui, à la lecture de la version du ms. *A*, souvent imprimée, irait bâtir toute une théorie sur l'attelage du XIIIe siècle! Les mss. *B* et *C* distinguent avec soin les paires de boeufs servant à tirer la charrue et les bêtes de somme. Quand on examine les dictionnaires, on observe qu'il n'est presque jamais fait mention du *roncin* comme d'un animal de trait. Le long article du Tobler-Lommatzsch n'en cite qu'un seul exemple: dans le *Moniage Guillaume* (3689). Partout ailleurs on voit le roncin destiné à porter des paquets ou à transporter des serviteurs (Tobler-Lommatzsch, VIII, 1453—56). On peut penser que le copiste de *A* n'a pas bien compris le sens du mot rare et archaïque *a son hues* et qu'il a été contraint dès lors à faire disparaître la rime précédente où il était question des *bues*. Tout le passage en a été modifié. L'explication présentée pour comprendre ce remaniement est confirmée un peu plus loin lorsque le texte emploie à nouveau la même expression *a ues*. Laissons ici la parole au ms. *B*:

    Li ami au vilain parlerent
    et au chevalier demanderent
    sa fille a oes lou païsant. (19—21)

A nouveau le ms. *A* ne conserve pas l'expression originale et use d'un substitut en écrivant *sa fille por le païsant*.

Bien souvent, dans le même texte le remanieur multiplie les leçons personnelles et les innovations. Quand une expression le gêne, il corrige hardiment. Pour ne prendre qu'un autre exemple, lorsque les messagers du roi demandent à l'épouse où ils pourront trouver son mari, les mss. *B* et *C* donnent un texte identique et disent:

    Dame, et o le troverons nos?
    — Vos lou verroiz tot a estros . . .

La tournure *a estros* 'aussitôt, tout de suite' n'a pas été comprise par le rédacteur du ms. *A*. Il modifie donc de fond en

---

[15] Cf. *Mélanges J. Frappier* (Genève, 1970), pp. 935—36.

comble les deux vers, en suivant sa fantaisie:

> Dame, ou le porrons nous trover?
> — Aus chans le porrez encontrer. . .

On pourrait allonger la liste des exemples. Au vers 30 de mon édition le ms. *B*, suivi d'ailleurs par le ms. *C*, évoque en ces termes le rapide mariage du héros:

> Et li vilains, a l'ainz qu'il pot,
>   fist ses noces et esposa. . .

L'expression *a l'ainz qu'il pot* n'a pas plu à notre perpétuel remanieur. Il écrit, à la place, "plus tost qu'il pot". C'est ainsi que disparaissent dans les textes les archaïsmes, que surgissent les modernismes, que fourmillent les leçons isolées!

Quand nous ne disposons que d'un manuscrit unique, nous ne pouvons pas voir la plupart de ces réfections. Mais lorsque la comparaison est possible avec un autre témoin, la lumière se fait. On pourrait dire aussi que divers signes trahissent le remaniement.

Les vers faux et les rimes inexactes en premier lieu. Le copiste-remanieur du ms. 837 a assez d'oreille et ne commet presque jamais de vers faux. Mais de temps en temps il ne se prive pas d'une rime approximative ou inexacte. Ainsi dans le fabliau du *Vilain Mire* la rime *feste: estre* du ms. *A* est un indice de réfection. Après la guérison de la fille du roi, une masse de malades se précipite à la cour. Les mss. *B* et *C* nous apprennent qu'ils y arrivent tous ensemble. Ensuite le ms. *B* déclare:

> Chascuns dist au vilain son estre.
> Li rois dist au vilain: 'Bel mestre,
> de ceste gent prenez conroi. . .' (299—301)

Le ms. *C* est un peu différent, et conserve à mon sens la leçon originale, mais il s'accorde parfaitement avec *B* pour la nature des rimes. Pour le rédacteur de *C*, les malades s'adressent d'abord au roi:

> Chascun li a conté son estre.
> Li rois a dit au vilain: 'Mestre,
> de ceste gent prenez conroi. . .'

Le ms. *A*, ayant commencé par supprimer le couple de rimes *semble: ensemble* et par modifier profondément les quatre vers précédents, n'a pu retrouver les rimes de la version primitive. Il a donc inventé, tant bien que mal:

Vindrent au roi a cele feste.
Chascuns li a conté son estre.
Li rois le vilain apela:
'Mestre, dist il, entendez ça!
De ceste gent prenez conroi. . .'

Dans la situation, le mot *feste* est particulièrement impropre. L'ensemble sent le délayage. La mauvaise rime trahit que l'on est en présence d'un passage refait.

Des rimes identiques révèlent souvent un méchant *rifacimento*. Ainsi à la fin de la *Bourgeoise d'Orléans*, le mari, roué de coups, finit par se lever et rejoindre ses gens. Le ms. *A* dit alors:

Enquis li ont comment ce vait.
'Malement, ce dist il, me vait.' (219–220)

On peut s'étonner de cette paire de rimes où revient le même verbe, avec exactement le même sens. Sans que nous ayons ici une preuve absolue, nous pouvons éprouver quelques soupçons. Le passage parallèle du ms. *C* confirme cette impression et suggère que les rimes de *A* ne remontent pas à l'original. En effet, le ms. *C* dit à cet endroit:

Demandent li comment li va.
'Mauvesement, fet il, m'esta.' (279–80 de *C*).

Le couplet de *C* est bien meilleur et a chance d'être la leçon authentique.

Les séries de quatre vers sur une même rime constituent un autre indice de remaniement. L'auteur du fabliau de la *Bourgeoise d'Orléans* nous peint au début du texte quatre *escoliers* qui arrivent, gros et gras, dans la cité d'Orléans pour y poursuivre, semble-t-il, leurs études. Le ms. *B* les représente ainsi:

cortois, chantant et envoisiez
et en la vile bien prisiez
o il avoient ostel pris.
Un en i ot de graignor pris
qui mout enta chiers un borjois,
sel tenoit an a mout cortois.
Et la dame meïsmesmant
prisoit mout son acoitemant. (15–22 de *B*)

Pour l'essentiel le ms. *C* donne la même version, avec quelques petites retouches et variantes personnelles. Le ms. *A* bouleverse profondément le texte. Il commence par faire disparaître le

vers *cortois, chantant et envoisiez*. Aussi modifie-t-il fatalement
la suite. Une réfection est rarement isolée. Elle entraîne souvent
tout une série de conséquences. On le voit bien ici dans la
version du ms. *A* :

> En la vile erent mout proisié, ·
> ou il estoient herbregié.
> Un en i ot de grant ponois,
> qui mout hantoit chiés un borgois;
> sel tenoit on mout a cortois,
> n'ert plains d'orgueil ne de bufois.
> Et a la dame vraiement
> plesoit mout son acointement.

Sans doute, l'apparence extérieure du passage est plus soignée
que dans le ms. *B*. Plus de *r* superflu à la préposition *chiés,* plus
de nasale faisant défaut dans la seconde syllabe d'*acointement*.
Mais le fond du texte a été profondément modifié. Le second
vers est une invention du remanieur. Les deux vers rimant en
-ois dans les mss. *B* et *C* ont été ici gravement touchés. Ils ont
été tellement tranformés qu'au lieu de trouver un couple de
rimes en *-ois,* comme il est normal, nous sommes en présence
de quatre vers sur la même rime. Signe patent de bouleverse-
ment et de déformation. Une autre preuve de la fâcheuse intervention du remanieur, c'est le mot *ponois*. Le terme ne se rencontre pas ailleurs dans les textes. Le dictionnaire de Tobler-
Lommatzsch le traduit 'Ubermut' (VII, 1637), comme s'il
s'agissait du mot parallèle *posnoi, podnoi,* rarement employé
et désignant l'outrecuidance, la prétention, la bravade. Mais
le contexte indique bien que cette acception ne convient guère
ici. Godefroy avait traduit 'puissance, haute position' (VI, 329).
En fait, nous avons affaire ici à un mot inventé, employé au
hasard, au petit bonheur la chance par un remanieur qui ne
songe qu'à boucher un trou et obtenir rapidement une rime. Le
contexte suggère que le rédacteur donnait sans doute au terme
le sens de 'valeur' ou 'importance'. Mais compte tenu du fait
que nous nous trouvons ici dans un passage déformé et remanié
sans vergogne, il est vain de chercher à préciser l'acception
exacte de ce vocable. Le remanieur se contente d'approxima-
tions. Faute de dictionnaires, il était d'ailleurs bien en peine
pour vérifier si le mot existait et si son sens s'accordait au passage.

Par la force des choses le rédacteur ne pouvait se fier qu'à son goût, qu'à son sens de la langue. Il vivait, à nos yeux, dans le flou et l'imprécis. Nul hasard si parfois il inventait à tort ou s'il se trompait. Un mot qui sémantiquement fait problème, qui détonne dans un ensemble, qui ne paraît pas à sa place ne doit pas être conservé avec un respect religieux, comme s'il s'agissait toujours d'une relique philologique, d'un précieux vestige, échappé aux désastres et aux ruines du temps. Il peut s'agir tout simplement d'un terme inventé ou employé maladroitement pour les besoins du mètre ou de la rime par un remanieur hâtif et peu scrupuleux.

Parfois les faits inquiétants s'additionnent et les soupçons de déformation fautive se renforcent. Une rime isolée est déjà un signe d'altération: le rédacteur a oublié la rime jumelle. Trois vers sur la même rime font également mauvaise impression. Lorsqu'on rencontre à la fois une rime en l'air et un mot qui ne convient guère en fin de vers, on peut être assuré que l'on se trouve en présence d'une faute manifeste. Il en va ainsi dans la version *B* de la *Bourgeoise d'Orléans* qui évoque en ces termes les illusions du mari:

> Hai, Deus! Com il savoit petit
> que la dame panse et muse,
> quar li uns d'aus panse une chose
> et li autres panse tot el. (104—7 de *B*)

Les perturbations apportées au texte original sont ici considérables puisque les mots *muse* et *chose* forment deux fins de vers aberrantes. Le mot *muse* ne convient pas pour le sens. La lecture du ms. *C* nous donne l'explication de cette bizarrerie. Le texte y est le suivant:

> Dieus, com cil savoit or petit
> ce que sa fame li porpose,
> que li uns pensoit une chose
> et li autres penssoit tot el. (136—39 de *C*)

Ici le ms. *A* donne un texte plus joli, qui semble une habile trouvaille du remanieur, car tous les rédacteurs n'étaient pas dénués de goût:

> Diex! Comme il savoit or petit
> de ce qu'ele pensse et porpensse!
> Li asniers une chose pensse,

et li asnes pensse tout el! (103—5 de mon éd.)

Un autre indice de remaniement sur lequel on n'a pas attiré
l'attention jusqu'ici me paraît un emploi incertain des temps
verbaux. On en voit quelques exemples de loin en loin. Ainsi
dans un passage du *Vilain Mire* propre au ms. *A*, qui décrit
l'arrivée des messagers du roi et de leur prisonnier à la cour
d'Angleterre. Cette addition se situe aussitôt après le vers 184
de mon édition. Le texte de *A* est le suivant:

Il li ont fet honte a plenté
et puis si l'ont au roi mené;
si le montent a reculons,
la teste devers les talons.
Li rois les avoit encontré,
si lor dist: 'Avez rien trové?
— Sire, oïl' distrent il ensanble. (193—99 de *A*)

Dans cette évocation originale, plusieurs vers sont amusants et
bien troussés. Mais on peut estimer qu'au vers 197, dans la
principale *Li rois les avoit encontré*, le plus-que-parfait n'est
guère à sa place. On ne s'attend pas à rencontrer ici un temps
qui marque l'accompli de manière durative. Mais il faut peut-
être se montrer prudent dans l'appréciation de la valeur du
plus-que-parfait. Il pourrait suggérer par parataxe l'antériorité
d'un événement ponctuel par rapport à la proposition qui suit
et qui donne les paroles du roi. En français moderne on parle
de l'emploi du plus-que-parfait comme 'fond de décor'.[16] On
pourrait soutenir aussi qu'une certaine valeur durative est
sensible dans la rencontre. Laissons les grammairiens disputer
du sens exact de cet emploi ici. *Grammatici certant*. N'oublions
pas que parfois dans l'ancienne langue un certain flou semble
apparaître dans l'usage des temps. On trouve parfois des imparfaits ou des plus-que-parfaits qui surprennent ou encore des
plus-que-parfaits coordonnés curieusement à des passés ponc-
tuels.[17]

---

[16] P. Imbs, *L'emploi des temps verbaux en français moderne* (Paris, 1960), p.
124.

[17] Voici quelques exemples de plus-que-parfaits: *Sis sires l'aveit esguardee,/Mut
durement l'en ad blasmee* (Marie de France, *Fresne* 43—44); *Quant il li aveit tut
cunté,/Enquis li ad e demaundé/S'il se despuille u vet vestuz* (Marie de France,
Bisclavret 67—69). J. Rychner a rassemblé un certain nombre d'emplois, qui lui

Contentons-nous ici de signaler quelques emplois qui suggèrent plus nettement une maladresse du rédacteur, un remaniement vite baclé. Il ne s'agit plus ici du ms. *A*. Dans le fabliau du *Meunier et les deux clercs*, un des deux clercs conseille à son compagnon d'acheter ensemble, en empruntant, un setier de blé. Ensuite l'autre répond. Le ms. *B* dit très normalement "Li autres a lors respondu" (v. 43 de mon édition). Au même endroit, le ms. *C* utilise un plus-que-parfait assez singulier "Enroment l'avoit respondu" (v. 35 de *C*). On serait tenté de juger défavorablement le remanieur du ms. *C* et de dire qu'il emploie à tort un plus-que-parfait, sans se soucier de la cohérence du récit. La comparaison systématique que l'on peut faire entre le rédacteur du ms. *B* et celui du ms. *C* ne plaide pas en faveur de ce dernier, qui multiplie joyeusement les contresens et les non-sens. Celui qui commet fréquemment d'énormes fautes n'est pas à un faux temps près! A la fin du même texte, dans un passage propre au ms. *B* et qui semble une addition maladroite, on rencontre également un curieux plus-que-parfait. Un des clercs sort de la huche au matin, quand il entend le coc chanter, se dirige vers son lit et finit par aboutir au lit du meunier:

A l'autre lit o se gisoit
li muniers, s'an va cil tot droit.
Dejoste li s'estoit cochiez:
ne s'est pas encor esveilliez
ne ne s'est mie aparceüz. (267—71 de mon éd.)

Dans ces vers 269—271, manifestement inventés par le rédacteur de la version *B* et qui n'ont pas dû lui coûter beaucoup de peine et de soin, il pourrait y avoir encore un emploi approximatif du plus-que-parfait. Le remanieur peut utiliser des formules dont il se souvient, même si elles ne conviennent pas très bien à la scène. Il n'est pas exclu également que pour obtenir huit syllabes il

---

semblent curieux, dans son édition des *Lais* de Marie de France (Paris, 1966; p. 246 en note au vers 739 de *Guigemar*). Il s'est demandé si ce n'était pas là un fait de syntaxe anglo-normand. Je crois qu'on peut répondre par la négative d'une part, et d'autre part qu'une grande partie de ces exemples peut s'expliquer: on retrouverait ailleurs des phénomènes semblables, y compris en français moderne. Comme exemple de plus-que-parfait coordonné à un passé antérieur on peut citer *Ipomedon* (éd. Holden, 359—60): *Kant du tout atorné se fu/E enveiseement iert vestu,/Sor un bel palefrai monta.*

emploie sans scrupule des formes verbales impropres. On se contentera ici de poser le problème. A la rigueur on pourrait justifier le plus-que-parfait comme indication vague du fond de décor par opposition aux verbes qui suivent et qui concernent le meunier toujours endormi. On se souviendra seulement que dans le domaine syntaxique, aussi bien que dans le domaine métrique, où c'est plus visible, des fautes peuvent être commises par des remanieurs pressés. Aucun aspect de la langue n'échappe à l'erreur: le système morphologique ou sémantique peut être violé de semblable façon. Il est souvent difficile aux critiques modernes de déceler certaines de ces fautes. Mais dans quelques cas privilégiés elles apparaissent clairement.

Que conclure? Le ms. 837 qui passe pour le meilleur recueil de fabliaux n'est pas exempt de défaillances. Sous une correction apparente, on relève bien des innovations, des retouches, des remaniements, parfois des déformations fâcheuses et des fautes patentes. Le nombre et l'importance de ces transformations varient selon les textes. Pour le ms. *A* comme pour les autres mss. de fabliaux on ne saurait dire que telle copie est continûment bonne ou mauvaise. Cela varie, semble-t-il, selon les histoires. Tout se passe, dirait-on, comme si le même manuscrit avait eu des modèles de qualité différente. On a l'impression aussi que le copiste est tantôt fidèle, tantôt inventif. Des appréciations nuancées ne pourront être portées qu'après des investigations très larges, qui manquent encore. Des manuscrits comme *B* et *C* sont tantôt très mauvais et tantôt joliment conservateurs. Jean Rychner estimait avec beaucoup de perspicacité que le ms. *B* mérite parfois confiance: "J'ai l'impression avec *B* d'un provincial un peu rustique, un peu fruste, mais qui se donne pour ce qu'il est, et plus honnête, peut-être, que le trop policé A".[18] En fait, pour des mss. comme *B* ou *C* la valeur de la rédaction varie selon les fabliaux. Dans la *Bourgeoise d'Orléans*, alors que le ms. *B* est impubliable en raison des grosses fautes qu'il commet à foison (vers déplacés, rimes massacrées, passages incompréhensibles, vers trop longs ou trop courts, lacunes), le ms. *C*, malgré quelques petites défaillances, n'est pas sans intérêt. En revanche, pour le *Meunier et les deux clercs* c'est l'inverse: le

[18] *Contribution à l'étude des fabliaux*, I *Observations* (Genève, 1960), p. 139.

ms. de Berlin nous donne un texte dégradé avec des rimes isolées, des rimes répétées, des vers repris de loin en loin, bref tout un ensemble d'altérations. Pour porter un jugement équitable sur les divers manuscrits de fabliaux, il faudrait pouvoir disposer de comparaisons d'ensemble. Au vu des textes examinés, il semble que le ms. *A* soit plus régulier. D'autre part, le responsable de cette rédaction évite les fautes grossières, si désagréables pour les éditeurs modernes, comme les rimes perturbées, les graves lacunes, les passages incompréhensibles. Les fautes qu'il commet, les déformations qu'il apporte au texte original n'en sont peut-être que plus dangereuses, car on a affaire à un habile homme qui prend des libertés avec son modèle, mais en se gardant des vers faux et des rimes trop inexactes. Mieux vaut un brave copiste borné et fidèle à un remanieur trop intelligent! Quand des témoins nous permettent de contrôler la version du ms. 837, on découvre qu'il ne faut pas toujours lui faire crédit. De temps en temps il abuse, il trompe, il donne le change.

Si le recueil le plus complet et le meilleur s'avère insuffisant, faut-il croire que tout moyen nous échappe pour retrouver le texte authentique des fabliaux? L'attitude exagérément conservatrice de Mario Roques et de ses disciples se fondait sur l'idée (illusoire) qu'il suffisait de publier un bon manuscrit avec le moins de corrections possibles. Mais il n'y a pas de manuscrit exempt d'erreurs et d'innovations. Le concept de 'bon manuscrit' est lui-même ambigu. Sans doute on peut appeler bon manuscrit une copie qui commet peu de fautes et demande peu de corrections. Mieux vaudrait dire en pareil cas qu'on se trouve devant un manuscrit correct et coulant. Le terme de bon manuscrit devrait être réservé aux copies à la fois satisfaisantes et fidèles. Comme le rappelait justement Alphonse Dain, le bon manuscrit est celui qui conserve les fautes sans les corriger et qui permet ainsi de remonter à l'état primaire des altérations et de retrouver le texte original.

Lorsque plusieurs manuscrits du même texte ont été conservés, il est vrai que la brièveté des fabliaux, la rareté des fautes communes (seul critère de classement indiscutable), la difficulté ou l'impossibilité de reconstituer un stemma assuré en raison de la multiplicité des variantes individuelles gênent sensiblement l'édition critique. Le lecteur moderne trouve qu'il y a trop peu de témoins et trop de variations entre les manuscrits. Mais il serait exagéré de soutenir qu'il n'y a que des remaniements dans cette littérature. On rencontre de tout dans la tradition textuelle des contes à rire: aussi bien des variantes légères que des modifications profondes, aussi bien des passages parallèles que des innovations individuelles.

Suivre aveuglément le copiste reviendrait à imprimer des leçons aberrantes. Un respect superstitieux du manuscrit médiéval est peut-être une solution de facilité pour l'éditeur, mais c'est aussi une démission de l'esprit critique et une renonciation à tout effort. Inversement, croire qu'on peut retrouver facilement la version originale et qu'on doit corriger immanquablement toutes les leçons isolées du manuscrit retenu est une chimère. L'éditeur de fabliaux, et peut-être tout éditeur de textes médié- vaux, doit éviter à la fois le désenchantement d'un pessimisme excessif et les illusions d'un optimisme naïf. Lorsque les diver- gences sont grandes entre les manuscrits, il est vain de vouloir rétablir le texte original, mais il est permis de corriger si la copie éditée commet des erreurs manifestes. De temps en temps la comparaison des variantes donne l'assurance d'atteindre le texte premier. Parfois l'examen n'aboutit pas: tout est obscur, la version authentique est brouillée. Parfois des corrections s'imposent d'elles-mêmes. Souvent, l'éditeur doit prendre parti pour améliorer un texte défectueux. Mais il ne faut pas s'en étonner. Après tout, l'établissement d'un texte est aussi une affaire de goût. Si nous ne pouvons pas tout savoir, si nous ne pouvons pas toujours rétablir le texte original, nous ne sommes pas toujours plongés dans des ténèbres inextricables. Un peu de lumière éclaire notre route. Nous avons le pouvoir et le devoir d'amender en partie les textes. Refusant les audaces des éditeurs qui voudraient tout corriger et les timidités des érudits qui ne veulent rien modifier, une critique plus mesurée, mieux tempérée tenterait avec prudence d'opérer les rectifications indispensables là où c'est visible, là où c'est possible.

GLIMPSES INTO OUR IGNORANCE OF THE ANGLO-NORMAN LEXIS

W. ROTHWELL

"There are probably more Anglo-French nouns in the *Oxford English Dictionary* than in Godefroy". This arresting claim is made by J. H. Baker in his *Manual of Law French*[1] and will certainly be amply vindicated with an abundance of detailed examples when Professor J. P. Collas publishes his voluminous collection of Anglo-Norman terms culled from the *OED*. Moreover, if Baker's claim is valid in respect of Godefroy, who made a genuine and quite remarkable effort a hundred years ago to cover the whole range of medieval French vocabulary,[2] it must apply with far greater force to the new Tobler-Lommatzsch,[3] which sets out quite specifically to record only the vocabulary used in what might be called the broad literary register, and that only as far as about 1350.

In practice, however, the problem of uncovering and recording the whole lexis of Anglo-Norman is more complex than Baker perhaps realized. The difficulty is not only that Godefroy fails to list many of the terms found in Anglo-Norman, but also that many words which he does list, but for which he has only Continental attestations, were, in fact, current also in Insular French, although they have not so far been noted by lexicographers. The true extent of the gaps in our knowledge in this area is difficult to gauge with any accuracy, since we often become aware of the existence of potentially wide stretches of ignorance only when perhaps one small corner happens to be illuminated by some chance revelation, thus giving a hint of the surrounding darkness.

---

[1] (Avebury, 1979), p. 31.
[2] *Dictionnaire de l'ancienne langue française et de tous ses˙dialectes* (Paris, 1880–1902).
[3] *Altfranzösisches Wörterbuch* (Berlin 1925–).

A modest illustration of this double difficulty is provided by the will of a certain Sir Fouk de Penebrugg from Tong in Shropshire.[4] This will is dated 1325 and deals largely with bequests of various pieces of knightly equipment, a transaction involving items that must have been in the possession of many a knight before and since his time. Yet the mere twenty-eight lines of this quite unremarkable will contain no less than eleven terms that had either not been picked up for inclusion in the *Anglo-Norman Dictionary*, or else, although listed there, had been incorrectly glossed. These terms are as follows: *barhuide* ('barehide'), *colret* ('neck-piece'), *coters* ('short coat, jacket'), *esquinebaus* ('leg armour'), *glasuers* ('scale armour'), *gossetes* ('gussets'), *palet* ('head armour'), *picer* ('chest armour for horse'), *poleyns* ('knee-pieces'), *teister* ('head-stall'), *waynepayns* ('gauntlets'). The majority of these words may be found in Continental works quoted by Godefroy, but were hitherto unknown in Insular French. Their chance occurrence in this brief will thus shows how a specialized French vocabulary of armour continued to be current in knightly circles in England long after the loss of Normandy at the beginning of the thirteenth century.[5] In addition to this general point, however, two of the terms quoted here call for more detailed comment, since they present difficulties and raise important issues regarding the approach to Anglo-Norman lexicography.

The first of these words is *barhuide*. Although listed in the *Anglo-Norman Dictionary*, *barhude* is incorrectly glossed, the translation 'board' being unacceptable in the light of the new context given by Sir Fouk's will. The sentence which led to the adoption of the incorrect gloss is taken from *The Gild Merchant*,[6] in which are set out the regulations for traders in Reading market. These regulations stipulate that iron or steel may be sold only from a cart, from a hurdle or wattle frame or from a

---

[4] MS London BL Stowe CH 622. I am much indebted to Professor Peter Rickard for bringing this will to my notice and especially for his perceptive deciphering and interpreting of it.

[5] This must not be construed as lending support to the naive opinion that "most people, down to the very poorest, were bilingual"; M. D. Legge, *Anglo-Norman Literature and its Background* (Oxford, 1963), p. 4. We are dealing with knights and lawyers, not with vileins or serfs.

[6] Ed. C. Gross (Oxford, 1890).

barhude rigged up within the shafts of the cart:

Nul ferour estraunge ne vende en marché de Redyng feer ne acier fors dé limunns de sa charette ou sur claye ou sur barhude deyns lé limuns (II, 206).

The editor's suggestion of 'barrow' for *barhude* here was clearly inappropriate, so 'board' was adopted as fitting quite plausibly into the general sense of the context. It is hardly likely, however, that a board would figure amongst the possessions handed down by a knight to his heirs, so *barhuide* in Sir Fouk's will posed a problem. The standard dictionaries of Medieval French offer no solution to the difficulty, but the *Revised Medieval Latin Word-List*[7] records *barhudum* 'barehide, cart cover' as early as 1172. We are dealing, then, with an English word latinized early for use in Latin documents at a time when English was not considered to be a fitting vehicle for the compilation of records. The *MLWL* led naturally to the *Middle English Dictionary*,[8] where the first entry turned out to be in French and taken — embarassingly enough — from the *Rotuli Parliamentorum*.[9] This key text is included in the List of Texts used for the *AND*, so *barhude* ought to have been picked up in the normal way for inclusion in the dictionary. To sum up: Sir Fouk's will had brought to light quite by chance an English word recorded first in Medieval Latin, then, some two and a half centuries later, in Anglo-Norman, which had followed Latin in becoming a language of record, and finally, no earlier than the fifteenth century, in English itself. *Barhude* provides an object lesson for the medievalist in the danger of failing to bear in mind the constant interplay of all three languages — Latin, French and English — in Britain during the Middle Ages.[10]

If *barhude* shows that it is dangerous to concentrate exclusively on the dictionaries of Medieval French in the search for the meaning of words in Anglo-Norman, another of the terms in Sir Fouk's will — *esquinebaus* — illustrates the incompleteness of our present knowledge of the lexis of Medieval French

---

[7] Ed. R. E. Latham (London, 1965).
[8] Ed. Kurath and Kuhn (Michigan, 1956–).
[9] Record Commission (London, 1767–77).
[10] See Frankwalt Möhren, 'La Terminologie de l'Agriculture en anglo-normand' in *XIV Congresso de Linguistica e Filologia romanza, Atti IV* (Naples, 1975), pp. 143–57.

generally, both continental and insular. Sir Fouk's *esquinebaus* are the same as Godefroy's *esquembaux* (III, 557b):

Ocrea, heuse ou estivaux, ou esquembaux
pour chaucier les gembes

For Godefroy the word was a hapax, this sole example being taken from an undated Latin-French glossary originally quoted by Du Cange. Although both the Latin and the French indicate as clearly as could be wished that *esquembaux* are 'leggings', Godefroy insists on glossing the term as 'sorte de chaussure'. Yet this incorrect gloss is not the essential point at issue here; what is more important for our present purposes is that a term found apparently only once on the Continent and therefore suspect, perhaps, as being possibly an error or a corrupt form, is seen to exist also in Insular French. In the Du Cange quotation, *esquembaux* is one of the words used to translate the Latin *ocreas*, so it must have been readily understood by French speakers who needed to have the Latin explained through the medium of their native speech. Similarly, here in England, Sir Fouk's will makes no attempt to provide an explanation for *esquinebaus*, so it is to be assumed that on this side of the Channel too the word was quite comprehensible in knightly quarters. What evidence there is in this case points towards *esquembaux*/*esquinebaus*[11] being a well-known medieval word that has almost escaped being recorded because it happened not to be used in literary texts, the register of literature being the only one thoroughly explored so far by lexicographers. Since the first Anglo-Norman wills are supposed to date only from 1347,[12] the chance discovery of Sir Fouk's will of 1325 inevitably raises the question of how many more such documents are still gathering dust in the great collections of official papers in London and perhaps elsewhere, and, more pertinently, how many more terms of this kind they might reveal if ever they were to see the light of day.

---

[11] Whether *esquembaux* is the correct form or not in the Du Cange text cannot be determined without re-examining the original document, but the obvious etymological link with the German 'Schienbein' and the English 'shin' would favour *esquinebaus* as the genuine form.

[12] J. Vising, *Anglo-Norman Language and Literature* (London, 1923), p. 24.

This kind of problem is not confined to unpublished material like the little will just examined. The text of the *Rotuli Parliamentorum* has been in print for over two centuries, yet its vocabulary is still far from completely understood.[13] For example, in the third volume reference is made to a mysterious *fluues*, a plural form indicating some form of ship:

> galeys, fluues, lynes & autres niefs (p. 303)

T. B. W. Reid spotted that if the minims are read only slightly differently to read *flunes*, the word would then be close to Godefroy's *flouin, fluin* 'vaisseau léger' (IV, 29a). The misreading of minims in the *Rotuli Parliamentorum* is a constantly recurring phenomenon, so that no violence whatever is being done to the original language by reading *flunes*. Support for this reading is furnished by the *MLWL* under *flunea*, where the additional forms given — *flunus, flunis* — are clearly very close to *flunes*. Once again, it would seem, a term thought to exist only on the Continent is shown to be recorded in Insular French; what is more, Godefroy has no attestation of the word before 1552, whilst the *Rotuli Parliamentorum* text is well over a century earlier than that, and the Anglo-Latin forms in the *MLWL* go back to 1254. A Renaissance vessel is thus seen to be really a product of the thirteenth century at the very latest.

Wherever the researcher looks in Anglo-Norman outside the well-known register of imaginative literature, an abundance of terms will be found that are not adequately covered either by Godefroy or the *OED*. For instance, Salzman's *Documentary History of Building in England down to 1540* (Oxford, 1952) contains many terms that are not officially supposed to appear in French or English until much later; others that are completely unknown. In his Preface, the author writes: "I am concerned not with artistic deductions from existing buildings, but with contemporary evidence on the actual processes of building. The amount of such evidence is prodigious: on a conservative estimate I have examined some fifteen hundred manuscripts..." (p. v). Unfortunately, he was able to publish only a fraction of

[13] For an attempt to make this most important text more accessible, see 'The French Text of the *Rotuli Parliamentorum*: Some Corrections' in *Bulletin of the John Rylands University Library of Manchester*, LXV (1983), 230–58.

these, a wealth of terminology from the rest being referred to only in passing, without the help of surrounding context, so that the bulk of this work will have to be done again before all Salzman's material is fully utilizable for lexicographical purposes. Dipping at random, however, into this rich store-house of neglected research reveals that, for example, *jamb* was being used for 'door-jamb' by 1292 at Dover (p. 94); that blocks of stone called *gobets* were being imported from Normandy by 1290 (p. 135); that, although modern forms of 'ogive' are late, as early as the 1290s forms such as *oguis, ogeyus* point clearly to the use of the concept in what appears to be Anglo-Latin and Anglo-French disguise (p. 116); that *coperons* 'copings, cornices' were in frequent use from the mid-fourteenth century (p. 109; cf. *AND coperun*); that another form of coping — *chapement* — was found from 1252 (p. 109), etc. On occasion, Salzman has to admit defeat, as when dealing with the group *cerch, serch, seerch, serge*, etc., of which he writes: "Although the term was in use over a period of about 300 years, it does not seem to have been recorded anywhere, and I am unable to explain its significance" (p. 109). Until the hundreds of documents referred to by Salzman are subjected to systematic combing, our knowledge of the terminology of medieval architecture in this country will remain fragmentary and our dictionaries incomplete.[14]

Nor is this incompleteness confined to the domain of architecture. To take just a few examples from the world of trade: The *Oak Book of Southampton*[15] was compiled in about 1300, so that the vocabulary which it uses must have been current from at least the thirteenth century. In this work we find that a kind of leather called 'basan' — *bazan* in the Anglo-Norman — was being brought into Southampton at this time on a regular basis, with a fixed duty payable; the earliest date given by the current dictionaries for the English 'basan', however, is 1714. In the later *Port Books of Southampton*[16] mention is

---

[14] For further examples from Salzman and other texts, see 'Lexical Borrowing in a Medieval Context' in *Bulletin of the John Rylands University Library of Manchester,* LXIII (1980), 118—43.

[15] Ed. P. Studer (Southampton, 1910—11).

[16] Ed. P. Studer (Southampton, 1913).

made of the importation of *cereate* (p. 42); the *Port Books* date from 1427—30, but the term is known to the English authorities only from 1543. Similarly, 'fangot' is given by the *OED* as coming into English in 1673, although it occurs on p. 50 of the *Port Books* and so cannot be later than 1430. The blue dye-stuff 'litmus' occurs in the Anglo-Norman forms *lytemoise* and *lyke-mose* on the pages of the *Liber Albus*[17] of London, a fifteenth-century compilation of documents that go back in many cases to the thirteenth or fourteenth centuries. The dye was being regularly imported into London, if the mention of duty payable is anything to go by, long before the sixteenth century, the earliest date given by the *Oxford Dictionary of English Etymology*. Finally, 'veneer' is mentioned as being brought into Southampton before 1430 — *ij rolles de venere* on p. 32 of the *Port Books* — although the word is listed in the *ODEE* only from the seventeenth century. The incompleteness of our knowledge of the vocabulary of English is attributable in large measure to our lack of knowledge of its Anglo-Norman component and to the arbitrary separation of the three languages that were so interwoven in England from the Norman Conquest onwards.

Any attempt by an outsider unversed in the language of English law to handle its many mysteries would be a hazardous undertaking, especially in advance of the appearance of Professor Collas's material referred to earlier, but perhaps one single reference may suffice to show that our knowledge is not complete in this sphere either. In a recent article in *The Law Quarterly Review*,[18] J. H. Baker tackles the puzzle of the medieval *pecunes*. He writes as follows: "It must be one of the most mysterious words lurking in those arcane volumes [*sc.* the *Year Books*], since it has almost entirely escaped the notice of philologists and lexicographers and has no recorded meaning or etymology" (p. 204). The *pecunes, pekenes* or *pekynnes* would appear to be — like *le cribbe* or *la crubbe* — 'some kind of enclosure at the side of the court where the apprentices stood to learn the law' (p. 206). Baker has posed the problem of etymology and origin, but who will solve it?

[17] Ed. H. T. Riley (Rolls Series, 1859—62).
[18] XCVIII (1980), 204—8.

Even on the fringes of the literary register, traces of our present lack of knowledge are not difficult to find. From the evidence of Bibbesworth's *Tretiz*,[19] it would appear likely that, by the middle of the thirteenth century, the English were eating haggis, crackling and suet, although this would not be the impression given by the current English dictionaries. For instance, in v. 1030 the pot-boy is told to take the haggis out of the pot with his hook:

Va t'en [*ed*. tue], quistroun, ou toun havez,
Estrere le hagis del postnez.

The editor's gloss *hachis* for *hagis* here will not stand, since minced meat cannot be lifted with a hook. Unless we are to cling blindly to the total separation of English and French in medieval England, it will have to be admitted that the *ODEE* is well wide of the mark in giving the fifteenth century for the introduction of 'haggis' into English. Again, at the end of his work Bibbesworth gives the vocabulary necessary for a feast. After mentioning the abundance of red and white wine, he goes on:

Puis tout autre foysen de rosté.
Checun de eus autre en cousté [*ed*. encousté],
Feyzauns, asciez e pardiz,
Grives, alawes e plovers rostiz,
Braoun, crispes e fruture (vv. 1121–25)

The editor's gloss 'fruitage' for *fruture* may be dismissed out of hand; even if it ever existed as a genuine French word, it would have to mean something like 'fruits', whilst *fruture* is in fact a form of *friture* 'pancake', as given in other manuscripts of the text and also in the derivative work *Femina*.[20] This means that there are two terms for 'pancake' in the same line — *crispes* and *fruture* — or else that *crispes* is the last in the succession of roast meat dishes, with *fruture* being the accompanying pancakes. If this is the correct interpretation, then *crispes* would mean 'crackling' and antedate the first official attestation in English by centuries. Finally, until Gille-

---

[19] Ed. A. Owen (Paris, 1929).
[20] Ed. W. A. Wright (London, 1909), p. 82, line 21.

land's little article in *ZfSL* recently,[21] the presence of 'suet' in Bibbesworth had passed unnoticed. Not that Gilleland quotes Bibbesworth, but simply that her perceptiveness in recognizing the true meaning of *siuet* in a cosmetic recipe roughly contemporaneous with Bibbesworth made it not too difficult to make sense of the puzzling line 703:

Du sueth l'em fet sueaus ('From fat one makes suet')

The Middle English gloss *heltre* over *sueth* has long been instrumental in making scholars attempt to base the sense of this line on the elder-tree — without much success.[22]

Again on the fringes of the literary register are the recently published records of the York Plays,[23] where we find a mixture of French and Latin setting down the activities of the medieval craft guild. There is not a great deal of French in these records, but sufficient to fill a linguistic gap in the history of our English 'pageant'. The *OED* and *ODEE* mention forms in Latin and English in their treatment of this word — *pagina* and *pagyn* — but none in French. The *MLWL* gives the Anglo-Latin forms *pagenda* for 1411 and *pagentes* for 1540. The York records, however, have two entries for 1387 and 1388 that show as clearly as could be wished the Modern English form in a French context:

expendront en la coillet de la moneie de lour pagent . . . (I, 4)
. . . lour pagent de corpore christi . . .   (*ibid.*, 6)

Since there appears to be no evidence for this word on the Continent, it looks as though we are again dealing with an English word, even though the surrounding context is French. The difficulty of separating English from French at this time is shown by a quotation given in the *OED* for about 1380, where *pagent* is mentioned as a variant of *pagyn* in a Wyclif text. The editors offer no comment on this form, but the York texts given above would suggest that it was current in England before

---

[21] XC (1980), 248–50.
[22] For further details and other examples, the reader is referred to 'A Mis-judged Author and a Mis-used Text: Walter de Bibbesworth and his "Tretiz"' in *Modern Language Review*, LXXVII (1982), 282–293.
[23] Ed. Alexandra F. Johnston and Margaret Rogerson (Toronto, 1979).

the end of the fourteenth century, whether interpreted as English or as French.

These same York records also provide a good illustration of the shift of meaning that has produced the English 'perform' from the Medieval French *parfournir*. As in the case of 'pageant', the standard dictionaries of Medieval French are of no help here, but it is clear from the York texts that the theatrical sense of the word was current in England before the beginning of the fifteenth century:

le juer & les pagentz de la jour de Corpore Christi les queux ne purrount estre juez ne perfournez mesme le jour   (I, 11).

Mention has been made earlier of the need to integrate the study of all three languages used in medieval Britain and of the difficulty in separating them in any useful way, apart from the superficial judgement by the form in which they appear in documents. Nowhere are these difficulties more obvious than in the domain of the bilingual and trilingual glosses. From the first half of the thirteenth century onwards, Latin, French and English came together increasingly in this kind of gloss, composed to assist those unable to cope with the Latin of texts which they had to study. Until recently, access to this material was severely hindered not only by the lack of modern, reliable editions of those glosses known to exist,[24] but also by the fact that it was not generally realized just how many of these texts were still lying unnoticed in many libraries. The publication of a number of glosses by Tony Hunt in the last few years[25] has

[24] The exception to this is the *Glasgow Glossary* in the excellent edition of A. Ewert, *Medium Aevum*, XXV (1957), 154–63.

[25] 'The Vernacular Entries in the *Glossae in Sidonium* (MS Oxford Digby 172)' in *ZfSL*, LXXXIX (1979), 130–50; 'Les Gloses en langue vulgaire dans les mss. de l'*Unum Omnium* de Jean de Garlande' in *Revue de Linguistique romane*, XLIII (1979), 162–78; 'Les Gloses en langue vulgaire dans les manuscrits du *De nominibus utensilium* d'Alexandre Nequam' in *Revue de Linguistique romane, XLIII* (1979), 235–62; 'Vernacular Glosses in Medieval Manuscripts' in *Cultura Neolatina*, XXXIX (1979), 9–37; 'The Anglo-Norman Vocabularies in MS Oxford Bodleian Library Douce 88. . .' in *Medium Aevum*, LXIX (1980), 5–15; 'Une Traduction partielle des *Parabolae* d'Alain de Lille' in *Le Moyen Age*, LXXXVII (1981), 45–56; 'The Old English Vocabularies in MS Oxford Bodley 730' in *English Studies*, LXII (1981), 201–9; 'The Trilingual Vocabulary in MS Westminster Abbey 24/11' in *Notes & Queries*, XXVIII (1981), 14–15.

brought them to the forefront of attention and greatly facili-, tated any new attempt to set them in the general linguistic context of medieval England.

The extent to which this kind of material was produced in medieval England bears witness, of course, to the widespread need felt here for help in reading Medieval Latin, but the date and form of these glosses yield less obvious and perhaps more important information about the shifting relationship of Latin, French and English. Hunt quotes Haskin's opinion that one of the glossed Latin texts, Nequam's *Sacerdos*, may be dated no later than the end of the twelfth century, whilst another, a Digby manuscript of the *Sidonius*, "can scarcely be later than 1200", and yet others are attributed to the first half of the thirteenth century.[26] These dates are significant pointers to the relationship of English to the two languages of culture — Latin and French — at that time, because amongst the glosses to Garland's *Unum Omnium* Hunt finds no less than 150 that are in English, not French. Nor is this an exception; in all the other glossed Latin texts that he has examined there are similarly English words in considerable number. The inference to be drawn from this unexpected fact must be that no later than the early years of the thirteenth century glossators were regularly using English mixed into their Anglo-Norman in order to explain Latin terms to English readers. The degree to which Anglo-Saxon and Norman civilizations must have blended even at this early date, at least as far as the lettered element in society was concerned, is indicated not only by the very presence of English terms, but — more significantly — by the evident uncertainty in the mind of scribes as to whether many words were in fact English or French. As Hunt says: "Even a cursory glance . . . at glossed grammatical texts of 13th-century England reveals a constant confusion in the application of these terms [*sc. romanice* and *anglice*] and a constant mingling of French and English forms".[27] A little later in the same paper he writes about "the lack of a clear demarcation between many Anglo-Norman and Middle English forms" (p. 133) and points out that "the English

---

[26] *Revue de Linguistique romane*, XLIII (1979), 236, and *ZfSL*, LXXXIX (1979), 131.
[27] *ZfSL*, LXXXIX (1979), 132.

glosses concern domestic terms which may have been most
familiar to the students, who were being taken through Sidonius's
text, in their native English rather than in their acquired French"
(*ibid.*). A brief selection of the kind of items referred to may be
useful at this point to illustrate the elementary nature of much
of the material listed in all the glosses: *orphanus*: gallice 'step-
chil'; *sinum*: gallice 'chesenet'; *hec facilla*: gallice 'sikel'; *remus*:
gallice 'hore'. When this kind of blatant error is found in respect
of large numbers of ordinary, everyday words from the beginning of the thirteenth century onwards, it is evident that the
upward thrust of English into the ranks of the literate must have
been very strong not much more than a century after the Con-
queror landed and gallicized the upper strata of the society of
this island. By this time England must have been well on the
way to reverting to its Germanic language, but with the happy
enrichment of the all-important Romance element that has
determined its character in modern times.

The uncertainty shown in many instances by the glossators
with regard to French and English finds an echo in the work of
those who provided glosses for the various manuscripts of
Bibbesworth's *Tretiz* and the later *Femina*. Although it would
be unsafe to base any definitive judgement on the evidence set
out in the present unreliable edition of the former work, it
would seem that here, as in the bilingual and trilingual glosses,
the separation between French and English is often far from
clear-cut. Further research on all available material of this kind
is an urgent requirement if we are to reach a better understanding of Anglo-Norman and Middle English.

Lest it should be thought that the kind of confusion just
referred to is confined to scribes constantly moving backwards
and forwards from one language to the other in their glosses and
so at times forgetting which one they are dealing with, it may
be as well to look for a moment at the case of 'key' as used
figuratively in two administrative texts of later Anglo-Norman:

A lour tresreduté seignour le Roy . . . supplient vos povres
tenantez de Noefchastell sur Tyne, un keye de North et
resset a vostre oest   (*Northumberland Petitions*, p. 222[28])

[28] *Ancient Petitions Relating to Northumberland* ed. C. M. Fraser, Surtees Society,
176 (London, 1966).

la dite ville est key & defens del paiis envyroun (*Rotuli Parliamentorum*, III, 639)

It is difficult not to take the view that *key(e)* here has been absorbed into Anglo-Norman, but whether the writers would have made a sharp distinction in every case between words in English and French is open to doubt, especially in the light of Hunt's findings.

The belated appearance of the complete *Anglo-Norman Dictionary*, even when — or perhaps if — supplemented by a much-needed volume of Additions and Corrections, will mark not the end but the real beginning of work on the lexis of Anglo-Norman. The dictionary will need to be used as a springboard for a much wider approach based on the material gathered by Professor Collas and the comprehensive list of Anglo-Norman manuscripts still being compiled by Professor Ruth Dean; full account will also need to be taken of both the *Middle English Dictionary* and the new dictionary of Medieval Latin now in process of publication.

LES SYNONYMES DANS LE *DIALOGUE DES CREATURES*, TRADUCTION PAR COLARD MANSION DU *DIALOGUS CREATURARUM*

P. RUELLE

L'ancien français n'ignore pas l'emploi redondant des synonymes.[1] Des types qui ont survécu jusqu'aujourd'hui s'y rencontrent déjà: *sûr et certain* (Tobler-Lommatzsch, IX, 592, l. 9 *seüre et certe*; l. 18 *seürs et certains*), *sain et sauf* (T.-L., IX, 66, l. 19 *sains e salfs*; l. 22 *sein et sauf*; l. 23 *sauf et sain*), *bel et bien* (T.-L., I, 963, l. 13–19 *bien et bel*), *feu et flamme* (T.-L., III, 1787, l. 51 *a foc a flamma*; l. 52 *a feu a flame*; 1788, l. 3 *a feu et a flame*; l. 15 *feu(s) et fla(m)me*). D'une manière générale, toutefois, l'ancienne langue use avec mesure de ce tour stylistique. Si l'on parcourt la *Chrestomathie* d'Albert Henry,[2] on est même frappé par le peu d'usage qui en est fait. Encore ne serait-on pas en peine de montrer que, dans des exemples comme les suivants, les différences de sens sont assez sensibles pour que les auteurs et les lecteurs ou les auditeurs en aient eu pleine conscience: *en proieres et en oroisons* (no. 59, l. 1), *qu'il li donast veoir et demostrast* (117, l. 3), *Et forsvoiié Et fors de voie desvoiié* (135, l. 46), *Li dei m'agaitent et espient* (ibid., l. 55).

En moyen français, l'emploi des synonymes redondants croît dans de notables proportions. Nous ne donnerons que quelques exemples, puisés dans la *Chrestomathie* de Peter Rickard.[3] Voici d'abord une phrase de Froissart: *Or regardez et ymaginez en vous meismes se j'ay eu bien cause de dire et traittier que le royaulme d'Angleterre en celle saison fut en grand peril et aventure que de estre tous perdus sans recouvrier* (no. 1, ll. 1–3).

---

[1] A. Stefenelli, *Der Synonymenreichtum der altfranzösischen Dichtersprache* (Wien, 1967).

[2] *Chrestomathie de la littérature en ancien français*, 6e éd. (Berne, 1978).

[3] *Chrestomathie de la langue française au XVe siècle* (Cambridge University Press, 1976).

Voici ce qu'on trouve sous la plume de Gerson: *un juge païen et incredule* (3, 1. 2), *telle . . . euvre est soustenue, alosee et deffendue* (*ibid*., l. 4). Et voici ce qu'écrit Thomas le Forestier: *pestilence peult venir et proceder de la vraye justice et pugnition divine a la raison de noz pechez et offences perpetrez et commis contre la volenté et commandemens de Dieu nostre createur* (54, ll. 2—4).

Autant que je sache, dans aucune oeuvre du XIVe ou du XVe siècle, le procédé n'a l'ampleur qu'il atteint dans le *Dialogue des créatures*, traduction réalisée vers 1480 par Colard Mansion d'un *Dialogus creaturarum*, sans doute écrit au XIVe siècle et d'auteur incertain.[4] Presque chaque phrase de ce long texte offre un et parfois plusieurs exemples d'emploi redondant des synonymes. Dans les pages qui suivent, nous allons nous efforcer d'analyser ce procédé qui n'eût pas manqué d'intéresser T.B.W. Reid et l'aurait peut-être fait sourire, habitué qu'il était à des problèmes plus compliqués.

Nous nous sommes limité aux six premiers dialogues, soit 202 paragraphes (§ § 157—359), dont les numéros seront mentionnés devant les exemples. Quand c'était possible sans altérer la syntaxe, nous avons ramené les substantifs et les adjectifs latins au nominatif.

Relevons d'abord les cas où la redondance du texte français résulte d'une traduction plus ou moins fidèle du texte latin, et ne perdons pas de vue que ce dernier paraît être du XIVe siècle. Leur nombre n'est pas négligeable: 162 *diffamer et mesdire — detrahere ac diffamare*; 164 *blasmes et vituperes — detrahis et blasphemas*; 165 *as en haynne et en repugnance — odis et impugnas*; 172 *convocqua et appella — clamavit aggregavitque*; 191 *de bas et plain lieu — de plano et infimo loco*; 202 *(nuee) espesse et grosse — (nubes) magna et spissa*; 234 *sentier et voye — limes vel semita*; 236 *seoir et reposer — sedere et quiescere*; 258 *engin*

---

[4] Le *Dialogue* est inédit. Force nous est donc de renvoyer à une édition qui n'a pas encore vu le jour mais que nous comptons publier prochainement. Le texte du *Dialogue*, comme celui du *Dialogus*, comporte un prologue et 122 'dialogues'. Chacun de ceux-ci se compose d'une fable assez brève et de commentaires moraux tout pénétrés d'une étonnante érudition, au moins en apparence. Nous avons divisé le texte en 3531 paragraphes, ce qui donne une idée de son étendue.

et conseil — ingenium et consilium; 261 *grandes et perilz —*
sollicitudines et pericula; 265 *souffisant ne prudent — luculentus*
et sufficiens; 273 *resplendeur et beaulté — splendor et pulchri-*
tudo; 280 *destruire et seichier — exsiccare et delere*; 281 *estre*
contemplees ne veues — contemplari et videri; 284 *germineroit*
ne produiroit aucun fruit — germinare et pullulare valeret; 285
droitture et choses raisonnables — ordinata et grata; 287 *justes*
et honnestes — justa et honesta; 320 *mauvais et cruel — malus*
et crudelis; 322 *contencion et discorde — contencio et discordia*;
329 *brisier et deffaire — terrere et frangere*; 340 *fureur et ire —*
ira et furor. Il faut, dans la même catégorie, faire une place à part
à l'exemple suivant: 173 *traire et lanchier — sagittas mittere et*
jaculis percutere. Il ne s'agit nullement, ici, de synonymie: *traire*
et *lanchier* sont des termes techniques et, respectivement,
traduisent exactement *sagittas mittere* et *jaculis percutere.*

A l'inverse, notons maintenant les cas où, parce qu'il s'agit
d'interpolations qui lui appartiennent, Mansion n'avait aucun
mot latin sous les yeux: 238 *murmure et tumulte*; 239 *folles et*
ydiotes; 266 *saige et discret homme* (mais c'est une expression
toute faite, courante dans les textes d'allure juridique); 268
moyens et soubtillitez; 288 *(vous) obtiendrez et aurez*; 311
vraye et juste (sentence); 318 *a leur honte et confusion*; 324
tenemens et heritaiges; 326 *paix et concorde* (mais c'est aussi
une expression toute faite); 328 *roideur et forche*; 329 *frater-*
nité et concorde; 336 *je prie et requiers*; 350 *chastoier et batre*;
352 *sainte et digne chose* (autre lieu commun).

Beaucoup plus nombreux, plus intéressants aussi parce qu'ils
montrent mieux comment procède la pensée du traducteur,
sont les exemples où Mansion a traduit par deux mots ou expressions un seul mot latin ou une seule expression.

Voici d'abord les cas, très nombreux, où la forme du mot
latin transparaît dans une des deux traductions françaises: 168
mauvaise et ingrate — ingrata; 169 *me laisse et permetz — per-*
mitte; 171 *animee et courrouchee — animata*; 184 *seignourir et*
dominer — dominari; 185 *personnes inferieures et basses —*
inferiores; 186 *dominer et seignourir — dominari*; 188 *soustenter*
et conforter — sustinere; 193 *sont conservez et gardez — con-*
servantur; 196 *est extirpé et confroissié — extirpatur*; 197 *superbe*
et tres orgueilleux — superbus; 202 *soi enfler et eslever en*

orgueil — se elevare; 215 *superbe et orgueil — superbia*; *dominer et seignourir — dominari*; 223 *muez et relaxez (en sept moys) — mutati (in septem menses)*; 236 *circuir et errer — circuimus*; 240 *(vous) vous desvoyeriez et fourvoyeriez — deviassetis*; 251 *muer ne changier — mutare*; 253 *regime et gouvernement — regimen*; 270 *qui appert au matin et amaine le jour — que apparet de mane*; 272 *tu as enlumineez et radieez — irradiasti*; 273 *supplantees et deceutes — supplantate*; 275 *n'est licite ne raisonnable — non licet*; 282 *choses injustes ne desraisonnables — injusta*; 284 *inundacions et vapeurs — inundacio*; 295 *retribue et donne — donet*; 303 *iré et troublé — iratus*; 307 *frere et ami — frater*; *honnestement ne bien — bene*; 311 *juste et souverain (Juge) — (Judex) justus*; 320 *(il) quiert et nourrist (rancunes et detractions) — querit (jurgia)*; 322 *ediffier et construire — construere*; *destruire et ramener a neant — destruere*; 334 *mon frere et ami — frater*; 336 *ma seureur et amie — soror*; 339 *discerner et congnoistre — discernere*; 342 *enflamber et avancier — inflammare*; 344 *prochains et amis — amici*; 355 *severes et crueulx — severa*. Ajoutons à cette série l'exemple suivant dont les deux premiers mots sont, dans le contexte, tout à fait superflus: 310 *pour moy contre toy — contra te*.

Il arrive que l'un des deux termes employés par Mansion évoque, sans plus, le mot latin qu'ils traduisent: 215 *tres hault et tres excellent Dieu — Excelsus*; 222 *deprioit et faisoit oraisons — orabat*; 248 *commencerent a elles repentir et desplaire — penituerunt*; 276 *(il) aourne et enlumine le jour — est diei ornator*; 280 *clarté et lumiere — lumen*; 333 *grever et degaster — aggravare*; 346 *est en fureur et en ire — irascitur*; 347 *attrempez et refroidiez — temperandus*; 356 *sentir les aiguillons de yre et de courroux — irascere*.

Les cas sont beaucoup plus nombreux où le couple qui vient à l'esprit de Mansion ne rappelle en rien la forme du mot latin à traduire: 166 *va arriere et te departz de ma presence — recede a me*; 177 *(je) te chastoieray et te corrigeray — sic faciam tibi*; 189 *sont portez et eslevez (en hault) — tolluntur (in altum)*; 192 *haulz et eslevez — in summitate*; 197 *petiz et humbles — parvi*; 203 *soi mettre et eslever en air — in aere se ponere*; 204 *(je) obfusque et coeuvre — obnubilo*; 228 *pour lui et en son lieu — pro eo*; 231 *est situee et assise — est*; 239 *(je) me lasse et traveille —*

me fatigo; 244 *se parti et s'en alla — recessit*; 251 *bon pasteur ou bon prince — rector*; 252 *nourrir et deffendre — fovere*; 262 *estre constitué en honneur et dignité mondaine — preesse*; 275 *vostre requeste et supplicacion — hoc*; 277 *germiner ne croistre — pullulare*; 284 *arousent et madifient — irrigant*; 285 *soient deboutez et n'ayent escout — propulsentur*; 290 *conserve et garde (a aucun) — confert*; 293 *je ne demande ne il ne me chault — non quero*; *quelle chose je puis et doy donner — quid me deceat dare*; 300 *pour et en la significacion de — propter*; etc.

Nous avons relevé deux curieux exemples d'une sorte d'hendiadys: 180 *vergoingneuse et esbahie — confusa in verecundia*; 187 *est un mal vituperable et tres mauvais — vituperabiliter malum* (adj.) *est*.

Notons enfin que, pour les 202 paragraphes examinés, nous n'avons trouvé qu'un exemple où Mansion a traduit un couple latin par un seul mot français: 205 *suppediter — offuscare et suppeditare*.

Le moment est venu de s'interroger sur une surabondance si contraire à nos habitudes et à notre goût. L'excès dont témoigne le *Dialogue* et la variété des cas examinés peuvent nous éclairer sur une pratique répandue à l'époque, même si elle est plus discrète dans d'autres oeuvres.

Observons d'abord que, si le modèle latin offrait à Mansion des exemples de redondance synonymique, ils s'y trouvent en nombre bien moins considérable que dans la traduction. Ils sont le témoignage d'un courant qui existait déjà au XIVe siècle et devait se manifester aussi bien en latin qu'en français.

La double traduction d'un seul mot latin est plus remarquable. De ce type, nous avons relevé trois séries d'inégale longueur.

Dans la première, l'un des deux mots français est un simple calque du mot latin. Trois fois sur quatre, à peu près (29/38), c'est lui qui se présente en premier lieu. Doit-on penser que le rôle de l'autre, quelle que soit sa place, est seulement, pour Mansion lui-même ou à l'intention de ses lecteurs, de préciser le sens du mot-calque? A relire l'ensemble de ces exemples, il semble bien que oui. Pour un homme du XVe siècle, à moins qu'il ne fût bon latiniste, *courrouchee* (171) est sûrement plus clair que *animee*, *conforter* (188) que *sustenter*, *confroissié* (196) que *extirpé*, *soi enfler* (202) que *soi eslever* (même complété par *en orgueil*), *enlumineez* (272) *que radieez, raisonnable* (275) que *licite*, etc.

Les choses sont déjà un peu moins nettes en ce qui concerne la deuxième série, où le mot latin n'est plus que vaguement évoqué. Rien de nous permet de penser que *soi repentir* (248) fût moins compréhensible que *soi desplaire, lumiere* (280) moins que *clarté, ire* (346) moins que *courroux*. Cependant, on notera que le mot qui n'a pas de correspondant latin est, en général, moins abstrait, plus proche de la réalité sensible, plus 'parlant': *deprioit* (262) comparé à *faisoit oraisons, soi desplaire* (248) à *soi repentir, enlumine* (276) à *aourne, degaster* (333) à *grever*, etc. On observera que *tres hault* (215), forme vulgaire, traduit exactement le latin *excelsus*, alors que le calque approximatif *excellent* ne signifie que 'qui excelle en son genre'.

Dans la troisième série, la plus nombreuse, Mansion n'a plus recouru aux formes latines et la comparaison en est rendue moins facile. Nous ne saurions dire s'il y a, pour Mansion et ses contemporains, une différence sensible entre *chastoieray* (177) et *corrigeray, honneur* (262) et *dignité mondaine, arousent* (284) et *madifient, conserver* (290) et *garder*. Mais on ne peut douter que *va arriere* (166) soit plus facile à se représenter que *te departz de ma presence, eslevez* (189) plus que *portez, haulz* (192) plus que *eslevez, eslever* (203) plus que *mettre, coeuvre* (204) plus que *obfusque*, etc. En revanche, on observera que *humbles* (197), mot abstrait, doublant *petiz*, est indispensable, dans le contexte (il s'agit des petits oiseaux comparés au lion), à une traduction satisfaisante de *parvi*. De même, *pasteur* (251) et *prince, je ne demande* (293) et *il ne me chault* se complètent pour une traduction convenable de *rector* et de *non quero*.

Il reste à examiner les interpolations. Ici, pas de point de comparaison latin, comme dans la plupart des textes français du XVe siècle, il va sans dire.

On peut laisser de côté les lieux communs: 266 *saige et discret* (on rencontre l'expression dès le XIIe siècle; T.-L., II, 1943, s.v. *discré*), 326 *paix et concorde* (on lit déjà *pais et concorde et amor* dans *Eneas*; T.-L., VII, 54, s.v. *pais*) et 352 *sainte et digne chose* (*chose sainte et digne* dans le *Roman de la Poire*, 1237–50; T.-L., II, 1927).

Dans les couples suivants, le second terme renchérit sur le premier, le renforce ou l'aggrave: 238 *murmure et tumulte*; 268 *moyens et soubtillitez*, 311 *vraye* (conforme à la vérité, c'est-à-dire, en l'occurrence, tenant simplement compte des faits) *et juste* (conforme à la justice), 324 *tenemens* (domaines que l'on tient en fiefs) *et heritaiges* (propriétés héréditaires), 328 *roideur* (caractère de ce qui plie difficilement, en l'occurrence un faisceau de verges) *et forche*, 336 *je prie et requiers* (réclame, demande avec insistance), 350 *chastoier et batre*. Dans trois cas, le second terme indique le fait ou l'état qui résulte du premier: 288 *obtiendrez et aurez*, 318 *honte et confusion*, 329 *fraternité et concorde*. Dans 239 *folles* (insensées) *et ydiotes* (ignorantes), il nous est difficile de voir une progression, mais il est possible que le second terme soit plus méprisant que le premier.

L'impression première que le *Dialogue* fourmille de synonymes redondants est trompeuse. Même un lecteur moderne, s'il a quelque habitude des textes en ancien et en moyen français, se rend vite compte que les mots formant un couple plus ou moins synonymique ne sont pas juxtaposés au petit bonheur. D'une manière générale, à un calque d'un mot latin est joint un mot populaire, un terme abstrait est glosé par un mot concret, les deux sens d'un mot latin utiles à une bonne compréhension sont précisés. S'il s'agit d'interpolations, le second terme précise le premier et presque toujours en le renforçant.

Que cette redondance ait fini par devenir un tic d'écriture, cela ne paraît pas douteux. Que les auteurs et les lecteurs y aient vu une sorte d'élégance, le long succès dont le tour a joui tend à le prouver. Qu'il faille toujours y voir une superfluité et une naïveté, les mécanismes psychologiques révélés par l'analyse nous ont montré qu'il n'en est rien. La redondance peut être, nous l'avons vu, le résultat d'une recherche stylistique consciente.

De l'examen, même attentif et détaillé, d'une seule oeuvre, surtout quand cette oeuvre est une traduction, on ne peut tirer que des conclusions limitées. Des travaux analogues à celui que l'on vient de lire pourraient être entrepris sur d'autres oeuvres écrites en moyen français et en latin du XIVe et du XVe siècle. Leurs conclusions, comparées, permettraient sans doute de retracer l'histoire du procédé du début à la fin et de mieux l'expliquer.

DEUX COPISTES AU TRAVAIL

Pour une étude textuelle globale du manuscrit 354 de la Bibliothèque de la Bourgeoisie de Berne

JEAN RYCHNER_____

L'étude des *remaniements* de fabliaux portait en général sur des fabliaux entiers et, même si elle envisageait l'ensemble du phénomène en vue d'une typologie, elle demeurait nécessairement une étude de cas. Elle n'aboutissait pas à une caractérisation des grands recueils qui nous ont conservé la plupart des pièces du genre, car les remaniements appartiennent à une préhistoire incontrôlable, au-delà de leur copie et de leur insertion dans un recueil, au-delà du travail sur les textes des artisans de ces anthologies. Il est pourtant certain que ce travail a existé et c'est lui qui a donné leur personnalité aux recueils que nous possédons. Pour en discerner les traces, il ne faut pas les chercher dans des transformations amples et profondes, mais dans la langue et ses graphies, dans la correction et le détail textuels, dans des variantes qui le plus souvent ne dépassent pas le couplet. Les lieux de l'observation ne doivent plus être, alors, les oeuvres en tant que touts; il faut sortir de la perspective monographique pour parcourir transversalement les collections, à la recherche des traits constants qui, dans des pièces de dates, de provenances, de genres littéraires divers, révéleront le traitement qu'elles ont subi ensemble, au même moment, lors de leur groupement en recueil. C'est ce que nous allons essayer de faire pour le deuxième en importance numérique des recueils de fabliaux, le manuscrit 354 de la Bibliothèque de la Bourgeoisie ou Burgerbibliothek de Berne.

On comprendra facilement qu'il ne puisse s'agir ici, vu l'ampleur que prendrait une étude complète, que d'exposer les résultats de premiers sondages, suffisants toutefois pour situer les questions et pour leur donner un début de réponse. On voudra bien garder en mémoire le caractère provisoire de nos observations sans que j'y insiste à chaque fois.

Voici la liste des pièces très inégalement sondées. Chaque titre y est précédé du numéro d'ordre de la pièce dans le recueil et suivi de la mention des éditions utilisées. Les principaux recueils de fabliaux seront désignés par leurs sigles habituels, à savoir *A* (Paris BN fr. 837), *B* (notre manuscrit), *C* (Berlin Bibl. nat. Hamilton 257), *D* (BN fr. 19152), *E* (BN fr. 1593), *F* (BN fr. 12603), *H* (BN fr. 2168).

1. *[Du foteor]*, fol. 1a–3d, 360 lignes.

> Texte de *D* dans *MR (Recueil général et complet des fabliaux des XIIIe et XIVe siècles*, publiés ... par Anatole de Montaiglon et Gaston Raynaud, Paris, 1872–90, 6 vol.), I, 304–17.

4. *De celui qui cracha sor ses morteres*, fol. 10c–11c, 136 lignes, ou *Le Vilain de Farbu*, par Jean Bodel.

> Texte de *H* dans Jean Bodel, *Fabliaux*, édition ... par Pierre Nardin (Paris, 1965), pp. 69–75.

6. *La Voie d'anfer*, fol. 12a–16b, 629 lignes.

> Textes des autres manuscrits dans *The Songe d'enfer of Raoul de Houdenc*. An edition based on all the extant manuscripts, by Madelyn Louise Mihm, Ann Arbor, University Microfilms International (London, 1982).

7. *Do chevalier a l'espee*, fol. 16b–26c, 1220 lignes.

8. *La Mule sanz frain*, fol. 26c–36b, 1067 lignes.

> Texte de *B* dans *Two Old French Gauvain Romances: Le Chevalier à l'épée and La Mule sans frein*, edited ... by R.C. Johnston and D.D.R. Owen (Edinburgh and London, 1972).

10. *De dan Denier*, fol. 38b–39b, 142 lignes.

> Textes de *A* et de *B* dans Jose Vincenzo Molle, *De dan Denier, contributo a un'edizione critica*, dans *Studi filologici e letterari dell'Istituto di filologia romanza e ispanistica dell'Università di Genova* (Genova, 1978), pp. 221–55.

11. *De la mere qui desfandoit sa fille vit a nomer*, fol. 39c–41a, 190 lignes.

> Texte de *A* dans *MR* V, 101–108.

15. *D'Estula et de l'anel de la paelle*, fol. 44a–45c, 193 lignes, ou *De Gombert et des deus clers*, par Jean Bodel.

> Texte de *A* dans *Les fabliaux de Jean Bodel*, édités par Pierre Nardin (Dakar, 1959), pp. 35–40.

> Texte de *C* dans Jean Bodel, *Fabliaux*, édition ... par Pierre Nardin (Paris, 1965), pp. 85–94.

16. *La Male Honte* (version de Huon), fol. 45c–47b, 209 lignes.

> Textes de *A*, *B* et *F* dans Jean Rychner, *Contribution à l'étude des fabliaux: variantes, remaniements, dégradations*, II (Neuchâtel/ Genève, 1960), 16–27.

18. *Do mire de Brai*, fol. 49c—52c, 348 lignes, ou *Le Vilain mire*.

Texte de *A* dans *Zwei altfranzösische Fablels (Auberée, Du Vilain mire)*, neu herausgegeben von Hans Helmut Christmann (Tübingen, 1963), pp. 44—57.

Texte de *B* dans *Fabliaux français du moyen âge*, édition critique par Philippe Ménard, I (Genève, 1979), 83—94.

Texte de *C* dans *Fabliaux*, selected and edited by R.C. Johnston and D.D.R. Owen (Oxford, 1957), pp. 56—66.

23. *De la damoisele qui n'ot parler de fotre qui n'aüst mal au cuer*, fol. 58a—59d, 210 lignes.

Textes de *A*, *B* et *D* dans Jean Rychner, *op. cit.*, pp. 120—35.

29. *Li Esbaubisemanz lecheor*, fol. 65d—67a, 141 lignes, ou *Les deux bordeors ribauz*.

Texte de *D* dans Edmond Faral, *Mimes français du XIIIe siècle; contribution à l'histoire du théâtre comique au moyen âge* (Paris, 1910), pp. 93—99.

30. *Coquaigne*, fol. 67a—68b, 137 lignes.

Texte de *A* dans Veikko Väänänen, 'Le fabliau de Cocagne' dans *Neuphilologische Mitteilungen*, XLVIII (1947), 3—36, avec les variantes de *E*.

40. *De la dame qui fist batre son mari*, fol. 78a—80c, 299 lignes, ou *De la borgoise d'Orleans*.

Textes de *A*, *B* et *C* dans Jean Rychner, *op. cit.*, pp. 80—99.

47. *Des trois larrons*, fol. 103c—108a, 514 lignes, ou *De Haimet et de Barat et Travers*, par Jean Bodel.

Texte de *D* dans *Trois fabliaux: Saint Pierre et le jongleur, De Haimet et de Barat et Travers, Estula*, éditions critiques par Martha Walters-Gehrig, Beihefte zur Zeitschrift für romanische Philologie, 102 (Tübingen, 1961), pp. 61—175, avec les variantes de *A*, *B* et *C*.

56. *D'Estula*, fol. 116b—117b, 139 lignes.

Texte de *D* dans *Trois fabliaux*, *op. cit.*, pp. 178—222, avec les variantes de *A* et de *B*.

Texte de *A* dans *MR* IV, 87—92.

62. *Do vilain qui conquist paradis par plait*, fol. 143d—145b, 172 lignes.

Texte de *D* dans *Twelve Fabliaux from Ms. ffr. 19152 of the Bibliothèque nationale*, edited by T.B.W. Reid (Manchester, 1958), pp. 19—22.

Texte de *A* et *C* dans Jean Rychner, *op. cit.*, pp. 179—183.

66. *De Tristan*, fol. 151d—156d, 594 lignes, ou *La Folie Tristan*.

Texte de *B* dans *La Folie Tristan de Berne*, publiée . . . par Ernest Hoepffner, Publications de la Faculté des lettres de l'Université de Strasbourg: Textes d'étude, 3 (Paris, 1934).

Les références seront chaque fois au manuscrit de Berne lui-même (éventuellement numéro de la pièce, puis folio, colonne et ligne), même pour les pièces qui en ont été publiées. Les sigles des autres recueils sont suivis, quand il s'agit d'un renvoi précis, du numéro que le vers porte dans les éditions que nous venons de citer.

L'histoire du recueil de Berne nous échappe depuis l'époque où il fut écrit, la première moitié du XIVe siècle, jusqu'au XVIe siècle, où trois de ses possesseurs ont écrit leurs noms au recto de son premier folio. Ce sont: *Quentinus Heduus* ou Jean Quentin, originaire d'Autun (d'où son *cognomen*), professeur de droit canon à Paris, mort en 1561; *Henri Estiene*, l'imprimeur humaniste bien connu (1528–1598); Melchior *Goldast*, historien et philologue suisse (1578–1635). Le recueil appartint ensuite à Jacques Bongars (1554–1612), humaniste et diplomate au service de Henri IV. Bongars résidait le plus souvent à Strasbourg et c'est au fils, Jacques, de son ami strasbourgeois le banquier René Gravisset qu'il légua sa bibliothèque. Jacques Gravisset, qui avait épousé en 1624 la fille de l'avoyer de Berne François Louis d'Erlach, fit don de cette splendide collection à la Bourgeoisie de Berne pour la remercier de l'avoir admis en son sein. Les livres furent transportés à Berne en mai 1632, de Bâle, où Gravisset les avait déposés en 1622 dans la maison que son père y possédait. Propriétaire de notre manuscrit depuis 1632, la Bibliothèque de la Bourgeoisie dut pourtant le racheter à un antiquaire français en 1837, après qu'il eut disparu durant vingt-huit ans, à la suite du prêt qu'elle en avait fait au gouvernement français, en 1809, pour que le grand connaisseur de fabliaux qu'était Dominique Martin Méon (1748–1829) pût le consulter, ce qu'il semble d'ailleurs ne pas avoir fait. Relevons à l'honneur de la Bourgeoisie que cet accident ne l'empêcha pas de mettre son précieux recueil à la disposition de Gaston Paris, à la Bibliothèque nationale, en 1896.[1]

[1] Sur l'histoire de la bibliothèque de Jacques Bongars, on consultera l'introduction au *Catalogus codicum Bernensium* de Hermann Hagen (Berne, 1875), et les trois volumes jubilaires de la bibliothèque de Berne: *Die Stadt- und Hochschulbibliothek. Zur Erinnerung an ihr 400 jähriges Bestehen und an die Schenkung der Bongarsiana im Jahr 1632*, herausgegeben von Hans Bloesch (Bern, 1932); *Schätze der Burgerbibliothek Bern, herausgegeben . . . anlässlich der 600-Jahr-Feier des Bundes der Stadt Bern mit den Waldstätten* (Bern, 1953); *Bibliotheca Bernensis 1974. Festgabe zur Einweihung des umgebauten und erweiterten Gebäudes der Stadt- und Universitätsbibliothek Bern . . .* (Bern, 1974).

La photographie a simplifié tout cela, et c'est en feuilletant tranquillement chez moi le bel album de fac-similés que M. Christoph von Steiger, conservateur des manuscrits de la Bibliothèque de la Bourgeoisie, a fait si aimablement confectionner à mon usage — ce dont je le remercie ici très vivement — que j'ai eu la surprise de constater que le recueil de Berne est l'oeuvre de deux copistes, ce que je n'avais lu nulle part. Hermann Hagen ne le signale pas dans son excellent *Catalogus codicum Bernensium* (Berne, 1875), mais j'en ai trouvé depuis la mention succincte dans les *Trois fabliaux* de Martha Walters-Gehrig (*op. cit.*, p. viii): "L'écriture est soignée et très nette. Le recueil a été exécuté par deux scribes." Il est possible, à vrai dire, que le second scribe de Mme Walters-Gehrig soit celui qui a copié le *Conte du Graal*, à partir du folio 208 recto. Cette seconde partie du recueil possède une certaine autonomie, par son contenu et par sa composition matérielle: l'ancienne foliotation ne la recouvre pas, les cahiers en sont numérotés à nouveau à partir de 1 et son copiste est, en effet, nettement différent. Elle provient cependant du même atelier que la première partie du recueil et devrait naturellement être prise en considération dans une étude complète. Je la néglige entièrement dans l'étude partielle que je présente aujourd'hui et l'on voudra bien me pardonner si, toutes les fois que je vais dire "le recueil de Berne", il faut entendre: "sans le *Perceval*".

Les deux copistes dont je parlais tout à l'heure ont donc été à l'oeuvre tous deux dans la première moitié du volume. Le partage du travail entre eux y a laissé des traces plus profondes que la simple distinction de leurs écritures. Pour en rendre compte clairement, je me servirai de la foliotation du XVe siècle, bien visible à chaque folio.

Le copiste B1 a écrit les 7 premiers cahiers du volume actuel, ce qui, à raison de 8 feuillets par cahier, fait 56 feuillets. Le dernier d'entre eux est cependant numéroté 55, car un feuillet a été omis dans la foliotation après le feuillet 13; une main moderne lui a donné le numéro 13a. Le travail de B1 s'arrête donc au bas du fol. 55 verso. Mais ce copiste avait certainement continué sur un autre cahier la copie du fabliau d'*Auberée* (pièce no. 19), interrompue en 55d, non reprise au fol. 56 par B2 et incomplète ainsi de 261 vers, à en juger par l'édition que

T.B.W. Reid a donnée de ce fabliau d'après *D* (*Twelve fabliaux,
op. cit.*, pp. 54—69). Signalons enfin, pour en finir avec B1, que
les feuillets 4 et 5 du recueil se sont perdus à une époque
postérieure à la foliotation.

La partie du recueil copiée par B2 commence aujourd'hui
avec le feuillet 56. Mais il s'est produit, avant la foliotation, une
importante interversion de cahiers, si bien qu'il faut en réalité
placer les 10 cahiers constituant les fol. 56—135 après les fol.
136—175 (5 cahiers). Après l'actuel folio 135 venaient les fol.
176—183 (1 cahier), qui se sont perdus après la foliotation. Puis
le manuscrit comprend dans l'ordre les fol. 184—274.

Les deux copistes avaient quelques habitudes professionnelles
différentes. Ainsi, B1 numérote ses cahiers au bas de leur
dernier verso, tandis que B2 lie le cahier précédent au suivant
par une réclame. D'autre part, je ne crois pas avoir observé sous
la plume de B1 le truc que B2 utilise pour bien remplir la
seconde ligne (parfois la première) quand il partage en deux
lignes un octosyllabe un peu long, truc qui est de répéter le
dernier mot; par exemple:

> Travers lo mostre et puis
> Son frere frere frere   47/103d 20—21[2]

Malgré ces différences, l'ouvrage de B1 et de B2 se ressemble
beaucoup, le texte y est également justifié en deux colonnes de
30 lignes par page, leurs écritures ont le même aspect général
(ce qui explique qu'on ne les ait pas distinguées) et leurs *scriptae*
ne diffèrent pas fondamentalement, encore que, comme nous
allons le voir, celle de B2 soit d'une teinte régionale plus marquée.
Il est donc certain que les deux copistes travaillaient dans le
même atelier au même recueil, ou à deux recueils semblables
dont les cahiers auraient été confondus au brochage. Les
rubriques (formules d'*incipit* et d'*explicit* des pièces réunies dans
le recueil) le confirment; elles sont, en effet, écrites de la même
main d'un bout à l'autre du volume ou, plus exactement, du
début jusqu'au moment où la rubrication cesse, c'est-à-dire avec
la pièce 68, au fol. 159b. Cette main, différente en tout cas de
B1, n'est sans doute pas celle de B2 non plus, mais elle use de la

---

[2] Voir encore, dans la même pièce 47: 106c 1—2, 107a 6—7, 107d 25—26, et
ailleurs: 144a 27—28, 151d 17—18, 154a 18—19.

même *scripta* que lui. On peut le vérifier sur les points suivants où l'usage de B2 diffère de celui de B1 : *an* pour *en* étymologique,[3] *aust* à l'imparfait du subjonctif de *avoir*,[4] et graphie *preste* pour *prestre*.[5]

Nous passons maintenant à l'examen des marques que les textes portent du travail auquel ils ont été soumis lors de leur transcription ou de leur admission dans le recueil. Nous prendrons d'abord les marques les plus évidentes et les plus faciles à relever, à savoir les traits qui constituent les *scriptae* respectives de B1 et de B2 et qui, tenant à la fois de la graphie et de la langue, donnent au texte de *B* son caractère le plus frappant. Nous en viendrons ensuite aux fautes et aux innovations attribuables à nos copistes.

Les traits les plus saillants de la *scripta* commune à B1 et B2 sont les suivants:

1. *iau* note les descendants de *ę* + *l* mouillé + *s* et de *ǫ* + *l* ou *l* mouillé + consonne. Ainsi, pour **melius**: *mialz* (15/44a 25, 29/66a 16, etc.); *miax* (6/16a 19, 16/46d 10, etc.); *miauz* (29/66b 3, 30/67b 8, etc); *lo miaudres* (29/66d 13); pour **vetulus**: *viauz* (15/45a 10, 18/49d 7). — Pour **voles**: *viax* (56/116d 26); pour **volet**: *vialt* (4/10d 5, 30/67c 6, etc.), *viaut* (8/31d 16, 30/67c 6, etc.); pour **oculos**: *ialz* (15/44a 26, 47/107a 11, etc.), *iax* (47/107d 21), *iauz* (15/44b 16, etc.). — Pour **-olus**: *filliax* (6/13a 19), *linciax* (15/44d 15), *morteriax* (de **mortariolum**) (4/11b 6). — La graphie pour *fou* est pourtant régulièrement *fox* (4/10c 25, 47/104c 12, etc.), et je n'ai relevé pour le futur et le conditionnel de *voloir* que des formes en *ou*: *voudré* (4/10d 22), *voudroie* (6/16a 28), etc. — La graphie *au* se rencontre dans *esmaure* (**exmolere**, 47/104b 4) et dans *sax*, participe passé de *saudre* 'payer' (1/3d 14).

2. La même graphie *au* correspond à *ę* + *l* + consonne: *li paux* 'le poil' (47/107a 14); les pronoms *ax* et *çax* (7/17b 16, 40/78d 25, etc.; 15/45b 16, 16/46b 2); *Richaut*, dans les rubriques de la pièce 58 (124c 10 et 135c 25); *fautre* 'feutre' (40/79d 18); *solaus* (7/16d 27). — Comme *-iax* correspond aussi à **-ellus**, les trois vers suivants résument bien les emplois de *-iax* et *-ax*:

---

[3] C'est le cas de *conmance* dans toutes les rubriques *d'incipit* sauf une: *et conmence de Brifaut* (3/9c 28). Je relève en outre *desfandoit* (11/39c 1), *escomeniemanz* (17/47b 21), *esbaubisemanz* (29/65d 19), *entandant* (43/90d 11), *Berangier* (64/146c 8).

[4] 23/58a 13.

[5] 41/80c 8, et 61/143b 13.

Cil descendent, si ont partie
La char Travers voiant ses iax:
.iii. monciax en ont fait entr'ax.　　　　　　47/107d 20—22

3. B1 et B2 mais, semble-t-il, B1 plus souvent que B2, notent *aign* les sons descendant de *e* + *n* + *yod*: *saignor* (1/3c 24, 4/10c 2, etc.); *laingne* 'bois' (18/52a 3); *viaigne* (30/68a 7), *bien vaigniez* (1/3d 1); *praigne* (30/67d 7); *daigniez* (1/3d 6), etc. Mais, inversément, *eign* se rencontre pour *aign*: *conpeigne* et *conpeignie* (56/116b 7 et 5); *seignerres* 'saigneur, qui fait une saignée' (29/66d 10).

4. Le son descendant de *ę* + *n* après labiale est souvent noté *oi: moins* (1/3a 24); *poine* ou *poinne* (16/46a 20, 30/67d 2, etc.); *avoinne* (7/18b 25); *moinne* (4/10c 21); *amoine* (56/116d 14); *enmoine* (40/79a 8); *pointe* 'peinte' (10/39b 10). — On remarquera la graphie *semoine* (30/67d 3), à la rime avec *poine*.

5. Les formes diphtonguées et non diphtonguées de l'ancien *ǫ́* libre alternent: *trove* (30/67b 26) et *trueve* (6/12b 11); *ovre* 'oeuvre' (29/66d 5, 40/78b 10, etc.); *nove* (20/66a 20); *avoques* 'avec' (30/68a 16); *volent* 'veulent' (30/67b 29), mais *iluec* (47/105b 21), *euef* 'oeuf' (47/104a 16), *eués* 'oeufs' (47/103d 19), *oés* et *eués* de **opus** (11/40d 28, 47/105b 7), *muert* (62/145a 25).

6. C'est également un *o* sans signe de diphtongaison qui note le plus souvent le descendant de *ǫ* + *l* + *yod: voil* (1/1a 11, 16/46d 7, 47/106d 12, etc.), *voille* (30/67c 15), *oil* 'yeux' (15/45b 21), *dol* 'deuil' (40/80b 12) mais *duel* (62/144b 11), *escuirol* (11/40a 24) mais *escuiroel* (11/40c 22).

7. La lettre *o* note encore à elle seule l'ancien *ǫ́* libre, surtout dans la terminaison -*or*, et l'ancien *ǫ́* entravé, témoins, par exemple, les rimes *labor: jor* (18/50a 19—20), et *prior: jor* (11/40a 7—8). Mais on recontre aussi *ou* et *eu: pooreuse: dotouse* (62/144a 5—6), *grevox* (56/116b 10), etc.

Parmi les consonnes, relevons:

8. l'absence assez fréquente du *d* intercalaire: *vanredi* (62/143d 27), *reponez vos* 'cachez-vous' (1/3c 13), les futurs *venré* (7/23c 12), *remanra* (18/50c 26), et les formes où un *d* étymologique s'est effacé après *n: responnent* 'répondent' (18/50c 25), *venenge* 'il vendange' (6/13d 15);

9. l'effacement de *s* devant consonne: *hate* 'hâte' (6/15d 3), *mellee* 'mêlée' (30/67d 18), *deites* 'dîtes' (62/144b 29), etc., ce qui donne lieu à de nombreux contrépels: *lastes* 'lattes' (30/67b 16), *moston* 'mouton' (56/116c 8), *costiaux* 'couteaux' (56/117a 17), *bascons* 'bacon' (47/105a 30);

10. la valeur sourde d'un seul *s* intervocalique: *sause* 'sauce' (6/15a 19), *grases* (30/67b 21), *puises* 'puisses' (29/66c 15), *eüsent* (6/15b 16), etc.

11. Quant à la morphologie, la forme *lo, lou* de l'article défini et du pronom personnel au cas régime singulier masculin couvre tout le recueil avec une grande constance; je n'ai relevé que 4 occurrences de *le*, 2 pour l'article, et 2 pour le pronom. *Lou* est plus fréquent que *lo* en B1 qu'en B2. Parmi les formes enclitiques, *do, dou* pour *de le*, et *o, ou* pour *en le* n'étonnent

guère, mais *no, nou* pour *ne le* (*no* en 7/18a 10, 10/38c 18, 66/152a 8, etc., *nou* en 1/3a 6, 1/3c 16) et surtout *sou* pour *si le* (7/17b 13) sont plus rares.[6]

12. Nous avons signalé plus haut les pronoms *ax* et *çax*; à côté de cette dernière forme se rencontrent *cels* et *cez* (*Cez entor cui ele se tient* 56/116b 9, *A cez cui povreté maintient* 56/116b 16).

13. Les secondes personnes du présent de l'indicatif de *estre* sont constamment *ies* et *iestes* (16/46b 27, 62/144b 27, etc.; 15/45a 10, 62/144b 29, etc.), et j'ai même relevé *iest* (*Dont Poitou est a la reonde Toz clos et iest itiex sa force* 6/12d 4–5).

14. La désinence *-oiz* est régulièrement employée au futur (4/10c 7, 31/68c 19, etc.) et parfois au subjonctif présent (1/1c 19, 16/47a 28).

15. La désinence *-on*, qui surprend dans l'ensemble de cette *scripta*, n'y est pourtant pas rare et ne s'expliquerait pas dans toutes ses occurrences par la chute de *s* devant initiale consonantique; cf. devant voyelle *devon* (18/50c 4), *laisson* (47/107c 9), *alon* (47/107c 10).

Tels sont les traits que B1 et B2 partagent. Voici ceux qui les différencient:

16. B2 préfère nettement la graphie étymologique *ai* tandis que B1 utilise souvent *e: faire* (56/117b 13) et *fere* (1/1a 11).

17. Inversément, B1 respecte le plus souvent la distinction étymologique entre *en* et *an*, tandis que B2 recourt de préférence à *an: gent* (16/47b 2) et *janz* (40/78c 16). On retrouve la même différence entre *en* et *an* dans les formes du pronom indéfini 'on': B1 préfère *l'en* (16/45d 3), B2 *l'an* (62/145a 25).

18. B1 écrit *-iex* la terminaison qui remonte à *-alis*, mais B2 l'écrit *-ex: ostiex* (1/1a 22), *menesteriex* (6/16a 10), *tiex* (10/39a 8), *quiex* (1/2a 10), etc.; *menesterex* (29/66a 28), *tex* (40/78b 22), *qex* (29/65d 30), etc.

19. Au français moderne *-eille* correspond *-elle* en B1, mais *-oille* en B2: *mervelle* (15/45b 3), *ourelle* (1/2a 5), *esvelle* (15/45b 4), etc.; *mervoille* (56/116d 5), *oroille* (47/105c 9), *esvoille* (47/107d 10), etc.

20. Sont propres à B2 les imparfaits du subjonctif *aüsse* (23/58c 21), *aüsses* (47/106b 11), *aüst* (21/58a 13), *saüst* (40/79a 15), le participe *aü* (47/106b 9), de même que *aürs* de **augurium** (47/107b 24) et *aüree* (30/67c 10).

21. B2 est seul enfin à diphtonguer *o* + *n* dans *boen* (23/59a 10, etc.) alors que B1 écrit régulièrement *bon* (1/2b 30, etc.), sauf à la rime, comme nous le verrons plus loin.

Ce n'est pas ici le lieu d'approfondir dans tous ses détails la question de la localisation du recueil de Berne. Je suis convaincu

---

[6] A côté de *sou = si le*, on rencontre la forme *sou = si vo(s)*: *Parlez, sou plest, ainz que m'esloigne* (1/2c 13); faut-il en rapprocher cet exemple de *vo* tonique sans *s* qui ne paraît pas être le possessif picard: *Vassaus, dist il, por coi menez Les levriers, quant il vo ne sont* (7/25a 23)?

que des relevés plus complets nous conduiraient à une localisation relativement précise de la *scripta* de B2 qui, plus marquée, donne plus de prise à l'analyse et à la comparaison. On sait que règne un certain consensus parmi les savants qui se sont occupés de telle ou telle pièce du recueil: ils en placent la confection dans la région orientale du domaine d'oïl et quelques-uns d'entre eux précisent: la Lorraine.[7] Avec Ernest Hoepffner,[8] je considère pour ma part la *scripta* de B2 comme bourguignonne. Je me fonde tout d'abord pour cela sur un argument d'autorité: le grand spécialiste des *scriptae* médiévales, mon collègue et ami le regretté C. Th. Gossen, concluait l'analyse des relevés que je lui ai présentés par cet avis prudent mais de poids: "Tout ce que l'on peut dire, selon moi, c'est que les textes offrent quelques traits typiques de la *scripta* dite bourguignonne, ou plus générale-ment du Sud-Est" (lettre du 30 novembre 1982). Je suis frappé aussi, outre l'accord général des traits principaux que nous avons relevés avec la *scripta* bourguignonne, par quelques coïncidences de détail.

E. Philipon[9] signale comme traits bourguignons la chute de *b* après *m* et celle de *r* devant consonne; or B1 et B2 les attestent sporadiquement: *amedui* (1/3b 20), *jame* 'jambe' (8/27d 24, 41/87a 21, 87c 6), *jamet* 'jambet, croc-en-jambe' (6/13ª b 22: *M'abat d'un jamet d'Engleterre*); *Fabu* pour *Farbu* (4/10c 3 et 11c 16), *matirs* 'martyrs' (62/144b 22), et graphie inverse *borc*

[7] C'est le cas, notamment, dans les éditions que j'ai citées plus haut de P. Nardin, de M. Walters-Gehrig, de V. Väänänen; le Nord de la Champagne a eu la préférence de Alfons Hilka (*Der Percevalroman von Christian von Troyes*, Halle, 1932, p. iii), suivi par Alexandre Micha (*La tradition manuscrite des romans de Chrétien de Troyes*, Paris, 1939, p. 57) et par M. L. Mihm (*op. cit.*), tandis que R.C. Johnston et D.D.R. Owen le rapprochent de la capitale en le plaçant dans la partie occidentale de la Champagne.

[8] "Des trois principaux dialectes de l'Est (lorrain, champenois, bourguignon), le lorrain doit être exclu. Le texte ignore entre autres complètement le trait le plus caractéristique du lorrain, le dégagement de *i* après une voyelle tonique, notamment après *e* issu de a. On hésitera plutôt entre le champenois et le bourguignon. La plupart des traits linguistiques que nous avons signalés ici se trouvent aussi bien dans l'un que dans l'autre de ces dialectes. Cependant, l'évolution de *ei* à *oi* devant *n*, ou en syllabe protonique (*roiaume* etc.); l'article et le pronom *lo*, toujours au lieu de *le*, de même *no*, *nou*, etc., pour *nel* etc., font pencher la balance en faveur de la Bourgogne." *Op. cit.*, pp. 28—29.

[9] 'Les parlers du duché de Bourgogne aux XIIIe et XIVe siècles' dans *Romania*, XXXIX (1910), 476—531, en partic. 527; voir aussi *Romania*, XLI (1912), 587.

'bouc' (30/67a 27). Les imparfaits du subjonctif *trovissiez* (*Ne trovissiez un grateor* 18/51c 8) de B1 et surtout *vossessent* de B2 (*Eles vossessent qu'il fust ars* 44/95d 11) ont une allure très bourguignonne: *vossessiens, vossissent* se rencontrent au XIVe siècle dans des documents de la région.[10]

De grandes similitudes rapprochent enfin la *scripta* de B2 de la *scripta* littéraire bourguignonne telle qu'elle apparaît dans les manuscrits bourguignons de *Floovant*[11] et du *Girart de Rossillon* en vers du XIVe siècle.[12] Au-delà de la rencontre sur tous les traits importants (y compris *iau* dans *miauz* < **melius** et *viaut* < **volet**), des détails frappent à nouveau. Le présent de l'indicatif *seut* de *suivre* (ms. *S* du *Girart*) rappelle *seust* de B2 (30/67b 23, 62/144a 11), dont le *s* provient sans doute d'une graphie inverse. *Chevoux* 'cheveux', en dépit de *ę + l + s* > *au* (cf. no. 2 ci-dessus), rencontre notre *chevox* (8/29a 25, 15/45b 22, 18/50b 9; cf. aussi *chevol* 66/155c 4). Le subjonctif *aüst* est attesté sans *h* dans le manuscrit *S* du *Girart* comme en B2 (cf. no. 20). *Giter, gitiés* du *Girart* sont analogues à *gitiez* (56/117a 16) ou *gistez* (40/80b 28). Les cas isolés de *ch* pour *g* dans la terminaison *-aige*, dans le *Girart*, évoquent nos *domache* (7/18a 13) et *fromache* (6/15a 7 et 8, 18/50b 3). Et les formes enclitiques *dou, nou* et *sou* (cf. no. 11) se rencontrent aussi dans le *Girart*. La chute de *l* devant consonne après *e*, attestée pour *Floovant* par des formes comme *ces* (**ecce illos**) ou comme *tinés* pour *tinels*, rappelle notre démonstratif *cez* (cf. no. 12) et les substantifs *soumés* 'sommeil' (15/45a 1) et *mantés* 'manteau'.[13]

A ces éléments de localisation empruntés à la *scripta* proprement dite de nos deux copistes, leur vocabulaire en ajoute

[10] Voir Ewald Goerlich, *Der burgundische Dialekt im XIII. und XIV. Jahrhundert* (Heilbronn, 1889), pp. 136 et 140.

[11] Montpellier, Bibliothèque de la Faculté de médecine, no. 441, publié par Sven Andolf, *Floovant, chanson de geste du XIIe siècle* (Uppsala, 1941); l'étude de la langue du manuscrit se trouve aux pages xcvi—clxxxiii.

[12] Montpellier, Bibliothèque de la Faculté de médecine, no. 349 (sigle *S*) et Paris BN fr. 15103 (sigle *P*), écrit à Châtillon-sur-Seine en 1417. Voir l'édition de Edward Billings Ham, *Girart de Rossillon, poème bourguignon du XIVe siècle* (New Haven, 1939); étude de la *scripta* des deux copistes bourguignons et de la langue de l'auteur aux pages 25—46 et 57—74.

[13] Il faut sans doute, en effet, lire la rubrique finale du *Lai du court mantel, ci fenit cormantes* (44/100d 23): *ci fenit cor[z] mantés*. La rubrique initiale en est: *Ci conmance de cort mantel* (93c 3).

quelques autres. Nous avons déjà signalé que l'auteur des rubriques écrivait *preste(s)*, comme B2, le mot *prestre*;[14] or cette forme, en dehors du Nord-Est, est bourguignonne surtout (*FEW*, IX, 357b, et T.-L., VII, 1824). Le mot *venenge* 'il vendange', écrit par B1 en 6/13d 15 (*Chascuns li venenge son orne*), doit être rapproché des formes sans *d* attestées en Bourgogne, en Franche-Comté et en Suisse romande (*FEW*, XIV, 465). B2 a remplacé le vers *Lors vont concueillir des sechons*, attesté par les trois manuscrits *ACD* dans la pièce 47 (*D* 395), par: *Puis vont querir des secherons* (106d 25). Est-ce un hasard si *secherons*, hapax dans les dictionnaires de Godefroy et de Tobler et Lommatzsch, est attesté dans les seuls patois de l'Yonne au sens de 'échalas de rebut', qui ne servent plus qu'au feu?[15]

Ces deux Bourguignons — laissons-les au bénéfice de cette honorable identité jusqu'à plus ample informé — il nous faut maintenant éprouver leur travail. Mais ils vont être saisis, hélas! bien plus facilement dans leurs défauts que dans leurs qualités: l'innocence ne laisse pas de trace . . . Encore devrions-nous ne pas les accuser de crimes qu'ils n'ont pas commis! C'est le grand danger qui nous guette, car les manuscrits qu'ils ont suivis étant pour nous perdus, la préhistoire des fautes que nous constatons nous échappe. Nous nous entourerons donc des précautions nécessaires sinon suffisantes en observant d'abord deux textes, un pour chacun des deux copistes, pour lesquels nous disposons d'autres manuscrits en nombre suffisant. Leur témoignage nous aidera à ne pas charger indûment les scribes du manuscrit de Berne. Pour prendre tout de suite un exemple tiré de la pièce 6 que nous choisissons comme échantillon du travail de B1, si nous lisons en 12c 6—9 ces quatre vers:

> Comment chascuns de ses parenz
> *Demande* et ausi demanda

---

[14] Cf. les rubriques des pièces 41 (80c 8) et 61 (143b 13); dans le texte de B2, voir 41/80d 4, 81c 30, 81d 5, etc., et 56/116d 14, 18, 20, 25, 30; 117a 20, 25.

[15] Cf. *FEW*, XI, 587a, et S. Jossier, *Dictionnaire des patois de l'Yonne* (Auxerre, 1882), p. 146.

Et de ce mes cuers li conta
Un conte qu'ele tint a boen

et que nous les comparons avec le texte de *A* 40—43:

Si com chascuns de ses parenz
Se *demaine* m'a demandé,
Et je li ai tantost conté
Un conte qu'ele tint a buen,

nous sommes tentés d'accuser B1 de la mauvaise lecture *demande* pour *demaine* qui rend son texte incompréhensible. La riche tradition manuscrite du *Songe d'enfer* de Raoul de Houdenc, disponible dans la bonne édition de M. L. Mihm (*op. cit.*), nous montre cependant que *B* partage la faute avec quatre manuscrits et qu'il n'en est donc pas responsable. Les risques d'erreur, qui subsistent, sont donc diminués par l'existence de neuf manuscrits conservés. Les fautes suivantes, que nous avons relevées et classées plus ou moins strictement, n'apparaissent toujours qu'en B1, cela va de soi.

Dans l'ensemble, B1 est tout sauf attentif. Il commet des fautes d'étourderie portant sur une ou deux lettres: *cil* pour *ci* (12b 7), *totes voie* (13d 11), *devoit* pour *devoient* (13ᵃ b 24), *monjoi* pour *monjoie* (14a 18), *sai* pour *sain* 'graisse' (15a 9), *prestres* pour *prestresse* (15d 7), *et du* pour *i fu* (16a 27), *contomenz* pour *contenemenz* (12c 5), *Haharz* pour *Hasarz* (13c 2), etc. Rares sont les fautes de ce type que B1 a remarquées et exponctuées, comme il l'a fait pour *tost*, par exemple (16a 23), qu'il faut lire *tot*.

Il oublie parfois des mots (ajoutons toujours: si c'est bien lui . . .), avec les conséquences qu'on imagine pour le sens: *s'ert* (12c 12, cf. *A* 46), *le* (13ᵃ d 15, cf. *A* 331), *en ot* (14d 2—3, cf. *A* 453), *en son tour* (13ᵃ b 20—21, cf. *A* 277). Omission plus considérable, un bourdon lui fait sauter les vers 543—548 de *A* (entre 15c 4 et 15c 5).

Une ressemblance phonique appelle *regardasse* pour *recordasse* (13ᵃ c 15, cf. *A* 301), et c'est peut-être une véritable dictée intérieure qui lui inspire en 13c 27 *Quant tost taverne de Paris* ('quant aux tavernes de Paris'?) pour un vers qui pourrait avoir été dans son modèle *Que tuit tavernier de Paris* (cf. *A* 183 et les variantes).

Une tendance continue à la répétition amène *Larrecin* à la place de *Cruauté* en 13ᵃ d 22 (cf. *A* 338), fait malheureusement rimer sur la même rime les vers 13b 19 et 20 (cf. *A* 143—144), 13ᵃ d 23 et 24 (cf. *A* 340) et 14a 1 et 2 (cf. *A* 350), et le conduit à reproduire la fin de 50d 27 à la fin de la ligne suivante.

Son indifférence au sens se confirme dans les mauvaises lectures qu'il fait de son modèle. Là où celui-ci devait commencer le vers *A* 47, comme tous les autres manuscrits, par *Sa gent* (graphié peut-être *Sa ient*), B1 confond le *S* majuscule avec le signe d'abréviation de *con* et écrit *Coniaent* (*Con* abrégé en *9*) sans se soucier d'une signification (12c 13). Au vers 72 de *A*, il lit *Quan aus* 'car en eux' *Qu'anors* (12d 8). *Estre sovent* (*A* 201) devient *Entre sont* (13d 10); *en son devant* (*A* 285) est lu *en son demant* (13ᵃ b 29); *S'en loerent* (*A* 507) se mue en *Si en orent* (15b 5) et *Mes ne remest* (*A* 638) en *Mes il ne m'est* (16a 20).

Il semble que B1 soit particulièrement inattentif au sens de ce qu'il copie quand il parvient au bas d'une colonne. En tout cas, c'est en cet endroit que se situent les deux mélectures suivantes. Au bas de la colonne 13a, il lit et écrit *chiés mi home* un texte qui devait être *chiés nul home* (*A* 124). La distraction du bas de la colonne 14b est plus amusante; là où son modèle portait *Sus el palais fet a ciment* (*A* 408), B1 lit *El palés fet anciaument*. Et c'est encore au passage d'une colonne à l'autre que se produisent les deux cafouillages suivants. Interversion et vers trop court entre les colonnes 15c et 15d: *Que langues de fax plaideors* [fin de colonne] *Sont molt chieres et amees Ne sont pas en enfer blasmees*, alors qu'on lit en *A* et dans les autres manuscrits: *Que langues de faus pledeors Ne sont pas en enfer blasmees, Mes chier tenues et amees* (*A* 574—576). Au bas de la colonne 15b, B1 écrit d'abord correctement avec les manuscrits de son groupe: *Des langues as pleideors sorent Fere li keu un entremés*, puis il perd le fil dans le dernier vers de la colonne: *N'onques de nul tens n'oï mes*, ce qui anticipe plus ou moins sur le premier vers de la colonne 15c: *N'oïstes mais parler a cort.*[16] On le voit, l'inattention peut aboutir au galimatias,

---

[16] Dans la pièce 10, c'est également au bas d'une colonne (38d) que B1 transcrit prématurément les deux vers *Sovent Il est li feus qui tot esprent*, qu'il copiera à nouveau à leur bonne place en 39b 13—14, conformément à *A* 143—144. Il se corrige

comme dans cet exemple encore, où le vers: *Nus a lor mengier
s'il n'aporte Ne vient, ce voit l'on en apert* (leçon des manuscrits
du groupe auquel appartient *B*, correspond à *A* 383) devient:
Ne voit en ce voi en apert (14b 5).

Ne quittons pas la pièce 6 de B1 sans mentionner la faute
curieuse qu'il commet au vers correspondant à *A* 57. Voici le
passage dans ce dernier recueil. Tricherie pose une question au
pèlerin de l'enfer, le *je* du récit: *Et Tricherie a un seul mot Me
redemanda esraument Que je li deïsse comment* Li tricheor
se maintenoient, Icil qui a li se tenoient, *Se le voir li savoie
espondre*. Au lieu des deux vers que je laisse en romains, B1,
qui sans cela porte le même texte, donne: *Li deciple de son
convent, De çax qui desoz lui estoient* (12c 23—24). Ces deux
vers ne riment pas et il manque un verbe, correspondant à *se
maintenoient*, à la proposition interrogative. Mais surtout, *Li
deciple de son convent* se retrouve beaucoup plus loin (*A* 324),
attesté par tous les manuscrits y compris *B* (13ᵃ d 8), dans une
question de *Larrecin* absolument analogue à celle de *Tricherie*.
Comment se fait-il que B1 ait eu ce vers dans la tête ou sous les
yeux dès le vers 57? Nous pourrions naturellement illustrer aussi
ces différents types de fautes de B1 par des exemples pris dans
d'autres pièces que le *Songe d'enfer*. Nous aurions à y signaler,
notamment, dans les pièces 1, 10, 11 et 16, des omissions plus
importantes.

Mais il est temps de passer à l'échantillon de B2, le no. 47,
Des .iii. larrons, conservé aussi par les recueils *A*, *C* et *D*, tradition
accessible dans l'excellente édition de M. Walters-Gehrig (*op.
cit.*), dont la base est *D*. Le tableau n'est pas très différent: on y
retrouve les fautes de quelques lettres,[17] les omissions de petits
mots,[18] les mots remplacés à tort.[19] Au chapitre des omissions,

_____

au haut de la col. 39a, en revenant au texte correspondant à *A* 98; l'omission de
quelque 40 vers est ainsi évitée.

[17] *nel* pour *nes* (107a 25), *sentiroie* pour *sentiroient* (105b 15), *doie* (?) pour
cuidoie (106c 30), *alument et* pour *alumé i* (106d 17), *aporteront* pour *aporteroit*
(107b 25), *au* pour *a* (103d 2), *le* pour *les* (104a 7), *laperçut* pour *saperçut* (104b 1),
etc.

[18] *sa* (107d 10; cf. *D* 509), *la* (106b 23; cf. *D* 334), *deniers* (104c 5; cf. *D* 97),
jor (104d 7; cf. *D* 131), etc.

[19] *a terre* (105b 19) pour *en l'aire* (*D* 203), *antroveure* (107c 30) pour *entroverture*
(*D* 487), *jus cheuz* (105c 7) pour *descenduz* (*D* 226), *mangiez* (107b 18) pour

la pièce 47 n'offre pas d'exemple de bourdon, mais bien celui, plus instructif encore, d'un bourdon évité de justesse. Après le vers *De sa fame dame Marie* (104c 21; cf. *D* 113), qui ressemble beaucoup à celui qui viendra 55 vers plus loin: *Fait sa fame dame Marie* (105a 15; cf. *D* 169), B2 passe d'abord à *D* 170: *Qui tote m'ont faite marrie* (104c 22), qui n'a aucun sens dans le premier contexte, puis il se reprend en revenant, en 104c 23, à *D* 117, non sans laisser tomber un couplet, *D* 115—116. Le bourdon a bien failli amputer la copie de B2 d'une cinquantaine de vers!

B2 avait peut-être le regard un peu moins inattentif que son collègue, mais nous le surprenons tout de même lisant *sa moiller* (107d 1) pour *someiller* (*D* 489), et, si nous ne pouvions recourir à l'exactitude bien connue du recueil *A*, nous ne trouverions sans doute pas la clé de son vers *Vint vers lui lo grant dune pas* (106a 18),[20] qui est: *le grandisme pas*. La pièce est surtout riche en exemples de mots plus ou moins rares remplacés par des mots plus communs. Mais ceci n'appartient plus aux fautes proprement dites, dues à l'inattention et plus ou moins inconscientes, et nous réservons le cas pour un examen ultérieur.

Pour avoir une idée plus complète des fautes de B2, on se reportera à l'analyse détaillée que E. Hoepffner[21] a faite de la copie par B2 de la *Folie Tristan* (no. 66). Rappelons encore pour notre part la copie très mauvaise de la *Bourgeoise d'Orléans* (no. 40),[23] les omissions qui déparent les pièces 29 (dont la transcription est pourtant bien meilleure)[24] et 30,[25] une tendance à la répétition qui rappelle celle de B1.[26] J'épingle dans la pièce 56 cette amusante haplographie: *Si apestula son*

---

veilliez (*D* 446), *dessaissi* (107c 2) pour *desgarni* (*D* 460), *Or tuit* (106a 4) pour *Orainz* (*D* 285), *cuit* (107c 22) pour *claing* (*D* 480), *ot* (104c 28) pour *fist* (*D* 122), *espiee* (105a 24) pour *encligniee* (*D* 178), *hurté* (105b 26) pour *luitié* (*D* 210), etc.

[20] Cette lecture me paraît assurée, mais M. Walters-Gehrig lit dans ses variantes *grantdime pas*, qui serait correct. *D*, lui, a en quelque sorte traduit: *plus que le pas D* 299; quant à *C*, il a renchéri: *Vint a lui grantdisime pas.*

[21] Edition de la *Folie Tristan, op. cit.*, p. 27.

[23] Cf. ce que j'en disais dans *Contribution* (*op. cit.*), I, 60, n. 2.

[24] Les deux omissions concernent les vv. 81—88 et 129—155 de *D*, base de l'édition Faral (*op. cit.*). Les vers qui suivent immédiatement la seconde de ces lacunes (66d 21—22) se rattachent pourtant à ce qui y est dit.

[25] Soit les vv. 65—72, 82—86 et 163—166 de l'éd. Väänänen (*op. cit.*).

chien (116d 6) pour *Si apele Estula son chien.* Et j'avouerai pour finir que certaines séparations de mots étranges me font douter que B2 ait toujours compris ce qu'il écrivait; je me demande ainsi si la lecture *si q'an tresoï* 'de sorte qu'on entendit distinctement', sur le modèle assuré de *A: si c'on tresoï* (v. 37), n'outrepasse pas, en entendement, la graphie *si qantres oi* (116c 10), ou si B2 savait en écrivant $\overline{q}$ *se deuoie* (56/117a 13) que son lecteur devrait lire *que, se Dé voie.*

D'un côté comme de l'autre, convenons-en, bien décevante est l'image. . . . Malgré la sympathie que l'on ressent tout naturellement pour ceux auxquels notre curiosité s'attache et qui, finalement, doivent l'existence à nos découvertes, on n'affirmera pas que les scribes du recueil de Berne aient été des phénix de la copie. Il est possible qu'en ne relevant que leurs défauts nous ayons chargé le portrait jusqu'à la caricature. Il se peut aussi que nous ayons attribué à B1 ou B2 des erreurs que, reçues de leurs modèles perdus, ils n'ont fait que transmettre. La qualité inégale de leur copie selon les pièces du recueil, si du moins une étude complète parvenait à fixer clairement les différences, inciterait peut-être à le croire: les copies exécrables pourraient tenir à la tradition plutôt qu'au relâchement de l'attention. Mais serait-ce beaucoup plus glorieux de les avoir transmises que de les avoir commises? Les philologues classiques peuvent certes se féliciter des copies naïves qui leur permettent de rétablir la lettre des textes mal cachée sous les fautes, mais, dans les traditions de langue vulgaire, faites de retouches constantes, le respect des fautes reçues ne voile plus la bêtise, pour l'appeler par son nom. Voici un cas où nous entrevoyons, semble-t-il, la préhistoire d'une faute: il confirme, hélas! le peu de discernement de B2. Le mari de la bourgeoise d'Orléans (no. 40) s'est mis dans une situation sans issue. Nous lisons de lui, dans un passage propre à *B* (79d 22–25):

> A ceste ore volsist il bien
> A saint Jasque ou otremer.

---

[26] Rimes sur le même mot à la suite de répétitions fautives: 29/66c 5–6, 62/144a 28–29, 145a 9–10; mots répétés dans le même vers: *Tant qu'il vint a l'ostel a l'ostel a preste* (56/116d 18); vers copié deux fois: 44/94a 23–24.

> Lors l'ont par mi une fener
> De desus un fumier flati.

Il n'y avait vraiment pas besoin d'être un très grand clerc pour ajouter *estre* après *otremer* et pour écrire *fenestre* à la place de *fener*, qui n'existe pas. Si B2 a reçu le texte en cet état et s'est contenté de le reproduire, que n'a-t-il montré cette exactitude partout! Mais si, comme on peut le penser, il avait sous les yeux un texte privé seulement du mot *estre* et qu'il a inventé *fener* pour la rime, ce n'est pas très brillant non plus . . .

Nous avons jusqu'ici examiné le travail de nos deux copistes sous l'aspect de ses manques, de fautes commises le plus souvent inconsciemment. Nous l'observerons maintenant dans ses manifestations intentionnelles. Les transformations qui résultent de ces intentions peuvent être considérées aussi, en un sens, comme des 'fautes' contre une transmission fidèle, mais enfin, si les textes en sortent très généralement détériorés, moins pleins et moins tenus dans l'expression, ils n'en restent pas moins le plus souvent compréhensibles et 'acceptables'.

L'attribution des modifications de ce type à B1 ou à B2 eux-mêmes est certainement plus problématique encore que celle des fautes. Pour beaucoup d'entre ces dernières, en effet, leur coïncidence avec l'acte même de la transcription ne fait pas de doute. Il n'en va pas de même pour les retouches volontaires, dont il nous est impossible de savoir si elles n'appartenaient pas déjà aux modèles de nos copistes. Nous pouvons néanmoins relever les transformations qui, dans l'état actuel de la tradition manuscrite, appartiennent en propre à *B* pour, précisément, nous interroger à leur sujet. Nous le ferons en les classant dès l'abord en trois séries selon qu'elles affectent la prononciation ou *scripta* proprement dite, la déclinaison ou le vocabulaire. Nous avons abandonné les variantes de syntaxe et d' 'écriture', dont l'examen, plus délicat, devrait porter sur un plus grand nombre de pièces pour donner des résultats pertinents.

Quant à la *scripta*, nous connaissons déjà la composition de cette sorte de badigeon, de ce superstrat régional qui recouvre les formes originales des textes d'origines diverses accueillis dans le manuscrit de Berne. Mais nous n'avons pas observé

encore comment cette couche, assez uniformément étendue
sur l'intérieur des vers, laisse subsister à la rime des éléments
du substrat originel. On le sait assez: c'est dans les rimes,
conservatrices par nature, que l'on va chercher d'habitude la
langue des auteurs; c'est naturellement l'inverse pour la langue
des copistes.

Quand la rime jure avec le vernis bourguignon qu'ils passent
sur leur texte, nos copistes réagissent de deux façons différentes:
ou bien ils se soumettent, ou bien ils la modifient. Voici tout
d'abord quelques exemples de soumission. *Mortax*, au lieu de
mortiex, rime avec *mareschax* (10/39b 16); *Richeut* (abrégé *Ri.*),
au lieu de *Richaut* qui se trouve dans *l'incipit* (58/124c 10),
rime avec *sueut*, de **solet** (58/133a 5); *valt*, de **volet**, au lieu
de *vialt*, rime avec *citoalt* (18/52b 19); *morterus*, au lieu de
morteriax, rime avec *nus* 'nul' (4/11c 7), ou encore *sodre* 'payer'
avec *codre* 'noisetier' (47/107c 23). B1 écrit *bon* à l'intérieur du
vers mais accepte *boen* ou *buen* à la rime avec *soen* ou *suen* (1/2d
25, 6/12c 9, 15/45a 18, 18/50d 27). Il conserve parfois à la rime
les graphies *mervelle* et *s'esvelle* qui lui sont familières (6/13ᵃa 7,
6/16b 17), mais se laisse ailleurs influencer partiellement et
sans nécessité par son modèle en écrivant *s'esvoille : mervelle*
(15/44c 7). Le pronom indéfini *on* n'apparaît sous cette forme
que lorsque la rime l'exige (7/18a 2 avec *non*, 56/116c 9 avec
moston), alors qu'il est toujours *en* ou *an* à l'intérieur du vers.
Et c'est encore à la rime que B1 reproduit l'imparfait en *-ot*
(6/13c 16, 7/24d 1, 18/51d 28)[27] ou le présent du subjonctif
en *-ge* (*amorge : forge* 4/10c 22—23), originaires de régions bien
différentes de la sienne, la Normandie et la Picardie.

Mais le manuscrit de Berne atteste aussi que 'quelqu'un', dans
la transmission de son texte, a eu une attitude moins passive qui

---

[27] Il est certes curieux que, dans ce dernier cas, *B* soit seul à attester l'imparfait
en *-ot* contre les manuscrits *A* et *C* qui ont la forme en *-oit*: *Car chascuns molt tres
bien sot Por coi li rois les apelot* (*B*), *Quar chascons d'aus moult bien savoit Por qoi li
rois les apeloit* (*AC*). Nous avons cependant toutes les raisons de croire que *B* trouvait
la forme en *-ot* dans son modèle; la syllabe qui lui manque n'est pas celle qu'il gagnerait
avec *savoit* pour *sot*, mais bien celle qu'il a perdue en oubliant *d'aus*; cf. *AC*. Quant à
la remarque de Ph. Ménard (*op. cit.*, p. 156) contre l'authenticité de l'imparfait en
-ot dans le *Mire de Brai*, elle ne semble pas pertinente puisque l'imparfait du v. 260
auquel il se réfère, *avoit*, n'appartenant pas à la conjugaison en *-er*, ne pouvait être
différent.

consiste à remplacer une rime trop manifestement étrangère. Comme nous l'avons remarqué, il nous est impossible de savoir si ce quelqu'un est l'un des deux copistes du manuscrit, mais il devait avoir du moins les mêmes raisons qu'eux pour récuser la rime. Quoi qu'il en soit, observons le cas particulièrement instructif d'une rime tantôt acceptée tantôt refusée.

La terminaison picarde -*ie*, descendante de *yod* + -*ata*, étrangère à la langue de B1 comme de B2, a été acceptée quand elle rime avec elle-même. Elle est alors graphiée tantôt -*ie* tantôt -*iee* (*mesnie : haitie* 8/34c 26—27; *haitiee : correciee* 18/50a 25—26, contre *haitie : corocie* de *CA*). Quand elle rime avec un -*ie* dans lequel survit un *i* long latin, elle est soit tolérée (*changie : charrie* 15/44d 18—19), soit remplacée; le couplet de Jean Bodel d'Arras attesté par *A* 113—114 et *C* 117—118: *Ainz ne li lut son nez mouchier S'ot esté trois fois assaillie. Or a Gombers bone mesnie* devient alors: *S'ot esté trois foiz essaiee. Or a Gonberz bone mesniee* (15/45a 6—7). Est-ce donc B1 lui-même qui, dans la même pièce, a tantôt reproduit tantôt modifié la rime picarde? Ce changement d'humeur, doublé peut-être du sentiment d'une difficulté plus grande dans un cas que dans l'autre, n'a rien d'invraisemblable. Mais nous n'avons pas la preuve que ces deux attitudes n'aient pas été en réalité celles de deux transcripteurs différents, la modification remontant alors à un état du texte antérieur à *B* et perdu pour nous.

Le mot *feu* appartient sous cette forme à la langue de B1 et de B2. A trois reprises pourtant, dans la même pièce copiée par B2, est acceptée la rime picarde *fu* 'feu' : *fu* 'il fut' (47/104a 11, 106d 15, 107b 4). Je trouve la trace possible d'un refus de la même rime dans un texte copié par B1; *La baissele esveillie fu, Son huis ovri, si fist du fu*, attesté par *D* 93—94, y devient en effet: *Si fu la beasse levee, Si se leva, fist sa foee* (1/1d 8—9). Si la forme *beasse* est bourguignonne, comme il le semble, il y aurait là un argument de plus en faveur de la responsabilité de B1 dans la modification de la rime, encore que *beasse* puisse avoir remplacé *baissele* dans un vers déjà modifié. De toute façon, le caractère très limité de nos premiers relevés nous recommande de ne pas différencier trop rapidement B1 et B2 face à *fu : fu*.

L'opposition entre -*z* et -*s* avait probablement perdu sa

pertinence pour B1 comme pour B2 qui tous deux écrivent parfois avec -*s*, à l'intérieur du vers, des mots dont l'étymologie réclame -*z*. Ils accepteront donc facilement des rimes qui réunissent -*s* et -*z*: *Gonberz : aers* (15/45c 5—6), *asazez : mez* de **mansus** (56/116b 21—22), *jus : esmoluz* (56/117a 16—17), *chaus* 'chauds': *chaus* 'chauves' (30/67d 4—5). Il semble même qu'en 15 B1 s'est montré une fois sur ce point plus conservateur (en dépit de sa graphie -*z* que l'étymologie condamne dans *ademiz*) que *A* et *C* en écrivant: *Ainz que li jorz soit esclarciz A son lit se rest ademiz* 'il s'est précipité dans son lit' (45a 24—25) contre: *Ainz que li jours fust escleriez A son lit en est reperiez* (*A* 133 et *C* 137). Aussi hésitera-t-on à mettre au compte de B1 l'innovation (si le texte a bien évolué dans ce sens) qui, dans la pièce 1, a rétabli une rime sur deux -*s*; texte de *D* 142—144: *Maroie, fait ele, que dist Li vallez qui tant a la sis? — Dame, ne me chalt de ses dis*; texte de B1: *Li vaslez qui tant a la sis? — Dame, a mon cuer n'en ai rien mis* (1/2a 25—26).

Un point de morphologie (qui concerne le compte des syllabes et non la rime, mais le cas est analogue) sépare B1 et B2, dans l'état actuel de notre documentation du moins. Le possessif picard se rencontre plusieurs fois dans la pièce 62, copiée par B2: *vo sairemant* (144c 1), *no mestre* (144c 4), *vo cors* (145a 24), tandis que dans la pièce 16 copiée par B1, *vo* disparaît au profit de *vostre*:

 A 82 Si la partez a *vo* compaingne
     Et aus chevaliers de *vo* table.

 F 130 Sel departés a *vo* compaingne
     Et as chevaliers de *vo* table.

 B 140 S'en donez a *vostre* compaigne,
     As chevaliers de *vostre* table. (46d 14—15)

 A 128 N'ai mes talent que *vo* cort sive
 F 180 N'ai mais talant en *vo* court voise
 B 178 N'é talant que *vostre* cort siue (47a 22)

Les choses semblent claires: B1 refuse *vo*. Mais que dire alors du cas suivant:

 A 125 Partir fist son avoir par mi,
     Vo part vous envoie par *mi*.

F 177 Si parti son avoir par mi,
    Vostre part vous envoiie *chi.*

B 175 Partir fist son avoir par mi,
    Vostre part vos envoie *ci.*   (47a 19—20)

Là, B1 rencontre *F* dans le remplacement simultané des deux formes picardes *vo* et *mi*;[28] si la rencontre n'est pas fortuite, ce serait que la modification a eu lieu avant eux (car l'un ne copie pas l'autre): B1 ne serait pour rien dans le dernier cas, que, en l'absence de *F*, nous aurions été bien tentés de lui attribuer.[29]

Au moment de quitter ces observations sur les rimes refusées et remplacées 'pour cause de *scripta*', remarquons que, si une étude complète du manuscrit de Berne confirmait ce que nos sondages révèlent peut-être trompeusement, à savoir que les modifications de rimes sont plus fréquentes dans la partie du manuscrit copiée par B1 que dans celle copiée par B2, il y aurait là une indication à retenir pour la solution du problème qui nous préoccupe. Cette plus grande fréquence, en effet, à la condition qu'elle soit suffisamment affirmée pour exclure le hasard, ne pourrait avoir d'autre raison que l'initiative de B1 lui-même. Et c'est justement en vue de solutions de ce type qu'une étude transversale nous paraissait souhaitable.

Quant à savoir si le même homme que nous avons vu capable des pires erreurs de copie dans une indifférence surprenante au sens l'était aussi de la réflexion nécessaire aux modifications intentionnelles que nous venons de voir, c'est une question que l'on ne peut esquiver et qu'imposent aussi les observations qui engagent la déclinaison et le vocabulaire.

Pour la déclinaison, on peut considérer que, dans l'ensemble, le manuscrit de Berne la conserve. Cela n'empêche pas que B1 et

---

[28] B2 a conservé le pronom personnel *mi* en 30/67a 14, à la rime avec *ami*, alors que *A* et *E* l'ont remplacé chacun à sa manière. V. Väänänen (*op. cit.*, p. 19) classe ce trait parmi ceux qui permettraient de localiser la copie *B*; en réalité, il n'appartient pas du tout à la langue de B2, qui conserve ici un trait de l'original.

[29] Je signale encore que B1 semble avoir rejeté par trois fois (dans le cadre de mes sondages) l'homophonie entre les sons qui remontent respectivement à ρ libre et ρ entravé (cf. C. Th. Gossen, *Grammaire de l'ancien picard*, Paris, 1976, p. 81). Les rimes remplacées étaient *jors : vavassors* et *soule : foule* dans la pièce 1 (vv. 15—16 et 155—156 dans le ms. *D*), et *eure : sequeure* dans la pièce 15 (vv. 53—54 dans *A*). Enfin, les rimes *place : saiche* (1, vv. 37—38 de *D*) et *mire : chire* (pour *chiere*, 18, vv. 173—174 de *C*) ne se retrouvent pas dans le texte de B1.

B2 ne laissent passer ou ne commettent eux-mêmes d'assez nombreuses fautes sous ce rapport. B1 partage notamment avec les manuscrits *A* et *C* les nombreuses rimes du *Vilain mire* (no. 18) qui négligent la distinction entre cas sujet et cas régime. En voici deux exemples:

> Et quant il sera esloigniez
> De sa meson, *lo chapelain*
> I ira tant hui et demain
> Que sa feme li foutera.   (50a 6–9; cf. *A* 48)

> Dist l'uns a l'autre: 'Bien sez tu
> Qu'il vialt avant estre *batu*
> Qu'il die ne bien ne voidie.'   (50d 19–21; cf. *A* 187)[30]

Il arrive plus souvent, dans cette pièce, que B1 ne partage la faute qu'avec *C*, très probablement à la suite d'une correction de *A*:

> Mes por feme qu'il ne prenoit
> Lou blasmoient molt *ses amis*
> Et tote la gent do païs.   (49c 29–49d 1; cf. *C* 8–10)

> Mes por fame que pas n'avoit
> Le blasmoient mout *si ami*
> Et toute la gent autressi.   (*A* 8–10)[31]

Quant à B2, il partage avec *A* la rime suivante de la pièce 40:

> Et seroit encontre lui la
> Qant il seroit bien anuitié.
> Li borjois l'ot, molt s'an fist *lié*. (78b29–78cl; cf. *A* 48,
>   *C* a refait le passage)

et celle-ci de la pièce 56:

> Si cuida ce fust *son compains*
> Qui aportast aucun gaain   (117a 10–11)

tandis que *D* corrige:

> Si cuida ce fust *ses conpainz*
> Qui aportast *aucuns gaainz*.   (v. 99–100)

---

[30] Cf. encore, dans l'édition Ménard, les vv. 117–118 et 343–344.
[31] Cf. encore les vv. 21–22, 49–50, 145–146, 201–202, 243–244, 281–282, 315–316, 353–354, 371–372.

Et voici maintenant des fautes que B1 et B2 commettent peut-
être eux-mêmes, en tout cas qu'ils ne partagent avec aucun
manuscrit conservé. Faute de graphie seulement dans les vers
suivants copiés par B1:

> Puis si s'est lez lou feu *cochié*,
> Bien s'est gratez et *aïsié*.   (18/51c 4–5)[32]

Faute plus profonde, atteignant la langue, dans:

> Ou Gomberz se gisoit, *son oste*.
> Et cil lo feri sor la coste   (15/45a 26–27)

alors que *A* et *C* écrivent correctement:

> La ou gisoit Gombers *ses ostes*.
> Cil le fiert du poing lez les costes   (*A* 135–136)[33]

Pour B2, il s'impose de citer ces quelques vers de la *Bourgeoise
d'Orléans*:

> Qanqu'il pooit tenir as poinz
> Estoit molt fermement *tenuz*.
> De Normandie sont *venuz*
> .iiii. *normanz clers escoliers*;
> Lor sas portent comme *coliers*,
> Dedanz lor livres et lor dras.
> Molt estoient *mignoz* et gras,
> Cortois, chantant et *envoisiez*
> Et en la vile bien *prisiez*.   (40/78a 15–23)

C ne commet aucune de ces fautes.

On s'étonnera dès lors que B1 et B2 soient parfois plus
rigoureux dans l'emploi des cas que les autres manuscrits. La
première pensée qui vienne à l'esprit est qu'ils ont cueilli là,
seuls, un rameau de la tradition remontant à l'original ou
redressé en cours de route avant eux. Mais est-ce tellement
sûr? Je soumets à l'appréciation du lecteur deux exemples

---

[32] Faute d'autant plus curieuse que *gratez* est accordé et surtout que, dans le texte
de B1, le premier de ces deux vers est écrit deux fois, la première fois (exponctuée
ensuite) avec *cochiez*. Les leçons respectives de *A* 253–254 et de *C* 261–262 sont:
Et s'est travers le feu couchiez, Si s'est gratez et estrilliez, et: *Si s'est delés le feu assis
Et s'est gratez et bien rostiz.*

[33] Cf. encore les fautes de B1 en 1/1d 12, 1/3d 12, 8/26d 2, 11/41a 3–4, 18/51c
8–9, 18/51c 31.

pour chacun des deux copistes. Les messagers du roi font part à la femme du vilain mire (pièce 18) de la maladie de la princesse:

> La fille le roi est malade.
> Il a passé .viii. jors *entiers* [entier *C*]
> Que ne pot boivre ne mengier,
> Quar une areste de poisson
> Li aresta ou gavion.   (*A* 144–148)

Telle est la leçon de *AC*, dans laquelle on a quelque peine à croire avec Ph. Ménard (*op. cit.*, p. 154) que *C* ait considéré *entier* comme un adverbe. Quoi qu'il en soit, les rapports étroits de *BC*, soulignés par le même éditeur (pp. 151–52), donnent du poids à l'accord de *AC* sur cette leçon. Voici celle de *B*:

> La fille au roi est si malade
> Qu'el ne puet boivre ne mengier.
> Il a passé .viii. jorz *des ier*
> Que une areste de poison
> Li aresta el gavïon.   (50c 6–10)

Il n'est pas certain, soit, que *des ier* et l'ordre des vers de *B* ne soient pas authentiques et que le texte n'ait pas été corrigé en *AC* par quelqu'un qui n'aurait pas compris qu'il signifiait: 'il y a eu hier huit jours que . . .'. Mais *A* et *C* seraient alors liés . . .

Dans la pièce 11, *B* n'a que *A* pour partenaire, mais on sait que ce recueil est souvent hypercorrect; de lui-même en tout cas, il n'aurait sans doute pas remanié un texte dans un sens contraire à la déclinaison. Or voici ce que nous y lisons:

> Tu as hurté de tel aïr
> Et tant feru et tant hurté
> Que .i. des oés est *esquaté*.
> Ce poise moi, c'est granz domages,
> *L'aubun* m'en cort par mi les nages.   (*MR* V, p. 107)

Les fautes soulignées ne figurent pas dans la copie de B1:

> Tu as feru de tel aïr
> Et tant as enpaint et hurté
> Que tu as .I. des oés crevé.
> Ce poise moi, *ce* est domage,
> *Ce* as tu fet par ton outrage.   (40d 26–30)

Texte correct, certes, quant à la déclinaison, mais déplorablement aplati quant au style, et presque certainement second. B1 lui-même est-il le coupable? La non élision de *ce* lui est en tout cas habituelle. Mais, toute plate que soit la modification, le copiste B1, l'auteur de toutes les fautes que nous avons vues, en eût-il été capable? Et c'est toujours la même question que posent les éventuelles corrections de B2, si modestes qu'elles soient, comme celle-ci, par exemple:

> Et a la dame vraiement
> Plesoit molt *son acointement.*   (*A* 21, soutenu par *C*)
>
> Et la dame meïsmesmant
> Prisoit molt son acoi[n] temant. (40/78a 28—29)

Pour prendre une vue juste de la pratique de B1 et de B2 à l'égard du vocabulaire des textes qu'ils transcrivaient, un examen plus complet que le nôtre serait encore plus nécessaire que dans les cas précédents. L'idée que l'on se fait de la fidélité ou de l'infidélité d'un copiste dans la transmission des mots est sans doute plus fortement marquée par la comparaison avec d'autres leçons que lorsqu'il s'agit des formes; les formes sont fausses ou justes, propres ou non à telle région, en elles-mêmes, tandis que les mots nous apparaissent plus rares ou plus communs, plus exacts ou plus vagues, par comparaison surtout. De sorte qu'une pièce conservée en dehors de *B* par un manuscrit seulement (pour ne pas parler de celles qu'il conserve seul) se présente dans d'autres conditions qu'une autre qu'on peut lire dans plusieurs autres recueils. Et ce n'est naturellement pas le nombre seul qui compte, mais la qualité: un manuscrit très fidèle fera ressortir les innovations sans cela invisibles d'un copiste qui l'était moins. Tout est relation. Ceci pour dire que, si la constance de certaines tendances de nos deux copistes ne fait pas de doute, il est encore plus difficile de les reconnaître avec certitude dans le traitement du vocabulaire. Nous pouvons bien observer certains faits, mais leur interprétation, et notamment l'appréciation de la part personnelle qu'y ont prise B1 et B2, demeure incertaine, même quand elle paraît s'imposer.

La comparaison accuse donc la supériorité ou l'infériorité de *B*. Le premier cas est, hélas! nettement plus rare que le second. Il se produit en particulier, en faveur de B1, dans le *Vilain de*

Farbu (no. 4), fabliau de Jean Bodel, dont le vocabulaire est clairement teinté du Nord. Le jeu de délation qui met aux prises les deux témoins de cette pièce, *B* et *H*, se termine sur le score flatteur pour *B* de 11 innovations présumées de *H* contre 4 pour lui-même, mais le match a sans doute engagé bien d'autres joueurs . . . Voici deux exemples de mots très probablement originaux conservés par B1:

> Çax [il s'agit de deniers] li lia en son *rigot*,
> Bien li a conté son escot.   (10c 12–13)

> Ceus en sa *borse* li bouta,
> Son escot bien li aconta.   (*H* 11–12)

L'autre exemple de *rigot* 'bourse' que citent les dictionnaires provient du *Dit des avocas*, très probablement originaire de Picardie aussi.[34]

Second exemple:

> O marchié devant une forge
> Ot .i. chaufer gité .i. fevres
> Por les fox et por les *chalevres*. (10c 23–25)

Les autres occurrences de *chalevre* 'sot, stupide' citées par Godefroy et par Tobler et Lommatzsch sont tirées de Gautier de Coinci (Soissonnais). *H* a remplacé le mot:

> Pour les faus et les esbahis   (*H* 24)

Mais la même pièce révèle des exemples contraires, où toutes les apparences sont favorables à *H*. Par quatre fois, par exemple, le verbe *rakier*, répandu en Picardie et en Normandie (cf. *FEW*, X, 35a), est remplacé en *B* par son synonyme *crachier*.[35] Autre exemple: en *H*, le père injurie son fils en le traitant de *puans quaistre* (*H* 112) 'puant marmiton'; le mot, originaire du Nord (cf. *FEW*, II, 1169), cède sa place en *B* à *puant mestre* (11b 22), qui n'a plus de sens.

Le cas du *Vilain de Farbu* était particulier. Dans l'ensemble,

---

[34] Si G. Raynaud, qui a publié le *Dit* (*Romania*, VIII, 1879), pense que *rigot* est un mot de l'Est (p. 101), c'est à la fois parce qu'il situait dans l'Est l'origine du recueil de Berne et parce qu'il croyait que le mot y provenait du copiste. L'origine picarde du *Dit des avocas* ne saurait faire de doute; un personnage y raconte notamment qu'il dînait l'autre jour à *Ailli sour Naie*, qui est un chef-lieu de canton dans la Somme.

[35] 10d 2, 11b 4 et 17, 11c 3.

comme nous l'avons dit, les mots propres à *B* sont en grande majorité plus communs et le principe de la *lectio difficilior* les condamne. C'est ainsi que *joïe* 'soufflet' est plus 'rare' que *envaïe, barate* plus que *trape, avoir le pïor* 'avoir le dessous' plus que *avoir peor* 'avoir peur', ou que, pour passer à B2, *demie* 'pain d'obole' est plus 'difficile' que *mie, perrin* que *solier, laigne* que *buche, envoisier* que *joer*, etc.,[36] étant bien entendu que dans chaque cas il faudrait s'arrêter aux raisons différentes de la 'rareté'. Il va de soi, par exemple, que le remplacement de *mais* par *plus*, de *el* par *rien*, de *enceis* par *avant* ou de *cuidier* par *croire*[37] procède d'une modernisation de la langue qui apparaît à bien d'autres signes.

Il arrive fréquemment que *B* ne soit pas seul à présenter un mot plus commun à la place d'un mot plus rare et qu'il ne constitue alors qu'un des rameaux d'une 'diffraction' multiple. Dans le vers suivant, il est clair que *a orce* 'à la dérive' faisait difficulté :

Tort va avant et droit *a orce*	(*A* 139)
Droiz va avant et torz *a orce*	(*D* 159)
Tors vait avant et droiz *acorce*	(62/145b 15)
Tort vet avant et droit *acroche*	(*C* 161)

Est-ce *escota* de *D*, 'demeura pour escot', ou *ahocha* de *A*, 's'accrocha', qui est la source de la diffraction dans ce vers d'*Estula* :

| Mais ses soupliz i *escota* | |
| A un pel, si qu'il i laissa. | (*D* 115–116) |

| Mes son soupeliz *ahocha* | |
| A .i. pel, si qu'il remest la. | (*A*) |

| Mais ses sorpeliz atacha | |
| A un pel, si qu'il l'i laissa. | (56/117a 27) |

La rime avec *parole* garantit l'authenticité de *carole* sous la

---

[36] envaïe 15/45b 20, cf. *A* 157 et *C* 162; *trape* 18/51d 14, cf. *A* 294 et *C* 302; *avoir peor* 15/45c 5, cf. *A* 172 et *C* 177; *mie* 30/67a 29, cf. *A* 16 et *E*; *solier* 40/79c 7, cf. *A* 165 et *C* 201; *buche* 47/106d 28, cf. *D* 398 et *C*; *joer* 40/79a 16, cf. *A* 127 et *C* 159.

[37] *plus* 1/2d 14, cf. *D* 224; *rien* 15/44b 19, cf. *A* et *C* 39; *avant* 18/50c 24, cf. *A* 162 et *C* 152; *croire* 30/67b 7, cf. *A* 24.

plume de Jean Bodel dans *De Haimet et de Barat*, tandis qu'elle condamne *riote* de B2:

Entrez sui en male *carole*   (*AC*)
"   "   " molt male *escole* (*D* 376)
"   "   " male *riote*   (47/106d 6)

Dans la même pièce, *carnaige* s'impose évidemment, pour le sens et pour la rime avec *barnaige*. Travers est rentré en possession de son bacon et Barat imagine qu'il doit s'en régaler:

Bien en doit faire son carnaige   (*D* 464 et *A*)

Corage, qui remplace *carnaige* en *C*, n'a pas de sens, et B2 ne nous offre qu'une longue cheville:

Jamais ne l'an feron domaje   (47/107c 6)

L'étude transversale du recueil de Berne montre que les mêmes mots ont parfois été récusés dans des pièces différentes. *Escopir* 'cracher', par exemple, attesté par *H* dans la pièce 4 et par *A* dans la pièce 11 est remplacé·les deux fois en B1 par *crachier*,[38] et *mehaing* 'mal, blessure', attesté par *D* dans le no. 56 et par *AC* dans le no. 40, disparaît ici comme là du texte de B2.[39] L'adverbe *lués* 'aussitôt' et la conjonction *lués que* 'dès que' semblent avoir été proscrits aussi bien par B1 que par B2.[40]

Ces analogies convergent, dirait-on, vers un seul responsable, mais ne nous hâtons pas trop de conclure: *pucele* nous invite à la prudence! Le mot figure dans d'autres manuscrits trois fois dans la pièce 1, cinq fois dans la pièce 11 et une fois dans la pièce 18 là où B1 place un autre substantif. Faut-il donc croire que B1 lui-même n'en voulait pas? Pourtant, en 1, l'équivalent de *pucele* est à chaque fois *baiasse* ou *beasse*;[41] une fois même, ce dernier mot figure aussi dans le manuscrit qui avait *pucele* les trois autres fois.[42] C'est donc probablement *baiasse* qui est original. En 11, où B1 est aux prises avec *A*, l'équivalent de *pucele* n'est jamais *baiasse*, mais *damoisele* ou *meschine*,[43] *pucele*

[38] 4/10d 11, cf. *H* 41; 11/40d 21, cf. *A* 185.
[39] 56/116b 10, cf. *D* 8; 40/80b 18, cf. *A* 234.
[40] 1/1c 2, cf. *D* 57; 1/1c 7, cf. *D* 62; 1/3c 7, cf. *D* 309; 4/10d 27, cf. *H* 57; 62/144c 7, cf. *C* 73. B2 comporte cependant un exemple de l'adverbe dans la graphie *leus* à la rime avec *heus* 'oeufs' (47/104a 9–10).
[41] 2b 23, cf. *D* 173; 2c 8, cf. *D* 188; 2d 25, cf. *D* 234.
[42] 2d 6, cf. *D* 216.
[43] 39c 7, cf. *A* 6; 39c 14, cf. *A* 16; 39d 13, cf. *A* 63.

étant évacué deux fois à la rime[44] et admis deux fois à l'intérieur du vers.[45] En 18 enfin, B1 répond à *pucele* par *meschine*.[46] Le cas de 1, d'une part, et de 11 et 18, d'autre part, ne sont donc pas analogues et nous ne saurons jamais, finalement, si B1 les aimait . . .

Bloqués dans cette impasse, nous éprouvons chaque pierre des murs dans l'espoir que l'une d'entr'elles cédera, avides du moindre indice. Et c'est en tâtonnant de la sorte que je fais encore, pour terminer, deux groupes d'observations contradictoires.

Quand les serviteurs du roi battent le vilain mire qui prétend ne rien connaître à la médecine et ne pouvoir soigner la princesse malade, il crie: *'Sire, merci! Je la guerrai, jel vos afi.'* Telle est la leçon de *C* 225—226, partagée par *A* 228. La variante propre à B: *Bon mire sui, jel vos afi* (51b 2) tient très probablement à l'intention de prêter au vilain la même réponse que lors de la rossée précédente, pour créer une de ces répétitions qui scandent le récit des contes. Mais, alors que *C* (*A* est ici aberrant) lui faisait bien dire alors: *"mire sui bon"* (v. 188), B1 avait précisément commis là une faute de copie (sous l'influence du vers précédent): *n'est mie boen* (50d 28). Il semble que l'on puisse en conclure que l'auteur de l'innovation *Bon mire sui* en 51b 2 n'est pas le même homme qui venait de commettre cette faute ou, du moins, que ce n'était pas le même homme dans le même temps.

Une autre variante de *B* autorise peut-être une déduction analogue. Un autre vilain, celui *qui conquist paradis par plait* (no. 62), se vante d'avoir été charitable:

> As povres donai de mon pain,
> *As mostiers fui et soir et main,*
> *N'onques n'amé tançon ne liure,*
> *Volantiers doné droite disme,*
> Les povres sovant saoloie . . .   (145a 11—15)

Les vers que j'ai soulignés appartiennent en propre à *B*. Or on y remarque une faute de lecture, *liure* pour *lime* 'querelle'.[47] C'est

---

[44] 40a 12, cf. *A* 89; *A* 97—98 est omis dans *B*.
[45] 40b 4, cf. *A* 111; 40d 14, cf. *A* 178.
[46] 51b 28, cf. *C* 256, *A* manque.
[47] Cf. *MR* III, p. 400.

donc que B2 copiait. Mais, d'autre part, la rime *lime : disme* suppose l'effacement de l' *s*, qui appartient à la langue de B2, comme si l'auteur de l'innovation était à la fois différent de B2 et parlait la même langue.

Avec l'observation que nous venons de faire sur l'*s* devant consonne, nous sommes déjà dans le second groupe de nos observations, qui illustrent, en effet, contrairement aux premières, la coïncidence entre une innovation et un trait de langue connu de nos copistes. C'est à nouveau l'effacement du *s* que suppose la rime du couplet suivant, propre à B2:

> Et sachiez bien, fame dol tel
> Ne mena con sa fame *fist*
> Quant ensi atorna [*lire* atorné] lo *vit*.   (40/80b 12—14)

Dernière observation: une des très rares fautes contre la dé-clinaison commises par B1 dans la copie de la pièce 16 se rencontre dans un vers inconnu de *A* et de *F*:

> Lors revint *lo vilain* avant   (47a 6)

Est-ce un hasard?[48]

Le mur ne cède pas, certes. Mais le jour filtre, je crois, par un interstice. Ces dernières remarques, comme l'ensemble de celles que nous avons faites, mettent en contradiction la passive étourderie des fautes et le travail intentionnel des innovations, tout en donnant l'impression que travail et étourderie ne sont pour ainsi dire pas très éloignés l'un de l'autre. Faisons dès lors l'hypothèse bien vraisemblable qu'une partie tout au moins des innovations propres à *B* ont été l'oeuvre d'un chef d'atelier, d'une manière de prote, ou du patron peut-être de l'entreprise, qui préparait les textes avant de les distribuer à ces manuels, les scribes. Mais sans pouvoir, ensuite, corriger les épreuves! Ou préférera-t-on croire que les copistes, avant de se mettre à la tâche matérielle de la copie, lisaient et préparaient les modèles en les annotant? Mais pourquoi, alors, si peu de soin et de discernement, de si mauvaises lectures, au second stade de leur travail? Les cas ont sans doute été divers. Dans le nôtre, l'hypothèse d'un préparateur distinct des scribes, mais de

---

[48] Même coïncidence entre faute contre la déclinaison et innovation de B1 dans les vv. 256—258 du *Vilain mire* (51c 7—9).

même pays et parlant la même langue, me paraît répondre le mieux à l'ensemble des observations.

Nous avons envisagé le travail de l'atelier dans une perspective rétrospective et peut-être négative, car nous avons été amenés nécessairement à juger les textes sur leurs fautes et leurs innovations par rapport à des modèles présumés meilleurs. J'aimerais en terminant prendre quelque distance, comme on fait au cinéma pour élargir la vision et placer la dernière figure dans un univers qui lui prête à la fois sens et poésie. Cet atelier bourguignon m'apparaît alors, là-bas, dans l'histoire, comme un relais sur les chemins de la littérature: les oeuvres s'y reposent un instant puis repartent, lancées vers de nouveaux publics. Ce serait le lieu d'évoquer le contenu de notre recueil, plus important, cela va de soi, que ses fautes de copie, ce choix surprenant d'oeuvres aussi différentes que la *Bourgeoise d'Orléans* et le *Conte du Graal*, le *Roman des sept sages de Rome* et la *Folie Tristan*, en passant par le *Songe d'enfer, Les Quinze signes* de la fin du monde ou les poèmes satiriques sur les clercs, les changeurs, les boulangers ou les tisserands. C'est toute une petite bibliothèque d'oeuvres le plus souvent courtes des XIIe et XIIIe siècles. De provenances diverses, datant d'hier et d'avant-hier, les voici recueillies dans notre atelier puis relancées dans le recueil qu'il fabrique pour un amateur du pays, qui a déjà passé commande ou que l'on compte bien trouver. Les innovations qu'y subissent les textes procèdent d'une intention de médiation, presque d'adaptation, de naturalisation de cette littérature dans un nouveau milieu. Ce n'est pas pour eux-mêmes, par simple plaisir ou par une opération de nature que notre prote et nos copistes habillent les textes à la bourguignonne et remplacent des mots plus rares, plus anciens ou étrangers à la région par des mots plus communs, plus récents ou plus familiers: ils pensent ainsi faciliter la lecture des oeuvres pour l'amateur peut-être pas tellement cultivé auquel ils destinent leur recueil. Sous cet aspect, leur travail, bien plus projectif que rétrospectif, prend toute sa signification dans l'histoire des conditions matérielles où s'est produite la rencontre indispensable de la littérature et de ses publics.

ANGLO-NORMAN AT WATERFORD

The mute testimony of MS Cambridge,
Corpus Christi College 405[1]

K. V. SINCLAIR_____

The most authoritative comment on the subject of Anglo-Norman in Ireland is available in the studies of Professor M. Dominica Legge. When suggesting that the poet Adam de Ros, translator of a *Vision of St Paul*, came from the port of Ross, north of Dunbrody near Waterford, she stated: "Anglo-Norman was used, naturally, in the Anglo-Norman settlements in Ireland just as it was used in England. Anglo-Norman documents written in Ireland survive; in all likelihood there was an Anglo-Norman literature also, and, as will be seen later, there is a possibility that an Irish-born friar was another important writer in French".[2] The author in question is Jofroi de Waterford,[3] about whom she commented further: "Anglo-Norman was of course the language of the English settlers, both military and ecclesiastic. It is therefore quite likely that Jofroi was born of English parentage at Waterford, and joined the Friary there. More than a century later, in 1423, another native of Waterford, James Yonge, translated his version of the *Secretum Secretorum* into

---

[1] Some of the ideas expressed in this paper were advanced in a public lecture which I gave by invitation in 1976 to the Medieval Society of the University of Pennsylvania, in Philadelphia.

[2] *Anglo-Norman in the Cloisters* (Edinburgh University Press, 1950), p. 54. We refer to this work by the abbreviation *ANC*.

[3] The bibliography for Jofroi is extensive going back to 1847 at least; here is a selection: V. Le Clerc, 'Jofroi de Waterford, dominicain' in *Histoire littéraire de la France*, XXI (1847), 216–29; G. L. Hamilton, 'The Sources of the *Secret des Secrets* of Jofroi de Waterford' in *Romanic Review*, I (1910), 259–64; M. Esposito, 'Notes on Mediaeval Hiberno-Latin and Hiberno-French Literature' in *Hermathena*, XXXVI (1910), 69–71; P. Power, 'Geoffrey of Waterford' in *Waterford and South-East of Ireland Archaeological Journal*, XVII (1914), 95–7; C. V. Langlois, *La Vie en France au moyen âge*. III. *La Connaissance de la nature et du monde* (Paris, 1927), pp.

English, without acknowledgement, so that all trace of him [Jofroi] was not lost in that part of Ireland".[4]

Professor Legge returned to the question of South-East Ireland thirteen years later in her *Anglo-Norman Literature and its Background*: "The Anglo-Norman colony in Ireland produced two works on the recent history of the island, both in verse".[5] The first of these poems is the *Song of Dermot and the Earl*,[6] about which she writes: "it was most certainly written by and for the Anglo-Norman community in Ireland, quite likely at Waterford, since in later times the manuscript is known to have been there, together with another containing an English translation[7] of the French *Secretum Secretorum* made by Jofroi de Waterford, a Dominican".[8]

The second poem mentioned is the *Erection of the Walls of New Ross*.[9] Professor Legge goes on to cite the existence of legal documents in Anglo-Norman relating to the lieutenancy of William of Windsor (1369–1376),[10] and she concludes: "One is on safe ground in saying that the Anglo-Norman colony in Ireland was just that, and reproduced on a small scale all the

---

71–121; J. Monfrin, 'Le Secret des Secrets. Recherches sur les traductions françaises, suivies du texte de Jofroi de Waterford et Servais Copale' in *Ecole Nationale des Chartes. Positions des thèses*, 1947, pp. 93–99; C. Pinchbeck, 'A Mediaeval Self-Educator' in *Medium Aevum*, XVII (1948), 1–14; J. Monfrin, 'Sur les sources du *Secret des Secrets* de Jofroi de Waterford et Servais Copale' in *Mélanges de linguistique romane et de philologie médiévale offerts à M. Maurice Delbouille* (Gembloux, 1964), II, 509–30. C. Segre calls Jofroi a "dominicain irlandais" in his profile of the work in *Grundriss der romanischen Literaturen des Mittelalters*, ed. H. R. Jauss & E. Köhler (Heidelberg, 1968 & 1970), VI/1, 100, and VI/2, 147, no. 2872. Hereafter, we use the acronym *GRLMA* for this encyclopedic reference work.

[4] Legge, *ANC*, p. 79.

[5] *Anglo-Norman Literature and its Background* (Oxford, 1963), p. 303. Henceforth we refer to this study as *ANL*.

[6] Ed. G. H. Orpen (Oxford, 1892).

[7] Ed. R. Steele, *Three Prose Versions of the Secreta Secretorum*, E.E.T.S. Extra Series, 74 (London, 1898), pp. 119–248.

[8] Legge, *ANL*, p. 304.

[9] First ed. by F. Madden, 'Anglo-Norman Poem on the Erection of the Walls of New Ross, A.D. 1265' in *Archaeologia*, XXII (1834), 307–22; and again more recently, but in an edition still leaving much to be desired, by H. Shields, 'The Walling of New Ross: a Thirteenth-Century Poem in French' in *Long Room. Bulletin of the Friends of the Library, Dublin, Trinity College*, XII–XIII (1975–76), 24–33.

[10] Ed. Maude V. Clarke in her *Fourteenth-Century Studies* (Oxford, 1937), pp. 146–241.

characteristics of life at home, including literature. It is perhaps not surprising that that great compendium, a private library in itself, Cambridge University Library Gg.I.1, which includes twenty-five items in Anglo-Norman, may have been copied in Ireland".[11]

The purpose of this paper is to suggest that a much larger number of Anglo-Norman works than hitherto suspected were known and read in Waterford in the thirteenth and fourteenth centuries; that they had most likely been transcribed in England, possibly for interested parties in the city, then taken there; and that minor texts were later added in Waterford by local scribes. The evidence for these contentions is, we believe, on the folios of a group of manuscripts unnoticed by historians of Anglo-Norman literature, even though individual texts have been edited at different times by modern scholars. The single-minded purpose of editors, namely to publish an unknown work, has for the most part eclipsed any perception of the Irish connection already alluded to. Moreover, although the cataloguer of the collection mentioned Waterford as a possible provenance, his authorial identifications had important lacunae, his bibliographical references were sparse, and, to complete the obscurity, he did not draw attention to Anglo-Norman textual characteristics and origins.

The collection of Anglo-Norman works to which allusion is made is now bound between one set of covers and constitutes MS 405 in the library of Corpus Christi College, Cambridge.[12] In describing the *recueil factice*, Montague Rhodes James

[11] Legge, *ANL*, p. 304. The provenance suggested appears to be attributable to Angus McIntosh; see *ANL*, p. 280, n. 1. I note that he indicates it himself in print much later in his joint paper with M. L. Samuels, 'Prolegomena to a Study of Mediaeval Anglo-Irish' in *Medium Aevum*, XXXVII (1968), 4, no. 39 in the classification "Unlocalized texts for which the evidence of Irish provenance is wholly or mainly linguistic". One presumes that McIntosh was writing in the context of the *Northern Passion* and the *Proverbs of Hendyng*. When the distinguished French philologist P. Meyer published his detailed notice of the codex, he said nothing about an Irish provenance for the Anglo-Norman texts; cf. 'Les Manuscrits français de Cambridge' in *Romania*, XV (1886), 283–340.

[12] My thanks go to the Master and Fellows of Corpus Christi College, Cambridge, for allowing a copy to be made of their codex for private study purposes. I am also indebted to their librarian, Dr R. I. Page, for facilitating my consultation of the manuscript.

distinguished six volumes.[13] A closer examination of codex V, however, leads to the conclusion that it is really two dissimilar manuscripts. We shall therefore refer to James's V as Va and Vb. The collocation of the volumes as a new integral manuscript had occurred by the middle of the sixteenth century, since a hand of the period scribbled on p. 2 a summary table of contents with page numbers which correspond with the existing ones.

On the question of provenance, James expressed the view that the *recueil* "evidently belonged to the brethren of St John of Jerusalem at Waterford".[14] Even the most cursory examination of the bulls, charters and memoranda copied on numerous folios of the component manuscripts allows us safely to endorse his observation.[15] Only two other scholars have made worthwhile comments on provenance, the first being P. Meyer and the other, O.H. Prior. Meyer called 405 "un recueil très précieux écrit en Angleterre",[16] while Prior believed its *Divisiones mundi* was "written in an Anglo-Norman dialect which contains distinctive features of the South, and even, more strictly speaking of South-West England".[17] The reconciliation of these statements can be conveniently made in spatial terms: some volumes, once separate entities, may well have been originally copied in the South-West of England and later conveyed to Waterford where they subsequently fell into the hands of the Knights Hospitaller.

The dating has been variously expressed. Meyer placed the collection "dans la seconde moitié du XIIIe siècle", and Vising did likewise.[18] James, however, had stated "several volumes of

---

[13] *A Descriptive Catalogue of the Manuscripts in the Library of Corpus Christi College, Cambridge* (Cambridge University Press, 1910–11), II, 277–88. On the life of this distinguished codicologist, see the recent study by R. W. Pfaff, *Montague Rhodes James* (London, 1980).

[14] *Cat.*, II, 277.

[15] It is echoed in A. Gwynn & R. N. Hadcock, *Medieval Religious Houses: Ireland* (London, 1970), p. 336.

[16] In *Romania*, XXXVI (1907), 111, when drawing attention to a sermon in our MS.

[17] See the bibliographical details below at n. 68.

[18] Meyer in *Romania*, XXXVI (1907), 111; and J. Vising, *Anglo-Norman Language and Literature* (Oxford University Press, 1923), p. 95, no. 255 with contents numbered 17, 23, 44, 88, 154, 184, 300.

cent. xiii and xiv early, all well written".[19] As codex Va contains
the largest number of texts that interest us, we record now that
it must date from the opening years of the fourteenth century.
Its first item (pp. 251—55) is a copy of a Latin Bull addressed
to the Grand Master and Brethren of the Hospital of St John of
Jerusalem by Boniface VIII in the sixth year of his pontificate
(1300).[20]

Codices II, III, IV and VI need not detain us for long. Sequen-
tially,[21] they give the texts of a Calendar in Latin and a Lec-
tionary in Latin. Volume IV contains the Waterford Custumal
in Anglo-Norman[22] (preceded by a *Carta confirmationis* dated
at Woodstock 4 Ed. II (1311)), charters in Latin for Bristol,
Drogheda and Haverford, a chronology in Latin of important
civil and ecclesiastical events in Ireland, Anglo-Norman recipes
reflecting principally military concerns for human coughs,
fevers, wounds, bleeding and dysentery, and for equine disten-
sions.[23] Lastly, in codex VI we meet transcripts of legal
memoranda in Latin regarding Waterford and Anglo-Norman
government in Ireland.

Codex I is a quire of ten folios in a book hand of the first
quarter of the fourteenth century, and it preserves on pp. 8—12
the text of *Prophecies* attributed to Merlin. These are not the
celebrated ones which a certain Richard of Ireland, it is alleged,
composed *c*. 1272—79 at the command of the Emperor Frederick
II.[24] Rather they are politically motivated, with specific reference to animal traits of the six monarchs who succeeded King
John, namely the Lamb of Winchester, the Dragon of Mercy,
the Goat of Caernarvon, the Boar of Windsor, the Ass with

[19] *Cat.*, II, 277.
[20] See A. Potthast, *Regesta Pontificum Romanorum* (Berlin, 1874—75), II,
1994, no. 24938.
[21] Details are supplied by James, *Cat.*, II, 280—83, 288.
[22] Published from this MS by G. Mac Niocaill in *Na Buirgeisi XII—XIV Aois*
(Dublin, 1964), I, 3—59.
[23] Transcribed by an early fourteenth-century hand on pp. 248—50. Given the
paleographical and bibliographical neglect of medieval recipes, I feel that I do not
have to apologise to readers for not being able to relate the wording of the Corpus
ones to other extant copies.
[24] See *Les Prophecies de Merlin edited from ms. 593 of the Bibliothèque Muni-
cipale of Rennes*, by Lucy A. Paton (New York, 1926—27).

leaden feet, and the Accursed Mole. It is a work of high imagination and colourful perspectives, seemingly composed in the
reign of Edward I. Latin, Middle English and Anglo-Norman
versions exist, the Latin being the oldest.[25] The Anglo-Norman
redaction still awaits the eye of a critical editor, the published
edition being based on a single defective manuscript.[26] The
incipit of our Corpus copy is: "Un aignel vendra hors de
Wyncestre que avera blanche lange et levres veritables et avera
escrit . . .".

Into the blank ruled lines on p. 12 where the prophecies end,
a later charter hand has copied a prose work and placed at its
head the rubric: "Ici comence le numbre de Adam taunt ke a
l'incarnaciun Jesu Crist, si cum desouz est escrit".[27] The
sixteenth-century indexer of the Corpus manuscript wrote
De sex aetatibus seculi against p. 12, and James's annotation
for the work reads "The tract is in Bede (XC 288)". The source
is indeed a text attributed to Bede, the *De temporibus liber*,
specifically, chapters xvi—xxii.[28] The work became an influential statement on cosmic Christian chronology, and it occurred
in many places. For example, Brunetto Latini distributed the
observations on the Six Ages throughout Book I of his *Tresor.*[29]

[25] Cf. R. Taylor, *The Political Prophecy in England* (Columbia University Press,
1911), pp. 48—57, and P. Zumthor, *Merlin le prophète. Un Thème de la littérature
polémique de l'historiographie et des romans* (Lausanne, 1943), p. 73.

[26] Taylor, *op. cit.*, pp. 160—64, prints the text of the thirteenth-century London
BL Harley 746. Professor Legge, *ANL*, p. 288, n. 2 does not mention this edition,
but refers to H. L. D. Ward, *Catalogue of the Romances in the Department of Manuscripts in the British Museum* (London, 1883—1910), I, 299—300 (for Cotton Julius
A.V.), 308 (for Arundel 57) and 309 (for Harley 746). Vising, no. 300, records these
three codices, along with our Corpus one, and Cambridge Univ. Libr. Gg. I.1., ff.
120r—121r, which P. Meyer had described in *Romania*, XV (1886), 295. Further
copies I have sighted are Cambridge Sidney Sussex College Δ 2.21, ff. 183v—185v;
London BL Royal 20.A.XI, ff. 137v—139r, and Royal 20.A.XVIII, ff. 336r—343r.
There are doubtless other Anglo-Norman transcriptions.

[27] James's title for the work is erroneous: *Table chronologique faite le 17 anne*
[sic] *du regne d'Edouard II*; he may well have derived it from T. D. Hardy, *Descriptive Catalogue of Materials relating to the History of Great Britain and Ireland
. . .*, Rolls Series (London, 1862—71), III, 382.

[28] See Migne, *P.L.*, XC, 288—91.

[29] Cf. *Li Livres dou Tresor de Brunetto Latini*, ed. F. J. Carmody (University of
California Press, 1948), pp. 33 ff.: "Et sachés ke quant Adan fu en aage de .ii.[c] et
.xxx. ans, ot il un autre fil de sa femme, ki fu apelés Seth. . .". The other five ages
are in chapters xxi, xxv, xli, xlii, xliii of Bk. I.

A contemporary compiler of a *vademecum* included them among statements relating to Adam,[30] while Jean de Sy in 1355 inserted them into his translation of the *Bible*.[31] Our copy represents a form of the tract that is found in isolation, and the incipit "Adam avoit .c. e .xxx. aunz quant il engendra Seth; Seth avoit cent e .v. aunz quant il engendra Enos. . ." is very similar to those of extant transcriptions in Continental French.[32]

The list of kings which follows on p. 14 in the same hand as the *Six Ages* commences abruptly, without a rubric, in the period of the Heptarchy, with mention of Ethelwulf (acc. 839) and continues with gaps to 18 Ed. II (1325). The Norman dynasty is announced in a special manner: "Ici commence [*sic*] les nouns des reys puis la venue Willyame le Cunquerour qe fu dit bastard. Primes: Williame le Cunquerour qe regna .xx. aunz et .xi. moins [*sic*] e gist a Cam. . ." The enumeration is confined to each monarch's name, length of reign, and location of his last resting-place. The Anglo-Norman origin of the regal silhouettes cannot be doubted. Some copies are fuller than the Corpus one, or commence at different points in time, or end diversely.[33] Until a critical edition is published, it would not be prudent to make any pronouncements about regional interests, historical accuracy, date of composition or manner of transmission of the information.

After the list of regnal years, the same charter hand has trans-

---

[30] Cf. F. E. Schneegans, 'Notes sur un calendrier français du XIIIe siècle' in *Mélanges de philologie romane et d'histoire littéraire offerts à M. Maurice Wilmotte* (Paris, 1910), II, 649–51, with the incipit: "Or dient li maistre qui la bible translaterent que Adam ot .cc. ans et .xxx. avant que il engendrat Seth".

[31] Cf. S. Berger, *La Bible française au moyen âge* (Paris, 1884), p. 239.

[32] E.g. Modena Bibl. Estense str. 29, ff. 5v–7r; Paris Bibl. de l'Arsenal 5201, pp. 227–28; Paris BN fr. 1444, f. 126v; fr. 2464, ff. 111r–112v; n.a.fr. 10554, ff. 41v–43r. See the references by P. Meyer in *Romania* XVI (1887), 62–63; J. Camus in *Revue des Langues romanes*, XXXV (1891), 195–96; R. N. Walpole in *Romance Philology*, VII (1953–54), 130; C. Segre, *Li Bestiaires d'amours di maistre Richart de Fornival e li Response du Bestiaire* (Milan & Naples, 1957), p. xliii. Vising has no entry for our tract.

[33] I notice similar wording in an early codex, the twelfth-century London BL Cotton Caligula A.III, ff. 146 *et seq.*, in the thirteenth-century Cotton Galba E.III, ff. 43r–51r, and in the fourteenth-century Royal 13.A.XVIII, item 10, where the words are placed in a genealogical table with circles or medallions.

cribed a Latin charm for lessening the effects of a lance wound; a Latin mensal account of lunar risings (pp. 15—16); and then an Anglo-Norman charm for keeping rats and mice out of standing corn.[34] The last of these three is not recorded by Vising; it does not have a Continental French congener among the numerous examples of incantations which P. Meyer edited.[35] However, it would be presumptuous to suggest that the Corpus copy is an *unicum*.

There follows next on pp. 16—17 a tract on the parlous days of the year, beginning: "Lé meystres, ky controverunt l'art, numbrerunt les malurés e lé perylous jours qe seunt e[n] le an, e ke en un de ces jours nestra, ne vivera mye longement. . .". This Anglo-Norman copy has close affinity with those made elsewhere by thirteenth-century Continental French scribes,[36] and is distantly related to the Parlous Days text transcribed by another Anglo-Norman copyist in the early fourteenth century.[37] A synoptic view of all the congeners would be welcome, and comprehensive critical editions would help determine if the Anglo-Norman redactions antedate or derive from the Continental French ones.

On the lower half of p. 17 is a short didactic work, not registered by Vising or adequately identified by James. It is in fact one of three Medieval French redactions of alphabetical schedules

---

[34] The incipit printed by James is somewhat abridged; it needs an additional extract to bring out the nature of the charm: "Ditez treis paternostres ou le noun du pere e le fiuz e le seint esperitz, e puis parnetz treis peres de creye e escrivitez le pere e le fiuz e le seint espiretz, e dunk ditez deux reys de tout le mound. . .".

[35] In particular in *Romania*, XIV (1885), 154, 491; XVIII (1889), 576; XXXII (1903), 77, 273, 289, 292—99, 453; XXXV (1906), 582; XXXVII (1908), 367—68, 516; XL (1911), 538.

[36] Namely: New Haven Yale Univ. Libr. 395 (*olim* Phillipps 4156), f. 183v, on which see P. Meyer, 'Notices sur quelques manuscrits français de la Bibliothèque Phillipps à Cheltenham' in *Notices et Extraits des manuscrits*, XXXIV/1 (1891), 237—38; a second copy is Oxford Bodleian Libr. Bodley 553, f. 39v, edited by Ö. Södergård, 'Note sur les jours périlleux de l'année' in *Neuphilologische Mitteilungen*, LV (1954), 267—71; a third one is in Paris BN lat. 770 and was published by P. Meyer, 'Bribes de littérature anglo-normande' in *Jahrbuch für romanische und englische Literatur*, VII (1866), 48—50. See further discussion in K. V. Sinclair, 'Anglo-Norman Studies: the Last Twenty Years' in *Australian Journal of French Studies*, II (1965—66), 113—55, 225—78, in particular 155. Hereafter this reference work is called Sinclair, *Twenty Years*.

[37] In London BL Arundel 220; ed. Meyer, *ibid.*, Södergård, *ibid.*

designed to interpret dreams. When he published it in 1957, Walter Suchier remarked on the unusual word formations and even unintelligible passages in this Corpus *unicum*, and opined that "der Schreiber hätte nur mangelhafte französische Sprachkenntnisse, vielleicht auch eine schlecht lesbare Vorlage gehabt".[38] He compared its readings with those in the Modena redaction (M), of Continental French origin.[39] Apart from word usage and order of explanations, M's author appears to have a different perspective: his alphabetical source is "un livre", whereas C requires the psalter; M is content with "la premiere letre que tu troveras au commencement de la premiere page", but C's point of reference is much more explicit: "la prime letre qe il trove de la part senestre" as one consults randomly the psalter. These considerations lead us to believe that C is an independent Anglo-Norman redaction derived from the same or a similar Latin original as the one employed by M's author.

The last of the Anglo-Norman texts in codex I is written on pp. 20—1 in the same clear, neat hand that copied a Latin tract on pp. 18—19.[40] James supplies the title *Incantation contre les maux et les périls*,[41] which is a reasonable description of contents, in line with the introduction, but which appears at first sight to be in contradiction with the explicit. The structure of the short textual matter is complex in that the first quarter sets out, in Anglo-Norman, uses for the document as a phylactery[42], then come passages in Latin supplying various Hebrew and Latin names for God, further brief comments in Anglo-Norman, additional sections in Latin, then the following: "Explicit epistola quam dominus noster Ihesus Christus manuscriptam[43] misit ad Abagarem regem qui eum videre desiderabit [*sic*]. Ihesus. Nazarenus. Rex. Iudeorum. Miserere·mei". Assuming

[38] Cf. W. Suchier, 'Altfranzösische Traumbücher' in *Zeitschrift für französische Sprache und Literatur*, LXVII (1957), 129—67. The Corpus text is on pp. 162—63.

[39] Published by J. Camus, 'Notices et extraits des manuscrits de Modène antérieurs au XVIe siècle' in *Revue des Langues romanes*, XXXV (1891), 205—6, from the fourteenth-century codex Modena Bibl. Estense str. 32, f. 24r.

[40] Entitled *De Vita Christiana ad cuius observanciam quilibet christianus obligatur.*

[41] *Cat.*, II, 279.

[42] The bearer's name is given in this copy as William: ". . . assistunt hinc famulo tuo Willelmo hoc scriptum portanti. . .".

[43] MS reading is *manum scriptam*.

that the explicit has been matched correctly by the copyist to
the text, we are in the presence of the Epistle which Jesus is
alleged to have sent to Abgarus, King of Edessa, in response to
a request for a leprosy cure. The Latin Epistle was well known
in England in the Middle Ages,[44] and is even found transcribed
among charms.[45] This manuscript tradition becomes confused,
however, when we meet the explicit and the incantation preceded by an Anglo-Norman preface which ascribes the text to a
Pope Saint Leo: "Seynt Leon apostoile de Rome escrit cest
lettre et dit: ky unkys le lirra, ja cel jour ne estout doter[46] sun
enimi de mort, de passiun ne de nul poysoun . . .". Presumably,
"escrit" has to be understood as meaning 'made a copy', but
even so, a pope of this name is not traditionally associated with
the Jesus Letter.[47] On the other hand, copies of the same
Corpus charm text do occur with a similar introduction in the
vernacular, and ascription to a Pope Leo.[48] But this is clearly
not the place to solve these problems of confused attribution.

Codex Va of the collection occupies pp. 251–462 and is
composed almost entirely of Anglo-Norman copies of literary
texts.[49] James lists eight, but he could not have known that one
of them was a continuation of its predecessor in the manuscript,
and that another text described as a single work was in fact two.
Vising took account of these anomalies, but chose to ignore the
anonymous poem about the Antichrist and the composition by
Perot de Garbelei.[50] A devotional work eulogising the Virgin

[44] See Cora E. Lutz, 'The Apocryphal Abgarus-Jesus Epistles in England in the
Middle Ages' in her *Essays on Manuscripts and Rare Books* (Hamden, Conn. 1975),
pp. 57–62, 152–53.

[45] *Ibid.*, p. 153, n. 26.

[46] MS *deter*.

[47] Five pontiffs of this name were traditionally considered saints by the time our
manuscript was prepared: Leo the Great (d. 461), Leo II (d. 683), Leo III (d. 816),
Leo IV (d. 855) and Leo IX (d. 1054). Although fact and fiction associated with early
popes of this name were examined by B. S. Lee, 'This is no fable: historical residues
in two medieval exempla' in *Speculum*, LVI (1981), 728–60, he did not discuss
charms or incantations.

[48] Namely, a fourteenth-century Book of Hours originating in England, London
BL Harley 1260, f. 230r; a Continental French transcription is extant in a fifteenth-
century *livre de prières*, now London BL Sloane 2356, ff. 58v–61r.

[49] I exclude here from my considerations of the literary texts a rhymed account
of the Hospitallers' Rule which I am editing for the Anglo-Norman Text Society.

[50] Cf. Vising, *ANL*, nos. 17, 23, 44, 88, 154, 184.

heads the list. The fact that most of the stanzas commence with "Ave" suggested to scholars of the last century that an appropriate title would be *Litany to the Virgin*. The text, however, is more distinctive than has been suggested. It celebrates five of the Joys of the Virgin, the five in fact for which worshippers in England had a predilection, the Annunciation, the Nativity, the Resurrection, the Ascension and the Assumption.[51] Our copy opens regularly[52] with the words:

Ave seinte Marie, mere al creatur,
Reine des angles, plaine de dusur . . . .

and contains (pp. 311—15) thirty-one stanzas, mainly four-line, but with supernumerary verses. It was once thought that the poem concluded with a Litany to Saints. James's observations on this point are therefore fully justified.[53] However, in 1871 Stengel had suggested that the encomium of saints and martyrs could be a different composition.[54] Vising listed it separately,[55] and Sonet followed suit.[56] In our manuscript it is transcribed without a break on pp. 315—17, and begins:

Gloriuse raine, de mai eez merci,
Pur amur seint Johan le vostre chere ami. . .

There are 72 lines, but without formal stanzaic grouping. The

---

[51] Middle English poems about the Five Joys are extant; see C.F. Brown, *Religious Lyrics of the Fourteenth Century*, 2nd revised ed. by G. V. Smithers (Oxford University Press, 1952), nos. 11, 26, 31, 122; and C. F. Brown, *Religious Lyrics of the Fifteenth Century* (Oxford, 1938), nos. 30, 31.

[52] That is, in the same manner as the other extant copies: London BL Addit. 46919 (*olim* Phillipps 8336), ff. 52v—54r; London Lambeth Palace 522, ff. 159r—162r with a second transcription on ff. 211r—215r; Oxford Bodleian Libr. Bodley 57, ff. 5r-5v; Digby 86, ff. 186v—188v. There is one Continental French copy in Paris BN fr. 12483, ff. 234r—235r. On all these, see J. Sonet, *Répertoire d'incipit de prières en ancien français* (Geneva, 1956), p. 27, no. 145, and the corrections and additional references in K. V. Sinclair, *Prières en ancien français* (Hamden, Conn. 1978), p. 35, no. 145. Edith Brayer in *GRLMA*, VI/1, 15, and VI/2, 40, no. 788, inadequately characterises the work as a "poème en forme de litanie".

[53] *Cat.*, II, 284.

[54] E. Stengel, *Codicem manu scriptum Digby 86 in bibliotheca Bodleiana asservatum descripsit excerpsit, illustravit* (Halle, 1871), pp. 81—82.

[55] Vising, *ANL*, no. 184 (151).

[56] Sonet, *op. cit.*, p. 120, no. 669, was incorrect in stating that the Corpus MS "n'a en commun avec ces quatrains que les deux premiers vers"; he also omits reference to the copies in Addit. 46919 and Lambeth Palace 522. The work is in Paris BN fr. 12483 on ff. 235r—236v; see Sinclair, *Prières*, p. 67, no. 669. Edith Brayer records the incipit from Sonet in *GRLMA*, VI/2, 37, no. 668.

variations among the readings in the extant copies point to scribal inadvertances and a complex textual tradition.

The opening lines of a new poem:

Ki vout saver l'afaitement
Ke Catun a sun fiz aprent . . .

announce a rendering of Cato's *Distichs* that occupies pp. 317—43. It is the version by the Benedictine monk Elie of Winchester, who is thought to have made his adaptation in the late twelfth or early thirteenth century.[57] Our copy is one of five to have survived.[58]

Items 25 and 26 of James's description, *Vers sur l'amour du prochain* and *Vers sur le jour du jugement* are in fact one and the same text, now called, for want of a better, medieval title, *Poème sur l'amour de Dieu et sur la haine du péché*. The Corpus copy (pp. 343—68) contributed variants for the edition published by P. Meyer, based on an Oxford manuscript.[59] The anonymous work must have been widely circulating in England, since it survives in two other forms. Vising and, more recently, Segre grouped all three redactions at one reference point,[60] but Meyer[61] had argued that the second version could be distinguished from the Rawlinson-Corpus one by a marked change in the wording of the exordium, and that the third version, as incorporated into certain codices of Book VI of the *Manuel*

---

[57] Cf. Legge, *ANC*, p. 16, and *ANL*, p. 182. See also Segre in *GRLMA*, VI/1, 88, 103—4, and VI/2, 153, no. 2940; and E. Ruhe, *Untersuchungen zu den altfranzösischen Uebersetzungen der Disticha Catonis* (Munich, 1968), pp. 117—47.

[58] Vising, *ANL*, no. 44, records only the Corpus, London and Oxford copies. Here are the details of the other four: Cambridge Pembroke College 46, ff. 1r—5v, an acephalous copy whose author was not identified by M. R. James, *A Descriptive Catalogue of the Manuscripts in the Library at Pembroke College, Cambridge* (Cambridge University Press, 1905), pp. 45—46; London BL Harley 4388, ff. 115v—119v, published by E. Stengel in H. Kühne, *Maistre Elies Ueberarbeitung der ältesten französischen Uebertragung von Ovids Ars Amatoria*, Ausgabe und Abhandlungen aus dem Gebiete der romanischen Philologie, 47 (Marburg, 1886), pp. 110—45; Oxford St. John's College 178, ff. 395—401r, discussed by A. Ewert, 'A Fourteenth-Century Latin—French Nominale' in *Medium Aevum*, III (1934), 13; Turin Biblio. Nazionale e Universitaria D.V. 29, ff. 366r—369r, noticed by E. G. Wahlgren, 'Rensignements sur quelques manuscrits français de la Bibliothèque Nationale de Turin' in *Studier i Modern Språkvetenskap*, XII (1934), 115.

[59] P. Meyer, 'Notice du ms. Rawlinson Poetry 241 (Oxford)' in *Romania*, XXIX (1900), 9—21.

[60] Cf. Vising, *ANL*, no. 154; Segre in *GRLMA*, VI/2, 105, no. 2244.

[61] See Meyer, 'Notice du ms. Rawlinson Poetry 241', 5—8.

des Péchés,[62] once attributed to William of Waddington, underwent rearrangement of line order. Sister M. Amelia Klenke sought to modify the conclusions of Meyer by attributing the second redaction to the celebrated Franciscan Nicole Bozon, and by including it among a selection of his poems.[63]

An anonymous verse sermon, now simply known by the opening line *Deu le Omnipotent*, occupies pp. 368–94. It disserts on the three Enemies of Man against which the Passion is the doughtiest of shields. The rubric *De Passione Christi* epitomises the content most appropriately. The importance of the text has long been recognised; it is one of the earliest verse sermons in French and is thought to date from the second half of the twelfth century.[64] In re-editing his father's 1879 edition which had been based on one codex only, W. Suchier[65] supplied the important variant readings from our manuscript and from a third copy discovered in the interval.[66] He also stated that he thought, on versification grounds, that England was the place of composition;[67] this may well explain the fact that the three known copies are by Anglo-Norman scribes.

[62] This version of the *Poème sur l'amour de Dieu* was last printed, and from one manuscript only, by F. J. Furnivall, *Roberd of Brunne's Handlyng Synne (written A.D. 1303) with the French Treatise on which it is founded, le Manuel des Pechiez by William of Wadington* (London, 1862), pp. 426–34. The problems related to our independent *Poème*'s place in the *Manuel* were discussed by C. Laird, 'Character and Growth of the *Manuel des Pechiez*' in *Traditio*, IV (1946), 268–70.

[63] In her paper entitled 'An Anglo-Norman Gospel Poem by Nicholas Bozon' in *Studies in Philology*, XLVIII (1951), 250–66, republished in her book entitled *Seven More Poems by Nicholas Bozon* (St Bonaventure, N.Y, 1951), pp. 1–16. The edition uses London BL Cotton A.XI as the base codex, and draws on variants from the Rawlinson copy already mentioned, and from Paris BN fr. 902. Legge, *ANL*, p. 231, mentions the attempt to add the text to the Bozon canon, but does not enter into a discussion of relationships of each redaction to the other. See also the questions which I raised in Sinclair, *Twenty Years*, p. 145.

[64] Cf. Vising, *ANL*, no. 23; Legge, *ANL*, pp. 180–81; Sinclair, *Twenty Years*, p. 141, n. 133; C. Segre in *GRLMA*, VI/1, 60, and VI/2, 103, no. 2196.

[65] *Zwei altfranzösische Reimpredigten mit Benutzung der Ausgabe Hermann Suchier, neu herausgegeben von W. Suchier* (Halle, 1949), pp. 123–44. The base MS is London BL Arundel 292, ff. 31r–38r; and the third MS is Harley 4971, f. 120v, a fragment of 66 lines.

[66] P. Meyer had first drawn attention to the Corpus and Harley MSS in his paper 'Sur la pièce strophique *Deu omnipotent*' in *Romania*, XXXVI (1907), 111–14.

[67] *Op. cit.*, p. 125: "Als Ort der Abfassung kommt nur England in Betracht". Legge, *ANL*, p. 180, seems to hold to an earlier view among scholars, when she writes: "Although all the extant manuscripts are Anglo-Norman . . . this appears to have been composed in Normandy. . .". Segre, *op. cit.*, writes "norm.".

The words *Hic incipiunt divisiones mundi*, placed in the right-hand margin on p. 394 against the line "Amen diez tuz", alert the reader to a new text. Its incipit is "Un livre de haut evre...;" it runs for some 935 lines and occupies pp. 394—425. The poem is derived from portions of the *De Imagine Mundi* by Honorius of Autun.[68] The poet identifies himself at line 20 at Perot de Garbelei, but he is silent about the fact that he has plagiarised scores of lines from an earlier verse rendering of Honorius, the *Mappemonde* by Pierre de Beauvais, who was active during the first quarter of the thirteenth century.[69] Both Vising and Professor Legge eschewed comment on Perot's work, yet its editor, Prior, had claimed that the author was an Anglo-Norman from Ireland.

The rubric *Hic incipit de Anticristo* on p. 425 heralds a new poem, but the apostrophes to "Meistre" suggest a dialogue between pupil and teacher, a format that is foreign to Old French texts on the Antichrist.[70] James cautiously observed that the work is "seemingly an extract from the French version of the *Elucidarium* of Honorius of Autun", but he made no pronouncement on the poet's identity.[71] Vising registers nothing for our codex number under Antichrist, Honorius, Elucidarium *alias* Lucidaire. It so happens that these 945 verses on pp. 425—57 constitute a composition by Gillebert from Cambres near Rouen,[72] which differs from the numerous other French redactions of the *Elucidarium* in that the poet confined his

[68] See *Cambridge Anglo-Norman Texts*, I, ed. J. P. Strachey, H. J. Chaytor and O. H. Prior (Cambridge University Press, 1924), pp. 34—62. Comments on the text are made by Segre in *GRLMA*, VI/1, 134—35, and VI/2, 194, no. 3676.

[69] Cf. G. L. Hamilton, 'Encore un plagiat médiéval: la *Mappemonde* de Pierre de Beauvais et les *Divisiones Mundi* de Perot de Garbelei' in *Mélanges de linguistique et de littérature offerts à M. Alfred Jeanroy* (Paris, 1928), pp. 627—38.

[70] An account of the rhymed Old French versions is supplied by P. Meyer, 'Légendes hagiographiques en français' in *Histoire littéraire de la France*, XXXIII (1906), 339ff.

[71] *Cat.*, II, 287.

[72] See H. Schladebach, *Das Elucidarium des Honorius Augustodunensis und der französische metrische Lucidaire des XIII. Jahrhunderts von Gillebert von Cambresy* (Leipzig, Diss. 1884); P. Eberhardt, 'Der Lucidaire Gilleberts' in *Archiv für das Studium der neueren Sprachen und Literaturen*, LXXIII (1885), 129—62; P. Meyer, 'Notice sur le ms. Ii.6.24 de la Bibliothèque de l'Université de Cambridge' in *Notices et Extraits des Manuscrits*, XXXII/2 (1886), 37—61, where the text is item 6 in a codex transcribed, it seems, at Caen.

translation effort to Book III where Honorius treated principally of the Antichrist.[73]

The hand responsible for all the transcriptions in Codex Va
concludes its work on pp. 457–62 with a copy of the *Vision
of St. Paul*, announced by the rubric *Hic incipit visio sancti
Pauli*. The opening words which James prints are those, as he
perceived, of the redaction by a certain Adam de Ros,[74] held
to be the first translator of the Latin *Visio*[75] into the French
vernacular.[76] Even though the earliest codex of this rendering
dates from about the middle of the thirteenth century, Adam's
composition is attributed by many scholars to the late twelfth
century.[77] Our Corpus manuscript preserves only the first 170
lines and the catchword of another, "Plus ke autre".[78] The break
occurs in the description of torments meted out to unchaste
maidens.

The interruption to the text after a catchword suggests to a
cautious reader that something may be irregular in the binding
or juxtaposition of the folios. On examining the ensuing sheets,
he discovers a new text by a different contemporary hand
whose line spacing and letter formation contrast with those of

[73] Yves Lefèvre, *L'Elucidarium et les Lucidaires*, Bibliothèque des Ecoles
françaises d'Athènes et de Rome, 180 (Paris, 1954), pp. 311–15 discusses briefly
our redaction, and refers his readers for the codices to A. Långfors, *Les Incipit des
poèmes français antérieurs au XVIe siècle* (Paris, 1917), pp. 367–68, where the
number attributed to our Corpus MS is 465. Segre includes the work in his review
of didactic tracts published in *GRLMA*, VI/1, 67, 140, and VI/2, 113, no. 2368.

[74] We defer discussion of the identity of his birthplace until our review of all
the Anglo-Norman works is concluded.

[75] The authority for the Latin sources is T. Silverstein, *Visio Sancti Pauli: the
History of the Apocalypse in Latin together with Nine Texts* (London, 1935), and
his paper 'The *Vision of St Paul*: New Links and Patterns in the Western Tradition' in
Archives d'histoire doctrinale et littéraire du moyen âge, XXXIV (1960), 199–248.

[76] Ed. L. E. Kastner, 'The *Vision of Saint Paul* by the Anglo-Norman Trouvere,
Adam de Ross' in *Zeitschrift für französische Sprache und Literatur*, XXIX (1906),
274–90. The Corpus MS readings are cited among the variants.

[77] Adam's composition, along with other French redactions, are discussed by
Legge, *ANC*, pp. 53–54; *ANL*, pp. 274–75, 304; D. D. R. Owen, 'The *Vision of St
Paul*: the French and Provençal Versions and their Sources' in *Romance Philology*,
XII (1958–59), 33–51, and in his study *The Vision of Hell* (Edinburgh, 1970),
pp. 51–55. See also the synopsis of Adam's work in *GRLMA*, VI/1, 201, 203, and
VI/2, 240–41, no. 4390.

[78] Not line 171 of the Kastner ed., but line 195, suggesting that the missing section
of the Corpus text had a gap at this point or contained lines out of order.

its predecessor. We are in fact in the presence of a new manuscript altogether. James considered it as the concluding part of V;[79] we shall designate it Vb. The two quires of eight folios contain an Anglo-Norman scribe's copy of a well-known and widely diffused Continental French didactic treatise, now usually named the *Livre des Moralités*.[80] The author drew his examples principally from the *Moralium dogma philosophorum* attributed to Guillaume de Conches.[81] The Corpus transcription breaks off: ". . . Dunc ly bons clers dit: Gard tey de conseiller e bien te purvoy de home loer ke". These words occur in a section on the role of servants in the household, exhorting them not to praise anyone to their masters who is unworthy of praise.[82] Thus, the last quarter of the tract is missing.

Our discussion of the Anglo-Norman components of Corpus Christi College MS 405 is almost at an end, and it is therefore appropriate to summarise our discoveries and suggest their importance. Of the eighteen texts which we have examined, twelve are by Anglo-Normans; of these, nine are anonymous and three by identified poets: Waterford Custumal, prophecies for six kings, profiles of select English monarchs, charm against rats among corn, explanation of dreams, five Joys of the Virgin, litany for saints, Elie of Winchester's *Cato*, poem on the love of God, the sermon *Deu le Omnipotent*, Perot de Garbelei's *Divisiones Mundi* and the *Vision* by Adam de Ros. The six remaining texts are not ascribable to Anglo-Norman authors: recipes, the *Six Ages*, the *Parlous Days*, introduction to a charm in epistolary form, the *Lucidaire* by Gillebert de Cambres and the *Livre des moralités*.

The regional attachments of the poet of the Virgin's Five Joys are uncharted, and the praises which he sings appear to

---

[79] *Cat.*, II, 287—88.

[80] Cf. *Das Moralium dogma philosophorum des Guillaume de Conches: Lateinisch, Altfranzösisch und Mittelniederfrankisch*, ed. J. Holmberg (Paris, 1929), pp. *30—*58, and 84—182, 194—97. In the introduction he describes 38 Old French copies; the number was increased to 47 by Edith Brayer, 'Notice du ms. Paris, B.N., fr. 1109' in *Mélanges Félix Grat* (Paris, 1946 & 1949), II, 240—42, but neither scholar mentions our Corpus MS.

[81] The ascription of the Latin original to Guillaume de Conches is not universally accepted; see J. R. Williams, 'The Quest for the Author of the *Moralium dogma philosophorum*, 1931—1956' in *Speculum*, XXXII (1957), 736—47.

[82] Cf. Holmberg, *op. cit.*, p. 158.

have no special merit for worshippers in Waterford. This is true of the sermon *Deu le Omnipotent* composed in England, but in an undetermined locality. The author of the *Poème sur l'amour de Dieu* was an Anglo-Norman, but the Waterford version occurs in only one other manuscript. Explanations are still needed to account for the popularity and rehandling of this poem by Bozon and by the compiler of the *Manuel des Péchés*. A similar veil lies over a likely Waterford interest in the Antichrist subject matter derived from the *Elucidarium* by Gillebert de Cambres. Admittedly, the Corpus codex does not contain the lines in which the poet identifies himself. One may reasonably assume that it was the text's subject matter, rather than its author, that was its principal attraction.

The three remaining poems whose authors are known do not appear to have any attachments to Waterford, at least until one becomes familiar with the region's history. The editor of Perot de Garbelei's translation of the *De Imagine Mundi* made these pointed comments about the toponym: "... no such place is to be found in France or in Great Britain. We have to cross the Irish Channel in order to locate it. And there we have "l'embarras du choix": *bally* is a frequent element in Irish place-names ... *Gar* as a prefix means 'short' or 'rough'. Garbally is the name of several places in Leinster, Munster and Connaught".[83] It is not surprising, we believe, that a copy of a work by an Anglo-Norman, hailing from a town of Garbally, was present in a collection of Anglo-Norman texts located in South-East Ireland.

The name Adam de Ros has been familiar to students of Anglo-Norman Literature since a claim was made for Ross-on-Wye in Herefordshire as his birth-place.[84] But in 1936 J. C. Russell published a biographical sketch of the poet, whose *Vision* he dated as early thirteenth-century, and he also adduced evidence that an Adam de Ros belonged in 1279 to the Cistercian Abbey of Dunbrody and in that year had represented his abbot

---

[83] Cf. *Cambridge Anglo-Norman Texts*, p. 35.
[84] Espoused by Kastner, the editor of Adam's *Vision* (see n. 76 above), taking his lead from H. L. D. Ward. More recently, H. R. Jauss, *GRLMA*, VI/2, 240, no. 4390, identifies Adam as a "moine de humble condition . . . originaire probablement de Ross-en-Wye en Herefordshire". Professor Owen, *Vision of Hell*, p. 51, gives prominence to the same origin.

coram rege.[85] This observation, juxtaposed as it is by Russell to
the Hereford connexion, implies that the two Adams are one
and the same person, yet there is no discussion of the identification in relation to a human life-span. Furthermore, he did not
perceive that there is a Ross twelve miles upstream from
Dunbrody on the Barrow River. It was Professor Legge who
drew the inference: "Obviously, the Dunbrody Adam came
from this Ross, a fact that Mr Russell overlooked".[86] When I
visited the abbey a few years ago, I found a structural skeleton
of great beauty, but I had difficulty in envisaging its glory and
importance seven centuries ago at the height of Anglo-Norman
influence. Ross itself has undergone name changes with time,
and is now New Ross or Ros Mhic Thriuin. The fact that we
have now established the presence of a copy of Adam's *Vision*
at Waterford in the early fourteenth century adds a little more
credence to the suggestion that he hailed from the city's com-
mercial rival of Ross on the Barrow. Nevertheless, regional
patriotism alone does not really bring us any closer to com-
prehending the Waterford citizens' interest in the textual
matter which Adam had translated.

Finally, there is need to comment on the existence in the
regional capital of a copy of Cato's *Distichs* in the Anglo-
Norman redaction prepared by a Benedictine monk of
Winchester, by name Elie. Of the three versions of Cato's primer
in Anglo-Norman,[87] why should Elie's be the one selected for
inclusion in the collection? Could the choice have arisen out of
cultural or religious links between Winchester and Waterford?[88]

---

[85] *Dictionary of Writers of Thirteenth-Century England* (London, 1936), pp.
9–10.

[86] Cf. Legge, *ANC*, p. 54; later, in her *ANL*, p. 304, she states: "Not far away
was Ross, where Adam de Ros, possibly a Cistercian of Dunbrody, who wrote
one of the versions of the *Vision of St. Paul*, may have been born". This origin is
still not widely accepted by scholars; see n. 84 above.

[87] Cf. Legge, *ANC*, pp. 13–17; *ANL*, p. 182.

[88] I remind the reader at this point that the *Prophecies* of Merlin concerning
the six kings, mentioned at the outset of this census, proclaims Winchester as the
Lamb's place of origin: "Ung aignel vendra hors de Wyncestre. . .", since the creature
in question is a descendant of Henry II, himself born in that city, if we are to believe
the text's own rubric: *Ci comencent akuns des prophetiez et des merveilles que
Merlyn dit en son tens de Engletterre et des rois que unt esté pus le tens le roi Henri
darreyn que nasqui a Wyncestre . . .* I would not wish, however, to suggest that these
associations imply that the political tract was composed under Benedictine influence.

Alternatively, may not the Benedictines themselves have been an influence? The annals of the Order and of the Waterford diocese offer evidence pointing in this direction. The first bishop was Malchus, consecrated in 1096 by St Anselm at Canterbury. Although subsequently appointed Archbishop of Cashel in 1111, Malchus was still in the canonicals of Waterford when he died in 1135.[89] It appears that he had been trained as a Benedictine at Winchester during the episcopacy of Bishop Walkelin (1070–1098). From the late twelfth century the Black Monks maintained a cell within the city walls of Waterford. It was dependent on the Cathedral Priory of St Saviour, St Peter and St Paul at Bath, had the status of a monastery-hospital, and was dedicated to St John the Evangelist.[90] Two of the priors became Bishops of Waterford, Walter from 1227 to 1252, and William between 1255 and 1274.[91] In the early fourteenth century the small cell was declining in prestige through mismanagement. A visit and investigation in 1306 by the Bath prior Robert de Clopcote[92] did not brighten the twilight years for very long. Clearly, the apogee of Benedictine influence had been in the mid-thirteenth century when two local priors were diocesans and when Anglo-Norman administrative control of ecclesiastical affairs in South-East Ireland was at its height.[93] Perhaps the inclusion of Elie's redaction of Cato in a manuscript destined for Waterford coincided with interest and concern for the Black Monks. The turn of the

---

[89] Cf. F. M. Powicke & E. B. Fryde, *Handbook of British Chronology*, 2nd ed. (London, 1961), pp. 322, 334; Gwynn & Hadcock, *op. cit.*, p. 100. See also the paper by A. Gwynn, 'The Origins of the Diocese of Waterford' in *Irish Ecclesiastical Record*, LIX (1942), 288–96.

[90] Cf. P. Power, 'The Priory, Church and Hospital of St. John the Evangelist, Waterford, in *Waterford and South-East of Ireland Archaeological Journal*, II (1896), 81–97. This paper by a local antiquarian is now somewhat dated and contains historical inaccuracies.

[91] Powicke & Fryde, *op. cit.*, p. 334; Gwynn & Hadcock, *op. cit.*, p. 108.

[92] Cf. Gwynn & Hadcock, *op. cit.* p. 108.

[93] For the circumstances giving rise to this hegemony, see two papers by P. J. Dunning, 'Pope Innocent III and the Waterford-Lismore Controversy 1198–1216' in *Irish Theological Quarterly*, XXVIII (1961), 215–32; 'Irish Representatives and Irish Ecclesiastical Affairs at the Fourth Lateran Council' in *Medieval Studies presented to Aubrey Gwynn* (Dublin, 1961), pp. 90–113. There is also an important article on the period that concerns us in the same homage volume, pp. 133–67, by J. A. Watt, 'English Law and the Irish Church: the Reign of Edward I'.

century dating for Boniface VIII's Bull at the head of codex Va would not weaken this inference.

However discursive these ideas may seem, our paper has retained its primary focus: to record the existence of a group of Anglo-Norman texts in Waterford in the reigns of Edward I and II. There has been no suggestion that the manuscripts themselves were executed in a Waterford scriptorium. What is clear is that codices containing texts of concern to civil, ecclesiastical and Hospitaller authorities in the city were most likely brought there, from South-West England, and that after this transference Anglo-Norman court hands added specifically regional memoranda on blank folios. These facts are worthy of inclusion in any future account which literary historians may write about the Anglo-Norman colony in South-East Ireland.

A FRAGMENT OF AN OLD FRENCH POEM IN OCTOSYLLABLES ON THE SUBJECT OF PYRAMUS AND THISBE

W. G. VAN EMDEN_____

Some years ago, I began research into the development in European literature of the Pyramus and Thisbe legend, and particularly into the influence of the twelfth-century French poem *Pyramus et Tisbé*, whose inclusion in the *Ovide moralisé* allowed it to influence, directly or indirectly, many later works of imagination.[1] It was therefore with particular interest that I later noticed the subject appearing in the contents of MS Paris BN nouv. acq. fr. 5094 which, among the fragments of *chansons de geste* for which it is usually consulted, contains two leaves of a poem in octosyllabic rhymed couplets on the Pyramus legend. The fragment consists of 123 lines which are not part of *P. et T.*; as far as I know, it has never been published.

The *Catalogue général* of the *Nouvelles acquisitions françaises* (t. II, Paris, 1900, p. 283) gives only the following entry:

VII (fol. 16—17) Double feuillet d'un exemplaire du [*sic*] roman de *Pyrame et Thisbé*. — 145 sur 200 millimètres.

Elsewhere on the same page, the dates of the miscellaneous fragments which make up the collection are summarised as

---

[1] My work on this poem (hereinafter *P. et T.*) has so far led to four articles: 'Sources de l'histoire de Pyrame et Thisbé chez Baïf et Théophile de Viau' in *Mélanges . . . Pierre le Gentil* (Paris, 1973), pp. 832—42; 'La légende de Pyrame et Thisbé: textes français des XVᵉ, XVIᵉ et XVIIᵉ siècles' in *Etudes . . . Félix Lecoy* (Paris, 1973), pp. 569—83; an edition, with variants from other versions, of the *mise en prose* as given in MS Paris BN f.fr. 137 in *Romania*, XCIV (1973), 29—56; 'Shakespeare and the French Pyramus and Thisbe Tradition, or Whatever Happened to Robin Starveling's Part?' in *Forum for Modern Language Studies*, XI (1975), 193—204. The *P. et T.* edition used for the present article is that of F. Branciforti (Firenze, 1959), which is established on the basis of the three autonomous MSS as well as those of the *Ovide moralisé*, with a full corpus of variants; for Ovid's *Metamorphosis*, the edition of A. Ludwic (Leipzig, 1909) has been used.

"XIIIe et XIVe siècle".[2] Linguistically, at any rate, our fragment is certainly to be placed not later than the former century,
perhaps, as will be seen, even slightly earlier, though the writing
of the scribe may well belong to the end of the thirteenth century.

The two separate pages mounted as "feuillets 16—17" seem
indeed to have been a double sheet, the middle of a gathering
originally arranged flesh, hair, hair, flesh, for the text is consecutive — provided the modern order is reversed. The text of leaf
17 clearly comes before that of 16 in terms of the well-known
story, and the last line of 17b is the first half of a couplet and
rhymes with a similarly orphan line at the head of 16a. Leaf 17
is physically larger than 16: they are respectively 222 by 144 mm.
and 214 (at the maximum point — 16 is cut irregularly and tapers
slightly towards the bottom right-hand corner) by 142 mm.
The writing occupies a rectangle of about 210 (200 in the case
of 16) by 80 mm.; only one or two lines exceed 80 mm. On the
versos, the column begins some 40 mm. from the edge; on the
rectos, the distance is only about 8 mm., the pages having
apparently been roughly cut out, so that the inner margins do
not match at all — a considerable stub must have been left. Both
have clearly been heavily cropped. They seem to have been used
as some sort of envelope, for leaf 16 has longitudinal fold lines
showing the recto to have been folded over the verso at about
22 mm. and 28 mm. respectively from the right and left margin;
on either side of, and parallel to, the left-hand fold, and about
two-thirds the way down the page, are two slits through which a
fastening must have been passed. Leaf 17 retains much less
pronounced traces of both creases. Irregular horizontal folds
buckle the text in two or three places and complicate the
reading of an already difficult text, since the writing is badly
worn on leaves 16r and 17v especially. These seem to have
formed the outside of the package; there are also a number of

---

[2] L. Delisle, *Manuscrits latins et français ajoutés aux des nouvelles acquisitions
pendant les années 1875–1891*, Parties I–II (Paris, 1891), pp. 257–58, mentions
Nouv. acq. fr. 5094 ("Fragments d'anciens manuscrits de poésie française"), but,
concentrating on the epic texts in it, ignores our fragments. They were, however,
certainly in the BN before 20 May 1886, according to a note on the title page of
the collection.

worm holes which correspond almost exactly in position on both leaves, as if something fairly thin had held them apart; they do not appear to have been made while they still formed part of a manuscript.

The text is written in a single column of 31 lines per page, except for 16v, which has only 30. There is no ornamentation of any kind, nor are there any enlarged initial letters. The ink, of varying shades of brown in general, has turned dark green, perhaps through some chemical reaction, in the first four lines of 17v; it does not appear to have been inked over on top of the original text.

Although the writing on the undamaged verso of 16 is easy to read, much of the rest is so badly rubbed that extensive use of ultra-violet light was necessary to decipher it, and even so a few words remain conjectural. In one or two places, the ink has completely disappeared, either by abrasion or worm damage. Italics have been used to indicate the letters added editorially in such places, as well as words which remain doubtful even after the use of the ultra-violet lamp and which have been extrapolated from meaning and/or prosody. In accordance with normal editorial practice, square brackets show letters inserted as a correction; but editorial interventions have been kept to a minimum, given the fragmentary nature of the text and the fact that it is of academic, rather than public, interest. Thus an editor of the complete poem for general use would certainly wish to correct line 110, which makes little sense in the context in which it stands. One might well propose:

> Dit Tybé: 'Amis, a nul fuer
> *Nulle chose ne veeroie*
> Que je certainement saroie
> Que vos a certes vousissiez.' 112

For the purposes for which I publish the fragment here, such an intervention would seem pointless. I have nevertheless punctuated the passage, supplied diacritics and capitals, separated *u* and *v*, *i* and *j*, for convenience. As *biax* 36 is not repeated, the value of *x* for the scribe is not absolutely clear and it has been left. Two cases of graphical hiatus (*de heure* 66; *de orens* 80) have been allowed to stand.

In so short a fragment, the linguistic evidence is necessarily incomplete and there cannot be many specimens of particular phenomena. Rhymes like *estre:feste* 102–3, and perhaps the four consecutive rhymes in *-ier* at 114–17, suggest that the poet was not excessively punctilious in any case. The rhyme *alaine*: *saine* 4–5 shows, not surprisingly, that the text is no earlier than the late twelfth century (Pope, § 467);[3] the fact that the endings of 4 and 5 imperfect and conditional at 79 and 80 (*voulïez, isirïon*) are dissyllabic is characteristic of the twelfth rather than the thirteenth century (Fouché, *Verbe fr.*, p. 242). These are the only two examples, however, and the second depends on assuming elision of *de* before a vowel (as certainly happens in 66). In any case, such forms occur in thirteenth-century texts too, though accompanied, as a rule, by more and more monosyllabic forms as time goes on.[4] The forms *derrenier* 53 and *vraiement* 99 are also in principle archaic in comparison with *dernier* and *vraiment* which begin to appear, respectively, "in the late twelfth and thirteenth centuries" (Pope, § 272) and "in the fourteenth century or even earlier" (*ibid.*, § 270), though their isolation in our short fragment weakens the force of the point, here as elsewhere.[5] There are no examples of ana-logical *-e* in 1 pres. ind. of First Conjugation verbs: *cuit* 20, *lo* 87, *pri* 44. The fem. adjective *tel* occurs in non-analogical form at 75, 76, *grant* at 33; there are no contrary examples. The declension system is generally well maintained, most of the 'errors' being attributable to the scribe, but *N'i a cil* 106 is

---

[3] The abbreviations used in this section refer to works so well known that full bibliographical details are hardly necessary. Suffice it to say that the latest editions have been used in each case.

[4] It is noteworthy that a text preserved only in a fifteenth-century manuscript, *Galien li Restorés*, has almost, though not quite, all the endings in question count-ing for two syllables. This poem, recently edited by D. M. Dougherty and E. B. Barnes, Purdue University Monographs in Romance Languages, 7 (Amsterdam, 1981), was thought by Jules Horrent to be based on a fourteenth-century *remanie-ment* of a post-1250 compilation which, in its turn, used the *Galien primitif* of around 1200, both the latter texts being lost; see *La Chanson de Roland dans les littératures française et espagnole au moyen âge* (Paris, 1951), pp. 404ff. The recent editors see no reason to disagree with Horrent's hypothesis; but the evidence of these endings suggests an earlier rather than a later date for the compilation and a pretty mechanical acceptance of much of its text by the fourteenth-century *remanieur*.

[5] *Vraiement* is the normal form in the *Galien*; cf. n. 4 above.

presumably the poet's, and he may also have written *parens*
(s.c.pl.) at 104—5, unless the rhyme *gens* was originally part of
*mauvaise gent.

Features which may point to a slightly more recent date are
still less numerous, but the main one, the equivalence of *s* and *z*
at the rhyme, suggests the reduction of the affricate group [ts],
which took place "in the course of the thirteenth century",
though Chrétien de Troyes already admits occasional rhymes
involving [ts] and [s] (Pope, § § 194—95; cf. Fouché, *Phon.
hist.*, p. 780: "On peut considérer que la réduction est complètement terminée dans le premier tiers du XIIIe siècle"). It
is, of course, possible to interpret the phenomenon as a Picard
feature, since this reduction took place earlier in that region
(Pope, § § N. xxi and 195). The rhymes which seem to attest
it, in spite of the graphy, are: *nulz* : *cheüz* 8—9, *nulz* : *chanuz*
64—65 and perhaps *orens* (for *orainz*[6]): *sens* 80—81. (It is the
scribe, at least potentially, who is responsible for many more
graphies suggesting the same reduction.) The rhyme *boivre* :
croire 78—79 attests an analogical infinitive of the former
verb which is characteristically present, according to Fouché
(*Verbe fr.*, p. 95) and Pope (§ 936(ii)), in late thirteenth-
century works like *Doon de Maience* or *Le Jeu de la Feuillee*,
but it appears also in the much earlier *Dialogues du pape
Gregoire* and *La Clef d'Amor*.

The evidence, such as it is, of the linguistic forms which
may be ascribed to the poet tends on the whole to support a
date earlier rather than later in the thirteenth century. In the
light of this, we may consider the rhyme *compere* : *chiere*
106—7 as Western (Pope, § § W. i and 512) rather than as
indicating a date in Middle French, which is where Pope (§ 510)
places the reduction of [je] to [e] after palatals and denti-
palatals in other regions. Fouché (*Phon. hist.*, p. 736) in any
case claims the beginnings of the process for the second half
of the twelfth century, though he sees the phenomenon as
becoming frequent in texts only a century later, and speaks of

---

[6] The form *ans* is quoted by Fouché (*Phon. hist.*, p. 175) as a variant of *ainz*
< **antius*. It seems that forms with -*s* for -*z* are not uncommon, so that this example
has certainly less force than the others.

the fourteenth for adjectives like *cher* (p. 264, Rem. III). If this rhyme is likely to be due to Western influence, the use of the possessive adjective *vo(s)* in the singular at 4, 43, 50, 92 and *nos* as the subject case masculine plural at 74, 104 is characteristically Picard (Pope, § § 853 and N. xxv; Gossen, § 68), though *vostre* 41, 46, 81 and *nostre* 100 are also found. The isolated form *haschiee* (= *haschie*) rhyming with *mie* at 74—75 is also typical of the Picard region, though the reduction of *-iee* to *-ie* is found in many areas, including the northern part of Normandy (see Fouché, *Phon. hist*, p. 268; Pope, § § N. v, E. iii and 513; Gossen, § 8). Finally, the elision suffered by the relative pronoun *que* for *qui* 66 corresponds to what Foulet (*Petite Syntaxe*, § 247) considers "un cas assez rare" which depends on the occasional analogical extension of the object case, a phenomenon which he ascribes particularly, though not exclusively, to eastern texts.

Overall, the fragment thus has no very pronounced dialectal features. The scribe is certainly not a Picard, for example, to judge by the universal presence of consonantal glides in the groups *m'l, n'r* and *l'r*, the absence of *le* for *la, mi* for *moi, c* or *k* for *ch* before *a* and the reverse before *e* or *i*. As to date, nothing speaks against the first half of the thirteenth century, or indeed the first quarter, for the poet, and the second half of the century for the scribe, as his writing suggests. Apart from his tendency to confuse final *s* and *z*, he is characterised by instability of pre-consonantal *s*: *pamez* 9 (but *pasmez* 15), *Tybe(e) passim, soupris* 40, and the occasional redundant letter: *nulz* 8, 64, *vault* 78, *leesce* 77, *enhuit* 88.

Two other features of the language of the fragment deserve mention: the poet uses *Tybé* or *Tybee* in three syllables for the heroine's name as metre requires, though the former is much commoner than the latter (only two examples: 10, 30). This does not happen in the *P. et T.* in either the twelfth-century version or in that of the *Ovide moralisé*. The trisyllabic form of the name seems not to occur in any verse version of the story known to me before the *Moralité nouvelle de Pyramus et Tisbee*,[7] a dramatised version which dates from about 1535

---

[7] Published by Emile Picot in *Bulletin du Bibliophile*, 1901, 1–35.

and depends on the *mise en prose* printed by Mansion and by Vérard at the end of the fifteenth century. Even in the *Moralité,* the form *Tisbee* counts normally for two syllables, though the author once rhymes it (pp. 27—28) with *espee* : *(gueule) bee.* The prose version, represented today by MSS Paris BN f.fr. 137 and London BL Royal 17 E IV, dates from an indeterminate period before 1480, and uses the form *Tisbee* throughout,[8] although Mansion and Vérard return to the form *Tisbe* or *Thisbe*, with only occasional examples of *Tisbee*. There is, as we shall see, no probability of the fragment's representing a lost version between the *P. et T.* and the *mise en prose*, which are closely related.[9]

The other point of interest is the use of the word *salle* 95 in the sense of a place shaded by trees. This meaning, which is occasionally found in texts of the seventeenth century and later, and which, according to the *FEW*,[10] is found in editions of the *Dictionnaire de l'Académie française* between 1694 and 1878, is entirely absent from the Old French dictionaries of Godefroy and Tobler-Lommatzsch, as well as that of Huguet for the sixteenth century; nor is Cotgrave's *Dictionarie* of any help. It is most curious to find this isolated example in a thirteenth-century text, and it is to be hoped that the problem raised here will lead to further investigation to bridge the long gap between our fragment and 1694.

Apparently at least some decades later than the well-known *P. et T.*, though considerably earlier than the *Ovide moralisé* which took up, and made the fortune of, the twelfth-century work, our fragment seems to be a parallel adaptation of the Ovidian *Metamorphosis*. Like the earlier French poem, it supplies at some, though lesser, length the speeches of the lovers through the famous chink, whereas Ovid, with one

[8] See my article in *Romania* cited in n. 1 above.

[9] For the text of the *mise en prose* corresponding to the part of the narrative covered by the fragment, see my article in *Romania*, 39—41.

[10] Vol. XVII, p. 9a: "übertragen nfr. *salle* . . . lieu entouré d'arbres qui forment un couvert". On investigation, the 1935 edition of the *Dictionnaire* continues to give this meaning for *salle*.

exception,[11] puts them into brief *oratio obliqua*. The question
of the relationship between these texts therefore arises: is the
fragment part of an independent *amplificatio* of Ovid's poem,
does it depend wholly on the earlier *P. et T.*, or does it use
both?[12]

The problem is complicated by the lack of what was no
doubt the greater part of the poem with which we are dealing,
and — as far as a comparison with Ovid goes — by the fact that
much of the fragment's text is dialogue invented by our author.
There are nevertheless at least two indications suggesting that he
did make independent use of Ovid. Though the context is
different, in that it is part of a monologue, line 4 of the fragment, with its desire to feel the "douce alaine" of Thisbe
through the chink, recalls line 72 of the Latin poem:

inque vices fuerat captatus anhelitus oris, . . .

Still clearer evidence is provided by the comparison with the
other two texts of lines 69—71 of the fragment:

Au matin chascun se leva

A la crevace qu'il savoient,

Ainsi qu'acoustumé avoient.

Here, unlike *P. et T.*, our fragment seems to pick up Ovid's
ad solitum coiere locum 83. In *P. et T.*, the decision to escape
is taken at what is only the second meeting at the chink (cf.
408—13), whereas our author (63—71), like Ovid (71ff.), stresses
that such meetings become a way of life before the decision is
made.

This point especially — and perhaps it would be unreasonable
to expect more proofs, given that the whole fragment corresponds to only some twenty lines of Ovid and happens to be
embroidering in a very different vein — makes it at least likely
that our author went directly to the *Metamorphosis*. Yet the
same piece of evidence seems to point to the influence of the

---

[11] *Ed. cit.*, lines 73—77.

[12] The problem of possible relationships with the other Latin and vernacular
texts which constitute the material of my continuing work on the development of
the legend is obviously too large to be properly treated here, but I hope to place the
fragment definitively in the tradition in a later study. For the moment, I see no
evidence in the texts known to me which would oblige me to go beyond the findings
of the present article.

earlier *P. et T.* also. There is a curious clumsiness, a sort of *dédoublement*, about lines 56—71 of the fragment, which seems to correspond to 411—12 of *P. et T.*, since the next line in both is very similar:

Piramus a premier parlé . . . 72

Primes parole Piramus: . . . *P. et T.* 413

(Ovid, of course, has no direct speech at this point; 83ff.) The author of the fragment insists, following the lead given by Ovid, as we have seen, on the repetition of the meetings (56, 59, 63), but when he comes to the fateful morning of the decision, he begins "Au matin . . ." as in 411 of *P. et T.*, where it is indeed the morning after the discovery of the chink. The turn of phrase of our poet, surprising as it is in the context in which he puts it, suggests a somewhat clumsy attempt to combine the narrative of *P. et T.* with that of Ovid's poem.

How far may this suggestion be supported by further evidence of knowledge of *P. et T.* on the part of our author? In my earlier work on the French Pyramus and Thisbe tradition, I have analysed a number of 'trace-elements' which allow the influence of the twelfth-century poem to be distinguished from that of Ovid.[13] It will be convenient to reproduce the first part of the analysis here.[14]

(1) The lovers are *of equal age*. (2) A *serf* tells of their love to (3) *Thisbe's mother*, who has her daughter locked up; (4) additonally, *the fathers quarrel*. (5) Pyramus *prays in the temple of Venus for help*. (6) *Thisbe finds the chink*. (7) She takes *the "pendant" of her belt* and attracts Pyramus's attention by pushing it through the chink. (8) *Thisbe suggests the rendez-vous*, where Ovid, l. 84, writes "statuunt"; I shall let (8a) designate the decision coming from Pyramus, as it does in other texts. (9) The lovers experience *alternate hope and fear* as they wait for nightfall. (10) Thisbe goes out in spite of *evil omens* and (11) passes a *"guaite" who takes her for a goddess*. . . .

Our fragment stops, unfortunately, before the story has reached many of the most characteristic and useful 'trace-elements', such as the lion in place of Ovid's lioness, and the particular noun used for the garment which Thisbe drops when

[13] See my article in *Forum for Modern Language Studies* cited in n. 1 above.
[14] *Art. cit.*, p. 195. The 'trace-elements' are numbered and the textually significant motifs italicised.

she flees from the beast. Like the twelfth-century poet, our
author has introduced at least one monologue (1–8 – Pyramus
clearly does not realise that Thisbe can hear him) as well as the
conversations referred to above. It is unclear whether Thisbe
had found the chink and marked it with the *pendant* of her belt
('trace-elements' 6 and 7), but Pyramus is certainly not speaking
to her at the beginning of our fragment, as he does in *P. et T.*
after he has seen the belt. It is possible that our author had the
young man finding the chink; certainly, in common with the
post-*P. et T.* tradition, he gives the decision to meet at Ninus's
tomb to Pyramus ('trace-element' 8a), whereas the twelfth-
century version ascribes the proposal to Thisbe (581–98). Ovid,
of course, simply says *statuunt*, just as he had earlier (67–68)
said *id vitium . . . primi vidistis amantes*, without more detail.
Unfortunately, one must make allowance for the probability
that the very talented author of *P. et T.* was unconventional in
his willingness to ascribe the leading role to Thisbe, and that
later authors may independently of each other have changed
this datum on the grounds that it was more fitting for the man
to take the initiative[15] – a reasonable supposition on the basis,
for example, of the parodic mockery of the reticent hero in
Aucassin et Nicolette. Certainly there is no evidence that the
manuscript *mise en prose*, which is preserved in two fifteenth-
century manuscripts and which was hitherto the earliest version
to show 'trace-element' 8a, knew our text in addition to its
obvious model in the *Ovide moralisé*, which it follows closely
over the narrative corresponding to our fragment; and the latter
is scarcely young enough to have known the *mise en prose*.

Apart from 8a, the fragment contains little or no direct
reference to the *P. et T.* 'trace-elements'. The insistent allusions
of Pyramus to the cruelty of their respective "peres" 74 and
"parens" 104 may possibly be a sign that our poem was influenced by the quarrel of the fathers (element 4) and the role of
Thisbe's mother (element 3) in *P. et T.*, since these are important
additions to Ovid's narrative; but the references could also be
extrapolations from the *Metamorphosis* (especially 61, 155).

---

[15] Those who used the *Metamorphosis* might in any case note the later suggestion
of a dominant role for Pyramus at 110–11 of Ovid's story.

The role of the "guaite" in *P. et T.* (11; see 615, 651—57) is
perhaps sufficiently striking to have inspired the allusion of line
90 in our fragment and the premonitory lines about the bright-
ness of the moon with which it ends, but one can hardly put this
forward as more than a plausible supposition.

Nevertheless, there do seem to be some textual resemblances
between our fragment and *P. et T.*, in spite of considerable
divergences in many respects. It is perhaps natural that, after
Pyramus's first speech, lines 10—13 of our text should resemble
P. et T. 364 ff.

> La pucele de l'autre part
> Est en escout et en esgart:
> De la parole entent l'effroi,
> Trait soi plus pres de la paroi,
> Met son oeil endroit la crevace: . . .   368

though the earlier poem does not have Pyramus unconscious at
this point, and its "Parler volt, mes ele ne puet" 370 contra-
dicts line 16 of the fragment, as does the sequel, for Thisbe takes
Pyramus to be dead in our version.

The resemblance of our line 48 to *P. et T.* 512—14 is still
more striking, especially as these lines come further on in the
narrative of the earlier poem and are a response to Pyramus's
claim (415) to be *navrez* on account of Thisbe, a point not
made in the preserved part of our poem:

> Bien sai, por moi estes navrez,
>   Pour moi
> Et ie por vos, en moie foi.   514

The stress on the lovers' leaving their houses as soon as night
has fallen (*P. et T.* 588, 595, 633; fragment 88—91, 119) is not
in Ovid; and one could draw a final parallel between lines 96—98
of our text and *P. et T.* 596—97, but here too the needs of the
narrative may be a sufficient explanation.

None of these parallels quite clinches the case for imitation
of *P. et T.* by the author of our fragment, but, taken together,
they do make such a relationship probable, and nothing seems
to demand a different conclusion. It seems likely that our
fragment represents an attempt to repeat the success of the earlier
P. et T. by the composition of a new vernacular version, which
shows signs of a return to the Latin source as well as a willing-

ness to borrow selectively from its French precursor. Our poet
seems to have made deliberate changes, if he did indeed exploit
P. et T.: the long lyrical speeches have been severely pruned, no
attempt has been made to imitate the metrical variety of *P. et
T.*, and our author has given the initiative to Pyramus, particularly as far as the fateful decision is concerned. His simpler
version obviously had less success, but readers may judge that
it is not without metrical and rhetorical competence and a
lyrical intensity of its own. The loss of the beginning and end is
a reason for real regret.

     '. . . Se vos fussiez ci *entre*soit   *f. 17r*
     Par d'autre part de la crevace,
     Tant que vos veïsse en la face
4   Et sentisse vo douce alaine
     Qui tant par est et bonne et saine,
     Et ensemble ci parlissons
     Et nos pensees deïssons;
8   Car ci ne nous entendist nulz.'
     Adonques rest pamez cheüz.
     Tybee d'autre part estoit,
     Qui sa complainte oïe avoit;
12   A la crevace en est venue
     Et si gete outre sa veüe,
     Et vit que Piramus estoit
     Pasmez, qui d'autre part gisoit.
16   Adonc commença a parler
     Et son ami a regreter,
     Et dist: 'Piramus, douz amis,
     Pour moi estes en tel point mis
20   Donc je ne cuit que vos soiez
     Ja mais nul jour par moi aidiez.
     Mes je en couvenant vos ai
     Se mors estes, pour vos mourrai.
24   Ja, par celui qui me fourma,
     Amours ne me reprouchera
     Que devers moi en soit li tors;
     Car se vos estes pour moi mors,

28 Pour vos mourrai, car c'est le droiz.'
Pyramus entr'oï la voiz
De Tybee, lors se leva;
Par la crevace regarda
32 Et vit Tybé, la simple et coie;   *f. 17v*
Donc ot a son cuer si grant joie
Que ne pot .i. seul mot parler.
Tybé le prist a apeler
36 Et dist: 'Biax amis, a que doit
Qu'a moi ne parlez orendroit
Tant diz que sommes andui ci?'
'Tybé, douce amie, merci,'
40 Fait Piramus, 'si sui soupris
De regarder vostre douz vis
Que je de parler n'ai poue[i]r
Quant vos cors puis *raperceveir*.'
44 'Et je vos pri, douz finz amans,'
Fait Tybé, 'ne soiez doutans:
S'amours a vostre cuer *blecié*
Le mien n'est de rienz *esparnié*.
48 Navrez estes, je sui navree;
Si n'iert ja ma plaie *sanee*
Se n'est de l'otroi de vo cuer.'
Piramus respont: 'A nul fuer
52 A nul jour garis ne serai
Se de l'otroi derrenier n'ai.'
Tant ont ensemble ainsi parlé
Que pour la nuit sont dessevré;
56 A l'endemain il rasemblerent
Et puis en maison s'en alerent.
Toute la nuit molt pensif furent
Et l'endemain, si comme il durent
60 Et com la couvenance fu,
Sont a la crevace *venu*.
Illec tiennent leur parlement;
Et cele vie longuement
64 Maintindrent que ne le sot nulz,   *f. 16r*
Granz ne petiz, jones, chanuz,
Tant que fortune, qu'en peu de heure

Torne celui desouz deseure,
68 Contre aus aventure torna.
Au matin chascun se leva
A la crevace qu'il savoient,
Ainsi qu'acoustumé avoient.
72 Piramus a premier parlé
Et dit: 'Douce amie Tybé,
Nos peres ne nous aiment mie
Qui soufrir nous font tel haschiee
76 Et nous font vivre a tel destrece
Que ne poons avoir leesce.
Mieuz ne nous vault mengier ne boivre;
Mes, se vos me voulïez croire,
80 Par tens isirïons de orens!'
Fait Tybé: 'Dites vostre sens;
Volentiers vos escouterai
Et de ma part l'otroierai.
84 Il ne me chaudroit ou je fusse
Mes qu'avec vos estre peüsse.'
Dist Piramus: 'Or m'escoutez:
Je lo bien, se vos le voulez,
88 Qu'enhuit, quant sera avespré,
Que tout sera asseüré,
Ainz que la gaite soit montee
Qu'issiez coiement, a celee,
92 De vo *p*orte et de vo manoir,
Que nul n*e*l puist apercevoir;
Si alez dehors la cité   *f. 16v*
A la salle d'antiquité,
96 Et m'atendez a la fontaine
Qui par est tant et clere et saine.
Desouz le mourier m'atendez,
Car vraiement m'i trouverez,
100 Et la nostre conseil prendrons
Pour savoir quel part nous irons,
La ou nous puiss[i]ens ensemble estre
Et nous jouer et mener feste.
104 Trop nous destraingnent nos parens,
Il en font que mauvaises gens;

N'i a cil de nous nel compere
De cors, de pensee et de chiere,
108 De cors, de pensee et de cuer!'
Dit Tybé: 'Amis, a nul fuer
Nulle chose je ne verroie
Que je certainement saroie
112 Que vos a certes vousissiez.'
D'an.ii. fu li plais otroiez.
Lors se departent sanz targier,
Pensis com pourront esploitier.
116 Ainsi sont si qu'a l'anuitier;
Et quant ce vint vers le couchier,
Que la lune fu haut levee
Et la gent fu asseüree,
120 Chascun se prist a esbahir
Comment il pourront hors issir
Pour la lune qui si cler luist.
C'est une chose qui leur nuist . . .

Notes to the Text

23. *pour* written p^u; the sense requires *pour*. 40. *si* conjectural: two badly formed letters, almost like two minims; *si* fits best into the context. 53. *n'ai* written as *uai*. 102. The ending could be *-ons* or *-ens*, as the scribe several times writes *o* in a very similar way to *e*. The final consonant is possibly a *t*, as if the scribe had thought of the 3rd person plural ending (cf. 105 for a contrary error), but on close inspection it seems to be a badly written *s*. 104. MS *destraĩgnens*. 110. The MS reading *v'roie* does not seem to leave room for doubt; but see pp. 241 above for a conjectural reconstruction.

THE PROBLEM OF EDITING *YVAIN*

BRIAN WOLEDGE

Tim Reid's edition of *Yvain* is one of the most valuable pieces of work which he produced. Ever since its first appearance in 1942, it has provided both students and specialists with a convenient, reasonably priced and scholarly edition of one of the finest works in Old French literature.

The actual text of Reid's edition is a photographic reprint of Wendelin Foerster's last edition, published in 1912. To this Reid added a compact but very informative introduction, a very full glossary, and a remarkable series of notes. These notes deal with difficulties that a university student is likely to meet, but they go far beyond this; they bring up to date Foerster's work of 1912 and they give us what is almost a running commentary on Foerster's interpretation of the poem, elucidating textual problems and giving a wealth of information on syntax (a subject that always fascinated Reid).

With Reid's corrections, Wendelin Foerster's edition of 1912, the last of the five editions which he published in twenty-five years, is the nearest we have yet got to the original text of Chrétien's *Yvain*. Foerster had a wonderful feeling for Old French idiom and vocabulary, and this edition is the fruit of thirty years' intense study of all aspects of Chrétien's work. But today it is certainly capable of improvement.

In all his editions of Chrétien's romances, Foerster followed the custom of his time and constructed a text that is not to be found in any single manuscript; he also used a normalised spelling. We cannot criticise him for these things, although most scholars use different methods today; what makes Foerster's editions deficient in spite of their great merits is the arbitrary and inconsistent way in which he treated his manuscripts, his failure to look in detail at textual evidence and his failure to tell his reader how he reached his conclusions. It is this that makes the production of a new edition of *Yvain* an urgent matter.[1]

Since Foerster's time, three scholars have made major contributions to the problem of editing *Yvain*, and they must be considered in turn; they are A. Micha, P. Jonin and Mario Roques.

Micha's comprehensive study, *La Tradition manuscrite des romans de Chrétien de Troyes*, appeared in 1939,[2] but was not available to Reid at the time when he produced his edition. Micha undertook a fresh examination of all the extant manuscripts of Chrétien's romances, and showed convincingly the shortcomings of Foerster's work.[3] In the last part of his study, Micha laid down the principles that he considered should be followed by a future editor of Chrétien and showed how these would work out for each of the romances. It is no exaggeration to say that Micha's book revolutionised the textual study of Chrétien's works.

In classifying the manuscripts of *Yvain*, Micha was able to confirm some of the results of Foerster's pioneering work: like Foerster, he made a basic division which can be summarised as *PH/FGASM/V*. In other words, the manuscripts divide themselves like this:

1. *P* (BN 1433)
   H (BN 794, copied by a scribe named Guiot).
2. *F* (BN 1450)
   G (BN 12560)
   A (Chantilly 472)
   S (BN 12603)
   M (Montpellier 252)
3. *V* (Vatican, Christine 1725).

All scholars seem to agree on this basic division, although they express it differently or qualify it in various ways; for instance, Foerster spoke of a twofold classification, *V* versus the rest, but

---

[1] The need for new editions of Chrétien's romances has been well put by Tony Hunt in 'Chrétien de Troyes: the textual problem' in *French Studies*, XXXIII (1979), 257–71.

[2] Reprinted ("2e tirage") as vol. 90 of *Publications romanes et françaises* (Geneva, 1966).

[3] See especially the chapter entitled "Le cas Foerster", pp. 18–27.

within the large group he gave a special position to *PH*. In the 1880s, Foerster considered *V* to be the best manuscript, the only representative of what he then called the alpha family, and accordingly he drew on it heavily for his first edition;[4] for all his later editions he made *PH* the alpha family and constructed his text largely from them.[5] Since 1891, the date of Foerster's second edition, in which he reduced the importance of *V*, the problem of editing *Yvain* has essentially been that of how to make the best use of the good qualities of *P* and *H*. The discovery of the Annonay fragments (758 lines in 1933 and 376 lines about 1953) provided valuable new evidence about the manuscript tradition, but did not alter the basic position: the fragments contain a text that is in many lines close to that of *P* and *H* and it is usually considered to be better than that of any of the complete manuscripts.[6]

One of Micha's most important conclusions was that there is so much contamination in the manuscript tradition of *Yvain* that any stemma that we construct will constantly break down. Foerster had already noted something of this, but Micha was the first to explore its full extent and to face its implications. He does risk printing a stemma for *Yvain*, but he immediately diminishes its importance by saying: "Tel est le schéma général. Mais ici vont surgir les exceptions multiples qui le modifient de façon continue" (p. 154). And later, in summing up the situation of all five romances, Micha wrote: "nos efforts ont été impuissants à établir des divisions nettes en familles absolument définies: chaque ms. 'oscille' plus ou moins, chaque cloison cède" (p. 195).

What is an editor to do when faced with manuscripts that refuse to stay classified? Micha (p. 391) rejects both the Lachmannian method used by Foerster, and Bédier's alternative of sticking to a single manuscript through thick and thin. He opts

---

[4] Halle, 1887, vol. II of *Chrestian von Troyes, sämtliche erhaltene Werke*, reprinted in 1965 by Rodopi, Amsterdam.

[5] *Romanische Bibliothek*, V (Halle, 1891); reprinted in revised form in 1902, 1906, 1912.

[6] These views were first expressed by the editors of the fragments: *Chrestien de Troyes: Le manuscrit d'Annonay*, ed. A. Pauphilet (Paris, 1934) (see in particular p. xiv), and L.-F. Flutre, 'Nouveaux fragments du manuscrit dit d'Annonay' in *Romania*, LXXV (1954), 1–21 (see 8–9).

for a commonsense compromise: give the text of the best
manuscript but remove its unsatisfactory readings, using other
manuscripts as a control.

> Après avoir établi, *même de façon aproximative*, les grandes divisions
> en familles, l'étude particulière de chaque ms. intervient: dans chaque
> groupe, nous établissons une hiérarchie, nous mettons à part celui que
> pour des raisons de clarté, d'intelligibilité, de respect relatif de son
> modèle, de qualité du modèle aperçu à travers la copie, nous avons
> jugé le meilleur. Cet examen de la valeur respective des mss. est tout
> aussi important que celui du classement, plus peut-être dans une tradi-
> tion où tout classement absolu est interdit. Nous arrivons ainsi à déter-
> miner le ms.-base: le meilleur ms. de la famille alpha.
> Notre principe d'édition serait alors le suivant: conserver le texte du
> ms., en le contrôlant par tel et tel autres mss. qui, à l'examen, auront
> paru aptes à ce rôle. Dans le désarroi général, ou simplement dans les
> divergences de presque tous les mss. sur un vers, c'est notre ms. base
> qui figurera dans le texte . . . On le gardera quand son texte, isolé, est
> meilleur que celui des autres réunis (ce que n'a pas fait Foerster) et on
> le laissera en note quand sa leçon, seule en face des autres, est mani-
> festement une réfection individuelle (ce que n'a pas fait Bédier). Dans
> aucun cas on ne pratiquera pas 'l'émendation', petit coup de pouce
> donné au texte du ms. base pour le transformer en texte lisible, ni on ne
> le maintiendra avec quelques regrets, sous prétexte de l'abandonner le
> moins possible. En résumé, c'est le texte du ms. base que le lecteur aura
> sous les yeux, mais corrigé de ses impuretés, de ses écarts évidents,
> grâce au contrôle de copies dignes de foi (p. 392).

Micha lays down these principles for all five of Chrétien's
romances and goes on to consider how they apply to each
romance in turn. I shall discuss his recommendations for publishing *Yvain* later. Micha himself did not publish *Yvain*, but he
put his ideas into practice when he edited *Cligés* (*CFMA*, 1957).

In 1958, P. Jonin published his *Prolégomènes à une édition
d'Yvain*.[7] Like Micha, he found a great deal to criticise in
Foerster's editions, and his criticisms are much on the same lines.
His stemma is in all essentials the same as Micha's (Jonin p. 90;
Micha p. 154),[8] and he also sees the importance of contamina-
tion:

[7] Aix-en-Provence, *Publication des Annales de la Faculté des Lettres. nouv.
sér. 119.*
[8] Jonin uses the siglum *A* (not *H*) for BN 794 and *C* (not *A*) for Chantilly 472.

Ainsi paraît se présenter le stemma général. Nous disons bien général, car, aussitôt la construction établie, il faut s'empresser d'accumuler les réserves. Nous voulons parler des multiples contaminations qui corrompent les rapports entre manuscrits, contaminations que M. A. Micha a minutieusement relevées et étudiées (p. 91).

But Jonin goes further than Micha in his conception of the effects of contamination, and rejects the idea of a base manuscript 'controlled' by one or more manuscripts of other families:

Peut-on dans ces conditions continuer à parler de manuscrits contrôleurs? Puisque les membres de chaque famille sont voués à la dispersion, les cloisons entre les groupes n'étant qu'apparentes, quelle valeur peut bien garder la notion de famille et partant la notion de contrôle liée nécessairement à l'autonomie des groupes et à l'étanchéité des cloisons? En fait, si les familles ne sont qu'illusoires, comme c'est le cas pour Yvain, le contrôle par des mss. de familles différentes devient également illusoire (p. 93).

There is therefore a clear difference of doctrine between Micha, for whom *le contrôle* has a definite part to play in the editor's work, and Jonin, who bans it. Jonin will stick more closely to his base manuscript and will abandon it only when its readings are "manifestement condamnées par le contexte" (p. 96); he will then take from one of the other manuscripts "la variante . . . qui nous paraîtra la plus adéquate au sens ou celle qu'impose la connaissance du milieu arthurien ou des coûtumes du siècle" (p. 96).

Jonin was not able to publish an edition of *Yvain*, but we can get an idea of how his method works because he included in his book 350 lines of text (numbered by him 5620–5970, corresponding to 5614–5964 in Foerster's edition and to 5608–5958 in the *CFMA* edition). Jonin's base manuscript is BN 794 (the Guiot manuscript, *A* in his system, *H* to Foerster and Micha), and in these 350 lines he departs from it only six times. In these cases Jonin's expression "manifestement condamné par le contexte" can be justified, and in all six it is easy to find a satisfactory reading in one or more of the other manuscripts. In four cases, the reading of the base manuscript is completely isolated. The following table gives some details:

Line nos. in Jonin	Foerster-Reid	*CFMA*	MSS used for emendation (Jonin's sigla)	Notes on rejected readings
5687	5681	5675	*GCS* (+ *V*)	Awkward syntax in *BN 794* and in *P*.
5733–36	5727–30	5721–24	*PGCS* (*V* missing)	Lines in wrong order in *794* alone
5761–64	5755–58	5749–52	*G* (+ *CS*)	Text remodelled in *794* alone, to compensate for missing line.
5861	5855	5849	*PGSV* (+ *C*)	*Quinzaine* for *quarantaine* in *794* and in *P*.
5891	5885	5879	*GCSV* (+ *P*)	*794* alone has *desapert*, of doubtful meaning.
5899	5893	5887	*G* (+ *PCSV*)	Awkward syntax in *794* only.

These are the kind of emendations that many editors would make, and Micha could hardly have acted otherwise if he were editing BN 794, since he wants to print his manuscript "corrigé de ses impuretés, de ses écarts évidents, grâce au contrôle de copies dignes de foi"; and it is noticeable that *G*, the manuscript that Micha chooses as a 'control' for *Yvain*, is heavily drawn on by Jonin, not because it is a 'control', or "digne de foi", as Micha would say, but simply because in these particular passages its reading is "la plus adéquate au sens". In these particular lines, then, differences of theory seem to disappear in practice. The difference between the two critics comes out more clearly in lines 5753–54 (Jonin's numbering; Foerster 5747–48, *CFMA* 5741–42), where the base manuscript has the inaccurate rhyme *painne*:*ainme* against *painne*:*mainne* in all the other manuscripts. Jonin keeps this rhyme, defending his conservatism in a note (pp. 118–19), but I suspect that Micha would have rejected it, regarding it as an "écart évident", to be got rid of along with other "impuretés".

The idea of an edition of *Yvain* that would stick closely to the readings of a single manuscript was carried to extremes by Mario Roques in his edition published in 1960; this forms part of an edition of Chrétien's five romances directed by Roques and in which he himself was responsible for *Erec*, the *Charrete* and *Yvain*.[9] The text printed is that of BN 794, the manuscript that Jonin had intended to publish. Of course, Roques was well aware of the complexities of the manuscript tradition of *Yvain*; he bypassed discussion of them, however, by pointing out that his edition was just one of the possible editions and that it did not prevent other scholars producing different ones. He says very little about such points in his Introduction, but it is significant that he admits that Guiot's copy "n'est peut-être pas de façon continue aussi excellente qu'elle l'est par exemple pour le Lancelot" (p. iii). He makes no reference to the work of Micha and Jonin.[10]

This claim of Roques to be producing just one of the possible editions of *Yvain* would be more impressive if his edition were a good one; unfortunately it is not. Perhaps the worst fault of Roques' edition is the lengths to which he goes in accepting the more surprising readings in the Guiot manuscript. There is a case to be made for accepting readings of the kind that I have listed above in speaking of Jonin's specimen. In such passages the manuscript does give some kind of sense, even though the grammar may be awkward or the sense not very satisfactory and the wording not that of Chrétien de Troyes. Roques does in fact print the text of his manuscript in the six cases I have listed; in such passages Roques is editing Guiot rather than editing Chrétien, and I suppose this is what he intended to do.

But where Guiot wrote nonsense it seems a pity to perpetuate his mistakes in print, yet this is what Roques did a number of times. For example, in lines 222—23, where Calogrenant is telling Arthur's knights how the vavasor called his servants to look after his guest, we have:

Je descendi de mon cheval,
et uns des sergenz le prenoit.   *CFMA* 222—23

---

[9] *Les romans de Chrétien de Troyes édités d'après la copie de Guiot*. I: *Erec et Enide*, ed. Roques, 1952; II: *Cligés*, ed. Micha, 1957; III: *Le Chevalier de la charrete*, ed. Roques, 1958; IV: *Le Chevalier au lion (Yvain)*, ed. Roques, 1960; V—VI: *Le Conte du Graal,* ed. Lecoy, 1973—75.

[10] In his introduction to *Erec*, the first volume of the series, he does however refer to Micha's work.

But Calogrenant had already dismounted a few minutes earlier
(*Je descendi*, 201). In the Foerster edition we have:

Li un seisirent mon cheval,
Que li buens vavassors tenoit.   224—25

The manuscripts are not unanimous here, and we cannot be
sure that Foerster has the exact wording used by Chrétien, but
at least he comes nearer than Roques. Unfortunately, in cases
like this Roques gives no indication of what is in the other
manuscripts.

A few lines further on, when Calogrenant is still talking
about his night at the vavasor's dwelling, Foerster's edition,
following the manuscripts other than Guiot, has:

Mout fui bien la nuit ostelez,
Et mes chevaus fu anselez,
Lués que l'an pot le jor veoir;
Car j'an oi mout proiié le soir;
Si fu bien feite ma proiiere.   269—73

Here again, the manuscripts have variants of detail, which
different editors would no doubt handle differently. But surely
no editor other than Roques would print Guiot's obviously
wrong version:

Molt fui bien la nuit ostelez,
et mes chevax fu establez
que g'en oi molt proié le soir.
Lors que l'en pot le jor veoir,
si fu bien fette ma proicre.   *CFMA* 267—71

Here are ten more examples of this procedure from the first
2000 lines of Yvain. The words in italics do not make sense in
the context and most of them are to be found only in the
Guiot manuscript:

373 se *ne* li randoies son droit
543 c'onques *nus* ne me regarda
730 'Di, va! fet il, *avoec* moi vien.'
946 *sanz encombrier et sanz grant mal* (910 repeated
                              instead of the appropriate line)
949 mon seignor Yvain *maintenant*
1037 *qu'an n'en voit point* (words repeated from 1029)
1101 mes il n'i ot a celui *siege*
1680 *Que* autresi boen ou meillor

1793 mes or li voldra *comander*
1847 Et *au demain* remanderoiz.

It occasionally happens that the surprising words in the *CFMA* edition are merely misreadings of the manuscript (or perhaps misprints):

790 tant d'enor con prodon *fet* feire.

The manuscript has *set feire* and apparently none has *fet feire*.

934—5 et mes sire Yveins *solemant*
        hurtc grant aleüre aprés.

The manuscript has *folemant*, and no variant for this word has been recorded.

Another weakness of Roques' edition is that the punctuation is often unsatisfactory; in fact it can hardly have been supplied by Roques himself, since it often suggests misunderstanding of ordinary Old French grammar. It would be tedious to list all the cases which I have noted, but here are a few examples:

1352   tant est Kex, et fel, et pervers,
1368—9 vangence en a feite greignor,
          qu'ele panre n'an seüst . . .

(*greignor que* is 'greater than').

2387—8 Puis l'enbraça par mi les flans,
          li rois, come cortois et frans,

(*li rois* is subject of *enbraça*).

2844 ss. (The hermit puts out food for Yvain:)
          et cil vient la qui molt covoite:
          le pain sel prant et si i mort;
          ne cuit que onques de si fort
          ne de si aspre eüst gosté
          n'avoit mie .xx. solz costé . . .

3934 ss. Mes sire Yvains onques ne fine
          de sopirer quant ce antant
          de la pitié que il l'en prant;
          li respont: 'Biax dolz sire chiers,' . . .

5731   Et vos comant! (this should be *Et vos comant?*)
5739   Desdaing, sire; (this should be *Desdaing, sire?*)

These two questions are both correctly punctuated in Foerster's editions.

Perhaps the anonymous assistant who put in the punctuation was also responsible for expanding the abbreviations, since here again there are suggestions of insufficient knowledge of Old French: abbreviated proper names are sometimes put into the wrong case (3628, 3692), and numerals are sometimes given their modern spelling (*six* 2476, *cinq* 2819; often the numerals are simply left as they are in the manuscript).

This is by no means a complete account of the shortcomings of the *CFMA* edition of *Yvain*, and it is sad to have to sum up by saying that it fails to give us a satisfactory text; we are better off with Foerster-Reid.[11]

But, as I said above, we can improve on Foerster-Reid. How are we to do this? I imagine that a future editor will not want a composite text of the kind favoured by Foerster, but will produce one that keeps close to a single manuscript (just how close is another question). He is unlikely to disagree with the view of earlier scholars (Foerster, Micha, Jonin, Pauphilet) that BN 794 and BN 1433 are the two best manuscripts and that they are closely related (if he rejects families and stemmata for the manuscript tradition of *Yvain*, he will at least agree that the text is similar in these two copies). No doubt he will also heartily agree with those who have thought 'If only the Annonay manuscript were complete!'[12] But as he cannot print a complete text from Annonay, he will have to decide between the rival merits of 794 and 1433.

This is not an easy decision. We will look first at some of the basic facts about the two manuscripts. First, BN 794. This is the

---

[11] I am here echoing some words of Reid's. In his article 'Chrétien de Troyes and the scribe Guiot' in *Medium Aevum*, XLV (1976), 1—19, he concludes a devastating review of Roques' edition of *Erec* with these words: "Whatever the editor's intention may have been, the text that has resulted is not really an edition of Chrétien de Troyes; if that is what we want, we shall still be well advised to go back to the 'antiquated' editions of Wendelin Foerster".

An attempt to remedy the faults of Roques' edition of *Yvain* was made by J. Nelson, C. W. Carroll and D. Kelly in an edition published in New York in 1968. They give the text of BN 794 modified by readings taken from Foerster's editions. The book is intended for undergraduates and has no scholarly value. The authors have removed some of Guiot's blunders, but they leave others; they also copy Roques' mistakes over punctuation and the expansion of abbreviations. They give no information about the source of their corrections and do not say where they have abandoned BN 794.

[12] This thought is implicit in the remarks of Pauphilet and Flutre (see above, n. 6) and of Micha (p. 295).

Guiot manuscript, called *H* by Foerster and Micha, *A* by Jonin and Roques.[13] Its date is between 1213 and the middle of the 13th century. It includes all five of the extant romances by Chrétien,[14] as well as Wace's *Brut*, the *Roman de Troie* and other works. The scribe Guiot worked at Provins (not Paris, as we formerly thought) and his dialect is Champenois; his spelling is exceptionally regular, and he seems to have given some thought to diacritics.[15] Foerster considered his language to be so close to that of Chrétien as revealed by rhyme and metre that he made Guiot's spelling the basis of his own regularised orthography. BN 1433, always given the siglum *P*, is a very different type of book; it is a de-luxe copy, with fine miniatures, of only two works, Chrétien's *Yvain* and the anonymous 13th-century Arthurian romance *L'Atre périlleux*.[16] Its dialect is a strongly marked Picard. With one exception, I have always seen it dated simply "13th century"; the exception is in the catalogue of an exhibition held at the Bibliothèque Nationale in 1955, where its date is given as "vers 1330" and its place of origin Paris.[17]

If, as seems probable, a future editor of *Yvain* has to choose between 794 and 1433 as his base manuscript, he will give very serious consideration to the work already done on this question by Jonin and Micha. Jonin, as we have seen, preferred 794 and used it for the specimen that he published. He justified his decision on pp. 64—87 of his *Prolégomènes* by a careful study of the lines where either of the two manuscripts is obviously unacceptable; he found about 50 of such lines in BN 794 (p. 68), but more than 100 in the first half of BN 1433 (p. 87). Even if one does not agree with every detail of Jonin's comparisons, it is difficult not to accept his conclusion that BN 974 should be the editor's base manuscript.

[13] *H* is the siglum used by Foerster when discussing *Yvain*; he calls the same MS *A* for *Cligés* and *C* for *Erec* and the *Charrete*.

[14] Not, however, *Guillaume d'Angleterre*, which of course may or may not be by Chrétien de Troyes.

[15] See Roques' very full description of the MS in *Romania*, LXXIII (1952), 177—99, especially 190—96.

[16] Ed. B. Woledge, *CFMA*, 1935.

[17] B.N., *Les Mss. à peintures en France du XIIIe au XVIe siècle* (Paris, 1955), p. 29. The evidence for localisation must be art-historical.

Curiously enough, Micha's views on this point are not entirely clear: he sometimes leans towards *H* and sometimes towards *P*. On the one hand he says "Le meilleur texte d'alpha est celui que nous transmet BN 794[18] . . . il est le moins remanié des mss., le nombre de ses variantes individuelles est bien moins élevé que dans BN 1433; plus souvent que ce dernier il a conservé le seul bon texte" (p. 228), and he gives statistics which again favour *H*: in *H* he counts 450 important individual readings and 23 'vers refaits'; for *P*, the figures are 650 and 36 (p. 228 n.); and again, on pp. 289–90, he says of *H*: "le ms. est le moins retouché de tous ceux d'*Yvain* . . . à maints passages, dans le désarroi général, c'est lui qui gardera la bonne tradition".[19] On the other hand, at the end of his book, when he comes to sum up on how each romance should be edited, Micha seems to have leaned away from *H* towards *P*. Whereas for each of the other romances he gives a clear preference to *H* (pp. 392–93), this is what he says about editing *Yvain*:

> Pour Yvain, le ms. d'Annonay confirme la valeur de BN 1433 que Foerster a fini par adopter pour son édition de la Romanische Bibliothek. Mais le BN 784 est très digne d'intérêt, et même le nombre des réfections individuelles n'est pas aussi élevé que dans le BN 1433. L'un et l'autre peut-être changent de position au cours du roman (cf. *PGAS*, *HV*). On obtiendra un bon texte en partant de BN 1433 (+ Annonay) comme base, et en le contrôlant par BN 794 et par BN 12560 [*G*], le meilleur des mss. bêta qui tire une sérieuse autorité de ses accords avec Annonay (p. 393).[20]

My own feeling is that a new edition of *Yvain* should be based on BN 794: in the present state of knowledge, it seems to me that, in spite of Micha's hesitation, the evidence which he himself accumulated, corroborated as it is by Jonin's work, leaves little room for doubt; but if I were going to do an edition, I should probably make some more comparisons before reaching a final decision.

---

[18] In Micha's classification, the alpha family consists of BN 794, BN 1433 and the Annonay fragments.

[19] Pp. 289–90 of Micha's book contain useful examples of both the good and bad points of Guiot's copy.

[20] Pauphilet had said something very similar in 1934 in his edition of the Annonay fragments (see above, n. 6): "On obtiendrait un excellent texte de base avec *P*, appuyé de notre ms. [Annonay] là où il existe, et contrôlé par *H* et *G*".

For example, I should take into consideration the fact that
P is better than *H* in dealing with hiatus at the end of words of
two or more syllables. It seems certain that Chrétien wrote
lines of the type

> qui mout la prisë et mout l'aimme   2419 ed. Reid
> (*PGSV*).

There are about twenty such lines in the various manuscripts of
Yvain and most of them are probably due to Chrétien himself.
Scribes differ in their handling of these lines; *V* has more
examples of non-elision than any other copy; *P* contains a few,
but *H* is the only manuscript to have none at all: presumably
Guiot, or his model, or the model of his model, objected to
this feature of versification and got rid of it by supplying an
extra syllable. Thus, in the line I have quoted, *H* reads:

> qui molt la prise, et qui molt l'ainme   CFMA 2421

On this point then, *P* is rather better than *H*.[21]

On the other hand, the contrast between the dialects of the
two scribes weighs in favour of *H*: as I have said, *H* is Champenois
and close to Chrétien's own language, while *P* has strong Picard
colouring. This is not such a trivial difference as it may seem. Of
course, other things being equal, a copy that gives us something
like the poet's pronunciation is to be preferred to one that does
not; but dialectal differences go much deeper than this and
concern morphology, syntax and vocabulary as well as pronunciation. It may be that in some of *P*'s readings Chrétien's
grammar or vocabulary have been Picardised. If examination
proved this to be so, I do not think there could be any case at
all for printing *P* in preference to *H*.[22]

Having chosen a base manuscript, how will a future editor
treat it? He will surely not repeat Roques' experiment of

---

[21] On such cases of non-elision see Foerster's notes, especially that on line 212 in
his 1887 edition, and B. Woledge, 'Notes on Rhythm in Chrétien's *Yvain*' in *The
Legend of Arthur in the Middle Ages: Studies presented to A. H. Diverres* (Cambridge,
1983), pp. 222–26.

[22] A good example of the modifications that can result from the scribe's copying
a work in a dialect that is not his own is Guiot's copy of Wace's *Brut*; see B. Woledge,
'Un scribe champenois devant un texte normand: Guiot copiste de Wace' in *Mélanges
. . . Frappier*, II (Paris, 1970), 1139–54. Again, when the scribe of *P* was copying
L'Atre périlleux, he got rid of some Norman rhymes that did not fit into his Picard
language (e.g. lines 1073–74, where *toloite: droite* is changed to *tolue :droiture*).

putting into the text the scribe's obvious blunders, but he will find himself up against many hard decisions when he comes to readings that look strange but which may go back to Chrétien. In that position, I am not sure whether I should allow myself freedom to exploit the other manuscripts as seemed fit on each occasion (Jonin's doctrine) or set up principles to guide me through the manuscript tradition, as Micha recommends. Perhaps only the experience of editing a few hundred lines could reveal which is the best method to follow.

The future editor of *Yvain* must give the reader copious notes explaining how he understands the text, why he has kept such and such a reading and has emended in such and such cases. He must provide variants, and it will be difficult for him to avoid the task of giving all variants except the most trivial, doing all over again the work that Foerster did with only partial efficiency. This means unfortunately that the edition will take a long time to prepare and will be very expensive; we shall probably need a cheaper edition of the text with selected variants.[23]

---

[23] I have not thought it necessary to discuss MS Garrett 125 at Princeton University, first described in 1963, since its text is of very poor quality; it is related to *FGAS* (see L. J. Rahilly in *Romania*, XCIX (1978), 1–30). There are also some unimportant fragments that I have not referred to. Among the editions of *Yvain*, I have mentioned only those that are significant from my point of view.

It is good to know that the Manchester University Press, after allowing Reid's edition of *Yvain* to go out of print, has now (June, 1983) agreed to reprint it.

TABULA COMMENDATORIA

Professor L.J. Austin
F.J. Barnett
Dr A. Bell
G. Bianciotto
Dr F. Bogdanow
A. Boursier
Professor H. Braet
Dr G.N. Bromiley
Professor G.L. Brook
V. Bubenicet
Dr G.S. Burgess
C. Ciociola
Professor P. Danchin
Professor Ruth J. Dean
J.N. Dickson
Professor A. Diverres
Sir Idris Foster
Pamela S. Gehrke
K.A. Goddard
Dr S. Gregory
Professor P.R. Grillo
Dr P.B. Grout
Professor C.A. Hackett
Dr Elizabeth Hackett
Dr J.P. Harper
Professor A. Henry
Christine M. Hill
F.W. Hodcroft
Professor A.J. Holden
L.D. Housley
T. Hunt
Dr Claire Isoz

Professor Karen Jambeck
Professor R.C. Johnston
Professor H.-E. Keller
Dr E.M. Kennedy
Professor W. Kibler
Professor J.C. Laidlaw
Professor J. Lawlor
Professor Y. Malkiel
Margaret Malpas
Sir W. Mansfield-Cooper
Reine Mantou
D.M. Marks
Professor J.H. Marshall
Dr M.T. McNunn
Professor D. McMillan
Professor Ph. Ménard
Professor B. Merrilees
Dr Evelyn Mullally
Professor R. Niklaus
Y. Otaka
Professor A.T. Patterson
B.E. Peters
Professor Rebecca Posner
Miss D.M. Reid
H.W.F. Reid
Professor P. Rickard
Professor P.T. Ricketts
Professor W. Roach
C.A. Robson
R. Rosenstein
Professor D.J.A. Ross
Professor W. Rothwell

Professor P. Ruelle
Professor D.W. Russell
Professor J. Rychner
Dr H. Shields
Professor I. Short
Professor K.V. Sinclair
M. de Smedt
Mrs D.A. Sneddon
Professor Mary B. Speer
Professor W. McC. Stewart
Professor G. Straka
Professor T. Takamiya
Dr J.H.M. Taylor
J.-C. Thiolier
D.A. Trotter
Dr K. Urwin
Professor W.G. van Emden
Kathryn Y. Wallace
Professor R.N. Walpole
Professor B. Woledge
F. Zufferey

Queen's University of Belfast
University of Bristol
St Catharine's College,
   Cambridge
University of Chicago
Royal Library, Copenhagen
University College, Dublin

University of Edinburgh
University of Hull
Keio University
University of Leeds
University of London Library
Queen Mary College, London
Université Catholique de
   Louvain
Institut National de la Langue
   Française, Nancy
University of Newcastle upon
   Tyne
Christ Church, Oxford
English Faculty Library,
   Oxford
Lady Margaret Hall, Oxford
St Anne's College, Oxford
Taylor Institution, Oxford
Trinity College, Oxford
University of Queensland
University of Reading
University of Southampton
University of Swansea
University of Toronto
Istituto di Filologia Moderna,
   Turin
Uppsala University
University of Warwick

SELECTIVE INDEX